My Father, Frank

Unresting Spirit of Everest

My Father, Frank
Unresting Spirit of Everest

TONY SMYTHE
Foreword by Doug Scott

bâton wicks

Bâton Wicks, Sheffield
www.batonwicks.com

MY FATHER, FRANK
TONY SMYTHE

First published in 2013 by Bâton Wicks.

BÂTON WICKS
Crescent House, 228 Psalter Lane, Sheffield, S11 8UT
www.batonwicks.com

A CIP catalogue record for this book is available from the British Library.

ISBN: 978-1-898573-87-6 (Hardback)
ISBN: 978-1-898573-88-3 (Ebook)

10 9 8 7 6 5 4 3 2 1

Designed and typeset in Adobe Garamond Pro by Rod Harrison — Vertebrate Graphics Ltd. — www.v-graphics.co.uk
Printed and bound in the UK by TJ International, Padstow, Cornwall.

TO SONIA

Contents

Foreword

By Doug Scott

At a dinner for Cumbrian authors I found myself sitting next to local grandee Willie Whitelaw who began his speech with the announcement that he was a traditionalist and that he was proud of it. I have to say that I too share his sentiments, particularly when it comes to discovering how the mountaineers of old pursued their craft. So it will be no surprise that when Tony Smythe's biography of his father Frank arrived I started to read with eager anticipation and hardly stopped reading until it was read.

Frank Smythe was the outstanding British climber during the inter-war period. He was not only revered by fellow climbers for the climbs he pioneered, but through film, radio, lectures and writing he was the best known climber nationwide. He, more than anyone, was responsible for educating the British public about mountaineering; Everest and Kangchenjunga became familiar beasts even before they were climbed at last in the 1950s.

I had forgotten what a fine writer Smythe was. And I had never fully appreciated the part he played in the development of Alpine and especially Himalayan climbing until I read this book. I suspect I had filed him away in my mind as the man who'd done a couple of new routes on Mont Blanc, had climbed Kamet, attempted Kangchenjunga and had gone a long way up Everest, and that was about it. Maybe I'd been side-tracked by his more romantic writings about spiritual and supernatural matters. So this book is timely. It is also well researched, helped by the privileged access to information available only to a family member. And it's well written with the authority of a committed climber; Tony, like his father climbed hard at home and abroad in all seasons with a variety of companions.

The reader will be watching to see just how objective Frank's son will be when dealing with events such as the feud that sadly developed between Frank and Graham Brown. And it isn't easy for a son to delve into his father's private life — particularly into sensitive matters such as his divorce. I compliment Tony Smythe on dealing with these and many other private issues in his father's life in the most even-handed way possible. Neither does he pull any punches when he comments for instance upon Frank's decision to choose Jim Gavin rather than the brilliant rock climber and proven Himalayan mountaineer Colin Kirkus for the 1936 Everest Expedition.

Tony is able to put a few ghosts to rest. It seems that Frank was not the sickly child that became a mountaineer against all the odds. He was quite athletic, a very good cricket player who also played football for his house. When he was invalided out of the RAF it was through eyestrain or 'glare' while training in Egypt (it soon cleared up afterwards) and not because of a heart problem. Not only was Frank fit, he had other natural advantages, one being an astonishing awareness of danger that more than once saved his life or those of others.

Tony reveals that it was Frank's ambition and pride that was the root cause of the notorious quarrel between him and Graham Brown — bad feeling that Brown could never forget or forgive. I have to say I found this one of the most interesting sections of the book for Tony's description of the climbing is riveting and his analysis of the disagreements masterful. The reader is left gripped and exhausted following the climbing and disappointed that after leading so much of the Route Major on Mont Blanc Smythe could not acknowledge Brown's contribution. How sad one feels for both but especially for Brown who as Tony points out, 'must have suffered more. It must be more corrosive to hate than to be hated'. Frank had the strength of character to apologise and let go of the quarrel whereas Graham Brown still bore him malice into his eighties.

The book does not lack humour and I found myself smiling, sometimes laughing out loud at Tony's observations in the Kamet film. The expedition 'gets to Base Camp by numerous shots of porters bowed under enormous loads, plodding this way and that … The porters grinned cheerfully but the sahibs usually had their backs to the camera except when the great length of Raymond Greene is seen stark naked, mercifully for an instant only, plunging into a pool … Holdsworth happily smokes his pipe while being carried across a raging river by a porter half his size … Frank commentates and a piano provides frantic music throughout.'

There are so many interesting facts, never known or half remembered, revealed in this book. John Hunt was rejected from the 1936 Expedition after the Medical Board decided, incorrectly, he had a heart problem. Later we find that Hunt and several other well-known mountaineers of the day were roped in during the war for mountain warfare training including Frank, who was posted out to the Canadian Rockies. Completely unknown to me was the fact that Frank was the first to spot Mallory's body when he was scoping the flanks of Everest in 1936 with a high powered telescope. In a private letter to Colonel Norton, the leader of the 1924 Everest Expedition, he wrote that he was convinced that he had spotted Mallory or Irvine's body but requested that 'It's not to be written about as the press would make an unpleasant sensation.' His discovery was only confirmed 63 years later by Graham Hoyland who was on the American Expedition that found Mallory in 1999.

Like many 'Everesters' Frank pushed himself to his limit on many other mountains, some of them quite technical, and all bar one, without guides. He was not just a big mountain man yo-yoing up fixed ropes for weeks on end. In the Garhwal he had a particularly productive season in 1937, making the first ascent of Nilgiri Parbat and Mana Peak. The first was made with two Sherpa friends after he had taught them the ropes, and he reached the summit of Mana Peak — at nearly 24,000 feet — solo after climbing the final 800 feet of rock on his own when his partner, Peter Oliver, became exhausted.

Tony's book has stimulated me into reading again Frank Smythe's great classics. Six of the best are to be found under one cover in Bâton Wicks' omnibus. As their publisher, Ken Wilson put it, they contain gripping adventures, a rich sense of period and a thread of mountaineering good sense. Above all Frank Smythe was a mountaineer who lived for mountains and was at his best amongst mountains. His son, Tony surely confirms this in his thoughtful and perceptive account of his father's life.

Doug Scott

Introduction

My father, Frank Smythe, born in 1900, had huge obstacles to overcome on his way to becoming probably the best-known climber and mountaineering writer of his generation. His father died when he was a baby and his mother went into a self-imposed exile, obsessively clinging to Frank throughout his early life. His schooling was a disaster. He was pressured into training as an engineer, work he hated. When that career failed his half-hearted efforts to make a fresh start in the Royal Air Force also collapsed. At the age of 26, an unskilled job loomed.

However, he had become good at the one thing he really enjoyed — climbing. Much of this had consisted of risky trips into the Alps on his own during engineering training in Austria and Switzerland, but he had survived to reach a high level of expertise, coping even with difficult and dangerous routes on rock, snow and ice. He also had a talent for writing about his adventures. He supplied stories to magazines. His first book was published. With the reluctant support of his mother, his chosen career in which climbing produced material for writing and writing paid for more climbing began to take shape.

In the process there were problems. He upset some senior members of the Alpine Club, who disliked the spectacle of a fellow member making money out of their gentlemanly pastime. And many in the climbing fraternity also felt that it was better to write for other climbers, not the general public. Traditionally it was bad form too, to let emotion play a part in the description of your climbs.

But Frank could never restrict himself in this way. All his life he wrote instinctively for the ordinary man who knew nothing about mountains, putting across his experiences with such conviction that a reader might easily feel he was there on the mountain too. It worked that way for me when I began to read his books as a boy. I felt the pain of frostbitten feet and the exhaustion, yet exhilaration of getting to the top of Kamet, the highest summit in the world reached at that time. I pictured the terrible ice avalanche on Kangchenjunga that killed an expedition Sherpa, and the simple heartfelt ceremony when his crushed body was consigned to a glacier grave before the party's retreat. Then there was Mount Everest, when Frank climbing alone got to within a thousand feet of the summit — a record height and an achievement that takes its place among the great moments of mountaineering history. More than once I read his description of how he slipped on the steep snowy rocks near the top of the Great Gully. And each time I vividly imagined myself hanging from my clutched ice axe, saved by its pick wedged in a crack above the yawning 8,000-foot drop of the north face.

He went on seven expeditions to the Himalayas, including his visit to the now-famous Valley of Flowers in Garhwal, a place of sublime beauty where he botanised and made outstanding climbs on the surrounding unexplored peaks. He became a highly regarded mountain photographer and ten albums of his pictures were published. He wrote a total of twenty-seven books within the space of twenty years, he lectured intensively, and his resulting popularity led to a level of fame and celebrity that in the days before television and the internet seems remarkable. However like most public figures of that era — the 1930s and 1940s — he kept the rest of his life strictly private. His writings were a blend of wonderful detail in the climbing and travel, tense descriptions of moments of difficulty or danger, a constant search for more profound ways of conveying his feelings for mountains, and wry humour at his own fallibility. But of his life at home and work he revealed almost nothing.

He died at the early age of 48 of cerebral malaria, a deadly strain of the disease, contracted on a trip to India in 1949 when I was 14. In the aftermath he was a hero to me. I was proud of his achievements and became a climber myself. I even, like him, lectured about my journeys and expeditions and wrote a book about climbing. It was sometimes suggested that I 'trod in my father's footsteps', and I dutifully agreed. But as the years passed I acquired a more thoughtful appraisal of him.

For although my two brothers and I had always admired him we'd never been able to form any kind of relationship, except perhaps in unremembered early childhood. After his marriage to Kathleen and the birth of each of us, our life together as a family had been disrupted by his absence on expeditions. And I was only four when he separated himself from us permanently after his marriage broke down. He left us to live with Nona, a nurse from New Zealand, whose own marriage had also failed. In those days divorce tended to be seen as shameful, so in my earlier years I pretended my famous father had not deserted us. Eventually I got over this, realising that Frank's marriage to Kathleen had probably been doomed from the start; they had been completely unsuited to one another. I started seeing him much as others saw him — a celebrated mountaineer who published a large number of books. But I also knew that his private life had been chaotic with great heartache for himself and those close to him.

I'd always turned down the idea of writing the story of his life. I was too busy, and the job seemed too daunting. But in 1999, when the mountaineering publisher Ken Wilson was putting together an omnibus of some of his books, I changed my mind. Harry Calvert's book, *Smythe's Mountains* had been published in 1985, but that dealt purely with his climbs. I knew there was so much more to be said about the man, his character and the private life behind his achievements. And the succeeding years of research became a fascinating voyage of discovery, adding to what my brothers and I knew already.

He narrowly missed being selected for the 1924 Everest expedition, the attempt when Mallory and Irvine were lost. He was sent to Argentina to work for a telephone company, but finding the job oppressive simply walked away and boarded a ship home, leaving his family to pick up the pieces of his broken contract. He rode the footplate as a fireman on the Southern Railway during the General Strike. After making two superb new routes on the Brenva Face of Mont Blanc — climbs that were the gateway to the rest of his mountaineering career — he fell out with his partner on the rope, Professor Thomas Graham Brown, and a bitter feud developed between them that split the Alpine Club and rocked the mountaineering establishment. A letter he wrote to *The Times* complaining about the film industry's reluctance to accept the movie he shot of his expedition to Kamet because of the lack of 'love interest' resulted in a summons by King George V for a private viewing of the film at Buckingham Palace (followed by a glass of whiskey with the King in his study). After that the film was accepted without further ado and became a runaway success for months to come in cinemas nationwide. He published a book about just one of his Everest expeditions — that in 1933 — but wrote plenty more about his companions during his three visits to the mountain, in diaries and letters that could not be aired in his lifetime. He planned three private expeditions to Everest; all were overtaken by events. He spotted Mallory's body through a telescope 63 years before it was found, but never disclosed this for fear of an 'unpleasant fuss.' He had several publishers, the Managing Director of one of them becoming a close family friend and Trustee to his Will. He obtained the help of a spiritualist to cure a severe digestive problem after a car crash, later communicating directly with her source, a seventeenth-century Sindh poet. Earlier his extraordinary psychic capacity had saved the lives of a group of men in a Bradford foundry. He was deeply involved in the later years of World War Two, commanding the training of elite mountain warfare troops, in Scotland and Canada, although he eventually suffered a severe breakdown in his health. After the war he invited my two brothers and me to join him and Nona in Scotland, a fascinating experience when at last we came face-to-face with the father we had never known.

His life was as much about his friends and climbing partners as the mountains he climbed. Geoffrey Winthrop Young, one of the most influential figures in British mountaineering had become a mentor to him when he was struggling to make a start as a writer. There were other renowned elders he had turned to in the absence of a natural father — Ernest Roberts of the Yorkshire Ramblers' Club during his early climbing in the Lake District, and in the run-up to Everest in 1933 the near-legendary Sir Francis Younghusband, explorer, soldier and leading player in the Great Game.

The list of interesting men he knew well goes on: the Everest leaders General Charles Bruce, Hugh Ruttledge and John Hunt. Colonel Philip Neame, VC, a climbing companion in the Bernese Oberland. Arthur Hinks, the formidable Royal Geographical Society Secretary for 30 years. And even his adversary Graham Brown should be included, a distinguished Professor of Physiology with a large following.

There were many other climbers who were with him in the mountains. Some of them are now significant figures in mountaineering history: Jim Bell, Eric Shipton, Graham Macphee, Colin Kirkus, Bill Tilman, Tenzing Norgay, Jack Longland, Noel Odell, Howard Somervell, Günther Dyhrenfurth, Ivan Waller. As custom required, they stayed largely out of sight as personalities in Frank's published writing. Clearly a biography was an opportunity to change that.

He loved hills and spent much of his short life among them. Despite his slight, even frail physique his determination and energy were awesome. Enduring fearful hardship at times, he found joy and inspiration on the heights but the nirvana he searched for always seemed just out of reach. In a small anthology of verse, *In Praise of Mountains*, selected by Eleanor and Geoffrey Winthrop Young, I came across some lines published anonymously in 1604 that seemed perfectly to sum up my father's life:

> As o'er the mountains walks the wandering soul,
> Seeking for rest, in his unresting spirit …

Tony Smythe
Staveley, March 2013

Prologue
Wycliffe, 1949

It's a hot Monday evening towards the end of June. In the Assembly Hall where the first two periods of prep are under way there's a general feeling of subdued gloom. It's the start of another week and amid the rustle of paper and creaking of chairs I try to concentrate on simultaneous equations, but I barely understand them and have a hollow feeling in my stomach. The hall is quite full because most people have their two occupation periods in the last half after the break; I've got a piano practice and a single period choral that will be a lot more fun than this. And it's likely there'll be a swim last thing, although you've got to be quick and you can get just about drowned in the rush before the whistle.

Suddenly the door on the far side opens and Stan, the Headmaster is standing there. There's a great rumbling of chairs as the School starts rising to its feet, but like a conductor quelling an orchestra with outstretched arms Stan signals for everyone to remain seated and Prune, who is supervising prep from the pulpit, booms 'Carry on with your work.' Stan's eyes rake the hall before he stalks across and has a low-voiced discussion with Prune. I am concerned to see both of them looking in my direction and then, to my horror Stan makes his way to my side and says quietly in that high refined tenor voice that's easy to mimic, 'Bring your things and come with me.'

Every eye is on me, red as a beetroot as I follow Stan out of the hall. He says nothing as we go down the main stairs, past the notice-boards and out into the quad in front of School House. My mind races as I rapidly survey all my recent misdemeanours and prepare my excuses and denials.

There is still no further word from the tall, loping and deeply-feared Stan, or 'Tiger' as he is occasionally called. Dressed as usual in his light-brown, hairy tweed suit, his keen profile, bared teeth in a small bullet-shaped head cutting through the evening air, he leads along the path by Haywardsfield, past Springfield's kitchen gardens, then past the San towards the grass tennis courts.

At last he comes to a seat. There is not a soul around.

'Sit down, Tony.'

This is a great relief. If I was in trouble it would be Smythe, and in really big trouble, a short staccato 'Smyth'. I sit on the bench and Stan sits next to me.

'You know, of course, that your father has been ill,' he says.

I feel an even greater sense of relief that this is definitely nothing to do with me. I remember my brother John telling me a while back that all had not gone well with Dad's trip to the Himalayas. He was unwell and he had had to come home.

'He was very ill and he got worse,' said Stan. 'He got much worse.'

There is a pause and Stan gazes into the distance.

'Tony, he died this morning.'

The words don't register for a moment but when they do I feel surprise rather than shock, almost as though I have been lagging behind in some kind of theatrical scenario and have failed to keep up with the script. As the meaning of what Stan has said sinks in, as well as amazement I even feel a flash of frustration that, after all the separation and pain for us, after the fatherless void in our family life, my father should now make his escape from us permanently, especially as only last summer in Scotland he was promising that when we were older he would take us to the Alps.

But there is shock in having the news thrust upon me at such close quarters by the formidable Stan, and to my embarrassment I feel tears rolling down, tears however that have less do with sadness than with the intensity of the moment and my behaving in a way that is perhaps expected of me.

'How well did you know your father?' asks Stan after a while.

'Not very well,' I mumble, feeling that this answer might not only be the one he expected from me but would avoid further questions.

Soon I am left on my own with my thoughts, and Stan makes his exit, no doubt with a feeling of relief. It is a beautiful evening and the sunset lingers late. But as well as thinking about Dad I am brooding about the complications coming up next morning when it'll probably be reported in the papers and the news gets out.

That's going to be the worst bit.

ONE

The Crevasse

On a fine afternoon in the early summer of 1922, a young English climber reached the top of a small peak in the Stubai Alps of Austria. He rested for a while, enjoying the spectacular view and feeling thankful for his break from work as a trainee in an engineering company near Innsbruck. He was 21, passionate about climbing and although his experience had been limited to rock climbing in the British hills, his arrival in the Alps had opened up a wealth of new and exciting opportunities. It was a pity that no companions were available and he was unable to afford a guide, but he was confident in his ability to explore the mountains on his own.

It had been an easy enough scramble up the sun-warmed rocks of the ridge to the summit, so the descent would be straightforward. But then some devil entered him and he decided to return by a different route. Below him the mountain fell away in a steep ice-face for several hundred feet to a snow-covered glacier rifted with numerous crevasses. This, he reckoned would make an excellent challenge and provide good practice in step-cutting. With scarcely another thought he hitched his rucksack into place, grasped his ice-axe and started down.

As he clumsily and laboriously hacked places for his boots in the ice slope the situation seemed suddenly to become serious, but he welcomed the feeling. It was quite novel to be up against a real challenge, although a small voice told him that he was violating every canon of mountaineering. He was a solo climber, it was late in the day, he would be taking a risk in crossing a crevassed glacier, and no one knew about his change of plan. But he was beyond common sense, beyond reason, and delighting in his crime. So he continued, his arms and knees soon aching from the unaccustomed process of step-cutting down steep ice. It was a long time before he approached the foot of the slope, his arms leaden with fatigue, his clothing drenched with sweat.

And now, previously hidden but coming into view, he saw the bergschrund.

He had come across this type of feature before. It was the natural gap or crevasse between a glacier and the mountainside it lay against. The ones he had seen had been mainly narrow or blocked with snow, and not difficult to deal with. This one was different. It was huge, a wide chasm of unknown depth, stretching out of sight to left and right. And somehow it would have to be crossed. With that cavernous rift below him the ice slope he was perched on now seemed unpleasantly steep and slippery. However, after cutting a few more steps to get a better view, he saw to his relief a snow bridge across the bergschrund that would provide a way over it. He descended to it, but his joy immediately evaporated. Even to his inexperienced eye it was obvious the snow bridge was sodden through and through, and would probably collapse beneath his weight. What then? The afternoon sun was reflected into the mouth of the rift where the névé or structure of the glacier was visible, with alternating layers of winter snowfall and summer dirt and debris. Fifty feet lower the gloom of bottle-green ice faded into the darkness of unplumbed depths.

The bergschrund would have to be jumped. Its width was about nine or ten feet. He'd been a useful long-jumper at school, but the more he looked at the distance he had to jump the less he liked it. It was a standing jump, which had to be made from a slippery stance on the ice slope. Supposing it failed? He'd land on the snow bridge, but if it collapsed … He glanced into the bottle-green depths. He told himself with the reckless confidence of youth that he was making an absurd fuss over something he could manage with the greatest of ease, and he set to work to cut out a wide and solid platform for the leap.

As he hacked away the sun in the west shone and salty sweat stung his eyes. It was profoundly quiet, but once or twice he heard and felt the vibration of thunder. Apart from that the only sounds were the thudding of his ice-axe and the tinkling of ice fragments as they skipped into the depths at his feet, sounds that grew fainter and fainter until they faded away into silence.

At last the platform was ready. It was a good one with plenty of room for both feet, but now everything was prepared, his doubts returned with redoubled force. Why not return to the top of the mountain? Even if he was benighted he would get down all right. No, the steps he had made would be melted away by the hot afternoon sun and he was too tired to remake them. Worse still was a perverse devil of pride. He had set off on a different route down, and he was going through with it come what might. What an idiot he was! Then came a loud rumble of thunder. It needed something outside him to force a decision.

The thunder, with its threat of approaching storm did it. He shuffled his boot nails well home into the ice, grasped his ice-axe in his right hand, its pick projecting outwards and away from his body, bent his knees, and putting everything he had into it, jumped.

His upper body landed on the far edge of the bergschrund. His feet struck the snow bridge, driving straight through the sun-softened snow into nothingness. But the ice-axe pick had driven well home into firm snow and the balance was in his favour. With a huge effort he heaved and levered himself forwards and upwards onto the solid lip of the bergschrund, and lay panting and trembling. At the same time he heard the fragments of the broken snow-bridge thudding into the depths of the bergschrund. He ought to have been thankful for a providential escape — he would never forget that feeling of useless legs, dangling in space — but his predominant feeling was shame at his stupidity. He deserved to be dead, but he was alive.[1]

Two

Childhood

On a sunny day in July 1897 a small wedding party emerged from the parish church of St Augustine's at Flimwell, a hamlet near Hawkhurst in rural Sussex. The bride and groom, together with the bride's parents, her six sisters and brothers, and the best man, made their way to a leafy corner of the churchyard where a photographer waited, his large camera on its tripod at the ready. A group was arranged. The photographer retreated to bury himself under his black cloth. He exhorted his subjects to keep perfectly still, and with a flourish of the lens cap he exposed the light-sensitive glass plate for the required seconds. And like a latter-day renaissance painting, the moment was captured for generations to come. It was the marriage of Algernon Smythe and Florence Reeves, the parents of my father, Frank.

Algernon, hands behind his back gazes steadily at the camera, quietly satisfied. The previous year his first wife, Rose had died from heart failure at the early age of 41 and the prospect of a solitary old age had been disheartening. He was 59 and the latest in his family to take control of a large timber business in Maidstone that had been run by Smythes since 1785. His bride's father, Francis Reeves was an old friend just four years his senior, and marrying his eldest daughter suited both men admirably. Florence however seems preoccupied. At 32 there had been a risk of remaining unmarried, but the age gap between her and Algernon was formidable. Marrying him had been a big step to take. And among all the photographs filling the albums in my family this one is perhaps the most poignant. For any doubts Florence harboured about the future would prove sadly prescient. Within a short time she would suffer calamities that would shape the rest of her life.

She had been born near Hawkhurst into a wealthy hop farming family. Several of the houses once occupied by her ancestors still exist, magnificent mansions lovingly restored by their twenty-first-century owners, with trims lawns and immaculate borders. The hop fields have gone, but her father had employed over 30 men and boys to tend 680 acres, roughly a square mile — an enormous crop feeding an insatiable brewing demand. He and her mother, Janet, had taken care to provide their seven children with a good education; Florence had attended an exclusive boarding school at Hackney run by a clergyman's widow with three governesses instructing a handful of girls. At the time of her marriage she was living with her family at the Hall at Wateringbury, near Maidstone, where her father was running a smaller farm in his later years. She had enjoyed a happy childhood in a big family ruled by loving parents who were strong Christian believers.

Frank's birthplace in Tonbridge Road, Maidstone stood a few hundred yards up the hill from the timber yard and offices of the Smythes' business beside the river Medway. When I visited a century later the yard had disappeared and in its place loomed a new Crown Court. Where there had been sheds and cranes and great stacks of logs, sawmills, and even a row of terraced houses for the workers, there was now a huge modern structure of concrete and dark glass and a car park. After decades of amalgamations and takeovers the company had finally been swallowed up by Travis Perkins, the giant building materials group who sold the site and established a branch downriver.

But the house up the hill was still there, a squat Victorian villa of yellow brick. It was no longer a private residence. High-powered lights, cameras and barred windows indicated that Number 32 served some more sinister purpose. I rang the bell. In a small reception room a woman explained to me that the premises were now operated by the Kent Probation Service. Any requests for further information would have to be made to the Home Office. There was no chance of my being given a guided tour of my father's birthplace. I stood on the pavement of the busy street again and thought of Florence. Her arrival here and her varying fortunes seemed to echo the problems of my own visit and search for glimpses of the past.

She and Algernon shared the house with the son and three daughters of her husband's first marriage. Bernard, aged 20, was working now with his father at the yard. Muriel, Kathleen and Evelyn were in their late teens. So while Florence was the new mother, the step-mother, the female head of the household, her role was unclear. When Algernon was there things should be straightforward, but when he was not ... Much would depend on the right kind of support from her husband. She was in a position that a modern agony aunt might write columns about.

Her first child, a boy, was born a year after her marriage. Whether or not an addition to his family appealed to Algernon he may have felt that a baby would help his young wife settle in her new home. And it would also be an interest for his daughters while he and Bernard worked at the yard. But within days disaster struck — the infant son died. What happened isn't known, but there are grim pointers. Maidstone had a reputation for unusually poor public health. There was its ancient sewer system and polluted wells. A recent typhoid outbreak had killed 130 people. There had been a wave of diphtheria, lethal for babies, and a measles epidemic. The infant death toll, usually one in every six births, had gone even higher. As often happened in those days the death went unregistered. No record exists of a doctor's visit. The baby wasn't even given a name.

Florence was devastated. It was a tragedy that helps to explain the difficult relationship she was to form with her surviving second and only child, another son.

He was born two years later, on 6 July 1900, and christened Francis Sydney. Studio photographs of him up to 12 years show him in a variety of costumes. A shepherd's smock and a seaside spade, the spade with a sailor suit, and weirdest of all, a Norfolk jacket and watch chain, Eton collar, knickerbockers, shiny boots, and a mournful dog on a plush chair.

The interesting thing about these images is that the young Frank looks thoroughly healthy. He has a fresh plump face and sturdy frame. He stands up straight and fixes the camera with a confident stare. The photographs do nothing to allay the suspicion that the illnesses he was supposed to have contracted in childhood were more the product of a worried mother's imagination than strict fact. It's easy to visualise the cautious family GP facing the anxious mother who'd lost her first child. And Frank himself in later life occasionally found it convenient to add an ailing childhood to the list of drawbacks he'd had to overcome as a successful mountaineer, although I don't think he ever seriously believed he'd been a weakling. Writing to his mother some 30 years later he quipped, 'Do you remember how you used to admonish me if I got wet feet and tell me to put an overcoat on? I believe you would still do it — and it would give me quite a thrill. Now I sweat and shiver and my wet feet dry on me — I'm scorched by suns and frozen by blizzards and in a little time I may be all out on that last thousand feet of Everest.'[1]

Algernon was the youngest of 10 children and had been head of the business since his brother, John died in 1895. In its first 120 years the company had produced paper, sawn and traded timber, and carted beer, slate and cement

— hard gritty work which seemed an unlikely background for the young Frank, destined for a somewhat different career. His mother though, must surely have nursed an image of a fulfilled life for herself, safe jobs in the business for the children God might see fit to bless them with, and peaceful final years for the husband she would look after in his retirement. She had married a man who had achieved everything he had set out to do. His business was prospering. He was a director of Maidstone's gas and water and other large companies. He was the vice-chairman of the Medway Lower Navigation Company. He sponsored the town's annual cricket week and the Carnival.

But there would be no golden years for Algernon. In those days men without a strong constitution tended not to survive a life of hard physical work beyond what is now considered late middle-age, and his decline began soon after Frank's birth. There are clues in the *Kent Messenger* report after his death on 25 January 1902:

> Mr Smythe had been in failing health for the past 12 months, and for some time had taken no active part in the conduct of his business, but until a day or two before his death had been able to go out and take exercise. The end, however, came with something of suddenness, and he passed away about 12 o'clock on Saturday night, at his residence, 32, Tonbridge Road. The deceased gentleman, who was 63 years of age, was well known in the district. In politics he took no part, and it was as a businessman that he was solely known.

So Frank was left without a father. He was 18 months old.

The doctor attending Algernon gave the cause of death as chronic nephritis and uraemia, an illness known as Bright's disease and essentially kidney failure, desperately debilitating if left untreated, with the blood becoming increasingly contaminated with urine. No therapies were available then and accumulating fluid would cause puffiness of the face or even bloating of the whole body; Algernon's plump-jowled appearance in his wedding photograph suggests he may have begun to suffer from the condition five years before his death.

The dynamics of the family now changed. Bernard became head of both business and household, and saw Florence as an interloper, an attitude confirmed by his son Percy a century later.[2] The infant Frank made things worse. At the end of a hard day Bernard did not enjoy coming back to noise and mess. The only mercy was that his youngest sister Kathleen was kind to Frank and helped look after him.

A much worse aggravation for Bernard was his father's Will. He inherited the business and a farm and a piece of land off the Tonbridge road. But no other property, and no cash. Florence was left most of the money, investments and the income from them, plus the rent from four houses and shops. The Estate was valued at just under £50,000 — the equivalent of about £5 million a century later. A serious quarrel erupted 25 years later when Frank broke his contract with an employer and his Maidstone relatives as guarantors were involved in legal action. Bernard's worst fears were realised. His step-brother was a liability, a black sheep who remained so in the eyes of these hard-working Maidstone folk, to whom writing books and climbing mountains could never be thought of as a proper way to earn a living.

The scene — a French train travelling south to Montreux on Lake Geneva. It's the end of a hot stuffy night in a compartment shared by an Englishwoman, her small boy, his nurse, and a Frenchman. They are all asleep except for the boy who steals to the window, raises the blind, lowers the window and peers out. He was to remember that instant for the rest of his days. There would be other moments pointing the way in life, but none quite like this:

> We were on a down grade and moving fast. A clean, cold air tore at my hot face. Above rose hills and forests. The dawn was putting out the stars. The train swung round a corner and passed clear of the hills and forests. I was suddenly conscious of space and distance. A plain was spread before me. But it was not that which caused a strange stirring of my blood, a quickening of life itself; it was that beyond the plain, and just visible in the dawn, I saw the Alps. So high they were and so remote, so distant, dim and cloud-woven, that to me, a child, gazing for the first time, it was as though God had chosen to manifest Himself by raising earth to sky and making of it a single step to heaven.[3]

The boy was of course Frank, and his mother was taking him to Switzerland. And as she dozed in the train she would have had no inkling of what a pivotal moment this was for her son. She couldn't have seen that with mountains in his blood, his schooldays would be a fiasco because of this distraction. Or that his half-hearted attempts to make a living doing things he wasn't interested in would cause her so much frustration and expense. She would never have dreamt that climbing would consume him, and that for the rest of her life she would endure the unending worry of his climbing not just on homeland hills and in the Alps, but in Asia on expeditions to the highest and most dangerous mountains in the world.

When Florence decided to head for Switzerland in May 1908, the reason she gave for the move was her son's health. Frank once casually listed an extraordinary set of illnesses that he believed he suffered from in childhood — chronic bronchitis, influenza, pneumonia (twice) and an enlarged heart. But he claimed all this came 'after enduring various scholastic experiments' after his initial education at preparatory school, which *followed* his spell in Switzerland. The only possible conclusion is that the ailments either didn't happen or were grossly exaggerated. The reality was that life for Florence in Maidstone had gone from fraught to impossible. Two of Bernard's sisters had married and moved away, and in a few weeks' time, in June that year, Bernard himself would marry. He had made it clear that he would not be moving. His bride would be coming to live with him at the family home. And so Florence had quit Maidstone, the beginning of a tortuous nomadic life.

Frank made many visits to Switzerland but none was as boring and frustrating as that at the age of seven. The Smythe entourage settled at a hotel at Chateau d'Oex above Montreux. There were walks and picnics, but it took months of pestering before he was allowed to go up a mountain. This was Mont Cray, a nearby hill for which he joined a group guided by a local lad aged 16.

It's a special moment in the life of a climber, the first walk up a hill. He remembered a calm September morning, dewy pastures and smoke rising from chalets. Then the forest, a part of the climbing experience that became sacred to him — forests were the link between the human world and the regions above of rock, snow and ice. They were places of changing mood, sunny and cheerful or gloomy and threatening, alive with birdsong or silent as a grave. In years to come he would rest among the trees late on a summer evening after a climb, or ski through their snow-laden ranks on short winter days. He would admire and photograph them, especially outpost pines that had withstood the storms. Sometimes the fringe of a forest was a place to rest; he believed the occasional lazy day was an important part of the mountain experience.

On Mont Cray he panted up behind his nonchalant young guide and discovered simple things that became instincts of a lifetime. How to walk up a hill — the placing of each foot, the smooth swing in balance from one leg to the next. The summit was a disappointment — an easing of the slope and a little heap of stones. He didn't join the rush to eat lunchtime sandwiches but found a quiet place to sit, enjoy the view and think. In years to come he would be accused of ambition, competitiveness and money-making, but he never lost touch with those early feelings for hills.

They were back in England in the autumn of 1909. His education could be delayed no longer, but where could they go? His mother did what many retired or widowed people did and still do now; she headed for the south coast. Hastings, Brighton, Bognor and Worthing were popular, but Bexhill had become fashionable and ideal for another reason. In those days of Empire many army officers serving overseas with their wives looked for boarding education for their children in England. And Bexhill obliged with a large number of private schools, particularly preparatory schools. They provided what was wanted — a good education with firm discipline. And the elegant town prospered. It saw itself as 'the last great Sussex seaside resort'. Florence remembered it from family outings of her own childhood. It would also be where she would return for the last years of her life.

THREE

Schooldays

'Shy, inattentive, and unable to make friends easily.' When Frank arrived at Devonshire House preparatory school at Bexhill in January 1910 he had missed the first term of the school year. He was a boarder so for the first time in his life he was away from his mother. That first school report told its own sorry little story.

In the town's public library I came across a description of the school by a former pupil, His Honour Judge Michael Birks. He told how in the schoolroom with its long oak benches and desks with inkwells and lids that lifted up there was a bookcase with a drawer containing a collection of Indian swords and daggers. 'In retrospect it is astonishing to think that such an armoury was left within the reach of boys,' he wrote, 'but I do not remember anyone coming to any harm.' Boys addressed one another by surname — Christian names were unthinkable. It was like 'a private house in which twenty-five boys happened to be living.' Black suits with long trousers were worn on Sunday. Hands were inspected before meals and the plentiful but stodgy food was served by maids little older than the senior boys. There were sports days, midnight feasts, hobbies, 'crazes' and home-made fireworks on Guy Fawkes night. But the Judge also remembered being bullied; there was too much leisure time, especially at weekends. 'There were only four or five boys who were natural bullies but it did not need much encouragement for the pack instinct to affect the rest, who then joined in with gusto.' He also remembered being punished by the Headmaster, receiving two strokes of the cane for the apparently simple offence of rampaging with a group through the lavatories. 'The strokes left raised red weals on one's bottom which gradually changed to purple bruises and could last a month or more. Nowadays this would be seen as sadistic torture and a terrible humiliation, giving rise to psychological injury. Such a thought never occurred to us. It was soon over, and preferable to being kept indoors.

At the same time we learned to accept pain and bear it with courage. The boy who let out so much as a whimper knew that he would receive no mercy from the other boys. If, on the other hand you took it in silence the bruises became a source of pride and earned the respect of the other boys.'

While Frank worked out how to survive at Devonshire House his mother stayed at Beach Towers, a private hotel about a mile away on the sea front. It was a smart area. The huge Metropole hotel loomed close by and good shops lay within a few minutes' walk. Along West Parade's beach the bathing machines lined up like tanks, ready to be drawn on their huge iron wheels into the sea, allowing females attired in swimming clothes with barely an inch of skin showing to step directly into the water. Other ladies rode bicycles along the Boulevard. Trams trundled, horses-and-carts clattered. The shops in St Leonard's Road sported canvas awnings to protect their windows from the English Riviera sun.

Boys from Devonshire House left when they were 13, usually to go to independent senior schools. One of these was Berkhamsted School in Hertfordshire, and Florence decided to move there and enter Frank as a day boy. It was handy for London, and the school, although mainly boarding, took a proportion of 'day bugs', as he scornfully called himself. But he appeared content with his new status, perhaps because he'd had a rough time as a boarder at Bexhill, the most likely reason for his mother withdrawing him from his prep school nearly a year earlier than normal, at the beginning of the spring term in January 1913 when he was still 12.

Progress at Berkhamsted depended on adequate performance in all classroom subjects, any weaknesses obliging a boy to stay in that form to repeat the syllabus for a further year, including even those subjects he did well at — in Frank's case, English and geography. 'Eventually,' he said, 'I drifted into the Remove, and there in company with other flotsam I remained for the remainder of my schooldays.'[1] He admitted he was lazy and daydreamed about mountains. Sometimes he felt he couldn't win. When he was asked the name of the highest mountain in Switzerland he replied correctly that it was the Dom, but on being told the answer was Mont Blanc he was severely reprimanded for arguing the point.* 'My schooldays,' he summed up, 'were not happy ones.'

But in saying this he ignored one thing he enjoyed and became good at — cricket. Playing in the school's first 11, he was a medium-fast bowler and not a bad tail end batsman. His finest hour came in June 1918 when, playing against strong opposition he took five wickets for only 20 runs. He was also superb at throwing the cricket ball; a special event in the annual Sports Day which,

---

*Frank and his teacher were both wrong! Switzerland's highest mountain is Monte Rosa.

in 1917, he won with a record throw of over 93 yards. He also played football for his St Bees House team. These reports again throw into doubt the image of an ailing lad beset by illnesses and forbidden by the doctors to take part in games — a scenario that he was content for others to accept.

One school contemporary was Bill Tilman, the outstanding explorer and climber. They confronted each another in a house cricket match, in which Tilman bowled Frank out who then got his revenge by catching Tilman. Raymond Greene was a good friend who became a climber and doctor and joined him on expeditions to Kamet and Everest. He discovered a heart abnormality in Frank on the Kamet expedition and decided it was nothing sinister — just a heart that had an unusual beat and not worth worrying about. Raymond and his family were well involved with Berkhamsted. His father, Charles was the headmaster, and he had two successful brothers at the school: Hugh, later a BBC Director General, and Graham, the novelist.

In August 1914 Frank returned from a holiday in Cornwall with his mother to find the First World War had begun. Berkhamsted was in turmoil. He jokingly remembered the German master being arrested and the tramp who slept in the school armoury and was nearly shot by a guard. Elderly 'local luminaries' advised the populace to stay indoors in an air raid since bombs 'nearly always slid off the roof'. But then for Frank, the fun died:

Somewhere, not very distant, the Great Killing went on. It was possible to hear the sound of it from a dell on Northchurch Common — a dull vibration as though something evil breathed. On Sundays aged clerics, specially imported for the occasion, ranted from the chapel pulpit. Soon we would be serving our country, perhaps dying for it. It was a Holy War. We were soldiers of Christ fighting against the forces of darkness and evil. Right was on our side. God would grant us the victory. Let us pray to Him. And day-by-day a line of black-edged cards along the chapel wall grew longer.

There was one boy. We called him 'Spider,' because he was long and thin, all arms and legs. He had a mop of sandy hair, and a freckled face in which was set a snub nose and humorous, mischievous blue eyes. Although in the 'Upper Fifth' or 'Sixth,' his mercurial, happy-go-lucky disposition was always landing him in trouble. One Saturday afternoon I found myself in detention school for laziness and inattention.

It was a glorious afternoon, ideal for cricket, and I had to copy several pages of irregular French verbs. I found myself next to the 'Spider.' He turned to me and whispered:

'I say, it's not much fun being cooped up here an afternoon like this. You know', his eyes were unusually serious, 'I've a feeling —'

But what the 'Spider's' feeling was I do not know, because the master on duty overheard him and ordered us to move apart. It was a pity that the 'Spider' could not have enjoyed that sunny afternoon, for a few months later when some more of those black-edged cards were posted up on the chapel wall, his name was on one of them.

Many school hours in those days were devoted to military training. We shot at targets that had a human figure in lieu of a bull's-eye. To say that school OTCs are not for training boys in the art of war, and that the only object of an OTC is to inculcate a habit of discipline and command, is as fantastic as it is absurd. They wear the trappings of war. They have field days which do nothing more nor less than mimic battles. Has any school the pluck to print in its prospectus: 'One of our aims is to teach your son to be a soldier. From 13 years of age onwards we will instruct him in the art of killing. He shall be well grounded in this before he has time to think for himself. Otherwise it might occur to him that it is disagreeable to kill his fellow men. Worse still, he might learn to prefer living to dying for his country. Horrible thought — he might even become a pacifist.'

This cynical piece suggests that Frank became a pacifist but he was simply expressing his disgust at the slaughter. It was a desperate time with 230 school-leavers losing their lives. Three sons of one family were killed. One boy became a pilot, flew his plane over the school playing fields, then crashed and died in front of his brother. On Armistice Night in November 1918 the headmaster refused to allow celebrations. The town was en fête, but the boarders had to sit down that evening and do their homework. It was a matter, said Greene, of preparing for a new future. But some townsfolk burst into the School, threatened to throw Greene in the canal, and persuaded the boys to break the curfew. Later that night Greene expelled 122 boys when they crept back into school, but next morning rescinded the order on all but two.

Frank missed recruitment for the war and almost inevitably the trenches, where casualties scarcely slackened before the final day, because of a chance piece of bureaucracy. At the end of the summer term in July 1918 he left school having turned 18 that month, and awaited his call-up papers. On 7 August however, Florence received a letter from his housemaster informing her that although he had served in the school's army cadet corps and even been promoted to Corporal the previous April, in order to comply fully with the current War Office Scheme he must return to school for a further term to join the Cadet Battalion. It's tempting to think that his housemaster, sickened by the slaughter, had been unusually diligent in discovering this, but his mother was happy enough to comply, and her relief in November when the last shot was fired can be imagined.

His final school report makes depressing reading. His positions in classroom subjects mostly bump along the bottom and the space for Examinations Passed remains blank. His cricket record is noted. Under Intended Profession someone has written 'Army (RFC.)' but subsequently crossed it out. The Royal Flying Corps was formed in 1916 as a branch of the Army. It was the fledgling Royal Air Force, and twice in later years the RAF would play a part in his life.

Frank saw his life at home and school as boringly trivial. He'd been given a pocket edition of Edward Whymper's *Scrambles Amongst the Alps* and read it so many times that when it came my way it had literally fallen apart. He read every book on climbing from the school library and pored over maps he bought with his pocket money, dreaming of what it must be like to venture into mountainous areas coloured dark brown, purple or white. His heroes were the great names of exploration — Whymper, Mummery, Conway, Freshfield, Scott and Shackleton. Switzerland was a distant memory and even the British hills were out of reach. Mountains offered fierce challenges but he had to be content with exploring the Chilterns on his bicycle. He had to persuade himself that scale didn't matter, and years later after going to the Himalayas decided this was true and never scorned even the lowliest British hills.

In the summer of 1915 he had a holiday in North Wales, his mother deciding it was easier to bow to her son's obsession than resist it. They stayed in a boarding house on the coast near Llandudno. From here he pushed his bicycle up a hill that reached the important 1,000-foot contour where he had a view of the distant range of Snowdonia. He was deeply affected by these far views — the rolling Weald during a picnic as a child, the Alps from the train when he was a bit older. Now the magic gripped him again:

> From the point where I ate my lunch the hills, patched untidily with stone walls and sprinkled with trees and cottages, extended northwards towards the valley of the Conway. Beyond this valley were the hills of Snowdonia …
>
> There came to me a great desire to tread those hills. I wanted to feel them beneath me, to see them around me, above me and below me. I wanted to be soaked by rain and dried by sun; to sweat, to shiver, to toil, to rest. There was something I had to seek. What it was I did not know. I only knew I had to seek it.

But it was another three years before the opportunity came to explore Snowdonia. He sometimes wrote about youthful rambles and early climbs in Wales, suggesting that even as a child he was cycling and exploring there on his own. It was wishful thinking. The fact is that after his months in Switzerland at the age of eight, which yielded only a bit of supervised walking, he was limited to seaside holidays and local walks and bike rides. The holiday on the North Wales coast was merely frustrating, and the year after that he wasn't allowed off the leash even though he was 16. This seems incredible nowadays but a century ago family ties were strong, the war put a damper on people enjoying themselves and Frank was the only child of a widowed mother who feared for his safety and couldn't understand why he wouldn't willingly stay at home and play tennis or enjoy a seaside holiday.

In 1918 the summer holidays at the end of his final school year beckoned. The war was dragging on towards its bloody conclusion and if he wasn't conscripted into the army he was going to have to decide on a career, although nobody seemed to know what it could be. Only one thing mattered to him that summer though: his mother agreed to another holiday in North Wales. This time it was to be Borth-y-Gest, a little village adjoining Porthmadog. A few miles south of Snowdon, it was as close as you could get to the mountains and still be at the seaside. And knowing that once they arrived she would probably see little of her son, Florence invited a friend from Berkhamsted, Mary Johnson, and her children to join them. It was a fateful decision. The two families already knew one another well, but the holiday brought them closer together. A decade later Frank would marry Kathleen, my mother and the youngest of Mary's three children.

The two women had much in common. Mary, known to her family and friends as Mollie, lived a few hundred yards and a couple of streets from Florence. She was also a widow, her husband, Alexander having died three years before. Like Florence's husband, Alex had been quite a bit older than Mollie but had retired early from his lucrative position as a consulting engineer in ships' boiler design. Just before his death he'd been fit and well but had got soaked in a rainstorm and caught flu which turned to pneumonia, and died with dreadful suddenness. It was a terrible blow for Mollie. She was 40, a qualified nurse and had worked in a North London hospital before her marriage. She would have become familiar with the fearful sight of a patient struggling for breath from pneumonia in the days before life-saving antibiotics. Now her own family was torn apart by the illness. But Mollie was a strong, decisive woman who went on to rule her family with matriarchal authority, and Florence, of a quieter, more nervous disposition, must have found her good company as two people of different natures but with problems in common sometimes do. They had originally met at the Mothers' Union. Both were staunch Christians. The two families had moved to Berkhamsted at about the same time. Mollie had been left with enough money for her children's education, at Berkhamsted School for the two boys, and the independent Girls' School for Kathleen. At the time of the holiday in North Wales Kenneth was just 16, Esmond 14 and Kathleen 10.

The Johnsons were more 'into' Berkhamsted than the Smythes. Mollie organised tennis parties — the photo album is full of shots of happy young players on garden courts, usually with Mollie in the background, smartly turned out in Empire-line dress, coat and beehive hat. There were picnics on the Common, swimming groups at Tring. The Johnsons had a wide circle of friends — the Hendersons, the Hawdons, the Squibbs's, the Forbes Milnes, the Ellerbys, the Pooles. Their garden was full of deck chairs, bicycles and a dog called Sam. They were often visited by Mollie's two sisters — my great aunts — who both lived to be a hundred. The sisters lived in Felixstowe and Mollie and her family had holidays on the pebbly beach there and swam in the freezing North Sea. There are pictures of older generations of Mollie's family, the Hellyers, one of whom, her father, was a very good wood carver. When he wasn't working on commissions for ship's figureheads and church screens he carved every piece of furniture he could lay his hands on. My birthday present from him when I was about four was a tiny stool with a depiction of a boy in a kayak named Tony and the motto 'Paddle Your Own Canoe'. He sent it by nailing on an address label and handing it to the postmistress. I have it still. The Johnsons lived a sociable life, mildly eccentric but somehow quite normal in the middle-class bourgeois circle they moved in. They were mainly impractical, propped up by their servants, but good manners and etiquette mattered more than anything. Emotion was something to be controlled and discussion about anything personal taboo, but they were happy to gossip about royalty or the Titanic or Bunny Austin losing his temper and throwing his racket into the crowd at Wimbledon. An extraordinary but typical piece of family lore that came my way as a child was the maxim that 'A gentleman is a man who uses a butter-knife when he is alone.'

Frank doesn't appear in the Johnsonian orbit, and I think that Florence, when she wasn't having tea with Mollie and talking about mutual school problems, lived a less sociable life. It was the difference between a fairly normal, jolly outgoing family who were carrying on despite the loss of husband and father, and a bereaved woman in a self-imposed exile worrying about her only son who was a failure at school, pined for mountains and seemed happiest with his own company.

The holiday went pretty much as imagined by Florence. Frank headed for the hills on his bicycle while the others enjoyed the beach. 'I cycled from Borth-y-Gest,' he wrote many years later, 'where I was undergoing what I have always detested, a seaside holiday.' But the Johnson album has one photo to prove that Frank joined the others, if only the once. It is a picture taken by him — as Esmond told us — of the others. The party is sitting in a sandy cove, their beach things strewn around them. Ken and Esmond are fully dressed apart from bare feet, as though they're about to go to school, long trousers and jacket, white shirt, school tie. Ken, looking up from a book smiles impishly while Mollie and Florence in their white blouses and sun hats have that frozen expression when the photographer has taken too long to press the shutter. Kathleen stares steadily into the lens of her future husband. Part of the snap is fogged. It's the earliest surviving photograph Frank ever took.

His first outing was to Moel Hebog, a hill above the Aberglaslyn Pass. It was his first summit and it could easily have been his last. Not wanting to reach the top by one of the easy ridges he took the face direct, deliberately climbing a rocky gully. It began to rain, the steepening rocks grew slippery and high up he became frightened, picturing, as every climber does, the consequences of a slip. He managed to conquer his rising panic and escaped onto easier ground. He had set himself up to be a statistic, a body the rescue teams pick off mountains everywhere, and shake their heads over, and talk about the foolhardiness of the victim.

Frank knew he'd been stupid. He had an impulsive streak in his nature that would often lead to rash acts. Like many climbers he would be endangered occasionally by his own impetuousness, incompetence or carelessness, and like all climbers he would always be potentially a victim of plain bad luck which, short of avoiding mountains altogether he could do nothing about. Risk however was a different matter. In the course of a lifetime in the hills he necessarily faced immense danger at times but he developed that ability to calculate risks with a fine sense of what made a route unacceptable and what made it a reasonable risk. The non-climber often can't understand the subtle difference between the two, and of course anyone can run out of luck in the end, as Frank well knew. But he gave himself an extra edge by careful obser-vation of how mountains behave. He educated himself about snow and ice and its stability in different conditions. He became entranced by its beauty, while knowing that it could wipe out a climber or a whole team in a sérac collapse. He took an obsessive interest in the potential for a slope to avalanche and witnessed more than once a mountainside that he felt wasn't quite right and therefore to be avoided, sometimes at the expenditure of much effort, breaking away in a deadly slide. He learnt about weather, the results of sudden temperature changes, and the signs of oncoming storms. He made the wry comment that Providence looked kindly upon the aspiring young climber, but he knew in his heart that for a novice to depend on this was reckless. A couple of times, on Kangchenjunga and in the Alps, he was accused of cowardice but although annoyed he didn't try to defend himself. In each case he was following his instinct for survival that at times appeared to have almost a psychic input. His record, his mountaineering CV, was hardly that of a coward.

If I have allowed myself to get off the subject of North Wales in 1918, it's to introduce the vital issue of mountain risk that for Frank began on the cliffs of Moel Hebog as a novice's terror, but continued as a threat to be mastered with a cool head and experience. His early ventures into the hills were all made solo, which in some ways increased the dangers, but that is assuming a companion would have had the skill and experience to make things safer. As it was, he had embarked on a learning curve and had survived the first dangerous moments. Compared with the guidance and supervision young novices usually receive today, it's a horror story, and there was a lot more of it to come in the Alps. But somehow, he would emerge a very talented all-round mountaineer.

He made several more expeditions from Borth-y-Gest. He rambled over the Glyders and Tryfan. He traversed the Snowdon Horseshoe, and returned there on another day to climb Lliwedd, the 900-foot crag forming the southerly arm of the horseshoe. This was a very ambitious scramble up a cliff that although broken is steep and exposed and needs care and some luck to find a route that avoids difficulties. Frank thought he had learnt a lesson after the scare on Moel Hebog but his elation as he neared the top received a nasty shock. As he pulled onto a ledge he surprised a sheep that immediately jumped away, skidded on a sloping slab and fell hundreds of feet to its death.

One last outing was over the little pointed peak of Cnicht, near Portmadog. 'I took one of my schoolmates with me,' he wrote, 'but he did not like mountain climbing and sat down and said he was tired. So I completed the ascent on my own.' The reluctant companion was Ken, who when the incident was described had become Frank's brother in law.

FOUR

Yorkshire Rambler

When Frank left school in December 1918 he was under pressure to decide on a career. It was said half-jokingly that he agreed to be an electrical engineer because the training would take him to the north of England, which would mean being near hills. Faraday House Electrical Engineering College offered a course in which the first year consisted of lectures and laboratory classes at the College in London, with the second year given to practical experience in a factory. Years three and four would be spent abroad, working for the diploma. Prospective students were not required to have strong academic qualifications. Frank duly enrolled, and on the morning of Monday 6 January 1919 he presented himself at the Electrical Standardising Testing and Training Institution in Southampton Row for day one of his new life.

Schools and Colleges are all about teaching. Dr Alexander Russell was the Principal Lecturer at Faraday House and had been on the staff since the College's foundation in 1890. He had a first class honours degree in mathematics and philosophy. He was a world authority on alternating current and electric cables. His list of qualifications alone was enough to send anyone running for cover; he was a Master of Art, Doctor of Science, Doctor of Literature, Fellow of the Royal Society and Master of the Institution of Electrical Engineers.

But he was also blessed with vitality and enthusiasm. He was a Scot, a large man with an open friendly face, and was known as 'Daddy' Russell because of his fatherly concern for his students. As a lecturer he achieved legendary status. A story goes that he was showing a method of calculating the length of a belt driving two pulleys of known diameters. He got so enthusiastic that he eventually covered two blackboards. What had started as a simple problem had developed into one of astronomical complexity. Hardly anyone knew what he was talking about. Then suddenly he turned round with a smile and said, 'Of course, if you really met this problem in a works, you would take a piece of string, pass it around the pulleys and measure the length required.'

He was fascinated by atmospheric electricity, and it was this that prompted Frank's interest in mountain thunderstorms, which he chose as a specialist subject for study. Some years later in the Bernese Oberland he gained unwanted experience by being caught in the worst electrical storm of his life.

In December 1919 he made his move north to Bradford to begin the second year. He lodged at St Luke's vicarage in East Morton, a pleasant little village perched on the edge of the moors north of the city and handy for his workplace at a factory in the Aire Valley below. When he wasn't working he was focussed on one thing only, the magical world that lay further north and west — the surrounding moors and crags of Yorkshire and the more distant hills of the Lake District. He had not only lived far from mountains but had totally lacked the company of other climbers. He had never known anyone else who was interested. His early years were a cocoon in which he matured slowly, educating himself with his mountain books and maps and nourished by his dreams. Now, in the north of England in his 20th year, urgently wanting to make up for a lot of lost time, he was about to break free.

The Yorkshire Ramblers' Club, founded in 1892, is one Britain's oldest climbing clubs, junior only to the Cairngorm Club and the Alpine Club. Its quaint name resulted from its first President, George T. Lowe, telling a friend that he would approach all the men he knew to be interested in 'rambling over our Yorkshire moors and fells with a view to forming a club and thus improving the chances of collecting larger groups for our outings.' Thirteen men attended the first meeting at a pub in Leeds and the Club was born.

I joined the YRC in 1954 while stationed near Darlington in the RAF. From the beginning I felt part of a big group of friendly men who all seemed to know one another and joked, laughed, drank beer, cooked huge quantities of food in the communal hut and planned the next day's climbing. Knowing that I was a newcomer they went out of their way to make sure I wasn't left out. When the conversation became general, at the table or round a huge fire, there were extraordinary stories told about the antics of earlier generations. Most of the others were older and many had responsible jobs in industry or the professions. If you needed information about anything, whether it was mechanical, financial, botanical, photographic, ornithological, or a replacement knee, there was someone in the YRC who was an expert. It wasn't a huge club

— the membership hovered at something under 200, of whom there were usually about 30 or 40 at meets. Some members, maybe most, were affluent, but subscriptions and levies for meals and hut fees were kept at a modest level. Monthly meets were arranged in all the mountainous areas of the British Isles with a yearly gathering in the Alps and the occasional expedition to a greater range. Unlike those aspiring to play cricket for Yorkshire, you didn't have to have been born in the county to be eligible for the YRC, although outsiders like me were probably in a minority. The club was men only, one of the last bastions of chauvinism in the climbing world, although now women are accepted. A song entitled 'Yorkshire' has been sung at the conclusion of every annual dinner since 1909. It has four solo verses, each followed by a chorus. The chorus, with respect, is excruciating, even after alcoholic dulling of the sensibilities:

> Here's a health, then lads to the Ridings three,
> To the broad acred shire in the North Countree:
> A health to bonny Yorkshire and all that she enfolds,
> From the Humber to the Tees, from the Pennines to the Wolds
> Here's a health, here's a health to Yorkshire!

This therefore was the club that Frank joined at the same age as me, some 35 years earlier. Like me he had made contact with the club within a short time of arriving in the North, and his arrival was remembered in a club journal article by a senior member, Ernest Roberts:

> It was one Sunday in December, 1919, soon after Frankland, Somervell and I had crossed Pool Bridge on our way to climb at Almscliff, that a cyclist overtook us and introduced himself as F.S. Smythe … Throughout that winter he climbed at Almscliff, and did his first Lakeland climb at Easter 1920 up Pavey Ark Little Gully. I found him to be exceptionally strong, and after a fortnight with him in August I reported that he had climbed the Eagle's Nest solo, and other severes, and that a new star had risen.

Of the three men Frank came across on his bike, the first, C.D. Frankland, was the best rock climber by far. Howard Somervell, ten years older than Frank, was a doctor, a quiet, energetic and deeply religious man who was to have a wonderful career, not so much in climbing — although he went twice to Everest and reached almost a record height — but eventually in treating the poor in India.

Ernest Roberts was the oldest of the trio and despite the age gap he became one of the best and most important friends Frank ever had.

Roberts was hugely respected in the Club. His record of climbing included routes in Wasdale in the company of legends such as the Abraham brothers, and a list of alpine ascents that qualified him for election to the Alpine Club in 1908, the same year that he joined the YRC. He held all the offices at various times in the 52 years he was a member. Even more than climbing he loved potholing, which has always been a speciality of the Club. My friend George Spenceley remembered travelling to potholes in Roberts' stately Armstrong Siddeley open tourer and as a very thin lad aged about 16 was sent down first, shouting from the depths at intervals to Roberts 'to prove that communication still existed.' When George returned from a wartime POW camp even thinner, Roberts decided that he was now the ideal shape to be the first down some exceptionally narrow and potentially dangerous unexplored rifts. 'It was very generous of him,' George assured me.

The Easter weekend of 1920 was Frank's chance to practice his skills on Lake District rock. This was much more serious climbing, where the leader then had little or no protection from a fall and where the climbs were much longer than at Almscliff. On his first climb he was relegated to last on the rope, but was happy with this:

> A mere novice's climb, but to me supremely enjoyable. I remember only vignettes: a thin mist that clung to the crags of Pavey Ark or poured inquiringly into the hollows, a downward glimpse between the dark walls of the gully to the waters of Stickle Tarn, and far beyond a dim brood of distant hills.

This extract from Frank's first book, *Climbs and Ski Runs,* gently revels in the homeland hills — rock-climbers' numb fingers in the rain, rests on sunny ledges on a precipice, shredding mist in a gale, the feel of soft turf underfoot, the delight of little streams, a dip in a cold tarn. But daydreaming had little place when he was introduced to rock-climbing. Like many climbers, once past the novice stage he became obsessed. The chat with friends, the pocket guidebooks with their little lists of climbs and standards, the need to test yourself and perhaps impress others — it was no different in Frank's day than it was in mine.

He was back in Langdale in May, climbing with anyone who was free, then in July went to Wasdale, again on his own. It was 20 years later when he admitted to a solo epic on the very hard Eagle's Nest Ridge:

Previously I had sworn that under no circumstances would I tackle any of those climbs relegated to the category of the 'exceptionally severe' but now my good resolutions went by the board. I removed my boots, and in another moment was treading the first steep rocks that lead up from one side on to the crest of the ridge. It was steep, steeper than I thought. I reached the point where it is necessary to pull up a vertical bit so as to gain the crest. Certainly it was more difficult than I had expected, the most difficult climb I had yet done, with or without a companion. I paused and looked down. There were some other climbers below, seated on the ledge known as the Grand Stand. They were regarding me intently; I dare say they were more than a trifle apprehensive as to the result of my antics. Youthful pride forbade retreat. Summoning up a show of resolution I advanced. The pull was made. In another moment I was on the crest of the ridge vowing that it had been perfectly easy. Now came the best part of the climb, a cat-like tread on stockinged feet from one small hold to the next on rough sun-warmed rock.[1]

Every rock-climber looks back for the rest of his life on such moments. A point on a climb when you're faced with a very worrying move and retreat isn't an option. Nowadays protective runners can be rigged almost anywhere, but those are not the situations I'm thinking of. The defining moments come when a long and probably fatal fall will result from a slip, and Frank soloing the Eagle's Nest Direct was such a moment. He appeared to restrict his soloing to a few occasions when he had no companion, but all one can say is that he was lucky, and unlike some he survived.

His apprenticeship in Bradford finished in the spring of 1921 and he went back to Berkhamsted for extra studies at Faraday House. He was keen to get back to the Lakes however, and an opportunity came in May. Again he made the pilgrimage by train and bus to Langdale, followed by the long plod with a heavy rucksack up Rossett Ghyll, over Esk Hause and Styhead Pass, and down to the climbers' 'doss' at the Burnthwaite Farm barn in Wasdale. Among the party was a young Scot, J.H.B. Bell.

Jim Bell was new to climbing. Like Frank he'd made solitary outings by bicycle to his native hills north of his home in Fife, and to Snowdonia from lodgings in Birmingham during his training to be an industrial chemist. But he was destined to become one of Scotland's finest mountaineers, making a huge number of new routes north of the border and climbing almost every summer in the Alps for two decades.

He and Frank teamed up, got on well and an enduring climbing partnership began. But it was a disconcerting beginning for Bell. Frank made few allowances, leading him up the climbs he had soloed the previous year including the Eagle's Nest Direct. Years later Bell wrote, 'He gave me an introduction to serious rock climbing and seemed to know all the best things to do and where to find them, even though it was his first visit to Wasdale.' Why Bell thought Frank was new to Wasdale is puzzling. Was his memory letting him down, or was his climbing partner playing a game to gain a psychological advantage? Whatever the answer to that, they agreed to join forces for more climbing at the first opportunity.

Frank was due to start the last part of his course at the end of the year, in Austria or Switzerland, and he viewed the prospect with mixed feelings. The Alps beckoned, but the need to persevere with his chosen career was depressing. It wouldn't have been so bad if engineering held the slightest appeal, but it didn't. During his year at Bradford he wrote to his mother often, but there was never a word about his work. He was good at shoving problems out of sight and out of mind until he had to face them. In September he arranged to meet Roberts for a final holiday in North Wales.

They stayed at a pub in Rhyd-Ddu near Beddgelert. Their intention was to explore a large cliff on Snowdon that had begun to be talked about but climbed on hardly at all; Clogwyn d'ur Arddu, the Black Cliff, or Cloggy as it has become known. Frank arrived a day early and set off to have a look on his own. Like every visitor, before and since, he was impressed.

The usual approach today is from Llanberis, a four-mile walk mainly following the Snowdon mountain railway until the cliff comes into sight and you branch off to its foot. From Rhyd-Ddu Frank took a path that meanders across the moors before crossing a low ridge into the cwm embraced by the great arms of the crag. Either way, nobody forgets his first view of Cloggy.

It is an enormous, awe-inspiring sweep of rock. Two great buttresses about 600 feet high form a centrepiece, with steep cracks, chimneys and walls on one, the east, and massive slabs, overlapping and overhanging one another on the west. Between them is a rake sloping up from right to left where men first ventured warily onto the crag, hunting for rare plants. The cliff faces north and apart from early or late on a summer's day when a low sun might touch its walls, it lies in shadow. A climber approaching its base feels that he is arriving in some great theatre. Everything becomes huge and the atmosphere funereal and forbidding. The east buttress looks desperately steep and the west buttress so undercut by its syncline strata that there seems no way of getting onto it. The rock is a silvery-grey, diamond-hard rhyolite and the wind blows coldly across the sharp vertical edges. Water drips from high overhead. The shouts of visitors echo eerily. The sunny slopes beyond the cwm suddenly have much greater appeal than this awful place.

Yet from the beginning Cloggy has exerted a powerful attraction on climbers and has been a venue for rock climbing at the highest level. It is an arena in which dreams have been realised, the impossible made real, reputations forged, epics endured and lives tragically lost. It has spawned half a dozen guidebooks, which have superseded one another as standards have risen. It has become a magnet for those dedicated to pushing the boundaries yet further, who train until arms and fingers, balance and brain have strength and understanding greater than ever before. It is a stage where technique, equipment, patience, a refusal to accept defeat, and skill and courage have resulted in climbs of ever-increasing grades on the blankest walls. It is for climbers the place where the rainbow ends, unique on the planet, legendary as Camelot.

And Frank, who later saw himself — and was seen — more as an all-round mountaineer than a rock climber, was to take part in the first ascent of one of the most important landmark routes in the story of man's duel with the crag.

But not this time. In three days he and Roberts, appalled by the main buttresses, found scrappy routes up the easier rocks of the Far West and Far East buttresses to which they gave the prosaic names, Giant's Trod and Non Such. It would be over six years before Frank returned to Cloggy to write his name in its history book.

FIVE

Alpine Apprentice

Frank left England in December 1921. A work experience programme had been fixed up for him at Baden in Switzerland, but this wasn't due to start until the following March and he'd persuaded his mother that he needed the extra months to improve his German. His real reason for leaving early, to go climbing and skiing in the Alps, he kept quiet about. Florence reluctantly agreed to the arrangement but decided they must go to Innsbruck for the interim since Austria was cheaper. And what's odd about this is not that they argued about the timing of their departure, but the fact that his mother was to be with him during his training abroad.

There would be little to interest her but she was in charge of the finances, and whether or not he preferred to be on his own, there was nothing he could do about that. Nowhere in his published descriptions of events during his year and a half in Austria and Switzerland is there any hint that his mother was there as well. Only in his letters to Roberts, who knew Florence, does she get an occasional mention, and she appears in one or two photographs. Frank didn't want to admit to having a clinging mother, but he wouldn't have been the first student to find himself in this position: dependent, and with no hope of independence.

But he was considerate towards her. Whenever they were apart he wrote to her. He wrote from camps up and down Mount Everest and from the Tibetan plateau. He wrote from boats to India and South America. He wrote from Scotland and from the Alps. He even wrote to his mother on the first night of his honeymoon. The letters sometimes revealed exasperation and embarrassment that she dogged him so pitifully. I was only four when Frank, and inevitably his mother too, separated themselves from our lives — a harrowing time that I deal with in this book when it comes. My older brother, John remembers her as a 'sweet and lovely grandmother' — very different from the fraught soul Frank was always trying to manage. In a photograph of her holding me on her knee she's wearing a polka-dot dress, a pearl necklace, and the wedding ring Algernon gave her. Her slightly frizzy hair is carefully arranged. She smiles, ignoring my squirming as Frank clicks the shutter. At 70 she has lots of lines round her eyes and the long nose, narrow mouth and long chin that Frank and I inherited.

Austria was much cheaper than Switzerland because of severe inflation after the First World War. The effects of this were starkly evident on their arrival in Innsbruck. The currency was falling in value almost daily. Tradesmen and hoteliers had to be alert to keep pace and even banks sometimes failed in their co-ordination, making it possible to change money at a profit. Tourists descended on the town and left in new fur coats and carrying suitcases stuffed with goods. 'Nothing short of plunder from a defenceless people fast sinking into ruin,'[1] Frank commented sadly. He was offered a valuable stamp collection for 'a mere song.' High-ranking Army officers could be seen doing menial jobs. There was a tall imposing man with a cavalry moustache, immaculate but always in the same suit, who had the 'saddest eyes' he had seen. Daily he appeared, slowly pacing the freezing streets and looking more and more pinched and drawn, until one day Frank saw him no more.

It was a sobering experience. Cushioned from the worst effects of the war by the English Channel he now came face to face with a people who had suffered military carnage and were destroyed financially. But there were crowded cafés and dance-floors in the evenings, and in the daytime skiers sought consolation in the open air. He was deeply impressed by the resilience of the Austrians and commented more than once on their stoicism, old-world courtesy and hospitality. It became the European country that was special to him.

His first venture into the mountains was on the Klein Brandjoch rising above the town, an undistinguished scramble but the first of the long list of climbs and peaks to support his application to join the Alpine Club. The next climb however, the Pfriemeswand, a 2,000-metre summit on the south side of the valley was a very different experience. He reached the top without difficulty but in trying to glissade down an easy slope found the wet snow sliding too, so he scrambled off the moving staircase and walked down in the wake of what became a wide avalanche. It seemed a harmless affair, just a grass slope with snow slipping down — until he came to the bottom. Here he found it piled in lumps to a depth of six feet, thousands of tons of the kind of snow that immediately sets like concrete, and if it doesn't crush its victim, suffocates him, even near the surface. The temperature had been rising all day, the Föhn wind was blowing, and he arrived back at Innsbruck bedraggled and thoughtful in heavy rain.

He had set himself to learn a lot, very quickly, including teaching himself to ski. As he slid up a valley in deep powder snow towards his next goal, an 8,000-foot pass, he became aware that the valley was narrowing and the sides steepening. Somewhere he'd read that these were classic conditions for an avalanche after new snow. He decided to go back but stopped at some hay huts to eat his lunch first. A little later he heard a rushing noise increasing to a roar. Not far up the valley an enormous powder-snow avalanche was thundering down from ledge to ledge, gathering huge quantities as it descended. On the opposite slopes the wind-blast bent large pine trees over like palms. The air was filled with a blizzard of icy powder obscuring the sun for minutes. He knew that had he continued he might have been overwhelmed. Perhaps acquired knowledge had saved him this time. Researching this first period of his big-mountain career — big as in Alpine — I was astonished by the number of potential disasters he survived, some by luck, some by a healthy instinct for self-preservation.

In February 1922 he and his mother moved 50 miles east to Kitzbühel. Here he joined Neil Hewett, another engineering student, and with Hewett's sister attempted the Gross Venediger, 3,674 metres, a climb that could be done largely on skis.

How often a young mountaineer's first high peak is a shambles. Everything went wrong for them. They skied in pouring rain with heavy rucksacks over the Thurn Pass, missed the train at Mittersil and slogged the rest of the way to Neukirchen, a total of about 30 miles. After an overnight stop at an inn they set off on a fine day for the Kürsinger Hut but lost the route and finished up at hay huts. They broke into one that happened to contain a stove, cooking utensils, mattresses and a supply of wood. Here they made a fire and ate all their food. Next day they set off early and at last climbed the glacier to the hut. But there were no blankets or fuel and in the morning, cold and hungry, anxious about the weather, they retreated.

But in time Frank would remember the fun, the banter, the summit that stayed out of reach. How often he dreamed about his youth and its foolishness! Then he would remember who he had become, a mature mountaineer and writer, cautious, critical and responsible …

In March 1922 he and his mother went to Baden, a small town near Zurich, and Frank reported for work at Brown Bowens, one of Switzerland's

biggest engineering companies. Faraday House had arranged the position of
trainee, with hands-on work experience when possible. But from the outset
it was a disaster. He described what happened in a letter to Ernest Roberts:[2]

> You will be interested to hear I have left my fourth-year firm. My short stay of
> a month there was a most unpleasant one … The heads of departments,
> foremen, etc. are Huns to the core, and as such delighted in making things
> unpleasant for an Englishman. The firm actually trade as a Swiss one, but is
> in reality owned by German capitalists … No interest whatever was taken in
> my work, which was of an unskilled navvy's variety, and no use to me at all.
> When I entered the firm I very foolishly signed papers that I improperly
> understood and did not read. So now it turns out I signed on to work as
> their unpaid apprentice.
>
> On the strength of this they repudiated any connection with Faraday House,
> under whose control I am of course. After keeping regular hours for a month, I
> ventured to ask for leave off one Saturday morning. The head of the department,
> a typical square-face, abused me. It was lucky for the Head of the Department
> that he was an old man. So I gave 'em my blessing and departed.

It was a setback but Frank seemed to take it in his stride. They were going
to stay in Baden. A Swiss engineer had promised him a job. He had begun
a postal course in surveying and levelling, which might lead to work in the
Canadian north-west. Whatever happened he could claim Associate
Membership of the Institute of Electrical Engineers.

Then he turned again to what mattered most in life. With a group above
Andermatt he had his first view of the riches in store — the Bernese Oberland
and even the distant spire of the Matterhorn. He reached the Clariden Hut
alone after an unfit English companion had to return, and next day skied
up the Claridenstock, 3,280 metres in marginal weather. From Zeigelbrücke
he climbed 10 minor peaks in three days, moving on his own from one rat-
infested hay hut to the next and enduring heavy rain, thunderstorms and
'a herd of howling Swiss rendering the morning hideous with their yellings.'

Neil Hewett had also moved to Baden and he and Frank climbed the Tödi,
3,614 metres (11,857 feet) the highest peak of the Glarus Alps. Frank described
the climb but his photographs capture the experience better. Hewett stands outside the Grünhorn Hut, a little boxy structure designed for about six people into
which 17 shoe-horned themselves that night. Then he's inside, grinning while
a row of men who've claimed their places on the long communal bunk look on.

This picture speaks volumes about the sleepless night to come, the sweating discomfort in the rough blankets, the sealed windows, fetid air, snores, farts and groans, and the rush to get dressed at last and swallow bread and luke-warm tea before exiting into the freezing night, all of which to this day is the rite of passage for the ascent of a popular peak in the high alps. In another shot you can almost breathe the clean cold air and feel the sunlight as Hewett stops near the summit, leaving only a tiring plod up the final snow dome.

Florence was very worried about Frank's prospects. The job in the Swiss engineer's business hadn't materialised, the chance of survey work in Canada seemed as flimsy as the paperwork of his postal course, and her son seemed more interested in climbing than earning a living. There were lively discussions. Finally it was agreed that they should go back to Innsbruck and look for a company that would give him the work experience needed for the Faraday House certificate. On 14 June 1922 they left Switzerland.

Frank was happy with this. His negative experience with the German employers at Baden had coloured his views on Switzerland. His letters to Roberts complained of the tourist crowds and the 'beastly Swiss ... the meanest-minded and rottenest people going'.[3] He soon calmed down, but remained forever suspicious of Swiss officialdom and hoteliers unless they proved themselves helpful.

They stayed at a gasthof in Telfes, a village in the Stubai south of Innsbruck and his fortunes picked up immediately. A large company at Landeck offered to give him a year's training in hydro-electric work and power-line construction. His mother was especially pleased that there was no premium to be paid. And with the summer climbing season just beginning he was even happier to learn that work wouldn't start until October.

Frank's first six months since leaving England had been a very mixed bag. His engineering work experience had yet to begin. His mountaineering had veered between alarming solo adventures and moderate plods with novice companions. Now at last there was the prospect of some better quality climbing. In July Jim Bell was joining him for two weeks. Since Wasdale days the Scotsman had spent much time in the mountains and was becoming a very accomplished rock climber.

When he arrived the weather in the Austrian Alps was poor so they headed for the Dolomites, to the Langkofel range, just beyond the Brenner Pass. They arrived at the Langkofel Hut in the early afternoon and rather than waste the rest of the day decided to do a short climb on the Langkofelkarspitz, a minor summit close at hand. Setting off at 3 p.m., they were soon enjoying the rough limestone with its plentiful holds where steepness seems to matter less than on other types of rock. Bell moved ahead, complaining good-naturedly about his companion's slowness. Finally they reached a point short of the summit and were astonished to find it was already 6 p.m. — two hours from darkness. They needed to start down immediately.

Frank led down what appeared to be an easy flank, but the angle steepened to a wall dropping into the depths of a gully. They were loath to retrace their steps and spend an uncomfortable if safe night on the ascent route, realising that if they didn't get down, the next day would be wasted. Bell spotted a way down via a difficult traverse; he succeeded, but it was almost completely dark by the time they were reunited on a lower easier section. But their troubles were far from over.

Again the wall steepened to the vertical, but Bell managed to reach a tiny ledge from which he thought they could abseil. Frank descended to him, using the rope doubled behind a spike as security but on reaching the ledge found the rope had jammed. In trying to tug it free he dislodged a large stone that grazed the back of his head. For a moment he swayed, stunned, and had he fallen, the slack between his waist tie and the jam would very likely have snapped the rope, resulting in a fatal plunge. Recovering, he climbed up to the jammed rope, freed it, and climbed down again — a harrowing experience in the near-darkness. From there an abseil took them into the gully. Again the rope jammed and this time they were forced to leave it for retrieval next day. A descent of a long rib of rock, groping for holds, brought them to the bottom of the face.

A crisis like that can ruin a partnership, particularly if there has been a breakdown of trust. But it can make it stronger. Jim Bell and Frank Smythe were at the start of their climbing careers. Bell was moving ahead in rock skill and sheer quantity of climbing. He would discover 70 new routes in Scotland, and like Roberts of the YRC, he became a doyen of the Scottish Mountaineering Club. But unlike Roberts he was of Frank's generation and their friendship was on equal terms.

Bill Murray, a famous Scottish contemporary described him as 'a short, stocky man with a bald head and a wicked grin.' A photograph of him on Ben Nevis adds to this image a pair of large nailed boots, neat long stockings, a tiny ruck-sack, and a face lit up with eagerness for problems to come, vertically overhead. Many were upset by his enjoyment of bad rock. 'Any fool can climb good rock,' he told Murray. 'It takes craft and cunning to get up vegetatious schist' — nasty stuff, which everybody admitted was abundant in Scotland. He used crampons in winter, when convention then ruled that this was cheating. He used ice pitons as daggers and made tubular ice pegs out of brass curtain rods. His climbing was decisive, and so was his response to his companions' problems. When a leader fell after a hold gave way on a route in Glen Etive and he crashed, stunned onto a heap of rubble poised above a drop, the next thing he heard was a rough voice bawling 'Stay where you are, you silly bugger!'

Bell had friends of all ages from all quarters and his climbs were of all standards. He drove a tiny Austin 7, wrapping a blanket round his legs as he trundled up to Glencoe in winter, and expounding to his shivering passengers on any subject from the theoretical to the metaphysical. According to Murray he was radical in his political views and could scandalise his more bourgeois fellow mountaineers. He once attended a Marxist rally with a Communist friend and on being invited to the platform to join assembled political revolutionaries, was introduced to an eager audience with the resounding call, 'DOCTOR J. H. B. BELL … THE SCOTTISH MOUNTAINEERING CLUB!' 'Even the flags must have blushed,' said Murray. 'But not Bell. He would have savoured the situation to the full.'

As an industrial chemist he regarded food as a fuel rather than a social nicety to be eaten in courses. Murray itemised the breakfast Bell made for his party at the CIC Hut on Ben Nevis. 'Oatmeal, sausages, kippers, tomato soup, peas and beans — all went into the pot. He persuaded me to share his burnt toast, on the grounds that charcoal was a bodily need. He expounded equations of chemical change to show how charcoal absorbed the troublesome gases of stomach and gut to our mutual benefit.'

My favourite story about Bell is one told by Frank. After a long hard climb on the Jungfrau they had stayed overnight at the notoriously expensive Jungfraujoch Hotel. Bell was muttering to himself about the size of the bill as they made their way next morning along a narrow path cut across steep snow slopes. 'There we came upon a stout Teuton,' wrote Frank. 'He was edging sideways like a crab along the path with shut eyes, digging his fingers into the snow. As we came up to him we heard him moan piteously: "Schwindel! Schwindel! Furchtbarer Schwindel!" Quick as a flash Bell turned to him and said: "Aye, man, you're right. It was a swindle, a f***ing swindle!"'

After the Langkofelkarspitz the rest of the holiday was uneventful, but for Frank the season wasn't quite over. Two terrible experiences awaited.

In the first of these two engineering students, A.W. Berry and H.H. Munro on holiday from their Faraday House courses joined him for a taste of Alpine climbing. Frank had nursed an ambition to climb the Olperer, 3,476 metres, the highest peak in the Zillertal Alps, and he persuaded the other two that it would be a fine objective. His companions had no mountaineering experience, but he made sure they were properly equipped with boots and ice axes. However Berry decided to stay behind, and when Frank set off with Munro the route he chose was a poor one. He soon found himself on an ice slope coated in slushy snow, and decided they must retreat. At that moment there was a loud crash and they were horrified to see a huge mass of rock detach itself from crags high above. They were unable to move from their ice steps, and nothing could save them from an enormous avalanche that thundered towards them, a black tide of death.

Then a miracle happened. The avalanche suddenly disappeared. It had been swallowed by large crevasses, which, unseen from below, split the slope higher up. A few rocks jumped the gaps and one of these, a chunk 'the size of a chest of drawers' flew between the two men with a noise 'like the scream of a high-powered racing car.' They were thankful to get off the mountain alive. 'Well, Smythe,' said Munro. 'In future I keep to terra firma — less terror and more firmer.'

The second incident was very different. Frank's objective was a range of peaks including the Wilder Freiger, a high mountain on the Italian frontier south-west of Innsbruck. It was the end of August when he reached the Nürnberger Hut above the Stubaital. A snowstorm lasting two days followed, in the middle of which to Frank's surprise, a party of three set off for the Hildesheimer Hut, a long day even in good weather over a complicated glacier system. The third day was calmer and tempted by a gleam of sun he climbed the Wilder Freiger by its easy north-east ridge, intending to continue to the Becher Haus, a nearby Italian hut.

On the Wilder Freiger however a following party of four comprising three Austrians and a German heading for the more distant Hildesheimer Hut invited him to join them and he accepted. But the weather deteriorated again, and on the ridge leading up to the Wilder Pfaff, which they had to traverse, they were hit by a ferocious storm. In seeking shelter on the lee side of the ridge they came across three ice axes, and buried in the snow, loaded rucksacks. Realising a disaster may have occurred, they searched briefly for bodies without success, then retreated, taking with them a few identifying things from the rucksacks — later finding that they belonged to the party which had set off in the bad weather from the Nürnberger Hut. Frank's group managed to locate the Müller Hut, a big old abandoned Austrian Alpine Club dwelling below the Wilder Pfaff, where after breaking in they found blankets but no emergency food or fuel. They burnt furniture to melt snow and keep warm, but their food quickly ran short. There was no question of pushing on in the storm to the occupied Becher Haus, even though it was only a short distance across a level glacier.

That night and next day the blizzard raged at hurricane force. Frank described how it was necessary to belay a man with ropes while he was collecting snow from the terrace, and the hut was bombarded with lumps of ice and stones blown off the mountainside. At last in calmer weather they reached the Becher Haus, taking two and a half hours to cover less than a mile in waist-deep snow. The hut keeper fed them and Frank's passport saved them from arrest by the Italian soldiers stationed there to guard the frontier. Then they set off to return to the Nürnberger Hut.

However on the Wilder Freiger they were beset by yet more bad weather — falling snow, thick mist and a rising gale. Trying to find the way down from the complicated summit the Austrian leader of the party confessed he was lost and the German sat down in the snow and said they would all die. Frank insisted that they should return to the summit and take a compass bearing to find the correct ridge down, and not brooking any argument, he started unroping in order to do this. The others all followed 'like lambs.' Steering carefully by compass from the summit, he recognised rock features from the ascent, and the party eventually reached the Nürnberger Hut safely. A search team later found the bodies of the three owners of the rucksacks and axes.

It was a horrific experience, but elements of a maturing mountaineer can be seen, particularly in his stubbornness in returning to the Wilder Freiger summit to take compass bearings in the storm. It was vitally necessary to do this, but when you're tired and have the false sense of security of being in a group, how easy it is to press on and hope for the best. Strangely enough I had the experience of being caught on the Wilder Pfaff in thick mist when I was traversing the mountain with my 17 year old son. The weather was otherwise acceptable but we were lucky to find the Müller Hut. It was the same huge dilapidated structure and we were the only visitors, although there was a guardian in charge. It was very cold but we weren't allowed to burn the furniture! We wrapped ourselves in 20 blankets each instead.

Frank's six-day epic marked the end of the 'summer' climbing season for him and he was rooted to the valley. He planned to write a guidebook to skiing in Tirol but it remained just an idea when at last, in October he began work at Landeck. This consisted of helping to build electricity pylons — 'Chilly but invigorating work on the mountainside from eight till five,' he told Roberts.

A month later however, his attention was caught by something of greater importance, and it needed action. On 10 November 1922 he wrote to the Royal Geographical Society:

Dear Sir,
I see from the papers that another expedition to Everest is contemplated next year or the year after … I am tremendously keen to have a chance of accompanying this. My age is 22½ and my climbing qualification is limited to the crags of Lakeland and Wales and climbs in the Central and Eastern Alps and Dolomites guideless, also high ski runs in Central and Eastern Alps. I am absolutely sound in wind and limb. As I am living in Tirol for the next year I spend all my spare time in the mountains.
Yours truly,
Francis S. Smythe (member of Yorkshire Ramblers' Club)

It was his first move towards the great mountain. In 10 years' time his ambition to attempt Everest would be realised, and his life would be changed forever in a way he could scarcely have imagined during that extraordinary period in the Alps.

Six

Rejected for Everest

Early in 1923 Austrian power line construction work came to a standstill in exceptional winter snowfall and Frank was laid off. Nervous that decisions about Everest were being made in his absence he wrote again to Hinks at the Royal Geographical Society, and learnt that the next expedition would not now go until 1924. But he also discovered that there would soon be a gathering of eminent mountaineers at the Army Staff College at Camberley, and Everest would be among the subjects to be discussed. His imagination went into overdrive. Other applicants would be considered in his absence! There was only one thing to do — he must join them. On 6 April he crossed the Channel, returning to England for the first time in over a year.

The Everest Committee was meeting at Camberley. This was a body that had been functioning since the first expedition to the mountain, the reconnaissance in 1921. Roughly half of its members were drawn from the Alpine Club Committee and the other half were senior members of the RGS. The Everest Committee had in turn appointed a handful of its members to form a separate Selection Committee to consider applicants for the next Everest expedition. And heading this tottering bureaucracy as Chairman of the Selectors was the mighty presence of Brigadier-General the Honourable Charles Granville Bruce, CB, MVO, President of the Alpine Club, leader of the 1922 expedition and leader of the expedition in the year to come.

Bruce was never going to allow any of these committees to get in the way of essentials. He was a huge man physically, with a boisterous personality that, even while he was alive, had become a part of mountaineering folklore. Aged 57, he had recently retired after a 32-year career in the Army, most of which had been spent in India with the 5th Ghurkha Rifles, a famous Regiment, of which he became Colonel in retirement. In the Himalayas he had accompanied Conway in the Karakoram, Mummery on the ill-fated first expedition to Nanga Parbat, and Longstaff to Trisul. Longstaff believed that no man had greater knowledge of the Himalayas at that time than Bruce. Even Everest had been in his sights as early as 1907 and 1910, although at the last moment these plans had become politically doomed. He had become fluent in Ghurkhali, even in some of its minor dialects, and his cheerfulness and sense of fun inspired great devotion from his men. 'I can still hear the yells of delight from a small band of natives who had recognised his thick-set figure from afar,' wrote Edward Strutt, a member of the 1922 Everest team. 'I can still see their greeting of him which was terminated only by Bruce catching hold of the foremost by the slack of his breeches and applying some resounding slaps, while volubly relating amidst shrieks of laughter a Rabelaisian story to the rest.'[1] Even the Head Lama of Rongbuk Monastery eagerly asked later expeditions after the health of the 'General Sahib'. And there are unnerving stories about Bruce's physical strength. He was reputed to be able to lift a man by the shoulders clear of the ground with outstretched arms. Horseplay was part of his make-up. Years later Frank photographed him in full Victorian rig, wielding an ice axe and candle lantern, a coil of rope round his neck, a telescope resting across his shoulders, a manic stare from behind large round goggles, and a bottle balanced on top of his head.

Even the confident Frank must have felt a qualm or two at the prospect of meeting such a man. But he seems to have got on well with Bruce, who a few days later in a letter to Sydney Spencer, the AC Secretary, wrote:

'I had a good time at the Staff College and [found] the youthful engineer, Smythe had come all the way over from Austria to talk about it [Everest]. I really believe he will do; but I shall appeal to Somervell and Mallory to test him.'[2]

Spencer wrote alongside this 'For Selection Committee', starting the process for Frank to be considered for 1924. It would be Howard Somervell who would 'test' him, later that year.

Bruce also introduced Frank to Philip Neame, a serving Colonel who had won the Victoria Cross in the First World War. He was a keen skier and had three weeks' leave starting later that month so Frank suggested they should meet in the Bernese Oberland for ski-mountaineering, to which Neame readily agreed. Frank then returned to Austria for a few days before travelling to Brig where he met Neame on 19 April. Then came an extraordinary session in the mountains, one which most climbers might look back on with a shudder, but which seemed almost routine for Frank. His laconic diary-style account to Roberts[3] tells the story of the first 10 days after they had moved up to Fiesch:

20 Apr.   Pelted with rain all day. Reduced to studying visitors' book and playing double-dummy auction bridge. The visitors' book went back to the '50s and '40s and there were some well-known names — Wills, Stephen, Hardy, Hinchcliffe, Ball, Kennedy, etc. etc.

21 Apr.   With two porters to the Eggishorn Hotel. One of the porters was actually a guide, but I didn't think much of him. There had been a metre of new snow and it was very avalanchy. He and his companion were so done, though they had little more weight than we had, that they wouldn't take the trouble to go up and come down a ridge to the hotel, but cut straight across a dangerous slope. We wouldn't follow them, but cut round by the safe way. Porters dismissed.

22 Apr.   Attempted to reach Concordia but were soon turned back by bad weather. Snow not safe.

23 Apr.   Bad weather all day — cold.

24 Apr.   Started for Concordia but turned back by severe blizzard.

25 Apr.   Went down to Fiesch for more grub and exercise — a good afternoon.

26 Apr.   To Concordia, reaching it just before a furious blizzard broke. Very cold. Everything in hut froze up.

27 Apr.   Blizzard etc. continued.

28 Apr.   Got to the Grunhorn Lücke in bad weather, and back.

29 Apr.   Went back to Eggishorn and back to Concordia in eight hours' actual skiing, carrying back five days' food — weather clearing.

I wondered what Colonel Neame thought of all this — and found out when I read his autobiography *Playing with Strife*, written in a prisoner-of-war camp in Italy during World War Two, when he had become a General. The cruel conditions of that holiday were no more than a passing inconvenience to him. Big game hunting in India was more challenging, especially when a tigress in her death throes, shot twice through the heart, plunged on him inflicting wounds and septicaemia from which he nearly died. Then there was the First World War. He had astonishingly spent all its four years on the Western Front without injury. The citation for his award of the VC describes what happened in prosaic terms:

Near Neuve Chapelle, France, on the 19 December, 1914, Lieutenant Neame, despite the heavy rifle fire and bombing by the enemy, succeeded in holding back German counter-attacks by making single-handed bombing attacks. He was covered by rifle and machine-gun fire from the trenches that had been recently captured from the Germans. During this act he killed and wounded many of them. He was able to delay the enemy advance long enough to rescue any of our wounded that were able to be moved.

The 'bombs' he used were a primitive form of grenade that unbelievably, he had to light with matches when he had no ordinary fuses left.

He was Frank's senior by 12 years. He rode Point-to-Point, played polo and was an Olympic gold medal rifle and Army revolver shot. His parents, who were cousins, were descended from a long line of yeoman farmers and landowners in Kent, so he and Frank found common ground for conversation while they sat out the bad weather. At the empty Concordia Hut, one of the most remote in the Alps, the temperature fell to minus 35 degrees celsius. The limited supply of wood had to be saved for cooking and melting snow for drinks so between these operations they buried themselves under blankets. These are demoralising times in mountains, and the two men were probably watching one another to see who would weaken. Neither did. Ten years later Frank had nothing to say about his companion apart from joking how a mouse ran over Neame's face one night, was brushed off and found dead in a corner next morning.

I used to wonder why he was so reticent about the people he climbed with. He liked to tell a good story at the expense of people he bumped into by chance, but climbing companions remained invisible, perhaps earning comic sympathy when they fell victims to some twist of fate. It was the convention to be discreet about the man on the other end of the rope, and Frank knew it. He sailed his literary ship close enough to the wind of establishment disapproval as it was. And his ordinary sensitivity to the feelings of his friends must have conflicted with many opportunities for good stories. The warts-and-all style still lay well in the future.

When the weather relented they climbed a couple of peaks. There was an extraordinary moment on the Finsteraarhorn. 'I was taking in the rope,' wrote Frank, 'when happening to glance towards the northern horizon I was amazed to see, floating in a blue sea, a large two-funnelled ship with details distinctly visible. Before Neame had time to get up and pay attention to it, it slowly faded away, but then as we watched, the blue sea appeared again with on it a whole fleet of battleships in line. They were quite black and details, masts, funnels, upper decks, etc. were perfectly distinct.[4] The fantastic sight lasted a quarter of an hour. It was a day of almost unlimited visibility, the atmosphere washed clear by the bad weather, with all the giant peaks of the Alps on view and the far reaches of the Black Forest visible some 150 miles to the north. The 'mirage' was directly in line with the North Sea coast 400 miles away but Frank eventually concluded that it had to be a cloud formation.

On his return to St Anton he had a huge row with his mother. She believed his training with the Landeck Company had been abandoned. Climbing was taking over. He'd been in England seeing if he could join the Everest expedition, and immediately after that he'd joined Colonel Neame for three weeks in Switzerland. Now he intended to spend a week skiing near St Anton. He'd made plans for the whole of July, August and much of September to climb with Somervell and then with Roberts in the Dolomites. There was no chance of getting the Faraday House diploma — the qualification for a 'proper' job — because he simply hadn't worked hard enough. She was tired of Austria and tired of spending large sums of money on her son for him simply to waste it on useless, dangerous mountaineering.

And having said her piece, and deaf to Frank's protestations, Florence went back to England, never to venture abroad again. She could not have guessed, let alone accept, that these two years of intensive alpinism 'indulged in' by her son were building a level of expertise that would be crucial in years to come. Just how concentrated his climbing had been is evident from one surviving document — his passport. During that period he shuttled across the borders of Austria, Switzerland and Italy more than 40 times. Writing to Roberts after this domestic earthquake, Frank merely added a postscript, 'Mother has just returned to England as her sister is seriously ill.' Whatever the truth of that, he was now severely short of funds and soon he fled penniless to England.

His life now seemed to be going nowhere. Looking back on my own life I can see the connections taking me from one point to the next, the mixture of preference and opportunity that played a part at each crossroads. If I am honest with myself, I know that the path bringing me to where I am now was unlikely to have been much different. I used to imagine that every step forwards in life was an unknown quantity to be hacked out, and fate and destiny were weasel words used by those who lacked the energy and inspiration to change things. Now I am not so sure.

When I began actively to investigate my father's life — a different process from accepting familiar facts about him — my astonishment that he had overcome his handicaps and reached the levels he did lessened. There were elements in his nature that routinely swept problems aside. He was optimistic and decisive. Even when he was wrong there was no dithering or regret. He often acted on impulse when others would have been cautious. He was usually brave and fortune often favoured him. He made his own luck.

So it's no surprise that when he got back to England he was awarded his Faraday House diploma. 'I still believe it was a mistake,' he wrote, 'or it may have been due to the kindness of Dr Russell.'[5] His mother was so relieved that, with no immediate job prospects for him, she agreed to his summer plans — that is, agreed to finance him. There's a hint in a letter to Roberts of his awareness of the need to economise: 'Intend to do camping as much as possible.' But life under canvas in those days was for expeditions or planned bivouacs. Few English gentlemen mountaineers camped in alpine valleys, and the spectacle of the impoverished British climber eking out his savings in a tent during a long alpine season lay decades in the future.

In early July he went to Italy to climb with Howard Somervell. Somervell had played a leading part on the Everest expedition the previous year, reaching with Mallory and Norton nearly 27,000 feet. Preparing now for the 1924 expedition, he'd come to the Dolomites to begin a strenuous summer in which he would climb 35 peaks in the same number of days. He had of course been asked by General Bruce to check out Frank but this was a job of incidental importance. He had arranged to meet his brother, Leslie for what he later described as a 'glorious mountain holiday.' At the end of the summer he would travel to India where, apart from taking part on Everest the following year, he would spend the rest of his working life at a medical mission among the poor.

Somervell's two accounts of the holiday, one for the *Alpine Journal* and one published much later in his book *After Everest*, give the impression that Frank's presence was fleeting and that they met by chance. 'Our party consisted of my brother and myself, occasionally with the addition of Frank Smythe, whom I found staying at Cortina,' he wrote, perhaps wanting to disguise the fact that there had been a serious purpose behind their climbing together. After a couple of routes alone with Somervell Frank joined him with his brother for the north-east face of the Langkofel.

This was and still is the classic route up to the highest point of the massif, a 'most enjoyable' 3,000-foot climb according to a 1960s guide book, but nevertheless a serious undertaking. Leslie Somervell seems to have been the star; where the others failed to make headway he led brilliantly and they reached the summit in the early afternoon. The descent was a minor nightmare of route finding — my guide book gives twice as much space to it as the ascent. Slowing them still more, Frank's boots, rope-soled *kletterschuen* had now fallen to pieces and he was descending painfully in near-bare feet. When they were finally off the difficulties Howard Somervell generously sped ahead to the inn on the Sella Pass to fetch his ordinary boots, a round trip of several hours.

They completed one more climb as a threesome, and then the two brothers went to Venice, while Frank rendezvoused with Roberts for Dolomites session number two. He bought new boots and probably wished by this time he could have new fingertips as well. The Dolomites are second only to Skye gabbro and perhaps Derbyshire gritstone, for their sandpapering effect on the skin.

He and Roberts polished off nine routes in three weeks. Roberts was a competent rock climber but his best years were behind him and he was content to be led by his protégé. Apart from one awkward moment on a wall on the Tofana di Rozes when Frank, leading out 60 feet could temporarily move neither up nor down, all went well until the end of the holiday. Then, on the Gröhmannspitze, a peak in the Langkofel group, there was an accident in which I believe Frank came closer to being killed than at any other time in his life. It was totally avoidable, one of those dreadful mistakes which mountains rarely forgive.

They had set off from the Sella Pass on a day when thick mist threatened to deny them a view of their peak but presently they were in the sunshine above a cloud sea. The route appeared to lie directly above. For hundreds of feet they climbed a steep but promising gully, but just before they could gain an easy ridge leading to the summit they were stopped by a large overhang. Leaving Roberts belayed on a ledge, Frank bypassed the overhang via a wall on the left. This brought him onto the broad ridge in the sunshine. Their problems were over.

He then made his near-fatal blunder. After a search he found a belay, a small but solid leaf of rock, but instead of attaching himself to it by the rope close to his waist he unthinkingly drew in the 20 feet of slack rope remaining between him and Roberts and wedged that round the belay. He then took a firm stance, called to Roberts to climb, and started drawing in the rope around his body in the approved way at that time.

Suddenly his enjoyment of the view was interrupted by a shout and a crash and at the same moment the rope he was drawing in tightened viciously. Roberts had stepped on a large boulder that had collapsed under him, and was falling with it down the gully. Frank was immediately pulled off balance by the rope and though he desperately dug in his heels and elbows he was unable to stop himself being dragged over the edge of the precipice. Headfirst he plummeted into the void. Suddenly with a jerk he stopped, dangling free. After a 20-foot slide and plunge into space the slack between him and the belay had been taken up and the rope had remained jammed behind the leaf of rock. Miraculously after such a fall the hemp rope, much weaker than a modern perlon rope, had not broken, and at the same moment Roberts had landed back on his ledge, unhurt. Frank, clawed his way back to the ridge having suffered nothing worse than a few cuts and bruises, and eventually Roberts joined him, unaware of what had really happened. Frank, highly embarrassed, enlightened him.

This appalling incident played heavily on his mind for a long time and he wrote about it in *The Spirit of the Hills*.[6] During the fall his immediate thought, as he shot into space, had been that the rope must have slipped off the belay:

I had assumed that I was as good as dead. I made desperate attempts to stop myself, and during this time a curious rigidity or tension gripped my whole mental and physical being. So great was this tension that it swamped all pain and fear, and rendered me insensible to bumps and blows. It was an overwhelming sensation, and quite outside my experience. It was as though all life's forces were in process of undergoing some fundamental evolutionary change, the change called death, which is normally beyond imagination and outside the range of ordinary human force or power ... I know now that death is not to be feared, it is a supreme experience, the climax, not the anti-climax, of life.

For how long I experienced this crescendo of power I cannot say. Time no longer existed as time ... Then, suddenly, this feeling was superseded by a feeling of complete detachment, indifference to what happened to my body ... Had the tenant already departed in anticipation of the wreck that was to follow? Was it merely a mental effect due to a sudden and intense nervous strain? It is not within my province to discuss that which only death can prove; yet to me this experience was a convincing one; it convinced me that consciousness survives beyond the grave.

Sometimes Frank was astonishingly aware of unseen but deadly danger. An example of this had already occurred in Yorkshire in 1920, although he waited many years before revealing the incident, perhaps unwilling to risk ridicule. The tale came in his final book, *Climbs in the Canadian Rockies*, when he was writing about the intuitive sense of danger some mountaineers develop:[7]

> This sense, possibly a sixth sense, is more developed in some than others. A striking instance occurred in my own case many years ago when I was training as an engineer at Bradford. I was talking one day to the foundry foreman when out of the tail of my eye I saw that a 20-ton casting was being raised by the overhead crane from a mould. Several men were guiding it up, and now it was aloft they were taking no particular notice of it and had closed in underneath it; after all, it was on a chain which was capable of taking far heavier jobs. But suddenly I knew that chain was going to break. I turned to the foreman. 'George,' I said, 'tell those men to stand back.' He was impressed by my tone and reacted immediately. He had a powerful voice: 'Stand back there,' he roared, 'you under that casting.' The men heard him, they looked up and quickly retreated from under the great swinging mass of metal. Next moment there was a tremendous twang! The chain broke and down it fell.
>
> The foreman turned to me with an ashen face. 'How did you know that chain was going to break?'
>
> 'I don't know,' I told him, 'I only knew that it would.'

He would also discover, when seeking unorthodox medical help after a motor accident, that he had a psychic capacity. But this he never revealed publicly, believing — probably rightly — that his image would be damaged if it became known. The story of it comes later. One fantastic moment he did write about was 'seeing' a Highland massacre. He had stopped in a grassy defile above the Falls of Glomach when a group of ragged people appeared, toiling up the path. Suddenly from both sides men appeared, brandishing spears, axes and clubs and with wild yells rushed down and after a short struggle slaughtered every one of the unfortunates. He had got out of the place as quickly as possible, convinced that he had been 'vouchsafed a backward glimpse into a blood-stained page of Highland history.'[8]

Howard Somervell eventually submitted his report on Frank before he left for India. After conferring with Godfrey Solly, the Alpine Club Vice President, he wrote a short note to Sydney Spencer in September 1923, lines which seem to have become part of mountaineering folklore:

F.S. Smythe

A bad mountaineer, always slipping and knocking stones down, and an intolerable companion; nobody in our party could stick him for more than a few days owing to his irritating self-sufficiency. However he is a very good goer for his age (?23 or 24) and carries on well without getting tired himself, tho' his incessant conversation makes others tired![9]

Somervell wrote a postscript asking that unless the Everest Committee seriously considered Frank for inclusion his note was 'best kept to yourself and torn up!' Frank wasn't and Spencer didn't. Somervell should have realised that secretaries have a habit of filing things.

Frank's rejection poses interesting questions, if only for idle speculation. He had got on well with Bruce and they remained good friends until the General's death in 1939, but he was perhaps unlucky that it was Somervell who had the casting vote in 1923. It's easy to visualise the negative impression the chattering Frank Smythe made (for 'self-sufficiency' read boastfulness) in his efforts to win over the quiet, powerful and cerebral Somervell, whom he knew could put in a good word for him. Sandy Irvine, Mallory's doomed companion had the 'right' background (Oxford, rowing blue), and was likeable, strong, a good mixer and as it turned out, vitally skilled with the oxygen equipment adjustments and adaptations. But Frank, nearly two years older, had hugely more climbing experience and ability than Irvine and he had the physiology to climb very high on Everest even without bottled oxygen as he proved in 1933. Would the outcome have been any different had it been Mallory and Smythe in 1924?

Ironically, 12 years later Frank would find himself in the same position as Somervell — vetting Everest candidates. But that story must wait.

SEVEN

Two Failed Careers

I am expecting to get a post with the River Plate Telephone Company, and if so will have a nine months specialised training (plus salary) in England before going to the Argentine. The engineering opportunities in this country are no good — no chance of getting on — and anybody with my ambition is forced to go abroad. If I get this job I have to sign a five-years contract, which is a long time, but on the other hand it is a very good opening in an A1 profession. With automatic telephones and long-range telephony, it is a highly specialised branch of engineering.

When Frank returned from the Alps he was job hunting for nearly a year; this message went to Ernest Roberts on 6 August 1924. Within days the post was confirmed, a contract was drawn up, the training course in London was scheduled to start a few weeks later, and he expected to leave for Buenos Aires in the autumn of 1925. It was a strange little piece, added to the end of a long letter about a holiday he'd had with Bell in Skye. After the frustrations that dogged him during the Faraday House course and his mother's nagging and worrying, he just seemed glad to get a job, even one that meant spending five years in Argentina. He was bowing to the inevitable, not reaching for the sky.

Days in the mountains were now numbered. In Skye he and Bell had tackled hard climbs and made new routes on the Cioch and Sgurr Sgumain, then traversed the whole Cuillin Ridge in a day. Christmas came and went without sight of a hill, but at Easter in 1925 he had a short break and climbed with Bell on Ben Nevis where they were defeated by severe winter conditions on Tower Ridge, and even struggled to reach the summit in a storm by the ordinary path. His third and final holiday sanctioned by Florence was in the Alps. Bell took his annual two weeks to coincide and they arrived at Wengen in mid-July.

How often the sight of great snowy peaks after a year or two of lowland Britain can tempt climbers to go for too big a route on the first day. And the pair proved the truth of this when they undertook the north face of the Jungfrau, a very long climb on the Oberland north wall. They endured many hours of gruelling effort and complicated route-finding, together with the unpleasant surprise of an electrical storm and a battering of snow and hail before they reached the safety of the Jungfraujoch and its hotel shortly before nightfall. 'Never so tired in my life,' was Bell's verdict, having casually informed Frank during the climb that his heart was doing 130 beats to the minute.

After a couple of days rest in the valley they traversed the Schreckhorn and Lauteraahorn, a fine outing on straightforward rock ridges. But the following day Frank had another confrontation with Nature in one of her deadliest moods.

Bell had been forced to opt out with a painfully swollen ankle. Two other climbers staying at the hut, Alexander Harrison and Charles Douglas had just set off for the Schreckhorn, so Frank, unwilling to waste the day caught them up and they invited him to join them. He persuaded them that the south west ridge, the climb he had just done with Bell, would be more interesting than their planned ordinary route up the peak, and the party changed direction. A few hours later they had climbed the ridge to within 500 feet of the summit.

At this point the weather, which had been doubtful after a lurid 'green ray' sunrise, suddenly turned bad. Black clouds rushed in from the north-west. The party had scarcely managed to scramble to shelter on a ledge below the ridge before the storm pounced. Lightning hit the crest above with loud bangs. Hail covered the rocks in a wintry coat. A full hour passed before the weather eased and they began to retreat the way they had come, reckoning this a safer bet than advancing over the exposed summit and down by the ordinary route. Soon however the weak sun disappeared and a rumble of thunder signalled the arrival of another storm. At this point they were negotiating slabs, the party was moving together and Frank was descending last. He wrote:

The slabs were sheeted with hail, so, with the object of securing the party, I placed the rope around a projecting rock. I had only just done this when I received a stunning bang on the head, and at the same moment was dimly conscious of a blaze of violet light and a loud report. I was only momentarily stunned, but I remember swaying out backward and would have fallen had not the rope been secured. Life was measured from death then by a second or two, for I am certain that if the rope had not been secured I would have fallen, in which case the party must have been dragged to disaster, for neither Douglas nor Harrison were in any position to arrest my fall.

Providentially the delay as the others waited for him to recover saved their lives for the second time when a couloir they were about to enter was swept by an avalanche of rocks. The temperature fell, freezing the water from the melting hail and coating the slabs with *verglas*. The wind rose and the lightning continued to strike the crest of a nearby subsidiary ridge, which would have made an easier and safer descent. It took another six hours to get down, even with Frank saving time sometimes by allowing himself to slide down the last few feet of a pitch, to be fielded by the strong and capable Harrison. Never was a mountain more aptly named than the Schreckhorn — Peak of Terror.[1]

Buenos Aires late in the year — approaching mid-summer — is a place to be avoided. I say this from personal experience having endured a few days there in early December waiting with my wife for a ship after a journey through South America. The heat and humidity caused cataracts of water to be ejected from the buildings by the air-conditioning systems. The volume of traffic, clamour of horns and murderous driving were unspeakable. That was in 1966. Maybe it's changed for the worse.

Frank arrived 41 years before us, on 16 November 1925, and it was a terrible shock for him too. Just a couple of weeks later, on 3 December he wrote to Hinks at the RGS, reminding the Secretary of his availability for Everest, and announcing his intention of quitting Argentina in the near future:

> This is to remind you with regard to the next Everest show, I shall be leaving BA in two or at the most three months, and my address will be c/o GPO Vancouver, British Columbia. I've no use for BA at all. The climate is bad, one always feels tired, and my present existence is a purely office routine. So I've decided to clear out and go to a cold climate and a decent country where one's outlook is not bounded by houses and there is something more than featureless plain. I don't think anyone at home can have any idea of the appalling monotony of this place. There is no country. So I am going to Canada, where I shall hope to get a job in the Government Survey, or at any rate something that brings me in touch with the wild and the fresh air. I hope to go prospecting up in the North West ... At all events whatever I'm doing you may depend on it that I shall be thoroughly tough when it comes to choosing the next Everest crowd. Nobody can be keener than I am to go.

It was an extraordinary letter for the distinguished and professional Arthur Hinks to receive from the youthful Smythe. He was 52 and as well as being one of the joint Secretaries of the Mount Everest Committee, had been

Secretary of the Royal Geographical Society since 1915 and would serve for 30 years. His work in astronomy had earned him the Gold Medal of the Royal Astronomical Society and he was a Fellow of the Royal Society. He was a highly regarded cartographer, but above all a tireless administrator, steering the RGS through the rocks and shallows of political and financial crises, watching Presidents of the Society come and go. Even the most eminent mountaineers and explorers treated him with care since within their closed world 'Hinksy' had formidable power and influence. It was fascinating to see in the correspondence between him and Frank over the years, signs of a gradual thaw, a grudging acceptance and recognition by the stuffy Hinks as Frank developed from the cocky young maverick into a seasoned and celebrated mountaineer.

Mail between England and Argentina at that time took at least two to three weeks to reach its destination. Hinks received Frank's letter just before Christmas and dispatched a short acknowledgement on 31 December. But Frank never received it — or not in Buenos Aires. On 5 January 1926, clutching a third-class 'steerage' ticket issued the day before, he boarded the Royal Mail ship *Andes*, bound, not for Canada, but for Southampton. He had scraped together the money for the cheapest passage home, and breaking his contract with his employers at the United River Plate Telephone Company had simply walked away. He had been in Buenos Aires just seven weeks and two days. He would never return to South America.

To say there was consternation in the Smythe and Reeves families when Frank arrived back in England would be putting it mildly, but much worse than the upheaval was the financial implication of the broken contract. The URPTC had invested a considerable sum in Frank's training, paid for his outward passage and faced substantial disruption after his departure without notice. As swiftly as a condor attacks its prey the lawyers and the demands for compensation descended upon Frank and then upon his sponsor, Florence.

Details of the outcome have never come to light. The legal tremors rumbled on for at least a year, and Bernard, Frank's step-brother and owner of the Maidstone timber business, reluctantly became involved. Opprobrium and scorn over Frank's behaviour flowed freely from the relatives. Somebody eventually picked up the pieces — the bill — and it wasn't Frank. He was, to put it bluntly, broke.

Nobody, least of all Frank, was keen on another stab at an engineering career, and different ideas for his future were floated. It was an astonishing situation for a man aged 25, and seemed to underline his immaturity and lack of worldliness. Certainly he understood economic realities and had social skills, but the forces which would drive him to success had yet to be generated. At that stage of his life, when he wasn't climbing he seemed to drift uneasily like a boat with an engine that wouldn't start. There would be no climbing for him at all that year, apart from a token few days at Coniston at Easter, and he was largely inactive for the first six months of 1926. It was as though he was under house arrest — which quite possibly, in effect, he was.

He and his mother moved to London, both feeling that his chances of work were better in the capital than Berkhamsted. Then in May he was involved in the country's General Strike. This began as a looming crisis after the mine owners, whose industry was in decline with falling prices, threatened the coal miners with a wage reduction. A stand-off to allow a Royal Commission to investigate had given the government plenty of time to prepare for a major dispute, and sure enough, with the Commission reporting in favour of the mine owners' action a country-wide strike affecting almost all industries began on 3 May. However, unlike strike action of later decades, there were no pickets left in place to dissuade 'black-leg' workers. In 1926 workers simply stayed at home and factories were left empty but in functioning order. A call went out for members of the public to respond to the country's woes and help where possible, and Frank, along with thousands of others, volunteered. On 6 May he reported at Waterloo Station and was signed on as a fireman on the Southern Railway.

Of course the country would have collapsed with or without the help of Frank and his shovel and all the other middle-class patriots who came to England's rescue, and fortunately negotiations brought an end to the strike in just nine days. Frank rode the footplate on the London to Brighton line and enjoyed telling everybody how inconvenient it was not to understand the signals. Even this was surely less memorable than the performance of a well-known racing driver[2] who signed on as a bus driver. Curious to see how fast a double-decker would go he lost all his passengers, who got out at the first stop after the descent of Hampstead Hill.

By the middle of May Frank had decided to join the Royal Air Force. The application form asked searching questions about his schooling, qualifications and sporting activities, and as usual the very process of compiling a CV invited economy with the truth and other little games and distortions. His '1925-1926' with the River Plate company on the heels of six years of engineering training was a delectable example. He also claimed as a 'prior occupation' a spell of photographic journalism, although he had had nothing published at that time. More interesting though is the question: why did he join the RAF?

He was silent about this, but the answer seems straightforward. There was great pressure on him to make amends after the Argentine fiasco. He had no qualification for anything other than engineering, which was now ruled out. He was out of a job and incarcerated in London. Recruiting offices everywhere were looking for suitable young men. Being a pilot sounded exciting, the life was glamorous, the pay was good, and there was a generous allowance of leave each year. At that time a large proportion of RAF pilot requirements came from an intake of Short Service Commissioned officers who were initially on a five-year engagement, with the offer of a Permanent Commission after that if they were good enough.

Frank's interview at the Air Ministry was on 28 June 1926, a Monday, and in a typically carefree way he spent the weekend beforehand walking in the Surrey Hills with a friend from the Yorkshire Ramblers' Club, Hugh Slingsby. From Slingsby's home at Ashtead on the Saturday they walked over Box Hill, stopped for a drink and Test Cricket talk with the proprietor of the Burford Bridge hotel, and in the overnight full moon and next day's sunshine covered 50 miles along the Pilgrims' Way and back along the high ground to the south. Frank wrote about this outing, an evocative piece underlining his fondness for this part of England.[3] It's no surprise to me that even before this was published he had moved — I should say we had moved, I was just a year old at the time — to a house in the wooded hills between Dorking and Guildford. But all this lay a decade ahead for Frank. It also lies a long way in the past for me, although I admit to still suffering a frisson of emotion on hearing names like Abinger Hammer, Holmbury Hill and Tenningshook Wood.

Events moved quickly after the walk. Within two weeks of the interview he had been accepted; the Medical Board had passed him 'fit as pilot', and he had been given instructions for joining his first unit, in Egypt. He was kitted with uniforms, packed a trunk, said his goodbyes, and at the end of July Pilot Officer (on probation) F.S. Smythe travelled across Europe and the Mediterranean and reported for duty at No 4 Flying Training School, Abu Sueir — an RAF station and airfield that quivered under a glaring sun in the middle of a desert at the hottest time of the year.

He was processed with unusual speed because a new intake of student pilots were due to start training in August, so he joined 34 others on the eleventh course at Abu Sueir since its creation as an FTS in 1921. It was situated halfway between Port Said and Cairo, and is elegantly described in *Pilot's Summer*, the memoirs of Frank Tredrey who was a pupil pilot there in 1930:

'There's only one place to learn landing. And that's at the RAF Flying School in Egypt. Miles and miles of flat, hard desert. It doesn't matter if you undershoot a mile or overshoot one — you're on the aerodrome just the same. Not good flying practice, I know. But nice for learning. You do practically all your flying between 0500 and 0800 hours each day, and eat your breakfast when you've done. Air as warm as milk and as smooth as silk. Nice steady breeze not varying 0.1 of a mile an hour. Not a bump if you searched for one down to the Sudan. And a horizon as clear cut as if someone had painted it against the blue with an ochre brush.'

The course was scheduled to last a year and was divided into two parts, the first of which would be spent learning to fly the Avro 504K basic trainer biplane before moving to the advanced stage of training on the De Havilland 9A. Frank's first letter home[4] reflects the excitement and determination a new trainee feels after the inspirational welcoming address by the Commanding Officer, the issue of equipment, the conducted tours and briefings:

I intend to work jolly hard and pass our exams well. That is the only thing to do if one wants a Permanent Commission or even to get on as a temporary officer. There is excellent tennis in the camp, an Officers' Club, swimming baths and cricket, which pleases me.

However, by the end of the month his enthusiasm seemed to be qualified:

This last week I have been doing the Observers' Course and have gone for cross country flights every morning on a big twin-engined Vickers Vimy bomber. It wasn't nearly so exciting as I thought — in fact pretty boring. We played cricket one day during the week but I disliked it. There is of course no grass and one plays on the sandy ground with a terrific sun trying to give you sunstroke and a frightful glare. It gave me eye strain, so I shall not play again. A lot have gone on the sick list for Gyppy tummy, which everyone gets.

Florence's heart must have sunk. A shake of the head, a silent prayer that things would work out. Later letters showed that she was right to worry.

He ate as little as he could to avoid a 'permanent gyppy tummy.' The mosquitoes made it 'next to impossible to sit down and write as they are after you all the time — huge malarial mosquitoes!' He fussed about the gramophone he asked to be sent and he scorned the formal social events at the officers' mess. Even more worrying was his desperation for leave, which must have sounded to his mother like a desire to quit. At Bradford and in Switzerland, in Austria and in Buenos Aires he had only complaints to make about his work, and now in Egypt, faced with the rigorous demands of a new career, it was the same. And at this point I have to declare an interest, and talk about myself for a moment. It's relevant to Frank's story, or at least relevant to my trying to write about this part of it.

I am an aeroplane. Almost before I could walk I had a pedal aeroplane. Not a pedal car, a pedal *aeroplane*. I remember my sadness when it disappeared. When we were older it was the war and my brother John and I made model aeroplanes, hundreds of them, cutting and sandpapering the balsa wood pieces of the kits and sticking them together. I can still smell the glue. We flew gliders and planes powered with rubber bands and noisy little diesel engines. When we were bored we set light to them and floated them out of the bedroom window and watched them crash in flames. Once I was a parachutist and jumped off the garage roof with an umbrella. Later, at school as an ATC cadet I got a ride in a Meteor jet. Later still, when I was called up for National Service the recruiting sergeant asked me, 'Army or RAF?' and then, 'Groundcrew or aircrew?' I joined a huge throng of would-be pilots and resolved to jump through every hoop held in front of me in order to become one. The training went on for the best part of two years while we flew all kinds of planes. It was fantastic, but always you had to keep learning to do new things or you were failed. The instruction and flight tests and ground exams went on all the time. It was the steepest learning curve I have ever experienced. I got used to my brain literally aching. The first take-off, circuit and landing in a jet was overwhelming, but a couple of days later the same thing had to be routine because there was more to be learnt than just getting in the air and back down again. Finally I joined my first front-line squadron and stayed in the Service for eight years, until a desk job loomed. After resigning, being an airline pilot didn't interest me; it would have been like driving a bus after Formula One. Half a century later I'm still somewhere up there, wondering if it really happened. Sometimes I've dreamed I could fly just by flapping my arms, and been stunned by disappointment on waking up. I most surely am an aeroplane.

So I couldn't understand Frank. How could all those petty problems *matter*? Did he think flying would worry his mother? It didn't sound like that to me. The truth was he was using the RAF as an escape route after Buenos Aires. So it's futile to expect him to share the magic that I found in flying. But it was something I found strangely difficult to accept. He wasn't *afraid* of flying, as has been suggested. He would have heard about the eight fatal accidents to student pilots in the previous two and a half years, including one who was killed on the first morning of his training, but he didn't let things like that bother him. He had the necessary fatalism and belief in himself to be a pilot. And in World War Two he flew a lot as a passenger, and found it fun, especially flying over mountains. More clues that his heart wasn't in it came in a letter to his mother after he found that she had been unwell. 'I am afraid it must be due to worry [about me]. If it is I will resign my commission at once. I can resign at any time while I'm on probation for the first six months.'

Fate has a habit of lending a hand to free us from commitments trapping us, and it was a divine intervention that was shortly to end Frank's fledgling RAF career. The process however, would be brutal. Florence recovered from her malaise, but she was alarmed to receive bad news:

> I have been rather ill. I can tell you now because I am convalescent, so there is no need to worry at all. It started with ptomaine poisoning which developed to what the doc calls pyelitis or inflammation of the kidneys. It's painful and one alternates between high fever and sweating attacks. I have been luckier than most people. More than half the officers are ill and the camp is in isolation! There are cases of typhoid, diptheria and many malarial. Some fellows are dangerously ill with an obscure internal complaint.

In a letter to Aunt Nettie from hospital in Cairo he said the doctors were puzzled. He wondered whether he would ever recover. He was getting frequent relapses combined with a high temperature. He was receiving injections with a special serum. It was thought to be some obscure kidney problem. There had been a typhoid epidemic in which 16 officers had been affected and one had died.

Eventually it was decided that treatment in England was needed and he was repatriated in late January 1927 to the RAF hospital at Uxbridge, where he underwent more tests. His own version of the results came in a letter to his mother on 15 February:

> [The pathologist] said I ought to take life very quietly and walk slowly upstairs so as not to strain my heart. He seemed to think I am very lucky to be alive considering that I was given solid foods all through my illness and after a week was allowed to get up and eat meat!

Frank later enjoyed telling how he defied the doctor's advice about the stairs, but his RAF records — the reports from five medical boards — tell a different story. His internal troubles were of no importance, but 'effects of glare', sustained in the Alps in 1922 and exacerbated in the desert, had caused a reduction in his visual capacity which although put at 'less than 20 per cent', was the main worry for the decision-makers. His heart was not mentioned.

By chance I came across a memo written five years later by Sir David Munro, Chairman of the Industrial Health Research Board, in reply to a request from Professor Thomas Graham Brown for details on Frank's health while in the RAF. Munro was in a position to obtain such highly confidential information and being a friend of Graham Brown obliged with the following note:

> On joining the RAF … [Smythe] was one of those sent out direct to a Flying Training School in Egypt.
>
> Immediately began to suffer from Glare. At his medical examination on entry [he] had not disclosed the fact that he had previously suffered from snow-blindness, and this fact was not elicited by the doctors.
>
> Condition got worse, and he developed severe blepharitis.
>
> Obviously he was unfit for the RAF with all its Eastern service.

Blepharitis is inflammation of the eyelids, but there were no lasting effects and Frank's sight eventually regained its acuity. However on 24 March 1927 he was sent home on leave and a month later formally invalided out of the RAF.

EIGHT

The Sentinelle

After the trauma of Egypt Frank quickly persuaded his mother that fresh air and exercise were needed, and in May 1927 he went to Corsica with Hugh Slingsby.

It was a disorganised romp. They slept on deck on the boat to Ajaccio. They had every kind of bad weather and ate in front of camp fires. The beech woods reminded them of Surrey and the rock climbing of Skye. A lizard shared their lunch. Their map was useless and they learnt the joy of standing in body on one mountain and spiritual intention on another, as Frank put it. A bus driver nearly took them over a cliff rather than kill a sleeping dog. When Slingsby's holiday finished Frank stayed on and from forest bivouacs tackled harder climbs. There was a steep peak, the Capo Tafonata pierced by a hole near the summit where the wind howled and where he crossed a snow slope so hard that lacking an ice axe he cut steps with his pocket knife. He had an agenda in mind, one that needed him to recapture his best form quickly — Mont Blanc. He had no way of knowing, but what he would achieve on that great mountain in the next two years would shape the rest of his climbing career, and his life as a writer.

The Chamonix Aiguilles soar thousands of feet above the valley, astonishing granite spires that turn blood red in the evening *alpenglow*. They form a ridge that is part of a great watershed containing the Géant Glacier, with its myriad crevasses, tortured ice-falls, and remote snowy bays. Lower down, the glacier become a single ice stream, zebra-striped with each summer's rock fall to mark its progress. At timberline on a shelf above the ice is the ancient Montenvers Hotel, served by rack railway from Chamonix. Countless tourists have come here to picnic, venture onto the Mer de Glace and admire the incredible west face of the Dru. Climbers have come this way since the start of alpinism.

Mont Blanc itself lies to the south-west of the cirque, a great massif, higher than anything else, with a remote and perfect snow dome forming its summit. From this supreme high point immense faces and ridges fall to the east and south, surely the most dramatic mountainside in the Alps, and even viewing it from miles away many will be awestruck at the thought of climbing there, and treading those final snows.

Of course the weather has the last word. The sky becomes too blue, the distances too clear. The forecast — accurate in modern times — deters the prudent from starting out. A veil of high cloud spreads from the south-westerly quarter and drifting fragments of a lower layer form mysteriously while the upper sheet obscures the summits. Climbers caught high up are attacked by a rising gale and volleying snowflakes. Descent, speed, escape are bywords for safety, for very survival, because this may not be a short-lived storm; it could be a week-long blizzard piling feet of snow on the rocks, a lethally cold blast even in mid-summer.

Much has changed since the 1920s. Visitors have multiplied — climbers, skiers, walkers, paragliding and hang-gliding enthusiasts, and ordinary holidaymakers. A road tunnel under the range and a cable car over the top connect Chamonix with Courmayeur in Italy. Chamonix has become a modern, traffic-choked town in one of the world's most spectacular valleys. The mountains aren't any bigger but the climbers' guidebooks list three and four times the original number of routes and there are usually queues on the popular climbs. The stylish clothes and bundles of safety gear worn by modern climbers would have been regarded with disbelief by their counterparts of a century ago. Rescues are accomplished in minutes by helicopters instead of hours or days by teams of guides. The glaciers are shrinking and recent record hot summers have caused the deep permafrost to loosen its grip releasing excessive rock fall. But despite all this the quality of the climbing remains magnificent, as good as anywhere in the world.

In 1927 the Brenva Face of Mont Blanc was one of the last great unclimbed prizes on the mountain. Facing east, more than half a mile wide and soaring some 4,000 feet from the Brenva Glacier its steep buttresses and ice ridges offered a more direct way than any other to the ice cap and summit snows. Frank had become interested in the face a year earlier when he met another London-based climber, Tom Blakeney. Blakeney had four Alpine seasons under his belt but like Frank he had never been to Chamonix and Mont Blanc. Of his meetings with Frank, he wrote:[1]

At that time, his ideas ran to the classic routes on Mont Blanc, such as the Old Brenva and the Pétéret; I suggested (and we studied photographs) that a route might lie up the left (ascending) side of the Great Couloir splitting the Brenva Face, and I heard from Smythe in Egypt later that he had not discarded the idea, though he was dubious about the crossing of the couloir, and about the ultimate ice-cliffs and exit on to the Col Major.

Agreeing to investigate they met in Chamonix in early June, 1927, but bad weather denied them even a glimpse of the Brenva Face. It was the end of Blakeney's holidays for that year, but Frank was back a month later intending to stay for the rest of the summer, and now with Jim Bell as his climbing partner.

Their first climb was an impressive one, the east ridge of the Aiguille du Plan, a route with an awesome reputation that had only been climbed once, in 1906 by the Irishman V.J.E. Ryan and his two famous Zermatt guides, the brothers Joseph and Franz Lochmatter. Frank and Bell were successful after a severe struggle beset with incidents — a slip and pendulum on an ice slope, Frank's jammed knee in a crack, the loss of Bell's ice axe, a bivouac and hours of uncertainty and hard exhausting climbing. It was a harsh Chamonix initiation for the pair.

On their return to the Montenvers they joined three other British climbers, George Bower, Ogier Ward and Graham Macphee and the whole group headed for the Old Brenva, a classic snow and ice route on Mont Blanc. The climb was useful for Frank since he could weigh up the possibilities on the unclimbed Brenva Face to his left. He noted that at the top it was capped by a menacing band of séracs — the edge of the summit glacier dome — which posed a serious avalanche threat, and made it vital to find a line up crests of rock or snow, since any falling ice should be diverted safely to the side of such features. After that, there would still be the problem of finding a way through the ice cliffs.

Bell and Ward went home, and with Macphee temporarily committed to climbing with another party, Frank and George Bower headed for the Grépon, a principal summit of the Aiguilles. Bower was a strong and experienced rock climber who had already done the Grépon by its classic Mer de Glace Face. However his party had avoided the strenuous final problem, the Knubel Crack, and he was determined to put this right. He and Frank climbed the easier Nantillons Face of the peak to the bottom of the notorious crack, and soon Frank found himself having to follow:

I must confess that, when my turn came, I was thankful not only for sustained hauling, but to have an additional rope let down as handhold. I was thus dragged like a lobster from beneath a rock, feebly gasping into the summit sunshine, where I congratulated Bower on his wonderful feat.[2]

Frank was 5 foot 10, of slender to average build, and had good stamina. But stamina is not the same as strength, and problems such as chimneys and cracks depending on sheer muscle were sometimes beyond him. Nowadays a committed rock climber will routinely train on artificial walls, or even on a purpose-built place in his own home, but Frank like nearly everyone then saw training for climbing as pointless. He was fairly inactive when not climbing, and he regretted his unfitness at the start of a holiday, but he dismissed physically strong climbers as 'supermen'. He achieved overall fitness by climbing, but that was all. Like most in his peer group he saw mountaineering as a distinguished pursuit, bulging muscles belonging to weight-lifters.

Soon Frank, Bower and Macphee headed for Mont Blanc again, now with a very challenging agenda — the Pétéret, one of the two longest ridges on the south side of the mountain. In its upper part it flanks the Brenva Face and from its crest rise two major peaks, the Aiguilles Noire and Blanche. Had Frank therefore abandoned the idea of the Brenva Face? Having seen it close up from the Old Brenva had he decided it was unsafe? Or as an 'expert ice man' (as Macphee referred to him in his diary) did he consider his companions not experienced enough? It was after all Macphee's first season in the Alps. Whatever the reason the Pétéret Ridge was a very ambitious choice. It had never been climbed in its complete length, and even the part they were heading for, from the Aiguille Blanche to Mont Blanc de Courmayeur, was still a huge undertaking and had only been climbed twice.

From Courmayeur's Royal Hotel they moved up to the small and primitive Gamba Hut, but the weather played cat and mouse; a bad spell forced them down to the valley, then it immediately cleared up again. It was the end of Bower's holiday, but Frank, enthralled by his first venture into the vastness of Mont Blanc's south side was intent on trying again. He and Macphee spent a night at a cheaper hotel, shopped for more provisions and set off for the Gamba once more.

The two men had already established a good relationship. Macphee, a Scottish dentist with a practice in Liverpool had started climbing only the year before at the age of 28, but after a lot of weekend climbing on British crags had become very proficient. Although not averse to leading, he was the ideal second

— a strong, square, watchful figure. He kept a diary and had done so from the age of eleven, almost never missing an entry, exactly filling the half-dozen lines available each day with his spidery writing. The entries were factual, spare with opinion, and when nothing much had happened Macphee still filled the lines, listing the ordinary events of the day. Almost every day began with 'J & CB', which stood for physical jerks and cold bath. The diaries were a reflection of their keeper, somewhat unimaginative and content with plodding routine. But he was reliable and generous. He had many friends and eventually climbed with luminaries such as Colin Kirkus and Menlove Edwards. He helped students start their climbing with the Liverpool University mountaineering club, of which he was President. When he married he was one of those quite rare people who keep their job, their friends, their wife and family, and their dedication to climbing all intact. Perhaps the most remarkable part of Macphee's life came early on. During the First World War he transferred to the Royal Flying Corps and served as a pilot. His diary impassively notes the vagaries of flying training:

> 30 July, 1917. After the fourth landing I was taxying along when the bus swung round and the undercarriage and prop were completely smashed and the left wing slightly strained. After breakfast I did panel signalling and gunnery. After lunch I went into Edinburgh with Erskine by the 1.14. We did shopping and had ices, and I went to the Clydesdale Bank to cash a cheque.

Then he was in France and with the same economy wrote about the crashes and inevitable losses of his comrades, until suddenly towards the end of 1917 the diary becomes blank. Officers had been ordered not to write diaries, and the following April Macphee had crashed behind enemy lines, surviving to be a prisoner for the last months of the war.

I wondered how he could get on with Frank, who had such a different temperament. Sometimes though the diaries seethe with anger, particularly when Frank was late, Macphee being the soul of punctuality. I understood from his daughter, Hermione that he made allowances for Frank because he saw a carefree spirit with uncommon ability on snow and ice. From Frank's viewpoint Graham Macphee was a man to rely on, a mountain partner who didn't get flustered or argue, a safe climber who was content to be second and accepted the Smythe way of doing things, a decent and honest man.

Frank knew the Pétéret Ridge would take two days and his plan was simple. From Courmayeur they would rest briefly at the hut then keep going until darkness came, probably somewhere on the Aiguille Blanche. At the bivouac they would brew, eat and rest until daylight, then next day should see them over Mont Blanc. It's not known whether they obtained a weather forecast, but anything available wouldn't have been reliable. Frank was simply hoping that in the middle of a poor summer the gods were going to allow two fine days to be strung together. It was a very risky thing to bank on, on such a climb.

All went more or less as planned that day. The sun beat down. The Gamba Hut, where they lay on the bunks until 5 p.m., was filled with people they knew and who wished them luck when they set off. Beyond the Col Innominata they were on new ground, a horrible loose descent to the Fresnay Glacier and then the difficult crossing of a 500-metre wide maze of séracs and chasms. On the far side, the couloir leading to the Dames Anglaises pinnacles, normally a death trap of falling rocks was now silent in the evening frost, and they stopped at the bottom for a quick meal. Frank complained that his rucksack was too heavy and on impulse hurled a 'large and unnecessary' lump of cheese into the bergschrund. However, as he wrote later, 'Macphee was startled out of his usual equanimity and he reproached me bitterly for the deed.'

A full moon assisted a rapid crampon ascent of the couloir until frozen snow gave way to ice, slowing them down. At last they reached rock, but it was the worst kind imaginable — the Aiguille Blanche was nothing but a collapsing ruin. For five hours they picked their way up the steep, complicated and desperately loose face of a tower, the Grande Gendarme until the moonlight failed at 2 a.m. when they stopped for a chilly rest, sheltering from a freezing wind in their Zdarsky tent-sack.

They were now about half way between the top of the couloir and the snowy crest of the Aiguille Blanche. The initial difficulties were behind them although they still faced the descent to the Col de Pétéret and after that, the complicated mixed climbing at high altitude up the Grand Pilier d'Angle to the summit of Mont Blanc de Courmayeur.

They set off at 5 a.m. and clambered up slabs to the ridge where there was a good view of the sky and the dawn. And at once Frank knew they were in trouble. The weather had 'gone to pieces.' It was an 'evil dawn of smooth grey cloud zeppelins and fierce bars of scarlet' and only a matter of time before bad weather swept in.

In a chapter entitled 'Fear' in his book *The Mountain Vision*, Frank reviewed that critical moment 14 years later — how their four options were equally appalling. Retreat by the route they had come was out of the question; the complexity and danger were too great. A descent from the Aiguille Blanche on its eastern, Brenva Face would be equally fraught — a Swiss climber attempting an escape there two years earlier had been killed by falling stones. Since continuing over Mont Blanc was unthinkable, Frank believed their only hope lay in a descent to the upper Fresnay Glacier from the Col de Pétéret ahead of them. He knew that a 1,000-foot buttress, the Rochers Grüber, had to be descended from the col, and he knew also that two men, Professor Balfour and his guide Johann Petrus had been killed trying to get down it after making what was probably the first ascent of the Aiguille Blanche. Worst of all he knew nothing of its problems, but instinct told him this was their best chance. 'Even now,' he wrote, 'I remember the anguish that preceded a decision on which our lives might depend, and the fears that inevitably accompany such a decision in which safety and danger are weighed on a knife-edge balance.'

The storm came in rapidly. They went wrong at one point. Nothing was easy, everything was loose. Snowflakes were flying out of the west. The wind gusted, dropped, then rose again, 'this time on a note of unrestraint, a wine-bibbing giant's roar of rage.' It was 1 p.m. before they reached the summit of the Aiguille Blanche, and the snow-plastered rocky descent to the Col de Pétérét took another two hours. 'A hurricane was now blowing on Mont Blanc,' he wrote, 'and the noise of it resembled the deepest note of a cathedral organ. The Col de Pétéret itself was a fearful sight. The snow came whirling through the gap in a furious *tourmente*, whilst ever and anon came the mad crash of rocks from the crumbling precipices on the Brenva side.'

The descent of the buttress to the Fresnay Glacier took another four hours. 'It was no time for half measures,' wrote Frank. 'We cut up our rope into loops, and using our hundred feet of spare rope swung ourselves down the pitches, drawing our rope after us.' With the light failing as they reached the glacier Frank's route-finding was at a premium and earned praise and a show of emotion in Macphee's diary. On the Col Innominata a thunderstorm broke out and in torrential rain and almost total darkness they somehow got down to the Gamba Hut — 'We could see our way by flashes of lightning,' wrote Macphee, a man not given to exaggeration. At 9 p.m., 36 hours after leaving Courmayeur they stumbled through the door, to the amazement of the occupants, who rallied round the soaked and exhausted men. 'The return of the Prodigal Son was a poor affair compared to ours,' mused Frank.

He was fated to endure at least one more terrible retreat in his climbing life, but his descent with Macphee from the Aiguille Blanche became regarded as one of the great escapes of that era, earning lavish praise from Geoffrey

Winthrop Young. Many victims of such an experience, while not disposed to swop alpinism for golf, might have done some hard thinking, but Frank's interest in the Brenva Face simply became more focussed. He knew that Young and Mallory had examined the possibilities of a route there. Two experienced climbers, an Austrian and a German had separately decided against an attempt on account of the sérac wall at the top of the face. And now two more climbers, Dr A.Grünwald and Herr D.Bischoff were actively interested in the Brenva Face. Not only that, this pair were staying in Courmayeur with the intention of making an attempt at the earliest opportunity, although Frank wrote that he had been unaware of their plans until after his own success.[3]

This is delicate ground to be treading. In the gentlemanly climbing world between the wars, the English were not supposed to admit to rivalry but the evidence suggests that the Brenva Face had become a race. When Frank wrote the story of his climb he listed others interested in the face. Grünwald and Bischoff get a mention, but only as climbers he happened to meet in Courmayeur, not as contenders. But if he met them did he discover their plans? Was he pretending later that there had been no competition? In any case he was now determined to attempt the Brenva Face at the first opportunity. His incredible escape with Macphee from the Aiguille Blanche had reinforced his confidence. But there was to be a dreadful twist in the story. Grünwald and Bischoff, whose plans may have acted as a catalyst in Frank's decision-making, were never to have their chance of competing. Later that month, after waiting in vain for suitable conditions, they died in a storm while returning to Chamonix over the Aiguille de Bionnassay, a peak on the far side of the same mountain on which Frank and Graham Macphee fought for their lives — Mont Blanc.

Macphee had a few days left of his holiday but Frank secretly thought him too inexperienced on snow and ice for the Brenva Face. They fitted in one more climb, an easy route up Mont Blanc (Frank's first time on top, at last) with the weather true to form, harrying them back to the Montenvers with an oncoming storm. And then it stayed bad for two weeks.

One by one Frank's friends all went home, and in late August, as the snow level crept down it would have been reasonable for him to quit too. But he had nothing to go home to — only a fretting mother, no job, and the memory of climbing nothing significant other than the Plan. This left him short of successful ventures to write about — for earning a living from writing had now become a consuming ambition.

He has been accused of a mercenary approach to mountaineering, and that his climbing was corrupted by money, but I've never felt that this was so. I believe that his climbing started as a daydreaming escape in childhood and mountains remained magical and mysterious throughout his comparatively short life. It was a kind of symbiosis. As a plant and an insect draw benefit from each other, so earning money from writing about climbing enabled him to do more of what he wanted most — to climb. His frustration and failures in Argentina and Egypt, his mother's worries and his relatives' scepticism simply hardened his determination to succeed in journalism, as he called it, at that point in his life. He put his position bluntly in a letter to Young:[4]

> The photos I've recently taken fetched 50 guineas, which means an overall profit of quite 100 per cent on a holiday. I don't know what the AC will think. It seems horribly professional, but my motto is, do anything (short of murder, arson, etc) which will take one to the mountains!

Then, at Montenvers, along came one of the most fateful encounters of his life. He was introduced to a man who was also short of a climbing partner, and who was prepared to stay on until mid-September if necessary — Professor Thomas Graham Brown.

Actually they had met a couple of weeks previously, after Frank had got back from the Old Brenva route. Graham Brown had recently begun a holiday in the area with Edwin Herbert, whom Frank knew, and two guides. That evening the talk had all been about the great classic routes on Mont Blanc and Graham Brown had listened carefully. He had also observed Frank, 'whose recent expeditions had excited much interest at Montenvers' he wrote later, 'and had aroused my own admiration.' The reason for his interest in Mont Blanc was quite simple. Graham Brown nursed a great ambition. Not only did he intend to climb the unclimbed Brenva Face of the mountain, but he knew exactly where his planned route on it lay, and the necessary timing of the ascent to minimise the dangers from ice avalanches.

Tom Graham Brown died in 1965 and I never met him. He started climbing quite late in life and in 1927, his fourth year of climbing in the Alps he was 45, virtually a generation older than Frank and most of the other British climbers at the Montenvers that year. Rather than attempt my own description of GB (as he was generally known) I offer one by Edwin Herbert. Herbert, who was a friend of both GB and Frank, was a solicitor, an average climber, modest, fair-minded and diplomatic. He later became a godfather to one of Frank's sons (my younger brother, Richard). Later still he was President of the Alpine Club. He wrote a piece in the *Alpine Journal* a few months after GB died that was part-obituary, part-unravelling of the dispute that festered for years after the Brenva Face saga:

> His was one of the most complex personalities I have ever known. There was the rigorous scientist whose work in physiology earned him a Fellowship of the Royal Society. There was a deep humility in the presence of the great mountains, amounting to awe. There was a deep capacity for friendship. There was a soaring ambition which quite naturally made him wish that the world should know that the great Brenva climbs were his. There was also a touchiness which made him at times a difficult companion and resulted in interruptions of friendship. I remember one fine morning, high up on Mont Blanc, I ventured to comment on the beauty of the sunrise. Receiving no answer and seeing GB with head bent over his ice-axe, I asked him if he was all right. The reply (without looking up) was, 'Yes, perfectly, except that I object to your conversation.' Fortunately, I then knew him well enough to realise that I had interrupted one of his deep meditations which were the mainspring of his actions.
>
> His physical characteristics were no less remarkable. He was very short in stature and had particularly short legs. In 1926 he was already in early middle-age, but weighed little over nine stone. He had had some experience of rock-climbing but little of snow or ice work. In 1926, helped by his minute weight, he was able to scramble up rocks quite well. On snow and ice he was really quite poor, and in addition was handicapped by his very short legs. His great strength was his ability to go on indefinitely without any apparent fatigue. I recall two descents of the Nantillons Glacier in one week in 1927 and the painful slowness of his descent of the dangerous passage. Neither in 1926 nor in 1927 was Graham Brown in my opinion fitted to lead a serious expedition. I mention these limitations, not for the purpose of detracting from Graham Brown's achievements, but on the contrary to emphasise the fact that his will and imagination were capable of transcending his own limitations and those of others.[5]

Herbert went on to describe GB's obsession with the Brenva Face of Mont Blanc, how the novel *Running Water* by A.E.W. Mason, which features a fictional ascent of the Old Brenva route, caused him to imagine the possibilities for making a route up the unexplored face to its left, even though he had never seen it, let alone done any climbing. In 1926 he saw the Brenva Face for the first time when he, Herbert and another climber, with their two guides travelled up the Val Veni from Courmayeur. From this distant view of it he picked out the rib running up the centre of the face towards the Col Major between the summit of Mont Blanc and its lower twin, Mont Blanc de Courmayeur, and this line which became known as the Route Major proved to be the finest and most important of the first three of the routes established on the face. From that moment, which had involved an instant rearrangement of his preconceived ideas, Graham Brown doggedly and perhaps optimistically claimed the climb as his own invention. Herbert affirmed: 'I am certain that it was an absolutely original conception on the part of Graham Brown and this I believe is an excellent illustration of the combination of his vivid imagination and his scientific mind.'

During the 1926/1927 winter GB, poring over his books and maps had proposed an expedition in which they would in short order climb the Brouillard Ridge of Mont Blanc, then descend the Pétéret Ridge to tackle the new route he had spotted on the Brenva Face. This lengthy and complex set of climbs would have been extraordinarily ambitious, even for top-class alpinists used to moving together at speed on difficult mixed ground. GB in the style of the Victorian mountaineers, used guides, directing operations himself from the rear, but given his and Herbert's lack of experience they might have had a problem persuading guides to take on such a programme.

In the 1927 season the succession of storms had scotched this 'southern zigzag' idea, and instead they had attempted without success to climb Mont Blanc via the easy Dôme route, before returning to Montenvers. And it was at this point, with Herbert's holiday running out, that GB and Frank bumped into one another for the second time, now both at a loose end.

Exactly what was proposed next varies according to whose account you read. Frank says that he suggested to GB that they should join forces on Mont Blanc's Brenva Face for 'the climb on which I had now set my heart'[6] — without specifying the route. Herbert simply says that he believed Frank was competent to lead 'the new climb'[7] (meaning the line GB had picked out, i.e. the Route Major). Blakeney later added fuel to the fire by declaring that the key climb, the Route Major, was the concept of both Frank and Graham Brown 'quite independent of one another.'[8] GB himself in his book *Brenva* states that Herbert, on the last evening of his holiday, 'mentioned my project on the Brenva Face for the first time, and suggested that 'we [i.e. himself and Frank] might try my proposed route.'

It might be wondered where all this is leading. After all, who cares who thought up a climb, so long as it is safely accomplished in good style?

The answer is, nobody particularly, but in view of the terrible outcome in relationships that followed the first two Brenva Face routes — and I have chosen those words with care — it will be seen that these skirmishes were important in that they marked the start of what turned out to be a collaboration between two men of utterly different personalities leading to a successful result but with an explosive aftermath that shocked and divided the Alpine Club.

Graham Macphee took a photograph of Herbert, GB and Frank at the Montenvers. The picture is a story in itself. All three are dressed in the 'smart/casual' of those days — suit or sports coat with waistcoat, shirt and tie. Herbert and Frank lounge on each side of GB, self-consciously laughing at one another, while GB, inches smaller than either stands upright between them, facing the camera, trousers at half-mast, jacket buttoned all the way up, a trilby on his head, a pipe in his hand, his expression an unblinking gaze into the lens. You feel that this small, contained man was in control, imposing his will almost before the handshakes had taken place.

When two people join up for an enterprise as committing as a big Alpine climb they will soon discover whether they are kindred spirits. If they are not, all is not lost. It just means that tuned to different wavelengths they must each work harder to avoid friction in the interest of a safe and successful climb. Frank and GB managed this after a fashion; the miracle is that they climbed together two years running. For this was a classic case of Art versus Science. If Frank, with his highly-strung and imaginative temperament was the artist, Graham Brown was at each and every waking moment a scientist. He was a man who measured and recorded things and wrote them down in a note-book, someone to whom exaggeration meant inaccuracy, and to whom those dynamic qualities of Frank's would become suspect. His book about the Brenva Face climbs contains precise descriptions of topography, and the photographs are all of views of the climbs with any climbers purely incidental. They have captions that minutely describe the features and record the date and the time the shot was taken to the nearest five minutes. *Brenva* is empty of emotion, sparing of opinion, and deals in facts. Graham Brown's currency, the fuel that powered him, was facts. When he died his archive, bequeathed to the Scottish National Library, was enormous because he had kept virtually every letter he had ever received and a copy of every letter he had written, as well as every other item of paperwork imaginable during the course of a long life. But I am getting ahead of the story. In 1927 Graham Brown was already a notable figure at Cardiff University where he worked, but the mixture of renown and notoriety that was to dog him in the mountaineering world still lay in the future.

The weather for the next six days was excellent and Frank and Graham Brown seized the opportunity to make their historic first ascent of the Brenva Face on 2 September. Frank published a short account in two club journals,[9] and the story appeared later in two of his books.[10] Graham Brown's book, *Brenva*, published much later, contained a chapter on the climb.

The descriptions together give a good idea of the problems and technical features of the climb. From the Torino Hut the two men were demoralised by soft snow on the glaciers, and the route on the face they had picked out and agreed on was reached late in the day. Crucially, it was not the Route Major, but a line further to the right between it and the Old Brenva route. Frank had vetoed the Route Major during their inspections from the Torino, deciding privately it was too risky, especially with an inexperienced second, and had initially opted simply for a variation of the Old Brenva. A compromise was reached when GB, after lengthy inspection with his monocular, persuaded his companion that a possible route with an exit existed up a curving ridge to the right of the Great Couloir.

The weather held, and after bivouacking safely underneath a small protecting buttress they called the Red Sentinel, they made an early start next morning. They were able to avoid most of the danger of avalanches with frost gripping the face. The upper part of the climb on the 'Twisting Ridge' was complicated and slow, with Frank cutting steps continuously, but the escape through the sérac barrier proved straightforward. It was a superb achievement, and the climb duly took its place in the record books. It became known as the Sentinelle route.

An important question remains. How did the pair get on during the climb and immediately afterwards? Frank complained later that GB had been slow, enlarging and adding ice steps to suit his short legs. And his use of a notebook and watch to record details during the climb was highly irritating — he noted for example that the climb had taken 27 hours and 25 minutes, of which 6 hours and 27 minutes were rests. But Frank seems to have kept his impatience and temper under control.

GB was the more equable, not allowing his enjoyment of the climb to be spoilt in any way. A letter he wrote to his close friend, George Gask, has an upbeat feel:

We — F.S. Smythe and self — got back yesterday from a first ascent of Mont Blanc by a new route! And you were so good in shoving me into the Club that I want you to be the first to have the news.

The slopes [near the top] were very steep and were composed of extremely hard ice. It looked as if there were many hours of hard step-cutting for Smythe (who led the climb — I'm too much of a rabbit at the game for that!) — perhaps four – six hours. However (to our great joy) we found a small fold in the ice — (a steep incipient gully) where there was two – three inches of snow on its north-east facing side. It was just possible for our crampons to hold and we were able to get up with comparatively little step-cutting (Smythe did about two hours' step-cutting on the final face — the ice was very hard).

We are both very uppish at the moment about this climb — tails well up. Knubel says it is one of the greatest. We think it is the only guideless first ascent of one of the great routes. It is the only face climb of Mont Blanc. It is a direct climb. It needs seven days of perfect weather — and we fitted it into the only seven days of perfect weather there have been here this awful season.

Please forgive this rhapsody — and my bad writing too (my fingers are very sore). 'Smythe is a great man!'

For GB the climb had been the partial fulfilment of a dream. On the upper reaches of the Sentinelle he had been aware of the soaring ice ridges and final rock buttress of the Route Major, immediately across the Great Couloir to their left. This was the pure route up the centre of the face that he felt was *the* one, and that night at the Vallot Hut he had again talked about it, even suggesting that they should return next day to the Torino for an immediate attempt on it while the good weather lasted. Frank had turned this idea down, but the two men weren't in a hurry to get home. They relaxed at the Montenvers, fitting in another two climbs between periods of bad weather, before heading for home on 15 September.

NINE

Route Major

The news of the breakthrough on the Brenva Face spread quickly. Traditionally a new route of such importance required the participants to write a description — a 'paper' — and read this at an Alpine Club meeting. It would also be published in the *Journal*.

Frank and Graham Brown had discussed this even before they did the climb. Frank had proposed that since he would be leading the route his partner should do the write up, but GB suggested the paper should be a joint effort. Back in England though, Frank told GB that he'd been advised by the Club Secretary and the Journal Editor that since his other climbs that summer were to be included in the paper it couldn't be done jointly; he must write and read it himself. GB accepted this, but a little later discovered that there was no such obstacle; it would be fine for them to combine, indeed Captain Farrar, the Editor personally thought it was a good idea. GB felt misled by Frank, who immediately backed down and agreed on a joint paper. Apart from a certain loss of faith, that might have been the end of the matter. Sadly it wasn't. Two weeks later Frank wrote to GB again, arguing that their writing styles were so different that a joint paper simply wouldn't work.

GB remained calm and patient. He reminded Frank what had been agreed before the climb and what Farrar and Spencer had said. In his own professional work papers were often produced jointly. 'Where there's a will there's a way,' he mused. And surely the climb would be nicely rounded off like this, leaving happy memories of the venture. But Frank was adamant, insisting that the Club opposed the idea of a jointly-written paper; it 'chose its victims' he said, and had chosen him. Then, amazingly, just three days later he wrote again agreeing after all to combine with GB. He was in a 'ghastly rush.' He'd landed a job as a *Times* Special Correspondent to report on a collapsing mountain in Switzerland.

The saga of the Alpine Club paper wasn't quite over. In the end Frank wrote it and read it to the Club on 7 February 1928, illustrating with slides made from Graham Brown's photographs. The *Journal* article was sub-headed 'Written in Collaboration with T. Graham Brown.' A photograph of the Brenva Face with a dotted line was captioned 'Mr Smythe's Route.'

This unsavoury episode demonstrated the gap between the two men. Graham Brown upheld the same principles in his recreational mountaineering as he did in his professional life. But Frank saw things from a different perspective. He was desperate to succeed as a writer. He had written more than a dozen stories about his adventures, ready for when he could find a publisher. The Sentinelle climb, the most prestigious of any he'd done, was a great opportunity for him. The word 'limelight' comes to mind. He needed this. The Professor didn't — he had a career already. If there'd been talk in the Alps about who would write the paper, it needn't be taken seriously now. More important things were at stake.

Graham Brown saw what was in Frank's mind. The younger man's ambition, the way he courted publicity, his plan to use mountaineering to make a living — all this was anathema to him. He saw the combined paper as the scholarly conclusion to a joint endeavour and although he was dismayed to see this arrangement rejected by Frank he became resigned to it. What he couldn't forgive or forget — although he kept his thoughts to himself — was Frank's pretence that he had been asked by Farrar and Spencer to write the paper on his own. Graham Brown saw this as a deliberate lie. It offended him that Frank unfairly claimed to have discovered the climb. Even a small thing like Frank putting his own name first in the *Journal* notes instead of following alphabetical order irked him.

But treasuring his memories of the climb, Graham Brown said nothing. By now he had summed up Frank Smythe and decided not to disturb the status quo. He knew the other man was a very good climber indeed and success on the Major next summer would depend again on him being at the sharp end of the rope. Frank, for his part, once he'd got what he wanted, wrote cheerful letters and chatted to GB as though nothing had happened.

Years later Herbert wrote that after the Sentinelle climb Frank had decided not to climb alone with Graham Brown again.[1] The pair however, seemed to have patched things up at the end of 1927. Their letters were friendly; the Professor came to stay with Frank and his mother at their home in Primrose Hill in December, and again in February for the AC meeting. They discussed climbing possibilities for the coming summer and Frank even talked about Mount Kenya and the Canadian Rockies, where they could 'go gold mining in their spare time'.

Frank was often in touch now with Geoffrey Winthrop Young. Young's activities had been severely curtailed after he lost a leg in the First World War, but his early Alpine pioneering, his partnership with great guides and stars such as George Mallory, and the publication of *Mountain Craft* and *On High Hills*, had already earned great respect. He was very approachable and enjoyed drawing successful young climbers into his orbit. In December 1927 Frank wrote to him, asking for advice about lecture agents:

> I hope to make my way with writing, lecturing and photography. It would be the ideal life as I detest commercialism and my greatest regret is not having had a classical education.

He described his plans for a book on guideless climbing. Would Young read the first drafts and provide a critique? 'Can literary ability develop after 27 years of age,' he asked anxiously, 'or must one remain mediocre?'

I met Geoffrey Young a couple of times in 1954. He was in Langdale, wearing his familiar cloak and trilby hat and invited me to join him at the Hill Inn in Chapel-le-Dale, but there he was surrounded by respectful admirers and there was no chance of a chat. So I wrote, and like Frank asked for his comments on an article I had written. My manuscript came back covered in pencilled suggestions together with a letter typed on a machine as old as the Grépon. 'Re-read after a few months,' he advised, 'when the thread in your own mind when you wrote is faded, and you'll begin to see how a *reader* is impressed by it. I used to rewrite *On High Hills* more or less once a year, for six years ... And used to be amazed each time how little I'd yet succeeded in making the *reader* see the picture.'[2] He seemed eager for my news, sometimes sending a postcard to restart things after a gap. I felt privileged, but GWY treated everybody as though they were special. Fifty years later when I looked into his archive I found files with letters from hundreds of people. Frank's correspondence with him was huge.

With their success on Mont Blanc Frank and GB both 'qualified' for an invitation to Young's 1928 Easter party at the Pen-y-Pass hotel in Snowdonia. He had been holding his gatherings since 1903, restarting them eventually after the First World War. About 50 climbers might attend, some at the forefront of British climbing, a unique collection of talent. Frank rode up to Wales on a motorcycle, possibly the first time he had used one and certainly the last, since on the way home the machine broke down three times before he reached Shrewsbury, the flailing chain ripping off part of the engine next to his foot and frightening him off motorbikes for life.

He had ten days in Snowdonia. The experienced climbers were expected to give some of their time to novices on easier climbs, and it was only in the final days that he was able to return to the cliff that had fascinated him six years earlier — Clogwyn d'ur Arddu. On 9 April 1928 a group including him and Jack Longland arrived at the bottom of the great cliff. A route had been made up a crack on the East Buttress the year before, but the taller West Buttress, with its awe-inspiring overlapping slabs, offered an even finer prize. It was Longland who now spotted the key traverse above the overhanging base of the buttress, to link with a long slab. They returned two days later to climb part way up the virgin rock until rain forced a retreat.

Six weeks later, on a fine day at Whitsun, a party returned to the cliff with Geoffrey Young, Frank driving him up the track from Llanberis in his recently acquired 'Baby' Austin 7. At the foot of the buttress they met Fred Pigott and two other Rucksack Club climbers who had started on the route not knowing of anyone else's involvement, but then found an abseil sling and sportingly stood down when they realised the original explorers had come back. Unselfish posturing on both sides followed, then the two teams agreed to combine. Longland was leader, Pigott second, then came Frank and the other Rucksackers, Bill Eversden and Morley Wood.

How much easier a climb is once it's in a guidebook, described, measured, and graded. Thirty years later John Cleare and I stood at the bottom of Longland's Climb, as it had become known. We'd recently done the Great Slab, over on the right-hand side of the buttress, also graded Very Severe, but had found it straightforward, apart from one tricky little move early on. We were on top form, shared the lead, and Longland's was glorious — a delicate tip-toe up an immense slab that leaned to the left and got narrower and narrower until you had to pull over its right-hand containing wall, exhilaratingly above 250 feet of space, to gain another slab and then the top. Wonderful. An hour and a half of pure pleasure.

In 1928 there was no chance of enjoying it this way. They had to work out a set of problems at the cutting edge of technical difficulty on one of the most forbidding cliffs in Britain. Longland and Pigott puzzled it out between them while the others had the luxury and the boredom of waiting, with rope-protected ascents to each stance, the tamest type of rock-climbing. But Frank's description holds images special to the tail end of a rope:

I gazed downwards for a moment … Two pink patches told of Geoffrey Young and his shirt, though at that distance it was impossible to tell which was which … Came another long wait. I looked up — two pairs of dissimilar breeches were actively defying gravity …

'Have you got the matches?' inquired Pigott from above. These matches were throughout the climb a constant source of anxiety to him, but on every occasion that we were together we forgot them, only to remember them when we were far apart again …

[The traverse] … was a brilliant piece of climbing. To my mind it is the hardest bit of the ascent, a long stride, the balance is critical, the handholds mere finger-scrapes, the exposure and the precipice beneath terrific … I have never seen a place that called more for a piton, and I must own to a vast feeling of satisfaction on finding myself attached to it …

The air was breathless and hot; a smooth slate-coloured cloud slid lazily over Snowdon; a dusky purple swept down the cwm … Longland settled the question by clinging up the overhang and gaining the platform above. The rest of us … crouched down out of the rain contentedly smoking, in the pleasant consciousness that Longland was sitting above and getting wet …[3]

Longland's Climb was a landmark in British climbing history. Fred Pigott thought it harder than his route on the East Buttress and more exacting than even the notorious Central Buttress of Scafell. Young saw the climb as 'the moment of change over from the older to the newer Rock Age,' and the deferring of the two parties to each other and then combining, was 'an example of mountaineering generosity that it is well to recall in a later time when the competitive spirit reigns and envy is known to walk abroad, even among mountaineers.'

These words were published in 1951, in his book *Mountains with a Difference*. Young had a high regard for Frank, although there were moments when his patience was tested. He preferred to see the positive side of a person. He wrote pen-portraits of many climbers including Frank:

I realised him first as a personality after our day's climbing on Lliwedd, during the communal ceremony of hot baths in the shack. He was perched on the back of the settle in the steam, wrapped in a towel, a faun-like figure, with reddish wavy hair, a hooked profile, and a red flame glinting behind the smile in his keen eyes. He was playing his mouth organ to himself, or broke into the talk in a laughing tenor with a slightly haughty intonation. He was sociable, but went his own way in life with independence and a restless enterprise. He kept a little apart from the ups and downs of personal relationship inevitable among explorers long secluded together; and this made him an admirable leader, seeing to everything himself beforehand, considerate and rarely interfering in action.

On 5 July 1928 Frank and Graham Brown went out to the Alps. Arriving in Kandersteg they ran into Ivan Waller, who was on his own, and invited him to join them. The three then went on to Chamonix.

The plan now was that Frank and GB would spend two weeks on training climbs before being joined by Ward and Blakeney for the Route Major. Frank had told GB in May that Blakeney would make a better fourth member of the party than Macphee since the latter had been 'very slow and weak' on the Pétéret Ridge the previous year when a storm had nearly destroyed them. But GB sensed that Frank was dithering. Not only was he substituting Macphee with Blakeney, who could take only a fortnight's holiday, but earlier he had revealed that the 'weak' Macphee was to join him in August for other climbs on the south side of Mont Blanc.

After a warm-up climb Frank, GB and Waller set off for a more testing route on a peak that had given Frank a hard time the previous year — the Grépon. This time he would suffer even greater embarrassment on a day he would never forget. Two factors combined to cause his downfall. It was the beginning of a holiday when he customarily struggled with unfitness, and he was climbing with Ivan Waller.

Waller, aged 21 was seven years younger than Frank and apart from some skiing in the Oberland had never been to the Alps. Sadly these things caused Frank not only to believe himself superior to Waller but to behave in a patronising way. What he didn't take into account was that Waller, although quite small, was very strong and fit, and probably the equal of Jack Longland in rock climbing skill. He was also the sort of person who was unimpressed by a man's reputation unless it was backed up by demonstrated ability.

He was a Cambridge student and had been one of those to stand aside in the assembling of the party for the ascent of Longland's in May. Yet his talent was prodigious. In 1927 he had made the first ascent of Belle Vue Bastion on Tryfan's Terrace Wall, a superb little 'Very Severe' that had defeated many attempts. He went on to shock the establishment by climbing it again next day solo, to musical accompaniment from a gramophone, and celebrated with a hand-stand on one of the mountain's exposed summit monoliths, Adam and Eve. Waller also had skills that would take him in other directions — as a skier, racing and rally driver, automobile engineer, and a wartime flight test engineer.

Peter Harding, a leading climber of the post-World War Two era, was employed by Waller for 10 years in an engineering firm. He remembered him as outspoken, but not a man to harbour grudges. He led by example. 'I remember a chimney they were knocking down,' he told me, 'and they couldn't get any of the demolishers to climb it. Ivan simply donned a pair of overalls, found himself a ladder, and led the party up the inside of the chimney. For a company director to do this … I think the owners were horrified!'

Waller, GB and Frank were tackling the Grépon by its normal route on the west face. Problems began when a party above dislodged stones. Frank, with a well-developed respect for avalanches warned Waller, who was leading, that his choice of route was dangerous. When the serious rock climbing began however, Waller was in his element and swarmed up the famous pitches one after another while the others laboured behind, sometimes needing help from the rope.

Frank relied on his friends to make allowances for him when he was not climbing well — his off-days he called them — but Waller afforded him no such indulgence. On the summit Frank, very tired now, wanted to rest but Waller insisted they move off immediately. After they had rappelled down to a ledge Frank stupidly attempted to continue before the rope had been untangled and Waller shouted, 'Come back, you silly c**t!' Finally on the glacier relationships broke down completely when the exhausted Frank, to slow the speeding Waller and GB yelled 'Stop, you bloody fools,' and sat down in the snow, bringing them abruptly to a halt on the rope. When Waller said, 'For God's sake come along Frank, this place is dangerous', he got the furious reply, 'Don't call me 'Frank' — I'm *Mr Smythe* to you.' And referring to the c-word, added savagely, 'I'm not used to being called the name you called me up there.' He told Waller bluntly that he would never climb with him again and Waller replied in the same vein. That evening there were more hard words said, and next day Waller went his own way.

Ugly incidents like this, usually due to a clash of temperaments or tiredness and stress, are possibly more common than climbers like to admit. It might be wondered how I am able to go into such detail since Frank never referred to it. The answer is — Graham Brown's archive. Four years later, for reasons that will become clear, GB re-established contact with Waller and persuaded him to recount his memories of that infamous day.[4]

Another problem lay in wait for Frank. After he and GB had spent a couple of days testing their new lightweight sleeping bags by bivouacking on the Aiguille Verte, they returned to find that although Blakeney had arrived, the fourth member of their team, Ward would not be able to join them. This was a setback. A party of three would be slower, not having the option of splitting into two pairs for speed, and it would be subtly weakened psychologically. However nothing could be done. Blakeney was allowed one training climb, then in continuing fine weather the party climbed the Géant Glacier to get a good view of the Brenva Face.

The conditions looked vastly different from the year before. I have on my wall a photograph of the face taken by Frank at that moment. The usual snowy amphitheatre with ribs of rock showing through has been transformed into a precipice dominated by black buttresses separated by icy couloirs. The diminished snow slopes after weeks of blazing sun have been scored by falling rock and ice. It is easy to picture the melting and refreezing that must have taken place, producing much wearisome ice axe work in the days when step-cutting was the only technique devised.

Frank immediately decided that new snow and colder weather were needed to put the face into condition, and to GB's dismay but with Blakeney's support he called for a descent to Courmayeur to bide their time. However on reaching the valley they ran into Eustace Thomas, who told them gleefully that he and his guide, Josef Knubel had just traversed the Pétéret, Brouillard and Old Brenva ridges, with a descent of the Innominata Face, all within a fortnight, and that Mont Blanc was in excellent condition.

Frank had been deceived. But it was no use lamenting the fact. In the morning they would go up to Moore's Old Bivouac, an overhanging rock high up the Brenva Glacier used by the pioneers, then next night they would bivouac at the Red Sentinel, and tackle the Route Major the day after that. However in a letter to Arnold Lunn many years later Blakeney wrote:

> Smythe told me later that year [1928] that he had had a conviction all along that he was going to be killed, and that it preyed on his mind the whole time. He was gloomy to a degree of the prospects of our Brenva Face route, though 1928 was a wonderful year in late June and early July … We ran into Eustace Thomas in Courmayeur and I remember how he told Smythe he was amazed to hear him advancing objections to every climb proposed. He had thought Smythe would be itching to do big things. Smythe replied, 'I am definitely nervous.' I have no doubt that part of his nervousness was simply that he knew that with GB in the party it would devolve too much on him.

Next morning they laboured up in stifling heat, GB and Blakeney no doubt

1 (above): The wedding of Frank's parents, Algernon Smythe and Florence Reeves in July 1897, attended only by the Reeves family — her mother, father, three brothers and three sisters, plus two unidentified gentlemen (at back, on left and on right).

2 (left): Enlarged image of the couple.

3, 4, 5 (below): Frank at ages two, nine and 12 years.

6 (above): Berkhamsted School Cricket 1st XI v Old Boys July 1918. Frank (back row in front of post) excelled as a medium-pace bowler (photo is part of a group shot of the two teams).

7 (left): Holiday with the Johnsons at Borth-y-Gest in 1918 — the earliest surviving photo taken by FS. From left: Ken, Mollie, Kathleen and Esmond Johnson, his mother Florence.

8 (right): Yorkshire Ramblers' Club. Ernest Roberts (left) supervising at a potholing meet.

EXPLORING THE ALPS SOLO DURING ENGINEERING TRAINING IN 1922

9 (above left): Setting out for a climb. **10 (above right):** A break from skiing.

CLIMBING WITH JIM BELL IN 1923.

11 (below left): Rope-wreathed in the Dolomites. **12 (below right):** Bell on Ben Nevis.

13 (above): The Somervell brothers, Howard and Leslie on the summit of the Langkofel when Frank joined them in the Dolomites.

14 (below left): Howard had been asked by General Bruce to test him for the 1924 Everest expedition — his report was discouraging.

15 (below right): Bruce posing years later for Frank's camera in typically exuberant style.

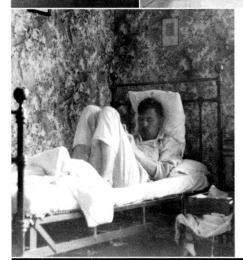

16 (above left): Failed schoolboy/qualified engineer seeks post — a 1924 portrait.

17 (above centre): En route to Buenos Aires in 1925 with new-found friend (right), where FS survived a job in telephone engineering for only 51 days.

18 (above right): Bernard Smythe, who became disenchanted with the wayward behaviour of his brother-in-law.

19 (left): During career number two as an RAF pilot Frank's health broke down in Egypt, leading to him being invalided from the Service after nine months.

20 (below): His flying training course — he is in the middle row, standing, third from right.

21 (above): The Péterét Ridge of Mont Blanc from which in August 1927 Frank and Graham Macphee were forced by a ferocious storm into making an epic escape.

22 (right): A 1937 picture of Macphee (centre) in Langdale with Colin Kirkus (right) and Piero Ghiglione. Two years earlier Frank had tested a group including Kirkus in the Alps for the 1936 Everest expedition. His rejection of Kirkus was generally regarded as a poor decision.

23 (above): A fateful meeting. Edwin Herbert (left) introduces Tom Graham Brown (centre) to Frank at the Montenvers in 1927.

24 (below): The Brenva Face of Mont Blanc. The Sentinelle route of 1927 runs up to the right of the Great Couloir splitting the face, the superb Route Major of 1928 lies immediately to the left of the couloir, following the series of ice ridges in its central section.

KANGCHENJUNGA — THE 1930 EXPEDITION

25 (above): The north-west face from Base Camp.

26 (below left): Gunter Dyhrenfurth and his wife, Hettie (central in the picture) with team members.
27 (below right): Frank in the specially designed heavy expedition boots he loathed.

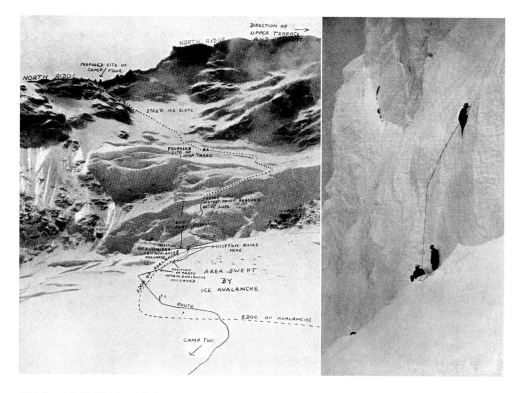

28 (above left): The intended route up the Great Ice Wall on the north-west face — the 200-metre-high unstable edge of a huge glacier terrace. **29 (above right):** Climbing the Great Ice Wall.

30 (below): An ice avalanche on the north-west face of Kangchenjunga. A collapse similar to this killed the sirdar, Chettan and led to the eventual abandonment of the attempt.

31 (above): Tennis at Berkhamsted. Frank's future wife, Kathleen Johnson (front centre) at a private party with her mother, Mollie (in dark hat at back). Her brother, Ken would later marry Gladys Waterfield, on Kathleen's right.

32 (left): Frank's mother, Florence (left) and Mollie Johnson in cheerful mood.

THE WEDDING

33 (right): Frank and Kathleen were married at St Peter's, Berkhamsted on 18th January, 1931.

THE HONEYMOON

34 (above left): Frank in the Ogwen Valley. **35 (above centre):** Kathleen on Snowdon.
36 (above right): In a sunnier clime, a Swiss hay hut.

KAMET

37 (below): The expedition at Ranikhet in May 1931. Standing: Greene, Holdsworth, Beauman, Shipton, Birnie. Seated: Nima Tendrup, FS, Achung.

38 (above left): Kamet (left) and the Mana Peak from Nilkanta.

39 (above right): Nima Dorje with the cinecamera, which he carried to within 500 feet of the summit of Kamet before becoming exhausted and going no further.

40 (below right): Holdsworth (left) and Shipton still with 2,500 feet to climb on summit day. The slopes of the snowy north face were much steeper than Frank's photograph suggests.

41 (below left): Lewa the sirdar reached the summit but, frostbitten, later lost all his toes.

42: Kamet, the last few weary steps at 4.30 p.m. on 21 June, 1931. The summit at 25,447 feet, 7,756 metres, was the highest in the world reached at that time.

EVEREST, 1933

43 (top left): Members at Kalimpong. Dr Graham and Hugh Ruttledge on left, FS on the right.

44 (top right): Frank rides his pony, Relling at the start of the 300-mile journey to the mountain, the reassuring presence of Shebbeare alongside.

45 (centre): On the Tibetan plateau. Shipton at the head of the table, perhaps dreaming of, and craving fresh eggs (see chapter 16).

46 (right): Raymond Greene with a couple of locals.

47 (above left): Camp 3a and the North Col, 2,000 feet higher.

48 (above right): Climbing the often dangerous and sometimes lethal North Col slopes.

49 (below left): Camp 5 — perched on the edge of the (unseen) north-east precipice.

50 (below right): Camp 6, at 27,400 feet (8,350 metres), well into the aptly-named 'Death Zone'.

51: View from 25,000 feet on Everest. This dramatic 1933 photograph of the graceful peak, Pumori (central in the picture), was overlooked by Frank until 1946, when he published it in his album, *Snow on the Hills*.

cursing that Frank's tactical blunder had cost them two days and much extra effort. And by the afternoon it all seemed to be going wrong again. Clouds billowed up, and at the bivouac there were rumbles of thunder. Hastily they lit a fire from old timber, had a brew and supper, got into their sleeping bags underneath the overhanging rock, and waited for the storm. Their climbing plans were in the balance, but they were about to see a great thunderstorm from a safe vantage point at 10,000 feet on Mont Blanc — a unique experience. Frank described it eloquently:

The lightning was ever nearer. The outlines of Mont Blanc and the Pétéret Ridge were wedged from the night by its quivering blue flames. We heard the storm strike the massif of Mont Blanc. The Brouillard Ridge was the first to receive its fury; then, without pause, it swept across towards us.

Weird beads of faint greenish light, like the watch-fires of goblins, danced and trembled on the spires of the Dames Anglaises: it was the brush discharge preceding the storm, a phenomenon known to sailors as St Elmo's Fires. I experienced a faint tingling of the scalp, and a feeling as though light cobwebs were brushing my face … A curtain of mauve fire descended; a crooked sword of intense light stabbed the crest of the Aiguille Noire de Pétéret; a tearing crack of thunder was flung from precipice to precipice, but before the echoes had been stifled amid the cirque of peaks the lightning slashed again. From individual reports the thunder resolved itself into one prolonged and mighty reverberation.

In a few minutes the storm was around us. Time and again the lightning struck but a few feet distant; it darted like fiery serpents into the Brenva Glacier … We counted 25 flashes a minute … The Pétéret Ridge disappeared, drowned in a torrent of hail and rain that burst furiously upon us; hail as large as marbles rattled about us; a gusty wind strove to pluck us from our shelter. Through the curtains of rain we no longer saw the lightning's spiteful stabs, but a confused and blinding glare … lightning and thunder were often practically simultaneous. Then we saw what none of us had ever seen before … The Aiguille Blanche de Pétéret poured forth its avalanches, and through the darkness we saw torrents of fire streaming down its cliffs as the rocks ground and crashed together on their flight to the Brenva Glacier.[5]

Next morning, with Mont Blanc coated in new snow, the weather forbidding, and Blakeney ill from drinking glacier water they retreated. It had become a shambles, but it could have been worse. Perhaps it crossed their minds that had they proceeded with their original plan of a night at the Torino Hut and a night at the Sentinel bivouac, the monster storm would have caught them somewhere high on the Route Major.

Let the last thought be for poor Tom Blakeney. To compound his miseries he lost his wallet and most of his money and decided to go home. He wrote in his memoirs:

> Of 1928 I can only think with shame. I threw away a golden opportunity with both hands, through sheer backbonelessness … I paid for it of course by naturally losing contact with Smythe as a climbing partner, whereas if I had only got that one big ascent under my belt I might have been in the running for a place on the next Everest expedition.

On 29 July Frank and GB, thrown together again as a pair returned to the Montenvers. Graham Brown wrote later that he suspected his companion's resolve weakening. Frank's insistence on returning to the Montenvers to 're-equip' and check his mail, and his suggestion that they should climb elsewhere in the interim were, in GB's opinion, delaying tactics, similar to the decision to descend to Courmayeur. This may have been true. When later a crisis began to develop on the Route Major Frank became very anxious compared with the Professor, who remained calm and clinical. But the real reason for his companion's nervousness was never recognised or at least admitted, by Graham Brown. It was simply that at heart, and especially when things became serious, Frank crucially lacked confidence in him.

Four days of unsettled weather limited them to easy local climbs. At last, on 5 August the sun shone, conditions were excellent, and they set off from the Torino Hut, a pre-dawn start being unnecessary since the Sentinelle bivouac could only be accessed safely in the evening frost. Eventually they reached the familiar place under the guardian rock and settled for the night.

People who knew of Frank sometimes remarked that I was 'following in my father's footsteps.' The cliché was relevant regarding the Route Major. Just before dawn on 5 August 1961 I stood with my friend Barry Annette at the edge of the Great Couloir just as Frank and GB had done 33 years earlier, within a day. My father was 28 years old when he did the climb; I came to it a year younger. Both of us had woken to a clear night, the sky a wealth of stars. Barry and I were lightly laden since we had started from the Col de la Fourche Hut soon after midnight intending to complete the climb in a day, while Frank and GB hefted heavy rucksacks after a night underneath the Sentinel rock with all their bivouac paraphernalia.

They were about to be the first humans ever to cross the Great Couloir; Barry and I knew that dozens had crossed since then. But both our parties faced the same danger of instant annihilation if there was a collapse from the enormous battlements of ice thousands of feet above. Like Frank and GB we were wearing crampons and clattered across the easy-angled rock slabs and patches of black ice, worn and polished from the avalanches. It was about 50 yards — far enough to have no chance if you were out of luck. But nothing fell; there was just an eerie drift of ankle-height powdery snow flowing down the runnelled surface.

Safely on the far side Barry and I soon gained the crest of the ridge which we would follow steeply upwards for the next few hours. It was divided into rock steps and buttresses, and curving snow arêtes. The dawn was coming now, a feast of colour on the horizon in far-off Switzerland and a few minutes later the sun painted the upper snows of Mont Blanc a delicate pink. There was not a breath of wind. After a quick snack we pressed on, moving together up frozen snow, perfect for cramponing. We couldn't believe our luck, the conditions were magical, and seemingly in no time we had reached the final rock buttress. We climbed the famous Unclimbable Corner — which seemed easier than any of the alternatives — gained the crest of the buttress, and found thankfully a straightforward way through the final ice cliffs to the mountain's upper snows. Here we sat in the sun at half-past nine in the morning. It was all over.

How different was the other party's experience! Recent snowfall had melted on the lower rocks then refrozen into *verglas*, slowing them greatly. Escaping at last onto the open snow ridges they rested for over an hour. But when they started again laborious cutting steps was necessary, and the hours started to fly. A freezing gusty wind blew, the arêtes seemed endless, the final buttress and ice cliffs with their unknown problems loomed more steeply overhead but never seemed to get any nearer. It was after midday when Frank called a halt to discuss whether they should go on.

It is at roughly this stage of the climb that the written accounts of both men begin seriously to differ. 60 years later John Hunt, who had climbed the Route Major and had known Frank well, commented, 'I have re-read Graham Brown's and Smythe's accounts of the 'Sentinelle' and 'Voie Major' climbs. Graham Brown, objective and factual, was probably more accurate than Frank's accounts (particularly of the 'Voie Major'), but I much prefer Frank's vivid story! I also knew Graham Brown and believe both men suffered from *amour propre*, which damaged the great merits of both men, and their great achievements.'[6]

This I think is a fair summing up. I wrote earlier about Frank's lack of confidence in his companion. That was understandable. Quite apart from his slowness and lack of experience on snow and ice, the Professor's coldly practical, unromantic approach to climbing and mountains generally was alien to Frank's way of thinking. GB had little time for the esoteric values that Frank held dear. There was a lack of rapport. But this was no reason for Frank consciously to overlook his companion's crucial part in the climb, which came during the overcoming of the final buttress. One is led to the conclusion that Frank was not prepared to give credit to Graham Brown where it was due. The reason for this is unpalatable. Frank, at this point in the climb was deeply worried. They were running out of time, it was becoming bitterly cold and the weather could not be relied on — smooth, evil-looking clouds lay on the horizon. He was horribly aware of the consequences of things going wrong on the upper part of Mont Blanc. He was looking to retreat, wanting an escape, but Graham Brown persuaded him that they should persevere for a bit longer. They eventually won through, and Frank suffered a blow to his pride. He could not accept that Graham Brown, whom he had considered inept, Graham Brown who grubbed absurdly with his ice axe, holding it halfway up the shaft and slowing them down by cutting extra steps for his short legs, Graham Brown who persistently made irritating comments while Frank was leading, and wrote in his notebook whenever he reached a stance, and was as humourless as an elderly hen … Frank could not stomach that Graham Brown, his unwished-for partner on the rope, had shown the courage and initiative that brought them victory. Frank could have been candid about the conflict of opinion at the foot of the final buttress — that he wanted to abandon the climb, and GB wanted to keep trying — but he chose to remain silent. He could have been generous about the Professor's effort that followed, but he begrudged it.

The drama began to unfold when they reached what is known as the Pedestal. This consists of a short rock rise that is topped by an ice slope, which in turn leads to the bottom of the final buttress. The buttress is massive, compact and vertical, even overhanging, but on the right its top slopes down to quite near the ice slope, and there is a vertical rock corner which, in about 10 feet, leads to easier ground. This is the so-called Unclimbable Corner which faced Frank and GB. The only apparent alternative was to traverse round a tongue of rock below on the right, but this looked repulsive, since the slope below it was hard ice and highly exposed above the Great Couloir. There was no telling whether a way could be found from round there to the summit of the buttress. They opted for the corner.

It was only short, but almost holdless and coated in *verglas*. After arranging a belay with ice axes rammed into the back of the corner where the ice gaped from the rock, Frank tried it, but could scarcely get off the ground. Graham Brown also made an attempt without success, and in his book *Brenva* he described what happened next:

> I offered to let him try to enter the crack from my bent back, although he would have to stand on it in his crampons, which we could not take off in that place.
>
> In order to make myself into a secure platform whilst standing in ice steps, I would have to wedge my shoulders into the corner, and grasp the upper edge of the ice with my hands. It would therefore be impossible to handle the rope, so I gave Smythe 20 feet or so of free rope from the axe belay, which was a little to the left and out of my reach. Then I set myself with shoulders fully bent, and Smythe climbed up on me in his crampons, thereafter standing upright and next mounting into the crack. After one upward half-glance, brief because Smythe's crampons were still within range, I kept my head down in the corner and tried to guess what was happening from the sounds. But these had ceased, and shortly thereafter Smythe, who was still a little short of the shelf, intimated urgently that a slip was to be expected at once. Had I stood up to try to steady his feet or to catch him as he fell, I would have had no security, and might in any case have been caught in the act of moving. There was nothing else for it but to brace myself and hope for the best.
>
> In such circumstances thought is rapid and clear. The danger to us both was obvious, because even were I not to be knocked off myself, the outward lean of the crack made it more than possible that Smythe might fall backwards off me, although the distance of his fall on to my back would be quite small. Were this to happen Smythe would slide down on to the clear *verglas* where it spread out just below us. Even if he alone went down, our two ice axes would be imprisoned by the taut rope, which would then hold him from the axe belay, and in this flash of thought it seemed (although perhaps wrongly) that that might be the end of us.
>
> Not more than a second or two can have passed as I waited in anxiety hoping that Smythe might recover himself or land safely if he slipped, but time seemed eternal. Then Smythe gave another urgent intimation and immediately fell. He fortunately landed on my back, half astride. One of his crampons carried away my left side-pocket with my pipe and tobacco, but without further damage. The prongs of the other crampon, however, went through my clothing, including a leather jacket, and into my side, but not deeply. In the excitement of the moment I did not feel this at the time, but did so soon afterwards. With his right leg bent under him and his crampons entangled, Smythe found his position on my back most awkward, but he kicked his crampons free of my clothes, and managed to slide safely off onto the ice steps.[7]

Their position can only be imagined. Thousands of feet above the Brenva Glacier they faced certain death if they fell. Yet remarkably, the horrific pantomime was repeated when Graham Brown stood on Frank's back and attempted the corner. He also failed, but managed to descend under control.

The situation appeared desperate. It was 2 p.m., they had been climbing for nine hours and the greatest difficulties might still lie ahead. Frank was overwrought — his anxiety getting the better of him after running into difficulties high up on such a serious climb with an inexperienced companion. Graham Brown said afterwards that he wept. Whether that was true or not Frank now wanted to descend some hundreds of feet, traverse across the Great Couloir and escape to safety via the top section of the Sentinelle route. Graham Brown however, deeply reluctant to abandon the climb, wanted to attempt the traverse round the rock tongue. Frank eventually agreed to this and remained in the corner to belay him.

GB then made his magnificent contribution to their success. Running out the full 110 feet of available rope he cut steps and handholds down across the glass-hard, olive-green ice, then once round the bottom of the rock tongue he could see that a route might exist up mixed ground to the top of the buttress. He moved up into good snow, took a belay and shouted for Frank, who eventually arrived, still somewhat demoralised. An hour and a half had disappeared during this one pitch, but the climbing went more steadily now, although the conditions were dreadful — their clothes became armour-plated in wind-blown snow and everything was covered in ice. In a minor way it was comparable, not technically but in its situation, with another great 'first' — the 'do or die' finish 10 years later up the exit cracks of the Eiger North Face in equally nasty conditions. They now shared the leading, although Frank, who had done all the step-cutting on the ice ridges, was so drained and suffering from occasional cramp in his arms that he had to hand over to GB for one strenuous little pitch that defeated him.

At last they stood on the top of the buttress, and to their huge relief the final ice cliffs were so broken that they presented no difficulty. All that remained was the late afternoon plod over Mont Blanc de Courmayeur and Mont Blanc to the Vallot Hut in the gusty wind and arctic cold. There, in the frozen and dirty interior of the emergency refuge they enjoyed a simple meal — hot tea, salami, bread and jam — and eventually rolled themselves up in many blankets for the night.

'I remained wakeful,' wrote Graham Brown, 'and wished for my lost pipe.'

TEN

Recrimination

The good weather that came at just the right moment for Frank and Graham Brown on Mont Blanc in 1928 allowed them to do two more climbs, on the Grands Charmoz and the Aiguille d'Argentière. It's surprising they continued together after the fraught situation on the Route Major, but the breakdown in their relationship wouldn't be delayed for long. It stemmed from an arrangement Frank had made to climb with Graham Macphee, which he then forgot about, leaving Graham Brown to pick up the pieces, which he failed to do.

Frank had invited Macphee to join him in Courmayeur on 9 August. However deciding that he'd have to get home earlier than that for a holiday with his mother, he had asked GB to climb with Macphee. GB had agreed to this although Frank, incredibly, did not tell him about the Courmayeur rendezvous. There was no word from Macphee, and GB regarded joining up with him as a very loose arrangement. Frank then apparently never gave the matter another thought.

Macphee duly arrived in Courmayeur and was shocked to find nobody there. He tried to make the best of things while he waited for Frank. He hired one guide who was slow and useless, while another didn't turn up as it was the day of a festival. His third attempt to climb was foiled by the weather. After five days, on 14 August, thoroughly frustrated he decided to go to Chamonix by bus. And at this point attention must be switched to Frank and Graham Brown.

A few days earlier they had been resting at the Montenvers after climbing the Grands Charmoz. While Frank lounged in bed Graham Brown ran into Alfred Zürcher, a Swiss climber whom Frank knew. Zürcher, hearing that GB would soon be on his own invited him to hire a guide and make up a foursome with himself and his own guide, Josef Knubel for the Brouillard Ridge on Mont Blanc. GB, delighted at this prospect told an approving Frank, and hired a guide, Alexander Graven. It was arranged that while Frank and GB were on their final climb, the Aiguille d'Argentière, Zürcher and the two guides would proceed on foot to Courmayeur via the Col de Géant, and GB would follow by road to join them.

However when Frank and GB got back to the Montenvers from the Argentière a postcard had arrived for Frank from Macphee in Courmayeur, the message a frantic *Where Are You?* Graham Brown found this 'very disturbing' but told Frank that sorry as he was, his arrangement with Zürcher would have to stand; the responsibility for Macphee was Frank's. There was a heated discussion. Next morning the two men went down to Chamonix and parted company, Frank returning to England, and GB going by coach to Courmayeur.

This is a tortuous tale, but in view of the outcome and the long shadow it was to cast on Frank's life, it needs to be told in detail. The focus now shifts back to Courmayeur. Macphee was about to leave by bus after his abortive few days when he ran into Zürcher, Knubel and Graven who had just arrived from the Col de Géant. Hearing that Frank had gone home but Graham Brown was due that evening he cancelled his trip and awaited GB's arrival.

When Graham Brown was confronted by Macphee he was apologetic, but said that he couldn't invite him to join him since he himself was Zürcher's guest. Overhearing this, the obliging Zürcher told GB that he had no objection to Macphee coming too; they could climb together with Graven on the planned route on Mont Blanc. But Graham Brown rejected this idea. There was a tense discussion in which GB insisted that Macphee had been let down by Frank, not him.

It is hard to fathom Graham Brown's mind-set at this point. He was a man of great integrity. To break an engagement was a cardinal sin. However since Zürcher was offering to release him from any perceived commitment some other factor must have been involved. Later he insisted he had no personal objection to Macphee. Perhaps he was angry with the disorganised Frank for landing him with the problem, or preferred to climb with Graven on his own. Perhaps Macphee had simply caught him off-balance after his long bus journey.

But he made efforts to help Macphee. He asked Knubel to inquire about the best available guide. He invited Macphee to join him in his hotel and have dinner with him. But the disillusioned Macphee accepted the offer of two Italians to climb with them and disappeared early next morning.

As it happened, poor weather ruined the rest of Graham Brown's holiday. But Macphee harboured a grievance, scarcely eased by his wretched final two weeks in the Alps when he endured storms, quarrelling companions, a lingering stomach ulcer and an accident to a partner, Eric Shipton, who fell into a crevasse on the Mer de Glace. He wrote to Frank complaining of shabby treatment by the Professor. His letter, forwarded to Frank in Cornwall provoked a strong reaction; Frank immediately wrote to GB. He was blunt and uncompromising.

The Professor had let down a fellow-member of his own club. Macphee was a fine rock-climber and iceman, so it was hardly a case of weakening the party. There was undoubtedly a personal objection. The whole business was wretched, especially if Macphee's statement was correct that although Zürcher had invited him to join them the Professor had objected. He had now written to Macphee pointing all this out. He, Frank, was not responsible for the Professor's refusal to help him.[1]

GB's response to Frank's blast was measured. He couldn't understand why Frank should think he had any personal objection to Macphee. He reminded Frank that after Macphee's surprise postcard had arrived he'd insisted that his arrangement with Zürcher and Graven must stand, and that Frank was responsible for Macphee. He listed the ways in which he had tried to help Macphee. He had made a definite engagement with Zürcher, and he kept his engagements. Graham Brown concluded his letter:

I want you to know this. When I was climbing with you I had an invitation to present a great man of science for an honorary degree to the Prince of Wales, who is the Chancellor of our University. It is considered a very great honour to perform such a function; but it would have meant leaving you alone for a week (and thus breaking my engagement to you), and so I refused it. I said nothing to you at the time, nor would I say anything to you now had it not been for the extraordinary terms of your letter.

I am very sorry about all this, and particularly that you seem to have allowed your emotions to run away with you a little. When you think it over calmly you will, I know, see that you have not been fair to me. But I want you to forget that and not to allow this sort of thing to mar the memory of our great climb.

Do like a good fellow send my films as soon as you can.[2]

Many mortals in Frank's position would have given up and made their peace with Macphee, who seemed resigned to what had happened:

'There appears to be no satisfactory explanation for my being let down so badly in the Alps,' he wrote in his diary, 'and my initial and final verdicts are now identical — carelessness and thoughtlessness on the part of Smythe, and downright selfishness on the part of the Professor.'

But GB's letter incensed Frank. He seized his pen again. His letter of 12 September ran to six pages of furious scrawl which I quote in full:

Dear Graham Brown,

I have just received your two letters and notes and hasten to reply. I have seen and climbed with Macphee recently and have also heard from Zürcher. You will be interested to learn that as a result of your not caring to change your 'arrangements' Macphee's holiday was ruined. With regard to Zürcher's letter, he explains that you asked him if he would take you on in his party. Like the good fellow he is, seeing you stranded without a companion, he agreed to take another member in his party, though I gather that he was not particularly anxious to do so.

As <u>he</u> asked Macphee and suggested that you and Macphee should form an independent party there was no question of him releasing <u>you</u> from any arrangement. There was not even the question of there being five people all together on the Brouillard, and even if you thought his addition a danger on that particular climb, it is obvious that you were prepared to ruin his holiday on the altar of your own ambition to do the climb. Zürcher's letter confirms Macphee's statements absolutely. Macphee considers, and rightly, your effort to find him a guide after refusing to climb with him, an impertinence. Therefore on the strength of Zürcher's invitation to Macphee, and preparedness to release you from any arrangements you had made with him (Zürcher) I cannot see why <u>your</u> arrangements had to stand at the expense of Macphee's holiday. As regards my own arrangements with Macphee which so unfortunately went wrong, Macphee has already forgiven me them, but he is not likely to forgive you.

I am sorry you missed the honour you suggested, but you have at least had the honour of being taken up two of the greatest climbs in the Alps — an honour which would not have occurred had you not met me — though I would have still done them — with someone else.

Macphee in addition has told me certain lies you have spread about me and the climb. One of these is that I wanted to turn back on the climb, but that you by your example and leadership saved the situation. I take it you refer to the 15-foot pitch, which after hours of cutting in steep ice I found myself unable to pull up owing to arm exhaustion — temporarily — but which I could undoubtedly have climbed without a rucksack after a few minutes rest. That I suggested retreat at any point on the climb is utterly untrue. Then Macphee says you continually referred to it as your climb and your own lead. By what right do you do this? As I say, had I not suggested your joining me last year you would not have done either climb. Then you say I was slow in cutting. Apart from having to do all the cutting bar six or so steps by yourself, with a heavy sack — I cut far bigger steps than I should have done with a more expert ice-man behind. As it was you were unable to utilise these steps and had to cut alternate ones and handholds — a job which doubled the time on the ice. A more expert man would have followed close behind on nearly all the climb, and not have allowed me to run out a long and heavy stretch of rope.

I see in your notes you place yourself first, for which your explanation is alphabetical order! I need hardly point out that the invariable custom of all climbing clubs and in particular in the *Alpine Journal*, is to place the leader's name first — the leader being the man who has led all or the majority of the climb. I have therefore written to Strutt, stating exactly how much of the climb was led by each of us, and asking him to amend this order of names. In addition, Strutt, a long time ago asked me for notes on the climb, and he has just written again asking for them in case he cares to publish them instead of yours, which he regards as provisional.

I will send your films off by registered post tomorrow, and in addition your sleeping bag and later a sum which I trust will be sufficient to cover the balance of my debt.

I have already made climbing arrangements for next season.

Yours truly,

F.S. Smythe

Graham Brown had responded to Frank's first letter calmly enough. But he saw this second one as something entirely different. It had gone far beyond a mere dispute about Macphee. Frank had set out deliberately to scorn and belittle him. The comment about 'the altar of your own ambition' and the jibe about the 'honour of being taken up' the climbs were grossly offensive, deeply insulting.

Graham Brown never forgave Frank for this letter. His response to it was an icy silence. The grapevine soon picked up what had happened and Frank's head of steam quickly dissipated. He was used to scraps and apologies, the rough and tumble of ordinary relationships, but he was uneasy to feel he now had an enemy. A year passed before he wrote again to Graham Brown:

I'm really sorry there's been such a row and I should much appreciate a restoration of those friendly relations which I so much valued before … I'm afraid that temperamentally we're hopelessly unsuited to each other on a mountain — I know that I want dry nursing a bit sometimes, and as far as I'm concerned I know that it was our hopeless failure to hit it off that spoilt the holiday for both of us. But that is one thing, and being on friendly terms another, and I'm sorry that anything on my part that I may have said or written should have resulted in a severance of these friendly relations.[3]

But there was still no reply. He waited another three months and in January, 1930 he tried again, this time apologising profusely and expressing deep regret for the 'pain' he must have caused. He asked for forgiveness.[4]

At last Graham Brown responded with a short letter:[5]

Dear Smythe,
Your quarrel with me was entirely on your side, and I cannot understand it, nor do I care to guess your motives. I have taken no part whatsoever in the quarrel, and if you want my forgiveness for the things you have done, your best and most sincere apology will be to undo them. But I feel quite impersonal in all this. Did you not really quarrel with the mountains — and can they forgive you?

I read your book *Climbs and Ski Runs* with great interest. Your photographs are splendid.
Yours etc.,
T Graham Brown

Frank may have been relieved to get a letter, but can't have drawn much comfort from its bleak message. Forgiveness in fact, was a long way from Graham Brown's thoughts. It has been difficult to work out not so much why he started his campaign of hatred against Frank — and I use those words with reluctance — but why he waited four years. But in 1932 he got to work.

In April that year he wrote a 48-page private analysis of Frank. It was divided into four sections with the titles, *My Estimate of Smythe, Smythe as a Climber, Smythe's Make-Up* and *My Own Doubts*. He also noted why he had written the analysis — 'For my own satisfaction, and to leave an accurate record, should I meet with an accident.' One passage is worth quoting, if only to illustrate his style:

But why climbing? I cannot answer this save by an untested hypothesis — which might fit the facts.

Smythe was taken by his mother to Switzerland as a child (age eight years). Such a trip would be an unusual event in the circle in which he moved, and Smythe would, no doubt, be regarded with awe by his little friends. He would soon come to be the 'authority' on Switzerland (being by no means repressed in this by his mother), and would come to 'possess' it. Switzerland, of course, is the place of mountains. No doubt, little Smythe was taken up some hill in Switzerland (Yes! See *Climbs and Ski Runs*, page 3). This would grow into a mountain — and little Smythe (if he was at all like the present Smythe) would fancy himself into mountaineering adventures for the benefit of his little friends. He would soon grow, in his and their esteem, into a mountain 'authority'. This 'possession' of mountains would last, and would serve to direct the grown-up Smythe's ambition towards them.

This is fantasy, but it will explain Smythe's intense mountain ambition in the absence (as I believe) of true mountain love on the one hand or of pleasure in climbing as an athletic exercise on the other.[6]

The analysis, neatly written in GB's tiny handwriting, was depressing — a monument to one man's intense dislike of another. GB also wrote memos of conversations. For two years, whenever the subject of Frank Smythe came up he remembered what had been said and by whom, and later wrote a detailed account, noting the date, time and place of the conversation, then adding his signature.

There was plenty for him to write. The Alpine Club in the early 1930s had far fewer members than now and it was a hotbed of jealousy and intrigue. It was the beginning of Frank's rise to fame but he was making money writing about what for many senior members was a kind of Holy Grail. This and his outspokenness made him a target for gossip.

Graham Brown however kept his feelings to himself for a long time. The delay is explained at the beginning of his 'analysis':

Although I was disgusted with Smythe and his behaviour, I was so impressed by my own possible bias in judging him that I did not discuss him with anybody at all for about two years … I never let myself even hint to anybody what my own estimate was, nor did I allow myself to criticise him to anybody. My opinion was that if I happened to be right, Smythe would repeat his behaviour to others, and that repetition (or its failure) would be the proof to me of the rightness or wrongness of my own judgement. If I was right, my silence would not have mattered; if I was wrong — it would have saved me from a great mistake, and a great injustice.

It seems that Frank 'repeated his behaviour', but there is another possible reason for GB starting in 1932 what amounted to a one-sided vendetta that he pursued unrelentingly until Frank's death — and even, whenever he had an audience, after that. By September that year Frank, with his Kangchenjunga and Kamet expeditions behind him, was the most experienced young Himalayan climber in Britain and an obvious choice for Everest in 1933. It must have been galling for GB to see the man who had insulted him and taken all the credit for the Route Major now so highly regarded. On one occasion Ogier Ward, after listening to GB's malevolent attack, warned him that he could ruin Frank. Frank's earning capacity might be reduced, and he had a young wife.

But by then GB could not resist talking about Frank. That summer during a train journey he unburdened himself to Edward Strutt, the *Alpine Journal* Editor. 'I was very glad to get it off my chest,' he wrote in his memo, 'and pleasantly surprised that Strutt knew of similar instances in Smythe's relations with other climbers.'

Later however he learnt that his long talk with Strutt had been ineffective. Neither Strutt nor Spencer had 'warned' Hugh Ruttledge, leader of the forthcoming Everest expedition about Frank, as GB had hoped, in fact Spencer advised him to commit the whole affair to oblivion. GB however was undaunted. He invited Ruttledge to lunch at the Athenaeum Club, and his written memo of the occasion amounted to an extraordinary rant:

> I said I regarded Smythe as a fraud who had been very lucky … He climbed only for himself, and would probably try to take the credit for things … He would do anything which could be written up in a dramatic way … He climbed on impulse and would probably have no 'guts' at high elevations … He worked up rows a day or two after a breakdown, and then called the spectator of it a coward in public … My mind was made up not to allow him to treat anybody else as he had me … Smythe thought of nothing but his own skin in time of danger, and would then sacrifice his companions (and their lives if necessary) for his own safety — but [he] was then off his head and did not do this in a calculated way … I told [Ruttledge] that what had caused me to speak to him (which I had not intended to do) was meeting Shipton on Saturday — when I felt that I could not let such a simple, modest fellow be sacrificed by Smythe because of my silence … [7]

There was more. Smythe was incapable of carrying a heavy rucksack. Others had experienced his 'breakdowns and panics.' He had abandoned a companion who had become ill. He was always nervous and frightened and did little of the leading 'unless something looked dramatic' but he always 'tried to go up first on rotten rock.' He told lies.

GB's memo suggested that Ruttledge said little in response. He promised that he would regard what he had been told as confidential, unless it was necessary to use the information for the safety of the expedition.

Graham Brown became regarded by many people as a curiosity — someone whose obsession had got the better of him. He wrote to Alpine Club committee members giving details of Frank's problems with Ivan Waller on the Grépon climb on the pretext that Frank might blackball Waller's candidacy which he had proposed. He also wrote two venomous letters to Frank,[8] prompting Frank to write despairingly to Young:

> To such an extraordinary extent does he dislike me that he went out of his way to write a letter on Xmas Eve last, timed to arrive on Xmas Day, and now another letter timed to arrive just prior to my departure for Everest. Both these letters were intended to wound as deeply as possible and were full of malice and uncharitableness such as I could not have believed possible in anyone who climbs mountains.[9]

Frank was so shaken by the Christmas Eve message that he threw caution to the winds and replied to it at length. His letter develops into a 'Cri de Coeur.' There is a hint of desperation in his retelling of the story of the Route Major as he remembered it, or perhaps as he *wished it to be remembered*, the key passage being his description of the ice traverse after they had failed on the Unclimbable Corner. He appears to claim that he led the traverse, whereas in his published account he acknowledges that Graham Brown led this section. The letter has typing errors, minimal punctuation and unusually for Frank, spelling mistakes, all suggesting that it poured out of him in his anxiety to consign the climb to history.[10]

The letter showed how far Frank was from understanding Graham Brown, who studied every part of it to 'prove' that Frank had dug an even deeper hole for himself. Then he dispatched a brutally abrupt reply, dismissing everything the other man had said as pure invention. He also rejected another offer of reconciliation, adding that he did not want any further contact. Finally he wrote a detailed memorandum about the whole episode which together with the letters takes up 51 pages in his archive. The papers he accumulated on Frank during 1932 alone amount to a staggering 315 pages.

The peak seemed to be reached in March 1933 when he wrote his famous 73-page letter to Strutt. I didn't believe it existed until I came across a copy in the Edinburgh archive. It was written in three parts and dispatched at two-day intervals, and is a testament to his obsession with the Brenva Face and the injustices, perceived or otherwise, done to him by the unspeakable Frank Smythe. Whether Strutt managed to read it is another matter.

Amazingly, Frank made yet another effort for a settlement the following year, suggesting a meeting in London.[11] But the letter went unanswered and Frank seems not to have made any further efforts.

Graham Brown went on to have a fine climbing career. His magnificent route up the Pear Buttress with guides in 1933 completed his 'triptych' on the Brenva Face. He climbed Mont Blanc by 18 different routes and many other classic Alpine climbs. He joined an American expedition to Mount Foraker in Alaska, and in the Himalayas was with Tilman's party on Nanda Devi in 1936 and with an expedition to Masherbrum in 1938.

From the people I contacted who had known him there was a mixture of opinion. Emlyn Jones, who had climbed with him in the Alps in the 1950s, found him 'not a very amenable chap'. Robin Hodgkin said that on the Masherbrum trip he was very friendly on the boat to Bombay, fitted in fairly well during the early walk-in, and was inclined to get edgy as they neared the mountain. He 'wanted his authority to be accepted, in what was a very democratic party'. When the expedition ran into trouble with a storm and avalanche GB became 'intolerable'.

Dr Charles Houston, the celebrated American mountaineer and high altitude physician was with him in the Alps in 1933, and then on Foraker and Nanda Devi. He remembered GB's 'scientific meticulousness'. He was impressed by GB's cheerful acceptance of a gruesome initiation ceremony at Zermatt in which he became an honorary member of the Harvard Mountaineering Club. What came across most of all when I spoke to Houston was GB's kindness to him in the early days of their friendship. Throughout their time together however GB poured out his malevolent opinions about Frank.

Several people described Graham Brown as cantankerous, and his appointment as Editor of the *Alpine Journal* in 1949 was followed by his sacking from the post four years later after colleagues found him too difficult to work with. However, when he retired to live in Edinburgh in the 1950s until his death in 1965 he generously invited impecunious student members of the University mountaineering club to stay rent-free in the basement of his flat. Robin Campbell, one of the guests, remembered with affection the pork-pie-hatted, gaberdine-raincoated GB in the local pub, 'removing his pipe and talking about the past, to the discredit of his contemporaries — Frank Smythe bearing more than his fair share of these calumnious attacks.'

As for Frank, his final letter to Graham Brown in 1934 suggested that he was tired of the situation and wanted closure. Apart from the slight risk to his Everest prospects in 1933 his climbing career did not appear to have been endangered. The climbing establishment was embarrassed by the feud, and Geoffrey Young told everybody that Frank wanted an end to it. And Frank had the strength of character to push problems, even one like this, out of sight and out of mind. He was just too busy to worry unduly about it.

Graham Brown on the other hand must have suffered more. It must be more corrosive to hate than be hated. Studying Frank Smythe and writing disparaging assessments, letters and memoranda and talking about him became paranoia. Harry Calvert in his book *Smythe's Mountains*, concluded that GB's 'crusade extending over decades [was] a disservice to Smythe, to mountaineering, and, most of all, to himself: he deserves pity rather than condemnation.'

ELEVEN

A Writer's Progress

When the row with Graham Brown began in September 1928, Frank cut short his Cornish holiday. He drove to the Lake District where Graham Macphee listened to his protests, didn't believe a word, and they went climbing on Gillercombe Buttress. 'It was wet and slimy,' Macphee wrote in his diary. 'Smythe was not much good coming second. It started to rain so we returned for tea.' A month later they were in North Wales, where Walter Amstutz, a Swiss climber and friend of Frank's, invited them to ski with him that Christmas at Mürren.

Amstutz, a wealthy entrepreneur was looking for a collaborator in a book on Mont Blanc. Nothing came of this, but the skiing was memorable. Macphee lost his skis, borrowed Frank's, smashed one, and Amstutz supplied them both with new pairs. They attended the Lunns' Christmas dances at Mürren's posh Palace Hotel. They slept in the bunkroom of the Jungfraujoch hotel, woke with splitting headaches from the altitude, and climbed the Mönch on a gin-clear morning with great views of Mont Blanc. They became the guests of the proprietor, Herr Sommer, who organised a bonfire and a bomb timed to go off at midnight on New Year's Eve.

They agreed to team up for the summer of 1929 in Chamonix, but in February Macphee had a bad accident. While climbing on gritstone he fell 20 feet, smashing his right foot and leg. Two days later as he lay in Manchester hospital he recorded his injuries with clinical detachment: 'Serious lesion — fractured astragalus, severe dislocation of the ankle and lower end of tibia in three pieces involving joint, and two spiral fractures higher up — what a miracle the fibula was not broken — all big sinews torn.' He was ruled out for the Alps, and Frank arranged to climb instead with Sandy Harrison, his companion on the Schreckhorn, and Charles Parry.

Frank had spotted a new route that potentially rivalled the Route Major.

From the Brenva Glacier a climb might be made up the great south-east face of Mont Maudit, which rose in a single leap to the ridge overhead at nearly 15,000 feet on Mont Blanc's northern spur. A careful study of photographs suggested it was feasible.

On their arrival in the Alps at the end of July the poor weather allowed only a couple of warm-up climbs during the first week. The Torino Hut offered alternative sport when Frank and Harrison received a violent shock from a nearby lightning flash while standing on the metal threshold in nailed boots. They were also warned by the hut's resident gendarme that it was forbidden to descend into Italy without permission, and that if they did so they risked being shot. Since they would have to cross the frontier ridge to reach the climb, an exciting expedition was clearly guaranteed.

At last on a clear day they could make final decisions about the route. A couloir linked with a long rock ridge leading to the top of the face. A useful-looking ledge alongside the couloir a thousand feet up would make a good tactical bivouac before the hard climbing.

Next day was fine and they set off, crossing into Italy some two miles from the trigger-happy policemen. A long lunch and laze on the Brenva Glacier was followed by an uneventful evening climb to the selected ledge, where they settled for the night in sleeping bags. The weather seemed perfect at first, but by midnight, even after the encouraging effects of hot rum punch, they became pessimistic about their chances — the stars were obscured by a creeping haze and there was a distant quiver of lightning. An hour later it was snowing.

It snowed all night and at dawn the deadly white blanket was still piling up, inch by inch. There was no hope of going on and escape was going to be a nightmare. The couloir was now a death-trap, but had to be crossed to reach the descent line on the far side, and Harrison, attempting it first was caught by an avalanche, luckily small enough for him not to be swept away, but he was exhausted by his efforts. They were very lucky to reach the glacier alive, with powerful slides thundering down all around them.

But worse was to come. With the return to France impossible in the conditions, they were obliged to descend the glacier into Italy with the disquieting prospect of an encounter with the Carabinieri. Suddenly there was a rumbling noise, and the others were horrified to see Parry caught in a mass of sliding boulders. While descending a rocky moraine he had stepped on a block which had tipped and started an avalanche.

He survived, apparently without serious injury, but was unable to walk.

Frank sped down to the valley where the Italian authorities luckily turned a blind eye to his illegal entry and he arranged a stretcher party. In hospital Parry was diagnosed with a badly strained knee, and eventually went home. But there was a sad aftermath; his spine was also affected. He eventually started climbing again, even accompanying Frank and Macphee in the Alps in 1934, but five years after that, complications from the original injury meant that his leg had to be amputated.

Frank wrote about their failure on the climb, finishing with a short epilogue:

> Many wild rumours had been circulated about Parry's accident, among which fractured thighs, broken ribs, and cracked skulls figured conspicuously. But perhaps the best of all emanated from an American who accosted me. 'Say,' he queried, 'do you happen to know that guy Smythe?' 'Intimately,' I replied. 'Waal,' he continued, with immense relish, 'I guess he's gone and done himself in at last.'

Climbs and Ski Runs, Frank's first book was published at last in October 1929. Victor Gollancz, who had recently started his publishing business, had hesitated to accept it, so Frank went to Blackwood, who had published five of his articles in their monthly magazine, and they agreed to take on the book.

Blackwood was a small family publishing business with a long and respected pedigree. The founder, William Blackwood had started in Edinburgh in 1804, and 13 years later launched the magazine of short stories and tales of adventure for which the firm became famous. *Blackwood's Magazine* flourished for over 150 years until the public's appetite for the genre began to fade towards the end of the twentieth century. For decades copies could be found in all corners of the British Empire — garrison messes, naval wardrooms, planters' bungalows and other colonial outposts. The articles tended to be gentlemanly well-crafted stories and memoirs by experienced travellers, sportsmen, civil servants and officers of the Crown.

Certain standards were maintained, and not just in the literary quality of the articles. I sent a piece about climbing in Scotland which was accepted, but only after the Editor had pointed out that a passage in which I described retreating in bad weather to a hotel and inadvertently allowing water from wet camping gear to drip through the dining-room ceiling would have to be removed. It was 'not at all the right thing to do' wrote Douglas Blackwood, and for a moment I was back in front of the Headmaster, whose office had mysteriously moved to 45 George Street, Edinburgh.

Frank's book was a collection of stories dealing with his early rambles on the British hills and his Alpine adventures, including the two Brenva Face climbs. A short piece at the end was entitled The 'Philosophy of a Mountaineer'. Geoffrey Young wrote a foreword and Frank dedicated the book to his mother. There was a generous allowance of 74 photographs. The book was priced at 21 shillings (£1.05) which was the equivalent of a steep £60 at the end of the century. But it sold well, and was reprinted four times in spite of the current economic slump. A number of newspapers published reviews for the general public, and others were written by climbers for their club journals. The reader of course, whether a climber or not, was the final arbiter. It's worth looking at this issue because it lay at the heart of Frank's success as a writer.

The book was enjoyed by the press reviewers because Frank had a winning formula for the general reader, for whom he wrote instinctively. His stories were a persuasive mix of excitement, danger, absurdity, wonderful mountains, unreliable weather and his penchant for becoming the victim of a malicious fate. He never assumed that his readers had any experience of mountaineering. Most books about climbing up to that time had been written with other mountaineers in mind. In earlier times a man who went up a mountain without a scientific objective, such as measuring the temperature or air pressure, was a fool, or even a heretic. Even when the Alpine Club was formed in 1857 and climbing became an accepted, if somewhat outlandish activity in its own right, it would remain for decades the preserve of professional men, such as doctors, clergymen and lawyers, who had no desire to write about mountaineering for the general public. The only writing most of them did was to describe their climbs in a journal, or write letters about them to each other. *Climbs and Ski Runs* appealed to people who had never been up a mountain but also interested mountaineers. I sense that whatever Frank's speciality might have been he probably would have brought this skill to bear when writing about it — of catching the attention of both the layman and the knowledgeable. The press reviews had hackneyed phrases like, 'gift for story telling', or 'can communicate to his readers that wonderful thrill of climbing', while the climbers duly settled to more thoughtful reviews. Tom Longstaff, a hard man to please, approved of Frank's 'remarkable suppression of self' and thought that the book might become a classic.

At the end of 1929 Frank appeared to have run out of ideas and was in need of inspiration from somewhere. When he crossed the Channel on 15 December, ostensibly to go skiing in Switzerland, it hardly seemed like part of a life-changing move. Afterwards he claimed it was purely by chance that a few days later, at the Suvretta Hotel in St Moritz, he met Professor Dyhrenfurth and the other members of his 1930 International Expedition to Kangchenjunga, the third highest mountain in the world. But the meeting had been secretly arranged. He was already in touch with two of the team, Hermann Hoerlin and Erwin Schneider. At that stage there were eight members — four Swiss, three German and an Austrian — and they were due to leave in just nine weeks' time. And Dyhrenfurth, who had been impressed by Frank's new routes on Mont Blanc had invited him to join them. There was only one snag. He was required to contribute £500 towards the expedition's costs, an enormous sum, the equivalent of about £30,000 at the end of the century.

He sent a postcard to his mother, not to ask for £500, which was well north of the financial line she had drawn in the sand, but to keep her informed: 'Do hope your cold is better. Love to Aunt Edith. Have been invited to go with German Expedition to Kangchenjunga (confidential). In awful rush. Your loving Frank.'

Then he got to work, with astonishing success. Within days *The Times* had commissioned him as their Special Correspondent on the expedition, financing him in full, at a stroke. However if the cash flow problem was solved he was soon to undergo the arduous, if useful experience of writing under pressure. From late February until June he was hammering on his typewriter. He sent dispatches from the high seas and from the plains of India, from tents pitched in sweltering jungles and on freezing glaciers. Native runners carried the reports to civilisation, and *The Times* published 500 column inches (or 40 feet) of them. He was disappointed however that the newspaper credited the dispatches not to him, but to their 'Special Correspondent', a mysterious person who dogged the expedition to report on its activities, including occasionally, those of the British member, Frank Smythe.

The weeks passed in a blur, but there was one job he wasn't expecting to deal with until he got back — a contract for a book about the expedition. He hadn't yet grasped how much excitement the expedition to Kangchenjunga would generate.

On 17 February 1930, four days before he left to join the team in Zurich, the expedition was announced with a flourish in the press. He was contacted that morning by the publishers A & C Black, and next day met Jack Newth, a senior executive at the firm's premises in Soho Square. No definite agreement was made but the day before leaving England he received their offer by post.

It was complicated, essentially offering an advance of £150, with royalties of 15 per cent. While he was mulling it over the phone rang. It was Victor Gollancz. They had a short discussion. Could Frank call on him that day?

Gollancz of course knew Frank from 1928, when he gave his proposed first book on climbing the thumbs down. Since then much had changed. Gollancz had found his feet, was ambitious, and on his way to becoming one of the most astute and respected publishers of the century. Frank too, hadn't done badly. *Climbs and Ski Runs* was a success, within the limitations of a smaller publishing house. And now, as Gollancz saw, Frank had somehow got himself onto a very big thing indeed in the Himalayas, and not only that, the expedition would be given enormous publicity with Frank's *Times* assignment, and syndication to other national newspapers. Gollancz was a decisive, well-educated man from an old Jewish family. He didn't hesitate. On the spot he offered an advance of £1,000 and royalties of 25 per cent of the published price.

The following morning Frank called on him at his office near Covent Garden, signed the contract which had been prepared overnight, posted his letter of regret to Jack Newth, and took a taxi to Victoria to catch the midday boat train.

TWELVE

Kangchenjunga

Professor Günter Oskar Dyhrenfurth had dreamed of climbing in the Himalayas since his youth. His wife Hettie, soon after she secretly became engaged to him in 1907 when she was 15, had written in her diary, '1911, we will marry. 1913, I shall have my first child. 1914, the first Himalayan expedition.' The first two things happened as planned, but the First World War had delayed the Himalayan expedition for 16 years, until he was 44.

They had both been born in Breslau, North Germany, where Günter from the age of 10 had been passionately keen on climbing, encouraged by his father. He became a geologist, worked in Switzerland for several years where job and mountaineering went side by side, then returned to Breslau to become a professor at the university. The war years saw him commanding a corps on the mountainous Italian front, where his expertise in snow conditions was invaluable. However during that time he had observed deep-rooted racial intolerance. Listening to some of his men pouring out bitterly anti-Semitic views when they were thrown together in mountain caves and bivouacs made him fear that after the war Germany would enter a new dark age. A danger lurked for his wife and children. For Hettie was Jewish. She was an only child and her father, Oskar Heymann, was president of a large chemical concern in Breslau.

In 1926 Dyhrenfurth took his family to Zurich, where they became Swiss citizens. He retained his professorship at Breslau, but when Hitler came to power in 1933 he refused to swear an oath of allegiance and resigned his university post. Interestingly, the two men came face to face at the Berlin Olympics in 1936, when Dyhrenfurth was awarded a gold medal for scientific and mountaineering achievements. Then, with Hitler standing in front of him, the German national anthem was played in honour of the country of his birth, and arms shot up in the Hitler salute.

Dyhrenfurth however, conspicuously and perhaps bravely, did not acknowledge the Führer, but remained at attention, arms at his sides.

By 1929 he was determined to delay the Himalayan trip no longer. He had become fascinated by Kangchenjunga, the great unclimbed peak of 8,586 metres on the border of eastern Nepal and Sikkim. But he was shocked to learn that Paul Bauer, a Munich climber had obtained permission to attempt the mountain that autumn. With entry to Nepal forbidden, Bauer's party approached Kangchenjunga from the east, from Sikkim, via the Zemu Glacier and north-east spur, but they found themselves committed to a very difficult ice ridge. Their high point was about 7,400 metres before terrible storms turned the attempt into a desperate retreat through two metres of new snow. The mountain was thus available for Dyhrenfurth's pre-monsoon attempt in 1930, although shortly before departure the expedition was in a critical financial state, and Frank's negotiation with *The Times* may have proved to be its salvation. This detail was revealed by Hettie Dyhrenfurth in her book *Memsahib in the Himalayas*. She was going too; her husband saw her as bound to accompany him. Her most painful moment was leaving their teenage children in the care of grandparents. Their son Norman, who became a well-known mountaineering film-maker, told me that climbing was of passing interest to his mother but she much preferred tennis, becoming one of the best mixed-doubles players in Switzerland. 'She was quite fond of rock-climbing. Her women's world record of about 24,000 feet in the Karakoram came about by chance, since my father didn't want to leave her alone at the highest camp.'

And so on 22 February 1930 an advance party consisting of the Dyhrenfurths and three other members including Frank assembled in Zurich. They caught a train to Venice and sailed for Bombay. Frank's accounts of his Himalayan expeditions rarely wasted any words on the journey — unlike Hettie Dyhrenfurth. From her you discover that at sea Günter required his team to rise at 6.30 a.m. to run round the deck. Duvanel, the cameraman filmed them climbing the mast, to the amusement of other passengers. Hettie took lessons in Hindustani from a young Indian, and she wrote that after she had danced with him one evening, 'Smythe explained to me that it simply wasn't done for a white lady to dance with 'coloured people', a viewpoint I found inexplicable.' She retaliated on the homeward voyage by digging Frank out of a bar in Aden, and ignoring his drunken protests that they could 'catch the next ship,' steered him back to the docks just in time.

In Bombay the expedition's six and a half tons of equipment and supplies were cleared through customs and dispatched to Darjeeling, and the party started the long train journey across India. Frank left for Delhi a day ahead, earning a fierce rebuke in Hettie's book for accidentally taking with him the bedding needed by the others for their night in the train. 'The good Smythe (he is always suspended in higher regions and is a nonplus-ultra of forgetfulness) will have experienced ringing in his ears as we, cursing him, prepared a pathetic bed from laundry and bath-robes.' In Delhi Hettie went on strike after being dragged round seventeen temples and palaces in a single morning by her tireless husband and Dr Richter, but rallied for a trip to Agra and the Taj Mahal. When the train arrived they tumbled onto the platform half-asleep then a little later saw the peerless monument in the moonlight. 'Our English expedition member, however,' wrote Hettie, 'declared that his strongest impression of Agra was when I stood on the platform in a pink nightgown. Regrettably I had to disenchant him of this overwhelming memory — the supposed nightgown was a very decent undergarment.'

I have to be grateful to Hettie for her memoirs. Frank presented himself as a tireless observer, perceptive but broadminded over the foibles of others. Drunkenness or bawdy remarks were ungentlemanly, the behaviour of the gutter. So it was a relief to discover that off-stage he was human, even if it was to Hettie's discomfiture. Her account suggested that Frank saw her as an attractive woman he felt good about; Norman Dyhrenfurth confirmed this and said that he wasn't the only lusty climber on the expedition to be attracted to his young mother.

Before I arrived in Darjeeling with my daughter some 70 years after Frank I had imagined a fabulous hill station perched above the forest within reach of the Himalayas, a historic settlement from where the Everest expeditions had set out. When we climbed out of our taxi a cold mist and a fog of exhaust fumes hung around the streets. There was an uproar of car horns. Tiers of buildings loomed on the steep hillside. For two days while we arranged a trek the greyness blanketed everything and we might have been anywhere. Then early on the third morning it was clear and we saw Kangchenjunga.

Artists have painted it; everybody's photographed it. Frank on a later trip saw the summit at dawn from a hundred miles away on the Bengal plain as a 'tiny point of golden light'. From near the Planters' Club[1] in Darjeeling, looking northwards, there's a ridge with trees forming a ragged skyline — or it looks as though it should be the skyline. But on a clear morning there's something floating above it, and it's a shock to realise that this strange white shape isn't a cloud. It's still a part of the earth, 50 miles distant — the ridges, glaciers and summits of Kangchenjunga, the Five Treasures of the Snow, so far above the ordinary world that it is like part of a dream. It is fantastic, one of the most incredible sights in the world. The disappointment of modern Darjeeling didn't matter so much then. Seeing Kangchenjunga that morning I had made the connection I was looking for; I understood a bit more why Frank came back to the Himalayas again and again during the rest of his short life.

By the end of March the other members of the expedition had arrived — George Wood-Johnson, a tea planter and climber who was to be a transport officer, Hoerlin and Schneider together with Marcel Kurz the Swiss deputy leader, and Ulrich Wieland, a German climber acting as meteorologist. The gear and food arrived late from Bombay and all 180 crates had to be repacked into 350 porter-loads, each weighing 27 kilograms. The special permission to enter Nepal was also delayed. Dyhrenfurth was not attracted by the eastern side of Kangchenjunga after Bauer's experience and he'd applied successfully to approach the mountain from the north-west, in Nepal. At last on 6 April, confirmation of approval came from the Maharaja's office in Kathmandu.

The march to base camp was beset with problems. The route was long and rugged with several passes to cross, the first being the highest, the Kang La, 5,015 metres, where deep winter snow caused some porters to desert and forty local men were hastily recruited to make up the numbers. Some loads disappeared and others suffered damage and pilfering. At Tseram the porters' food ran short, nothing could be bought locally, and Dyhrenfurth had to call for a double march to Ghunsa before their supplies ran out. Fortunately a Subadar, a Maharaja's representative joined them for this section, and fearful of repercussions promised that porters' food would be available from then on.

Many years later I walked part of the route and marvelled at the beauty of this remote corner of Nepal. In April the massed rhododendron blooms had a background of snow and blue sky. I saw the open glade with its smooth green sward that Frank had assessed as a potential cricket ground, comparing it favourably with the 'gasometers of the Oval and the sulphurous vapours of Bramall Lane.' I came to one of the Buddhist water-driven prayer wheels that earned his admiration for the 'lazy but ingenious' locals of Ghunsa. I photographed the village in the valley below and his shot from the same spot shows little change.

The expedition's respite from difficulties was short. No food or additional porters had arrived from the lower valleys and the weary Subadar assured

Dyhrenfurth that all would be well; he would speak to the Head Man. Frank's description of the showdown next day shows that he was now familiar with the way things worked in the East:

> [Wood-Johnson had] the disagreeable task of getting blood out of a stone, or in other words, food out of the Head Man. That individual, lulled doubtless into a sense of security by the patronage of his house by the sahibs the previous evening, had done nothing. Probably, this was due not so much to wilful neglect, as to native inability to appreciate the value of time. What mattered a week, or two weeks, or even a month to the sahibs? What was their hurry? Why were they so anxious to undergo hardships on the mountains when every day was bringing the summer nearer? Such was his philosophy — the same sort of philosophy in these regions that decrees that when you are invited to a wedding you find it usually more convenient to turn up two or three months after the ceremony.
>
> We repaired to the Head Man's house to find him peacefully tilling his garden. The Subadar was furious. He saw his reputation destroyed, his authority set at nought, possibly even his head removed on his return to Kathmandu. He grasped the cowering Head Man, seized some rope lying handy, and proceeded to lash him up to a post. 'Produce the food, or have your head cut off' — that appeared to be the gist of the conversation for the next few minutes. Of course we interceded. We had no wish for our way through Nepal to be littered with the heads of Head Men.[2]

The final three days from Ghunsa to Kangchenjunga's northern base camp are memorable. From woods full of primula and sweet-scented shrubs you glimpse jagged snowy spires, and at the village of Kambachen there are views of the colossal North Face of Jannu. Higher up you might chance upon a grazing yak, a wary and possibly ill-tempered beast — perhaps a descendant of the one that Wood-Johnson tried to ride with a bone-jarring lack of success, as gleefully observed by Frank. At Lhonak you're drawing level with the bottom of the mighty Kangchenjunga Glacier, and dominating everything is the Wedge Peak soaring overhead, its ice ridges so thin that the sun can shine through them to form a fringe of fire. Further up you realise that the glacier is flowing from a huge amphitheatre at the heart of the north-west face of Kangchenjunga itself.

When I arrived at the grassy shelf known as Pangpema, where every expedition to this side of the mountain has made its base camp, it was a day of worsening weather. Layers of cloud obscured the summits and draped the

mountainside, allowing only glimpses of the sérac walls defending the
north-west face. These ice cliffs, each hundreds of feet high, were pale green
in the drifting mist and very forbidding. I was thankful to be going no further,
but for Frank and his companions the real work would soon begin on one
of the most dangerous mountains in the world.

Most of the porters were now paid off. A small village sprang up — a tent
for each of the Europeans, a kitchen, large mess tent, medical tent, store
tents, photographic processing tent, toilet tents and for the porters, tents and
constructions from stones, turf and canvas. Each 'sahib' had his personal
servant. General Bruce, who was remembered with reverence in Darjeeling had
provided Frank with a letter introducing him, 'flatteringly if inaccurately',
as his grandson. 'This charming fiction,' wrote Frank, 'was of inestimable
advantage to me personally, and I was soon known among our porters as the
Nati-sahib (Grandson).' His servant was Nima Tendrup, who had been with
Sandy Irvine on Everest in 1924. Frank had doubts about him at first.
Nima was fairly old for a native, and personal servants were expected to carry
loads and fend for their masters in high camps. He had been to 25,000 feet
with Irvine, but that was six years earlier. Frank's employment and care of
porters were key issues on his expeditions. His chapter entitled 'Friendship'
in *The Spirit of the Hills* captured the essence of his rapport with Nima
Tendrup, the first and perhaps the best man he ever hired:

I interviewed him on the terrace of the Mount Everest Hotel. It was more of an
inspection than an interview, as I could not speak Tibetan, Nepali or Urdu.
Nima stood there rigidly at attention, and the first thing I noticed was that on
his breast, gleaming as the result of the daily and loving care expended upon it
was the North-West Frontier Medal. His countenance was cast in a heavy mould.
It had not the expression of a man of action, and was not indicative of a super-
abundance of grey matter, but there was an underlying strength of character which
was amplified by a pair of unusually large candid brown eyes. He wore a soiled
green wind-jacket, a relic of a former expedition, and a pair of brown breeches
which were neither riding breeches nor plus fours, but something in between.
His legs were encased in a pair of woollen stockings that had been darned and
darned again until they were almost all darns, and on his feet were a pair of
ancient climbing boots. Lastly, he carried in his hand the inevitable Homburg
hat, of which the Tibetans are so fond. In physique, he was heavy and looked
doughy and out of training. A solemn-faced fellow he was, with a permanent,
slightly puzzled expression. It was natural solemnity, a lack of expression ingrained,

perhaps, by military service. What his age was I do not know; I doubt if he knew himself. I should have said 35, and that is getting on for a Bhotia; they live hard and die young in Tibet.[3]

Frank described Nima Tendrup's 'old soldierly' laziness, seeing what he could get away with at first. He was adept at camping. After dinner Frank would find his tent with the candle lantern lit, his sleeping-bag, mattress and pillow arranged. In the morning, believing that the spirit needed time to return to the body after sleep he would call gently, 'Sahib! Sahib! Sahib!' slowly raising his voice until Frank woke, before handing in a steaming mug of tea. If the Sahib lost or broke anything, somehow a replacement would be found. Frank ended his Friendship chapter:

> It may be that you who read these lines may go one day to Darjeeling. Possibly, you may hire a rickshaw. If among those drawing it there is a broad-shouldered, solemn-faced man with a brightly polished medal suspended from his breast, you may be quite certain that it is Nima Tendrup, the 'Old Soldier.' You will know that you are being drawn along by one who has been on four expeditions to Everest, two expeditions to Kangchenjunga, and expeditions to Kamet, Nanga Parbat and other of the greatest peaks in the world. You will know that beneath that polished medal and its stained and dirty ribbon, and the ragged jacket to which it is pinned, beats a brave heart, endowed with qualities of faithfulness and loyalty; a heart which responds instinctively to the call of comradeship and adventure, that exists in close communion with the noblest aspects of nature, that strives in the cause of others, upwards and onwards, through sweat and weariness, through heat and cold, through hardship and peril. A man to admire, respect and love as a friend.

Such a lavish tribute might make people uneasy today. There is no longer an Empire or — in theory at any rate — a large gulf between employer and employed. The welfare of porters and climbing Sherpas is being addressed. It's unfashionable to describe hired men as faithful or loyal as this is thought by some to be demeaning, resurrecting the spectre of colonialism, exploitation, and masters and servants.

But employing a man to help you climb a Himalayan peak is not the same as hiring someone for a job in a town. The uncomfortable fact is that in the Himalayas a sizeable proportion of climbers from the developed world, possibly still the majority, use local help beyond the base camp. The Sherpas of Nepal particularly, have developed climbing skills far in excess of those of their forebears in Frank's day. And there are numerous cases of self-sacrifice among Sherpas helping employers who have got into difficulty in high dangerous places. Different words might be used to describe their bravery and loyalty, but the admiration and regard for such men is as real and deserved today as it was for Nima Tendrup in the 1930s.

At the base camp climbing equipment was unpacked and distributed. Frank was horrified by the boots issued, which were calf-length, heavily insulated and nailed, and weighed three kilograms per pair, with the crampons another two kilograms. He continued to wear the lighter boots he had used for the march in, calculating that the full set of equipment and clothing provided, weighing nearly 15 kilograms was nearly a quarter of his own body weight. He wore the expedition boots just once. 'I shall not easily forget the effort of lifting them at an altitude of 23,000 feet,' he wrote. 'Weight does not spell warmth, and it is over the graves of former mistakes, and not on the wings of new ideas, that the greatest Himalayan peaks will be conquered.'[4] The comment antagonised Dyhrenfurth, especially as Frank held him personally responsible for the designs. And he couldn't come to terms with other aspects of Dyhrenfurth's style. Each member had been issued with a small national flag of his country to be flown on his tent; Frank joked that it solved a problem when he ran out of handkerchiefs. To rouse the expedition in the morning Dyhrenfurth blew three blasts on a small horn; Wood-Johnson managed to steal the horn, but unbelievably a spare was produced. However these were minor peculiarities. The biggest gap between Frank and his leader concerned their attitudes towards risk on the mountain, and that lay in the future.

The relationship between the two men started well. Frank had invited Dyhrenfurth to join the Alpine Club and seconded General Bruce's formal proposal. The Club respected Dyhrenfurth's international aims in the xenophobic climate developing in Germany. All had gone well as far as base camp — apart from the transport and supply problems — and in a letter to his mother Frank wrote, 'I like the Professor immensely — he's a real good chap.'[5]

Viewed from five miles away the north-west face of Kangchenjunga rose in a succession of three glacial terraces and it was judged that if the upper of these could be reached an assault could be made on the final rock pyramid and main summit. Dyhrenfurth commented:

Smythe himself found this route so obvious that he at first cheerfully exclaimed 'How easy!' I was never so optimistic myself, but I confess that I too, with all the others, was fully convinced that the ascent was possible.

However it was soon realised that the ice cliffs forming the outer edges of each of the terraces presented a serious obstacle. The first terrace was particularly well defended with a line of séracs between 600 and 800 feet high stretching three miles — right across the face it seemed, although a reconnaissance was needed to view a hidden section at the left edge of the face. If the ice cliffs petered out there the first terrace might be reached safely, and with luck the adjoining North Ridge would provide access to the third terrace and the summit.

Books about Himalayan expeditions often give the impression that it's not much more than a measured build-up of camps in a kind of super-Alpine setting with the outcome dependent on the weather. For each individual though, the experience is deeply personal. He runs out of breath in the thin air, his feet are numbed by freezing powder snow, the glare is terrific, everything is exhausting. He will suffer from a string of aches and pains — pick any six from sunburn, eyestrain, sore throat, diarrhoea, headache, backache, piles, minor injuries and sores, thirst, a lack of appetite and poor sleep.

Frank saw the Himalayas as something much more than a large version of the Alps. He seemed to be aware of a greater force that could empower him, or just as easily if the mountain gods chose, crush him. Doug Scott experienced this extra dimension during a harrowing retreat from high on the north-west face of Kangchenjunga during a lightweight attempt in 1979, the first expedition there after Dyhrenfurth's. He, Pete Boardman and Georges Bettembourg had reached the third or Great Terrace when they ran into the 100 mile-per-hour westerly jet stream that had battered the mountain for weeks. They managed to find shelter on the Sikkim side of the frontier ridge but the wind changed direction during the night eventually tearing their tent to shreds. At 4.30 a.m. they were forced to bale out, descending five miles and 10,000 feet in one push to safety. 'It had been the closest call I've ever had,' wrote Scott, 'the finest line I'd drawn between being here and not being here, and yet it was curiously exhilarating. During the struggle I was transformed from one state of being into another, transcending the ego and freeing energy to face the unknown with adrenalin running high — wonderful stuff.'[6] Incredibly, a few days later Scott, Boardman and Joe Tasker returned to reach the summit, one of the really great Himalayan achievements.

Dyhrenfurth's hopes of easy progress to the North Ridge were dashed and he directed that a route should be made to the first terrace at its eastern end, where the ice cliff was lowest. He and Kurz fell ill and retreated to base camp leaving Frank, Wieland and Wood-Johnson to work on the sérac from a nearby camp. There were incidents. A porter, Ondi wandered from the camp, fell into a crevasse and was discovered two hours later. He was hauled out near to death, but recovered. Wood-Johnson was called to sort out the retrieval of expedition food still languishing near the Kang La. Meanwhile Frank and Wieland continued to work their way up the ice wall, fixing ropes, with following porters hacking out steps 'large enough for an elephant.' But for all the camaraderie they knew the place was fraught with danger. They were climbing on the outer edge of a hanging glacier that must sooner or later obey the law of gravity and break off in an avalanche, perhaps of gigantic proportions. Hourly, day and night, they'd heard the thunder and boom of falling masses of ice somewhere in the amphitheatre of the north-west face.

On 6 May Schneider arrived, and a day later Hoerlin too. Success would normally depend on this powerful pair, on Schneider particularly. He had a record of hard climbs in the eastern Alps and he had been to the Pamir where he had polished off eight 6,000-metre peaks plus a first ascent of Pik Lenin, 7,135 metres — and he was still aged only 24. Frank and Wieland took a day's rest, and a day after that the route had been pushed nearly to the top of the ice wall. It was expected that next day all the porters would go up with loads and establish a camp on the terrace above. It was midnight before Frank finished writing his diary and a report for *The Times* and blew out the candle, but sleep would not come.

> The night was curiously warm, in fact, the warmest night we had had since we arrived at the Base Camp. Now and again came the long-drawn-out thunder of avalanches. Perhaps it was the atmosphere, or maybe some trick of the imagination, but the sound of the avalanches seemed dull and muffled. It was as though Kangchenjunga was choking with suppressed wrath. My body was ready for sleep, but my mind was not. It was troubled and restless, groping in a catacomb of doubt and fear. I have known fear before on a mountain, but that was fear of a different nature, sharp and sudden in the face of an immediate danger, but I have never known what it was to lie awake before a climb, tortured by the devils of misgiving.[7]

When he slept at last he was troubled with terrible dreams in which the porters were always getting into an impossible position and appealing to him for help that he was unable to give. He put his fears down to brooding about the risks to the detriment of his nerves, which had become 'temporarily unstrung.' It was, he wrote, 'a more logical explanation than the acceptance of the premonition theory, which is dependent upon a belief in psychical phenomena.' However in letters to Slingsby, Roberts and Young some months later he appeared to know that there would be a catastrophe. To Slingsby he had a 'foreboding on the day of the accident,' to Roberts he was 'certain — a premonition practically — that there was going to be a smash,' and to Young he had 'a conviction that there was *bound* to be a disaster.' In his book *The Kangchenjunga Adventure* Frank puts his fears down to gut feeling, not psychic capacity, in spite of earlier incidents in the Bradford foundry and during the walk to the Falls of Glomach in Scotland. But those events and the disaster about to occur on Kangchenjunga all pre-dated an episode in 1934 during a struggle for health after a car crash which seemed to prove beyond doubt that he had ability for what can only be described as extra-sensory perception. I prefer to wait until I get to this point in his life before I tell the story of it. It's worth mentioning now though, that apart from this one episode, which he revealed privately and only because he thought he could help another person in trouble, he never admitted outside his immediate family that he'd had any psychic experiences. Confronted with strange phenomena he would look for a scientific explanation, and if there wasn't one he preferred to put it down to something prosaic he hadn't thought of. He was wary of being ridiculed.

The morning of 9 May was warm and they sat outside for breakfast. But Frank felt tired and unfit to climb. Eventually everyone except him and the cook left, plodding up the track leading to the ice wall — Schneider and Chettan, the sirdar who was a man of great strength and experience, then Duvanel with three porters carrying cine gear, finally Hoerlin, Wieland and eight porters carrying large loads.

Frank returned to his tent to write letters but an hour later was startled by the roar of a large avalanche. With a terrible realisation he knew at once that it came, not from the usual direction of the north-west face but from much closer at hand — the cliffs where they had been working. He dashed outside and never forgot the horrifying sight:

An enormous portion of the ice wall had collapsed. Huge masses of ice as high as cathedrals, were still toppling to destruction; billowing clouds of snow spray were rushing upwards and outwards in the van of a huge avalanche. On the slope below was the party, mere black dots, strung out in a straggling line.

They were not moving. For an instant, during which I suppose my brain must have been stunned, the scene was stamped on my mind like a still photograph, or perhaps a more apt comparison would be a ciné film that has jammed for a fraction of a second. Then everything jerked on again. I remember feeling no surprise, it was almost like a fantastic solution to something that had been puzzling me.

Now the dots were moving, moving to the left; they were running, but how slowly, how uselessly before the reeling clouds of death that had already far out-flanked them; they were engulfed and blotted out like insects beneath a tidal wave.[8]

Realising that the avalanche could reach the camp Frank yelled to the cook to run for it, but they only managed 20 yards before heart and lungs gave out. The avalanche came to a halt 200 yards away. They grabbed ice axes and set off upwards, finding that the track vanished under the debris of ice blocks piled several feet high. They skirted the edge, not expecting to find anyone alive, but through the thinning veil of snow cloud to their huge relief they eventually saw figures. Nima Tendrup was among them, poking about among the ice blocks with an ice axe. When Frank asked him whether there was a man buried there, he replied, 'Load, sahib, I look for load.' In running to escape the avalanche he had dropped the load entrusted to him, and this mattered to him despite the horror. Soon the survivors gathered; only Schneider and Chettan were missing. Then a hand was seen protruding from the blocks and Chettan was dug out. He was dead, having been carried down several hundred feet and crushed. Artificial respiration was administered for an hour in the forlorn hope of reviving him. During this Schneider appeared, having had an incredible escape. 'I heard a crack,' he said, 'then down it came, huge masses of ice from hundreds of feet above. I thought I was dead, but I ran to the left, and the avalanche missed me by five metres.' Chettan had been too far behind Schneider to save himself.

The rest of the party had extraordinary luck. The track they were following had been entirely obliterated except at one point where it took a zigzag to the left out of the path of the avalanche, and they had happened to be at that place. Their escape had been so close that several porters had been bruised by ice blocks. Part of the route on the ice wall had disappeared, and the area of snow slopes covered by debris was estimated to have been nearly a mile square, with the avalanche weighing 'scarcely less than a million tons.' The ice wall now appeared more unstable than before, new cracks had appeared, an even greater avalanche could occur. They buried Chettan's body after a short but moving ceremony, and the whole party in deep despair retreated to Camp 1. Years later Schneider wrote that during their descent from the ice wall the evening before the avalanche Chettan had stopped him, pointed to the cliff and said: 'Sahib, no good!' then attempted by signs to indicate how dangerous he thought it was.

Dyhrenfurth, Kurz and Richter came up the following day and a discussion was held. Frank wrote that those who had been at base camp were in favour of renewing the attempt on the ice wall, but 'this was very properly rejected by all those who had shared in the attack.' Eventually Dyhrenfurth decided to attempt the mountain by the north-west ridge. This was bristling with difficulty and if anything, even more ambitious than the route they had failed on. And there was almost no chance of reaching Kangchenjunga's main summit, which was at the far end of a line of intermediate peaks. Frank told Dyhrenfurth that he believed the north-west ridge was hopeless and later overheard conversations in nearby tents, in which he was referred to as 'the English coward.' He was naturally disgusted, but the feelings of the others are perhaps understandable. His outspokenness about the dangers was resented. They had a job to do; they were all in the same boat. But the north-west ridge was nevertheless abandoned quickly. By way of consolation Schneider and Frank made a mainly ski ascent of the Ramthang Peak, 7,105 metres, a shapely but easy summit adjacent to the Wedge Peak.

The report of the avalanche in *The Times* left little to the imagination, and Frank, mindful that his mother would read it, made a brave if somewhat grotesque attempt to rationalise it in a letter to her. 'For heaven's sake don't worry about that beastly accident,' he wrote. 'We don't intend to have another. There is no doubt it was a dangerous route, but not nearly [as] dangerous as it proved.'[9]

Dyhrenfurth had planned to return to Darjeeling by going north and east over the Jonsong La into Sikkim so completing the circuit of Kangchenjunga, and he also wanted to climb the Jonsong Peak, 7,420 metres, higher than any summit reached at that time. It was an ambitious programme. The pass was very high and with only 75 porters retained, relaying was necessary.

Two parties reached the Jonsong Peak summit. It was a straightforward climb mainly on snow, but Frank failed to make the first ascent alongside Schneider and Hoerlin when his partner, Wood-Johnson felt unwell after leaving the top camp. The latter insisted Frank should go on, and he did so, but became exhausted in hurrying to catch up with Schneider and Hoerlin and abandoned the attempt. On the return he discovered that Wood-Johnson had actually collapsed and needed help to get back to the tent. Frank was later criticised for allowing his anxiety to reach the summit to take priority over Wood-Johnson's welfare. This could have been an unfair accusation if only because Wood-Johnson, according to his own account was so anxious not to spoil Frank's chances he concealed the true seriousness of his malaise, which was food-poisoning. He recovered, and Frank completed the ascent with Dyhrenfurth, Wieland and Kurz some days later.

There were interesting moments on the return to Darjeeling. Gorges had to be crossed by bridges made of branches and string. Hettie was nearly drowned when she was persuaded by her guide, who was lost, into taking a piggyback ride across a powerful river. Shoulder-deep and almost too late he managed to retreat. Frank was mysteriously struck by a stunning blow on the back of his neck in a haunted bungalow, and he awoke that night to find himself trying to climb out of the window while standing on top of Wood-Johnson. In Gangtok the expedition was invited to dine with the Maharaja of Sikkim, and here Frank's and Hettie's accounts vary. Wine and champagne flowed freely during the excellent meal and for Frank it was an exceptionally convivial evening in which the Maharanee, who spoke excellent English, translated his risqué stories into Tibetan for a stout gentleman opposite, who turned out to be the Holiest Lama of Sikkim. Afterwards in the salon Hettie happened to see Frank 'turning green.' As though 'bitten by a tarantula' she jumped up, announced that it was time for them to leave, and in the general departure Frank managed to escape into the garden unnoticed. Afterwards he admitted that he would remember her presence of mind 'on his deathbed.'

THIRTEEN

Rising Star, Married Man

When Frank stepped ashore at Dover on 19 July 1930, he had just eight weeks to deliver the manuscript of his Kangchenjunga book to his new publisher, Victor Gollancz who with entrepreneurial zeal had contracted a deadline with an eye on the Christmas market. It would be a relentless schedule, 2,000 words a day, week in, week out.

There were other obligations. Earlier that year the literary and lecture agents, Christy and Moore had signed him up. Gerald Christy ran the lectures and was a leader in the business with a list of nearly 200 speakers including many household names. Leonard Moore of the Literary Agency wasn't short of celebrities either, both budding and established — George Orwell was a client, soon to have his first major work published, also by Victor Gollancz. Moore had nothing left to learn about driving a deal; even Gollancz was wary of him. Later the publisher, realising he had miscalculated his costs for a popular edition of *The Kangchenjunga Adventure* wrote to Moore begging him to persuade Frank to accept a slightly reduced royalty. He played his only card. If Frank agreed, he would advance £100 immediately instead of in 10 months' time. Moore may have been tough, but he was fair. He replied without preamble. 'If you will send me the cheque for £100 on account, Smythe will be glad to have it.'

But regardless of the work overload, Frank was already making plans for next year. He was confident he could organise an expedition of his own in 1931. And he knew exactly which mountain he intended to climb.

Kamet was a beautiful and distinctive mountain in the Indian Garhwal Himalayas. At 7,756 metres (25,447 feet) its summit was higher than any mountain climbed at that time. Frank had heard of it from the Yorkshire Ramblers' Club, who had regarded it as 'their' mountain since a member of the Club, Morris Slingsby, had made two attempts on it before the First World War. Hugh Slingsby, another of that great mountaineering family, had become a good friend. Due to its accessibility Kamet had attracted no fewer than nine expeditions launched by luminaries such as Tom Longstaff, General Bruce and Charles Meade, with the earliest attempt made in 1855 by two brothers, Adolph and Robert Schlagintweit. All had been rebuffed by combinations of bad weather, uncertainty about the best route, and cruel conditions on a high, cold mountain — its summit being not far short of the notorious 8,000-metre level. In 1931 it was an ambitious target.

But Frank's ambition was unlimited. Even then he saw Kamet as a stepping-stone, his real interest being Everest. In India he'd learnt that the political tension following the 1924 expedition had eased, and the Tibetan government might be receptive to another application to attempt the world's highest peak. On 11 August he'd written to the Alpine Club hierarchy about it. He thought that permission might be granted by the Maharaja of Nepal for the short cut through his country to the north col of Everest via the Arun valley. He urged speedy action because he believed plans were afoot for an international expedition to Everest — a reference to the possibility of Dyhrenfurth mounting an attempt — and he added, 'I am sure you will agree that there are very strong sentimental reasons why Everest should be climbed by a purely British party.' In the meantime, he said, Kamet would be an 'ideal training ground for a nucleus of Everest candidates'. *The Times*, already contracted for Kamet, would pay 'a large sum' for news rights on Everest. And so Frank — thought pushy by some — set about positioning himself for the time when the world's highest mountain should appear again on the agenda.

Paying for an expedition to Kamet was a daunting prospect. He wrote to Bernard, his half-brother and owner of the Maidstone timber business asking for help, even suggesting that his mother had been unfairly treated in Algernon's will and that a contribution was still legally owing from the estate. But Bernard had already been involved in Frank's Argentine fiasco four years earlier and viewed his wayward antics with scepticism. On 30 August he sent a frosty reply:

My dear Frank,
I am glad you got back safely from India, etc. Re the Will and the point you raise, it seems to me that until a person is entitled to the money no action can be taken, but [if] you take action the Trustees will have to get opinion and if

necessary defend it or fight it with your Mother's money, and if I receive any letter from a lawyer on the matter I shall hand it over to the Trustee's solicitors. Please give our love to your Mother.

Yours ever,

Bernard

Frank made no further move in this direction. Instead he became engaged to be married.

Florence, living in London had rather lost touch with her Berkhamsted friend, Mollie Johnson, but recently Mollie had rented a flat in Baker Street where she could provide accommodation and support for her daughter Kathleen, who was studying the piano at the nearby Royal Academy of Music. The two mothers saw one another occasionally and it was during one of these get-togethers that Frank and Kathleen met again for the first time in 12 years. Kathleen was no longer the boring child; she was now 22 and an attractive young woman.

This is a part of Frank's life I have not been looking forward to dealing with. How can you probe your own parents' relationship and marriage? It was obviously an enormously important part of Frank's life, and Kathleen's as well, and the fact that their marriage didn't survive, leading to anguish for them and their surrounding family, including of course my two brothers and me, means that I need to look at everything from the beginning and try to see where problems lay.

After leaving school at Berkhamsted Kathleen had spent a year at a 'finishing' school in Vevey on Lake Geneva. Further study of the piano at home and at the Academy led to her becoming a very good pianist indeed. She might have reached concert standard, although her self-effacing temperament could have been a handicap. Getting married to Frank ended any hopes in that direction.

She was a calm and gentle person, having inherited none of her mother's rather dominant manner, although there was a stubbornness lurking there, common to the Johnson family. Her father had died when she was seven, but her mother brought her up and her brothers with inflexible discipline. Kenneth and Esmond effectively escaped when they went to college, but Kathleen stayed within her mother's orbit. And at home, with servants, she remained woefully impractical. Her life consisted of music practice, helping her mother with charitable and church work, visits to or from elderly relatives, picnics, swimming and tennis parties, and more music practice.

How different from Frank's world! She saw a restless young man with gingery hair, a bit shy, a leaner and more weather-beaten version of the boy they had known at Berkhamsted and Borth-y-Gest. But he had an intensity that captured her interest. And when she went for walks with him in Regent's Park he talked about mountains. It must have sounded amazing to her. Sleeping in mountain huts, camping in remote valleys full of flowers, walking on glaciers, watching thunderstorms at close quarters, climbing the rock towers of the Dolomites. The forests of the Himalayas. The icy precipices of Kangchenjunga. Kathleen couldn't have stopped thinking about the fantastic life described to her, and the man who was living it, a man who had become famous and moved in exotic circles.

It was easy to see what attracted her to Frank and the opportunity for escape from her rather predictable life, but it wasn't so obvious what he saw in Kathleen. Or to be blunt, what he saw beyond her good looks and her friendly nature. This seems a harsh thing to say about one's own mother, and I don't mean that Kathleen was lacking in character; the fact is that she and Frank had almost nothing in common and were of such entirely different temperaments that they were unlikely ever to have any real understanding of one another. In our society today relationships usually develop in stages. The 'chatting up', the 'seeing' one another, and the 'going out with' are words used for the first contact, the early dates, and the deeper friendship which in most cases incorporates a sexual relationship as well as the intensive exchanging of ideas and experiences and building of closeness. All of which might lead to living together, starting a family, with marriage taking its place as an option before that, or later on, or not at all.

Frank and Kathleen were handicapped. They were heavily chaperoned by their mothers. Florence even insisted on being present in her son's study when he dictated to a secretary employed to type the publisher's draft of his book, a quite extraordinary situation. They were inhibited by their upbringing and by the attitude of society at that time. That they turned out to be incompatible over physical sex became sadly apparent after they were married. But the most telling factor was not just that Frank had rushed into asking Kathleen to marry him — their engagement was announced in *The Times* on 10 October 1930 — but that he wanted the wedding to take place very quickly, in January before he went to Kamet. A letter he wrote to his good friend, Graham Macphee on 19 September is somehow significant. Macphee had got married the previous June and Frank, who had not been in touch for over a year, wrote:

Have only just heard of your marriage. Why didn't you tell me you were going to be, you blighter? All of the very best and many congratulations … When are you likely to be in Town? Mind you let me know …[1]

I got the feeling that Frank saw marriage at this stage of his life simply as a Good Idea. In July he had become 30. Marriage was the perfect way of escaping from his mother. Kathleen was a wonderful girl, and if he waited until after he got back from Kamet he might lose her to somebody else. He liked to look and plan ahead. Climbing and expeditions were things you fitted into your life, and a wedding was the same. I believe that sadly, Frank was focussing more on the concept of marriage and its advantages to him, than on the person who would fill the role as his wife.

Both mothers were opposed, but they were helpless to prevent the union. Mollie saw Frank as unreliable, he lacked a 'proper' job, he was rather old for her daughter and in any case January was much too soon to marry. Indecently so. The old saying 'Marry in haste, repent at leisure' probably crossed her mind. She disapproved of a man who could leave his wife — *her daughter* — on her own for months on end while he gallivanted on the other side of the world. She never did get on with Frank, never did accept his chosen way of earning a living, and in the future lay a morass of trouble and heartache in which she would play a significant part.

Florence was against the marriage for an entirely different reason. Although she had sometimes urged Frank to 'marry some nice girl and settle down', when it was actually about to happen — the marrying part if not the settling down — she became distraught. She talked about the 'parting of the ways' and the loneliness she would have to endure. Frank could not contain his irritation when they were together, but he was full of remorse when they were apart. Once he received a letter from his mother during a lecture tour. From a Sheffield hotel he replied:

You have been a dear and wonderful Mother to me and I can never repay you for all you have done, and for all the sacrifices you have made, and the worries you have endured. But you mustn't write such a letter as though you were saying good-bye forever — it's absolute rot. Of course we shall see heaps of each other and it's absurd to write as you do.[2]

Frank was three weeks late with his manuscript, but at the end of October the energetic Gollancz had produced a prospectus and order form.

And incredibly, just one month later, on 28 November, it was published —
a fat volume of 464 pages, 48 photographs and priced at 16 shillings (80 pence).
And if *Climbs and Ski Runs* had been lift-off for Frank's writing career *The
Kangchenjunga Adventure* took it into orbit.

Even Gollancz seemed shaken. A week after publication sales were
already 'well over 3,000'.[3] Frank was not the first to introduce the public to
Himalayan mountaineering — the three Everest expeditions of the 1920s
had each been followed by a book written by its leader. But their accounts
were more like reports than stories, and Frank felt that the public would
only warm to one person's story, and that person had to be him. It was the
difference between an official survey of big game shooting in northern India
and Jim Corbett's terrifying stories of his night outings to hunt down man-
eating tigers.

I am not the person to assess my father's writing. But I will say that when I have
dipped into one of his books — to check something perhaps — I've tended
to read on. And on. I accept this may not mean anything. Nostalgia comes
into it because these are the stories I read when I was a boy.

In 2000 Ken Wilson and his company Bâton Wicks published an omnibus edition of six of Frank's books. It was a bold venture since the books he
chose to republish had been sold in such large numbers that there was no
shortage of them in second-hand bookshops. And Frank's writing had to
some extent fallen out of favour by the 1960s. His lapses into purple prose,
his dated attitudes and style, the new waves of Himalayan exploration, the
before and after effect of World War Two on everything, and Frank not living
long enough to become a respected elder — all these things had apparently
consigned him to a historical and literary bottom shelf. But Ken believed in
Frank's importance as a climber and writer between the wars and had been
waiting for the opportunity to produce the omnibus as one of his series of
these weighty volumes — Tilman and Shipton having already been 'dusted
down and shown up in lights.' On publication he lobbied assiduously for the
climbing world to take note. So how, as one reviewer asked rhetorically,
would Frank Smythe fare now?

Some biographers see the historical view of their subject as an integral part
of their remit. Others become absorbed in his lifetime while they're writing it,
as though the future has no relevance. It's tempting to avoid distractions by
taking that second route, which is what I have tended to do with Frank, but
there are moments when you have to emerge into the light of day. You need

to remind yourself that a reader is going to find the bygone era into which you have comfortably immersed yourself, strange. I had imagined the omnibus reviewers as critical and ruthless young guns, impatient of the bad old days, happy to put Frank Smythe back in the pigeon-hole he had occupied since his death. But I was wrong.

Gordon Stainforth's *Alpine Journal* review was the longest and most comprehensive. He duly acknowledged Frank's climbing record, then said that the biggest revelation was 'the quality of Smythe's writing ... At his best a no-nonsense Englishness is miraculously combined with the intensity of a poet.' He admired the breadth and depth of his interests beyond climbing, which 'raises Smythe's writing well above most mountain literature.' He empathised with Frank's approach:

> He is also something of a philosopher. And it is here, traditionally, particularly among his colleagues in the Alpine Club, that Smythe has been held to have come unstuck. Lord Shuster said his observations were 'neither as original nor as profound as he seems to think,' while Sir Arnold Lunn condemned him for attempting to 'construct a religion out of his mountaineering experiences'. And very recently I have heard another critic describe his ideas as 'wacky'. Looking at his writings again, I think this is very harsh, indeed entirely unsustainable. Smythe's wackiest idea is that he believes in God, an idea that has never gone down well with the scientific reductionists. I think also the fact that he was — as he himself confessed — an 'incurable romantic', interested in flowers and sunsets, made some of his contemporaries regard him as a bit wet. Smythe tells us that Ruttledge called him a blooming sybarite, only he did not use the word 'blooming', and he admits that he 'runs the risk of being labelled 'sentimental' — a red rag this word to the bull of materialism.'
>
> I think the so-called 'philosophical' aspect of Smythe's work needs to be looked at a little more closely. While he was certainly a religious aesthete he was scarcely the mystic that some have branded him. God is mentioned extremely infrequently, and then only in a very abstract way. Fascinated by one particularly delicate mountain flower, he simply remarks: 'Heaven knows how it grows — and that I think is the correct answer.' There is nothing remotely intellectual or obscure about his beliefs. 'A clever friend once told me,' he says, that 'the trouble with you is that you feel more than you think.' If this is so, thank God for my disability ...I am content to accept with childlike faith and delight the infinite beauties and grandeurs of the universe.' If this is a philosophy at all, it is a very gentle philosophy.[4]

But the historians' verdicts lay a long way in the future as *The Kangchenjunga Adventure* hit the Christmas bookshelves in 1930. Gollancz had arranged for advertisements in the newspapers and the first one to appear caused a shudder to run through the Alpine Club. It's so bland that it's hard to imagine how offence could have been caused. But Frank wrote anxiously to Gollancz that he had received criticism; Arnold Lunn considered it 'foul bad taste'.[5]

Gollancz's guffaw at this might have been heard the length of Henrietta Street, but he handled Frank with care:

My dear Smythe,
I am completely at sea ... The fact that Arnold Lunn considers it 'foul bad taste' moves me not at all: but the fact that you seem half to share his opinion, and that you have had other complaints, disturbs me. I don't think I am usually obtuse in these things, but I have looked at it again and again, and simply can't see what the objection is. Will you enlighten me?

You must also realise that, of course, the advertisement is not meant in the very least to appeal to mountaineers. Such mountaineers as intend to buy the book will buy it anyhow ... But if you are going to appeal to mountaineers only, you can't begin to get any real sale — not a quarter of the sale represented by the advance. The only possible way to get a really big sale for such a book is to appeal to the general public ...

It suddenly occurs to me that the idea may be that it is bad taste for you to boast that you climbed the Jonsong Peak. This is grotesque. You are not boasting. Nobody imagines that you write the advertisement for your own book![6]

Nowadays few writers would feel this to be a dilemma, but it was a worrying moment for Frank. From inside the cold embrace of the mountaineering establishment he had to choose between the devil of public appeal and the deep blue sea of obscurity and perhaps poverty as a climbers-only writer. He'd been faced with this quandary in the aftermath of the Brenva Face, but had restored the approval of his peers with *Climbs and Ski Runs* published by the dull but respectable Blackwood. Now he stood on the brink again. But he replied to Gollancz's letter the day he received it, and I believe it took only minutes, even seconds to make up his mind. 'You are absolutely right,' he wrote. 'It's only the old-fashioned purists who scoff at advertising ...'[7]

Kangchenjunga however continued to haunt him, as he revealed in a tactless outburst to Geoffrey Young. He'd had a letter from an 'eminent' member of the Alpine Club, suggesting he'd been responsible for Chettan's death.

Another offered to 'clear' him with the 'Inner Circle' of the club. The AC, wrote Frank furiously, was almost dead. It was a 'sort of inquisition.' Why not a rival club of younger men? He would willingly 'put up a bit of hard cash' to see it fulfilled ... [8]

But Frank stayed loyal to the Alpine Club all his life. He loved the Tuesday night meetings, the gossip. He knew the Club was essential to him, providing the contacts to smooth his path to anywhere in the world. The club atmosphere however, could be stifling. The author and climber Scott Russell described his own first visit to the premises in 1935 after he'd become a member. On arrival he met Sydney Spencer, who talked about the Club and asked him which members he particularly wanted to meet. Russell mentioned Winthrop Young and George Finch, and Spencer told him that Young was approved of but not Finch. He would not like Finch, nobody did [he had committed the 'crime' of giving unauthorised lectures about the 1922 Everest expedition]. Spencer then said, 'I hope your proposers told you that in addition to being the oldest mountaineering body in the world, the Alpine Club is a unique one — a club for gentlemen who also climb.' Pointing out of the window at a street-sweeper in Savile Row, he added, 'I mean we would never elect that fellow even if he were the finest climber in the world.'

Of the five men Frank invited to join him for the Kamet expedition the only one who had climbed in a greater range was Eric Shipton, who after climbing Mount Kenya was at the threshold of his outstanding mountaineering and exploring career. The others, all with climbing experience, were Dr Raymond Greene, his Berkhamsted schooldays friend, Bill Birnie, a captain in the Indian Army and ideal as transport officer, Bentley Beauman, an RAF Wing Commander, and Romilly Holdsworth — known as 'Holdy' — a Harrow School classics master who was an expert botanist and an Oxford cricket blue, two talents which appealed to Frank.

It was an odd little team in which hardly anyone knew anybody else. That it functioned so well may have been due to Frank's preference for a group of men with easy-going natures and a variety of interests. He was proud of the fact that they stayed friends afterwards. He asked for a contribution of £300 per person, the Yorkshire Ramblers' Club gave him £105 and the Ski Club of Great Britain £80. *The Times* appointed him as their Special Correspondent again, this time publishing his name at the head of each dispatch.

After Kamet Frank climbed with Shipton on three Everest expeditions. Both had failed to make headway in ordinary jobs and embraced mountaineering and exploring and earning a living from writing — full-time for Frank, part of a living for Shipton. Without question, Shipton's exploring career was one of the greatest. For over 50 years he went on lightweight ventures to China, Pakistan, Tibet, Nepal and Patagonia. He wrote eight books, contributing to five more, a smaller output than might be expected after such a life, although he produced many articles for journals. Like Frank he was an Everest 'nearly' man in the 1930s, but when in 1951 a wave of exploration of the mountain began from Nepal, his dismissal from the leadership of the ultimately successful party, together with events in his personal life, resulted in a five-year hiatus before he got going again.

Shipton's father, like Frank's, died when he was a baby and he too had a poor relationship with his widowed mother and had a difficult time at school. Both men were happiest on small expeditions. But there the common experiences seem to end. There was a disparity in temperaments. Shipton was sociable and agreeable, Frank more volatile. In Shipton's partnership with Bill Tilman he was sometimes content to let Tilman call the shots; Frank was never at ease unless he was in charge. But he liked Shipton and throughout his correspondence and diaries I came across only one disparaging comment. On Everest in 1936 after an apparently safer route to the North Col had been found on its west side he wrote, 'Had Mallory discovered [this] seven lives would not have been lost in 1922. And had Eric done his job properly last year instead of climbing other peaks and enjoying himself [a reference to Shipton's leadership of the reconnaissance] we might have been successful this year.'[9]

As climbers they seemed pretty well matched but Shipton's feelings about his companion were qualified. Privately he regarded Frank as 'about the worst traveller I have ever met,' and after Frank's death he wrote that although he was an agreeable companion he was 'not a stimulating one, for he lacked originality, and tended to talk and think in clichés.' He added that Frank's 'prolific writing also suffered from this defect, which caused some of his critics to accuse him of sham sentiment.' This last point is perhaps relevant regarding their lack of real closeness. Shipton was one of the body of climbers who were jealous of or resented Frank's success. In 1938 in a letter to his friend, Pamela Freston he bemoaned the £75 advance he received for his second book, adding, 'It's OK for blokes like Frank who get £700 down before they start writing!'[10]

Frank and Kathleen were married on Saturday 17 January 1931 at St Peter's Parish Church, Berkhamsted. Bernard sank his differences and attended, signing the register as a witness. The Berkhamsted Gazette reported on the bride's dress, the César Franck and Bach played by two of her music teachers, the reception in the Town Hall, the gifts of a silver fruit stand from the Mothers' Union and a table from General Bruce. The newlyweds left for their honeymoon, which was to be spent motoring, the bride wearing a scarlet and black three-piece suit and a fur coat, a present from her husband.

The motoring took them to North Wales where, inspired by Graham Macphee who had spent his honeymoon on Rannoch Moor, Frank introduced Kathleen to the demands and delights of walking in Snowdonia in mid-winter. They stayed at the Pen-y-Gwryd hotel and the family album proves that the weather could have been worse. Frank shot pictures of grey mountains with scudding clouds and shafts of sunshine. They went to Idwal where Kathleen smilingly posed a few feet up the Slabs, then to the jaws of the Devil's Kitchen, and to the top of Glyder Fawr. They walked up Snowdon where Kathleen, clinging in a gale to an ice-festooned signpost on the railway track near the summit and still dressed in beret, raincoat and stout shoes, looks absolutely frozen and badly needing the fur coat. Frank took pity on her with lunchtime sandwiches in sheltered coves on Anglesey. She snapped him sitting on a boulder at Ogwen, gazing at her reflectively and perhaps wondering how long it will take to make a climber out of her. The last picture was taken in the Betws-y-Coed woods where she is standing on a branch halfway up a tree.

In London they began their married life in a flat in Hampstead which Frank had previously occupied with his mother. Florence moved out to live a few streets away and become a forlorn nearby presence for her son and daughter-in-law.

The final weeks before Frank left for Kamet were frantic. He invited Gollancz to take on the book, and in a rush of confidence that left Leonard Moore trailing, offered to accept a reduced advance in the event of failure to climb the mountain. Gollancz was happy to write this into the contract.

On 28 March, with the other expedition members travelling later he caught the midday boat train. Kathleen was to have a few days' skiing with him in Switzerland before he continued to Venice and India, and Brian Lunn, younger brother of Arnold went too, to ski and escort Kathleen home. Frank noted in his diary that they were seen off by 'Mother and M.I.L.' — a brusque reference to his mother-in-law.

Kathleen had been caught in a six-month whirlwind. Rest and recovery were almost at hand, but not just yet. Next day they had reached Kleine Scheidegg underneath the Eiger where Frank purchased 24 pairs of snow-goggles for his porters and an ice axe for himself, and next morning in brilliant sunshine and a bitterly cold wind they set off from the Jungfraujoch to ski up the Walcherhorn. This involved crossing a pass, weary miles of snowfield, a final icy climb, and the long return, all at 3,500 metres or more. For Kathleen, unfit, unacclimatised, and with no recent skiing, the result was awful, as Frank recorded:

> I was surprised to see how well K ran. She has any amount of grit and pluck, when she can do her turns she will be first class. An icy blast greeted us on the summit. A very tiring plug back over Mönch Joch. Altogether too long a day to start with, and as I saw K getting dreadfully tired and only doing a few steps at a time but never complaining, I cursed myself for a fool. It was a tired worn out party that crawled through the Sphinx Stollen hole into the Jungfrau Joch. Cheery evening. A long and learned argument on religion with Brian.

Next day Kathleen felt too tired and sick to venture more than a few yards from the hotel. Frank stayed with her while Brian went on his own, and the day after that, with Kathleen still unwell the two men skied and climbed the Jungfrau.

The Walcherhorn was the first, and the last mountain Kathleen ever climbed, apart from some hill walking, so Frank's hopes for a wife who could share some of his adventures in the mountains were dashed. There would be a moment when he tried to persuade her to come with him to the Himalayas. But that was more a desperate ploy to breathe life into a failing marriage. And by then it was a choice for her of off-loading two very young children onto relatives, or staying to look after them herself. She stayed, although years later more than once she told us that she wished she'd gone with Frank.

> 3 April. It was our last day together. Caught 4.15 p.m. train to Lauterbrunnen and went via Interlaken and Spiez to Brig. I forgot my ice axe and left it in hotel I think. Did not let K come to see me off. It was bad enough parting as it was.

Fourteen

Kamet

On 14 May 1931 the Kamet expedition party assembled at Ranikhet, a hill town in Garhwal some 50 miles south of the Himalayan snows. It was a magical spot. From a forested ridge there was a view through trees of wave upon wave of blue foothills, with the peaks of Nanda Devi, Trisul and Kamet jutting up over the horizon. Frank was awestruck. 'In that magical hour of dawn,' he wrote, 'all that I knew of mountains was forgotten, and I saw them again as I had seen them when I was a boy.'

He and Shipton, who had joined him in Bombay from Kenya had arrived in advance of the other four. It would be at least another three weeks before the high passes would be clear of snow and it was useful to have time in hand since social life in the elegant summer retreat meant that nothing could be hurried. His diary shows how preparations became entangled with invitations:

Dined with Marshal. I am suffering from hill 'trots' slightly. It must be the water, which is full of mica. Dinner was fearfully boring. Men wore tails and one man, formerly a Guards officer, with a silky moustache and a face like a sheep, wore white gloves. The women looked at one when one asked them for a dance as though one was attacking their virginity. I retired to the bar and remained there until the end.[1]

They visited Government House to arrange for porters:

A very hot tramp up to Naini Tal … Dinner a cheery affair — no women present and not Lady Hailey. Looked at maps in billiards room afterwards. Sir Malcolm Hailey keenly interested. A pleasant room to sleep in, but bathroom decorated with a huge spider which Nema pursued very half-heartedly.

Strolled round grounds before breakfast … Saw Lady Hailey. She showed me her Tibetan pictures. Not thinking of anything to say, I blurted out, 'Fine open country it looks,' which amused her intensely. Glad to escape. I'm no social wallah, though I seem to be let in for a devil of a lot of socialites.[2]

Shipton described how after one formal dinner-party Frank 'sauntered' out of the dining-room with the ladies, and sat in the drawing-room for a quarter of an hour, chatting to his embarrassed hostess, before noticing his gaffe.

Other distractions included sleeping on the bungalow veranda and being woken by 'the screams of animals being slaughtered by leopards', and conversation with the Forest Officer, who told them about an Indian philosopher who lived at 18,000 feet, completely naked, spoke perfect English, and when cut off by snow survived weeks without food. 'We must look him up,' Frank remarked. He and Shipton continued to be plagued by 'hill trots' but Frank eventually discovered a remedy. 'Three-quarters of a wine glass of castor oil topped up with whiskey. Effect terrific, a three-hour sitting. Felt half dead, but managed to get to sleep by midnight.'

Preparations complete, on 18 May they rode 60 miles to Baijnath in a decrepit lorry with bandaged tyres. They joined up with their porters who had left with the stores a week earlier with the sirdar, Lewa, an experienced Sherpa who had been on Kangchenjunga the year before. The approach lay over the Kuari Pass, up the Dhaoli River, and finally up a great gorge to set up a base camp immediately east of Kamet, before tackling a route recommended by Charles Meade.

They were as pampered as any modern-day trekkers, although there were incidents. Beauman sat on the gramophone records sadly reducing their number. The expedition adopted a baby musk deer, stolen by one of the men from its mother to Frank's annoyance. They tried to feed the animal from a syringe, but it died within a few days. At villages Greene was called on to deal with cases of syphilis, gonorrhoea, cancer of the stomach, malaria, intestinal ulcers and blood poisoning. He was about to remove the tonsils of a terrified little boy when it became clear that it was his father who needed attention. At one camp Lewa was sent to buy a sheep.

He returned later leading one on a halter, and explained that, as he had been unable to find the owner he had appropriated the sheep from the pasture on which it was grazing!

The sheep was slaughtered in a masterly fashion by Budhibal Gurung. This had scarcely been done when we observed a gesticulating and agitated figure, its rags flying in the breeze, running along the ridge towards the camp. It was the shepherd of the flock! What was he to do? As soon as he reached us the floodgates of his eloquence were unloosed. The sahibs had taken his sheep. What would his master say? He had betrayed his trust. He was a ruined man.

Laughingly, Birnie took hold of his shoulders and forced him into a kneeling position. 'Now,' he said, 'be quiet or we will cut off your head too.' But this little pleasantry was lost on the shepherd; he still chattered volubly.

'All right, then. Cut off his head,' Birnie ordered Budhibal Gurung. I looked at Budhibal Gurung. There was no trace of a smile in his eyes. 'Cut off his head,' re-iterated Birnie. Budhibal Gurung's hand seemed to tighten on the hilt of his reeking kukri; there was a curious look in his eyes; these men are used to obeying orders. I don't think we realised at the time how near that order came to being carried out … [3]

It was settled amicably, the sheep was paid for, and there was a welcome change of diet for everybody that evening.

Thirty yaks were hired for the rugged last 20 miles to base camp. They were powerful animals, able to swim rivers where necessary, and apparently docile. However, as Frank wrote later, the sight of a European, 'particularly one with a reddish beard' could unnerve them without warning:

One yak bolted. Two or three others immediately followed its example … In the general mêlée, several boxes fell to the ground, and one of them rolled down the hillside … The lid of the box was torn from its hinges and Shipton's pyjamas emerged; they were caught by a bush and remained bravely fluttering in the breeze. The gramophone shot out and bounded valley-wards … Lewa pounced upon it. We thought it must be irreparably damaged, but from another unbroken box we unpacked a record and placed it in the machine … It was with profound thank-fulness that we heard Caruso's passionate 'O sole Mio'. Whether this had a steadying influence on the yaks I do not know, but thenceforward they proceeded soberly. [4]

They established their base camp at 15,000 feet near the Raikana Glacier with Kamet some 10 miles distant. Frank's plan was to make an Advanced Base further on, then go for the summit using about three camps en route. The topography of the mountain supported this idea, since the climbing difficulties came higher up on a thousand-foot wall of mixed rock and snow. Then easier ground led to Meade's Col on the ridge between Kamet and a lower peak to the north, the Ibi Gamin. The final slope above the col, some 2,000 feet high, was the only part of the route which had not been climbed by a previous expedition. It seemed to lie at a reasonable angle and consisted of snow and ice.

In war plans are said never to survive contact with the enemy, but Kamet cooperated benignly with Frank's programme. In four days they had set up their Advanced Base. In a further five days a route straightforward enough for loaded porters to follow via fixed ropes had been made up the thousand-foot wall. And in another three days from a camp above that, a party consisting of Frank, Shipton, Holdsworth, Lewa and another Sherpa, Nima Dorje, reached Meade's Col, ready for a single day's push to the summit.

Frank knew this was dangerously fast, but the weather was on their side with plenty of fine days. He'd resolved not to rush the mountain, to allow for acclimatisation, but the fear of bad weather and the oncoming monsoon remained.

Of course it hadn't been *that* easy. Frank's theory that ice avalanches were more likely to be detached from their parent hanging glaciers at the first touch of the sun had been false and had caused a delay on a section of the East Kamet Glacier. They had headaches and poor sleep when they reached 18,000 feet, but all the Europeans except Beauman acclimatised well. After being threatened on the wall by falling rocks, they had to find an alternative line.

But the final slog to Meade's Col was tough, especially for porters carrying supplies for the top camp. More than once Lewa was seen to take the load from an exhausted man and add it to his own, making a total of about 80 pounds — 'A *superhuman* effort,' Frank commented. However in spite of his admiration for his sirdar, Frank never believed he or any other Sherpa could lead a party on a mountain. This wasn't through a lack of confidence in their technical skills — they could learn those — but because he thought they lacked the western climber's understanding of the need for self-discipline when the going got tough. Subsequent developments proved him wrong.

Frank observed the men he employed. He saw how the Darjeeling porters paid local men to carry their loads, not because they were lazy but because it gave them prestige in the eyes of the local girls. He described how the cook, Achung told him 'with an unholy gleam in his eye' that a vital part of the mincing machine was lost, and how after Shipton had carved a wood replacement plug, 'we would see Achung seated on the ground, turning the handle round and round with the dull, hopeless look of a beaten man, once again a slave to the mincing machine.' He admired Nima Dorje's unflappability at a dangerous moment on the climb: 'His broad grin came up from the depths like a fine day in an English summer.' He saw that Budhibal Gurung was 'a serious young man, which is unusual among Ghurkhas. He seldom spoke unless addressed, but his speckless, tropical uniform, his wide-brimmed rakish hat, and his quiet air of efficiency betokened a good soldier.'

A cold dawn filtered into a cold world. With a conscious effort I heaved myself to my knees. The sleeping-bag cracked sharply; it was sheeted with ice deposited by my congealed breath. With numbed fingers I fumbled at the frozen tapes securing the flaps of the tent and peered outside. A cloudless sky was shot with green and orange; the peaks stood from the night like pallid statues. Dawn was gilding the crest of Kamet. Now was the time to start, but it was too cold — the coldest morning I ever remember in the Himalayas. The world almost creaked in the cold. To have left the comparative shelter of our tents would have meant certain frostbite. It was essential that we should start comfortably, with a hot breakfast inside us, and cooking and eating under such conditions were impossible. I slipped my hands back into my sleeping-bag and busied myself restoring the circulation to my numbed finger-tips. How easily circulation is lost at high altitudes, and how slowly and painfully it returns![5]

It was the morning of 21 June — the summer solstice, summit day, the culmination of many months of planning, effort and dreams. Eventually the party set off, climbing on two ropes, Shipton with Lewa, and Frank following with Holdsworth and Nima Dorje, who carried the heavy cine camera.

From that camp the final slope of Kamet rose, gently at first then steepening to its skyline ridge, with the highest point, the summit, at the right-hand end. It was the north face, it was mainly unbroken snow and it appeared to be less difficult than the other sides of the mountain, which were defended with cliffs. The face might lie at a shallower angle at its right-hand edge, but Frank thought that this route, catching the westerly winds would be icy and involve too much step-cutting.

The snow to the foot of the face was almost level, although it was soft and littered with blocks of ice fallen from higher séracs. After that the slope steepened remorselessly. Their progress slowed. When they stopped for a rest in the sun it needed a huge effort of will to start again. Frank filmed Shipton and Lewa setting off, and wished he had not burdened himself with making a movie. He vowed that he would never do so again — a promise he kept. Soon the two ropes had closed together again. The three Englishmen took turns in front, stamping snow steps, cutting footholds in bare ice. In a quarter of an hour the leader would thankfully make way for the next man.

Climbing at high altitudes without supplementary oxygen is like the functioning of a battery not long before it runs flat. There's not much energy left. Frank's account talks not just of fatigue, but growing anxiety:

We arrived at a point where the slope steepened abruptly. Ice-walls and soft snow forced us diagonally to the left towards the edge of the eastern precipice. Now, for the first time since leaving the camp, we could see the final slope, 400 feet high, separating us from the summit ridge. From the camp it had looked steep, and we knew now that it *was* steep. Everything depended on its condition. Supposing that the rippled, wind-blown snow covering it concealed hard ice? If step-cutting[6] was necessary throughout its entire height it would be impossible to overcome it without pitching a higher camp. Time would defeat us; it would take many hours — a whole day's work at least. And supposing the slope consisted of snow ready to avalanche if disturbed? There was no avoiding it. Ice-walls barred approach to the right, sheer precipices fell away to the left. Then indeed we should be beaten. Supposing it proved necessary to pitch a higher camp; was there a ledge on that inhospitable slope of Kamet where a camp could be pitched? We could see none. Were the porters capable of carrying up equipment? It was doubtful; they were already tired from their exertions between Camps 4 and 5.[7]

Nima Dorje became exhausted and could go no further. Frank decided he could wait for them on a convenient snow ledge behind a boulder, or if he wished, return alone safely since a slip from the stretch of ice they had just climbed would result in nothing worse than a landing in the softer snow below, and the track after that was easy. Lewa shouldered the rucksack with the cine camera and they went on. And now, to their great relief, the ice gave way to firm snow into which they could kick steps.

The slope steepened until it was practically a wall. We advanced in turn. A few feet at a time was enough, and we would then stop to gasp for oxygen. I remember that as I leaned forward to rest on my in-driven ice-axe, I could see my feet, a few yards of wind-caked snow-slope, and then the East Kamet Glacier, nearly 7,000 feet beneath. By the boulder sat the solitary figure of Nima Dorje.[8]

At last Frank found himself sprawling face downwards across the narrow summit ridge. It was 4.30 p.m. and the final 400 feet. had taken two and a half hours. The others came and they made their way along the sharp crest.

The ridge rose up into a sharp point … The summit was almost within our grasp; surely it could not escape us now? We gained the point and gazed over and beyond it. At our feet the ridge sank down to a shallow gap. Beyond the gap it merged gently into a small cone of snow — the summit!

We seized hold of Lewa and shoved him on in front of us. As I clutched hold of him I could hear the breath jerking from him in wheezy gasps. I do not think that he quite understood what we were doing. And so he was the first to tread the summit. It was the least compliment we could pay to those splendid men, our porters …[9]

The final 1,500 feet had taken over seven hours. They lay in the snow, spent. Holdsworth smoked his pipe and Frank impressed by 'this offering to the Goddess Nicotine,' photographed him. He'd already had his camera out for the last bit as they neared the summit. One of these shots was published in both *The Times* and the *Illustrated London News* as double-page spreads nearly half a metre wide.[10] It became an iconic image of their success. Two figures toil up the narrow crest of the ridge, sunlit on one side and shadowed on the other. Behind them and far below, a glacier curves out of sight. To the right rises the graceful pyramid of the Mana Peak, nearly 24,000 feet high and waiting to provide Frank, six years later, with one of the greatest solo challenges of his life. From the Mana Peak a row of lesser summits fall like a roller-coaster ride across the breadth of the picture. They conceal the mysterious Banke Plateau behind, but the camera position is so high that range after range of distant peaks can be glimpsed over their crests, and further still the view seems limitless over the clouded foothills into India. It is a wonderful picture, a symphony of sun and shadow, clouds and mountains, depth and distance. It is a heartening yet humbling image, a celebration of man's achievement, but also a reminder of his frailness confronted with the enormity of space and time.

They stayed on top for half an hour. Frank rigged up the cine camera and filmed the party, the view and the summit itself, but by the time he had finished his fingers were white and dead. Replacing his gloves he beat his hands together until he felt the agony of returning circulation. They started down. In three hours they would be overtaken by darkness and there was a terrible temptation to hurry the descent of the slope overlooking the eastern precipice, but steadiness, which meant slowness, was crucial.

Rope length by rope length, they approached safer ground. Not surprisingly Nima Dorje had already gone down. Frank and Holdsworth stopped to await Shipton and Lewa, but the latter was in trouble:

He was moving very slowly and was obviously distressed. His face was greenish in hue, his eyes rigid and staring from exhaustion. He groaned out that he was in great pain, and pointed to his stomach. There was nothing we could do for him save to encourage him to continued effort and to relieve him of his load.[11]

The descent became a nightmare of breakable crust, deep powder and icy board snow on which their nailed boots skidded. The cold became severe. There was an extraordinary sunset in which the sun, shining from the horizon through a collection of peaks, cast bars of shadow like wheel spokes into the east. Finally they closed on the camp and Birnie and Greene came out to help them to the tents.

> Intense cold during the descent had wreaked its will upon us ... The removal of [Lewa's] boots and stockings revealed feet frozen and immovable, the whiteness of which was already changing to a dark purple. Men were immediately set to work to try to restore their circulation, but though they massaged for an hour or more his feet were far beyond the initial stages of frostbite, and circulation would not return.[12]

Shipton and Holdsworth had slight frostnip in their toes but Frank had escaped, due he thought, to his habit of constantly bunching and releasing his toes when numbness threatened. But it seems remarkable that they all did not share Lewa's fate. Leather boots and wool stockings are now considered hopelessly inadequate for extreme cold.

A second ascent of Kamet by the other three Europeans had been planned for the morrow, but this was delayed a day to allow acclimatisation at the high camp and to arrange for Lewa's immediate descent to base camp — Greene believed that in the denser air and increased oxygenation of the blood lay the only chance of saving his feet. Budhibal Gurung had come up and Frank put him in charge of a party of porters detailed to help Lewa get from camp to camp down the mountain.

Meanwhile Frank and his partners of the first ascent waited at the top camp in support of Greene, Birnie and Kesar Singh who made their summit bid on yet another fortuitously fine day. Birnie and Greene suffered slight frost-nip but Kesar Singh, the only porter prepared to go with them after Lewa's dreadful experience, escaped completely. He rejected boots in favour of the traditional wrapping of his feet in layers of sacking and rags, although unsurprisingly he had problems coming down steep ice steps and relied heavily on Birnie, who protected him by going down immediately in front. Astonishingly they had dumped their rope to save weight for the last bit, making the descent somewhat perilous.

Next day all the Europeans, together with the rest of the porters went down, carrying everything that could be salvaged. Lewa was stretchered onwards to base camp, although the locally-hired porters whom he had bossed and bullied earlier in the expedition initially refused to carry him. Nima Dorje argued on his behalf, while Shipton and Holdsworth, the only Europeans with him at that moment and speaking no Hindi could only look on and hope. Later a pony was obtained for Lewa and Frank described his proud sirdar's anguish:

> The tears were streaming down his cheeks, and he was sobbing bitterly, not, I believe, so much from pain as from what he felt to be an undignified position and thoughts of the future. He was but a shadow of his former self, and we could not help but perceive in his moral breakdown and distress the essential difference between the European and the native. Had one of us been seriously frostbitten he would at least have *tried* to bear his misfortune with stoical calm and fortitude. But a native cannot control his feelings; he is a child.[13]

Lewa was regarded as an unfortunate casualty in the conquest of the mountain. In more recent times however the plight of hired men on those early Himalayan expeditions has come under scrutiny. Jonathan Neale, in *Tigers of the Snow*, a book about the history of the Sherpas, took a hard look at Lewa and his fate on Kamet. He pointed out that he could expect little compensation from the Himalayan Club and no pension if he was incapacitated. He also criticised the decision to send Lewa down from the top camp unaccompanied by a European. 'They were all excited by the second summit attempt the next day,' he wrote.

Frank had confidence in the Ghurkha appointed to supervise Lewa's descent and felt it was important for the first party to stay at Meade's Col in support of the second bid for the summit. Neale however believed that in the circumstances there ought not to have been a second ascent, that Europeans should have supervised Lewa's descent, and he should have been carried [although it was likely that would have been impossible, at least on the 1,000-foot wall above the intermediate camp]. Referring to Lewa's breakdown on the pony, he wrote:

> Faced with Lewa's pain and fear, Smythe had strong reasons to shut his eyes. Smythe had been one of the people who had kept the frostbitten Lewa in Camp 5 an extra day. He had sent Lewa down to Camp 2 alone.* He would not be giving his faithful sardar (sic) a pension. All this meant that Smythe couldn't take on board the full human force of Lewa's tears. Instead Smythe took refuge in paternalism. In good times, paternalism means that the white

---

*In fact there was no delay in Lewa's descent — he went down from the top camp the morning after his climb. And he did not of course go down alone.

man is the father, the servant a faithful son, and the father looks after the son. In bad times paternalism means that the European is a man, the native is a child, and the white man does not have to look after a whining child.

None of this is to imply that Smythe was a cold or unsympathetic man. Among climbers of his generation, he was notable for his fondness for Sherpas. His books are a good source on Sherpa history precisely because he noticed individual Sherpas, talked to them, and wrote about them. Because he was actually looking at Lewa, Smythe could see him crying. Because he almost felt what Lewa felt, he had to turn another man into a child.[14]

But if Neale thought that Frank's heart was in roughly the right place he was cynical about his attitude towards India:

> Smythe had taken on board the colonial stereotype of Hindus — weak and unable to govern themselves properly. Luckily another race of men had come from across the seas to do the job for them. But Smythe was also nervously aware [that] most Indians wanted independence. Once the Kamet expedition got into the mountains, 'we were no longer in range of Gandhi's activities, and after the insolent stares of the 'Congress Wallahs' of the lower hills and plains, it was pleasant to be greeted with a respectful and friendly 'Salaam, Sahib' or 'Salaam, Huzoor' from the villagers we met on the path.'

There is no doubt that Frank, like virtually all of his generation, believed passionately in England and the Empire, and their power and potential for good in less developed parts of the globe, although he was discriminating about individual Englishmen he met on his travels. Sometimes though, he allowed his imagination a free run in his conviction that India could not be trusted to govern herself. After lengthy consideration of the dangers posed by religion where 'fanaticisms and hatreds are always simmering, like a molten, subterranean lava lake,' he wrote:

> India is not, and cannot be for centuries, fit to rule herself, and to abandon her would be equivalent to putting all the animals of the Zoo in one cage. The strong would survive, but the agonies of the weak would be too terrible to contemplate.[15]

The lurid comparison of Indians with animals in the zoo came back to haunt Frank, or rather his memory. One reviewer of *Tigers in the Snow*, Charles Clarke, taking a sideswipe at him found the remark 'priceless.'

However we are children of our own time as Frank was of his, and were he to view the world today from a cloud-couch he would be able to console himself with the thought that our generation will probably be followed by another who find some of our most treasured convictions, whether about India's politics or anything else, equally hilarious.

Lewa was sent to hospital at Joshimath where he began the long and painful road of amputations and recovery. He lost the top joint of all his toes, but continued to work for expeditions and would later return as sirdar on the Everest expedition of 1933. One month remained before Frank and his party were due back at Ranikhet and he planned to explore and climb in the Badrinath Range, west of Kamet. However it amounted to little more than a holiday dressed up as exploring, although Shipton in particular found this part of the trip more rewarding than the rigours of Kamet. But it was an anti-climax. The expedition meandered to a conclusion, crossing passes, climbing easy peaks and camping in delightful valleys. Birnie made a map, numbering the glaciers one to 12.

Before their return to England there was a delectable moment that lingered in Frank's mind and was the inspiration for his return to the Garhwal in 1937. His party had crossed the little-known Bhyundar Pass en route to Badrinath on a wet, cold miserable day after the monsoon had broken:

> Within a few minutes we became warmer as we lost height. Dense mist shrouded the mountainside and we had paused, uncertain as to the route, when I heard Holdsworth exclaim: 'Look!' At first I could see nothing but rocks, then suddenly my gaze was arrested by a little splash of blue, and beyond it were other splashes of blue, a blue so intense it seemed to light the hillside. As Holdsworth wrote: 'All of a sudden I realised that I was simply surrounded by primulas. Forgotten were all pains and cold and lost porters. And what a primula it was! Its leek-like habit proclaimed it a member of the nivalis section. All over the little shelves and terraces it grew, often with its roots in running water. At the most it stood six inches high, but its flowers were enormous for its stature, and ample in number — sometimes as many as thirty to the beautifully proportioned umbel, and in colour of the most heavenly French blue, sweetly scented.'[16]

Frank never forgot that moment and it generated an interest in Alpine plants that he followed for the rest of his life.

FIFTEEN

Hammering on Everest's Door

When Frank got home from Kamet in September 1931 he had a book to write, a film to edit, a mountain of correspondence to deal with and lectures to give. He had tributes to respond to including the prestigious election to Honorary membership of the French Alpine Club. He had a young wife he'd scarcely seen since their marriage to have a holiday with. But one matter took priority — Everest.

Among the messages of congratulation was one from Sir William Good-enough, Royal Geographical Society President and Chairman of the Everest Committee. Frank saw this as an opportunity to resurrect the Everest issue. There had been no progress, although an application had been lodged with the Tibetan Government. So plunging in where most would hesitate to tread, he wrote to the Foreign Office asking them to apply for a private expedition to the mountain. And in August 1932 the good news arrived at the RGS that the go-ahead had been granted for the following year.

It was, of course the Everest Committee's application which was successful, not Frank's, although his bold move was mentioned at the end of the letter from Mr J.C. Walton of the Political Department:

I should add that Mr. F.S. Smythe enquired early this year as to the possibility of an Expedition on a small scale ... We informed Mr Smythe that any request of this sort to the Tibetan Government would certainly be refused ... Now that this unexpected change in their attitude has occurred, we should like to tell Mr Smythe as a matter of courtesy that consent has now been obtained in favour of an Expedition organised by the Mount Everest Committee ... We should of course be glad if Mr Smythe were asked to co-operate ...[1]

Frank could console himself with the thought that despite this wooden response to his independent effort, his pestering may have done something to stir up the India Office. Walt Unsworth in his history of the mountain, *Everest*, poses the possibility that simple chauvinism, a fear of a politically unstoppable German demand to attempt Everest forced the India Office to press the MEC's request more strongly. This seems as good a theory as any for the 'reluctant permission' for 1933 given by the Dalai Lama.

But this is jumping ahead a little. After his return from Kamet, the most pressing of the demands on Frank (apart from holiday with wife) were the speaking engagements, some of which had been arranged a year previously. These were either after-dinner speeches, or slide lectures. And from a speaker's point of view there's a big difference between the two.

Everybody has attended some formal event where a speech is given. Within seconds you know whether you're going to enjoy it. It's a talent possessed by few people, and they're outnumbered by the mediocre and the awful. It's obviously a challenging situation for those asked to 'say a few words'. The members of their audience might prefer to go on chatting to each other, or get to the bar, or go home. The person introducing the speaker can put him at a disadvantage with a long preamble. There might be distracting crashing noises from the kitchen with waiters still speeding around serving coffee. In a big room with a thick carpet and low ceiling the acoustics can be terrible. At a climbing club dinner a few dodgy jokes go with the territory.

An after-dinner speaker needs to relate to his audience. He needs to be a confident, outgoing person with a good sense of humour, and a reasonably thick skin. He will poke fun at himself, make eye contact with his audience, think on his feet, and know when to sit down.

Frank didn't fit this profile. He was a private person with a small circle of close friends. He had a guarded nature, took offence easily, was happy in his own company, and more at ease with one or two friends than a big group. It was said that his temper improved with altitude. If this was so it was not because he was necessarily better at coping with people at altitude but probably because there weren't going to be many up there with him anyway! At sea level his social ineptitude — to which he readily confessed in his diaries — caused him to distance himself from strangers. Having to speak at a function wasn't something he enjoyed, and it was bound to show in the performance he gave.

Evidence of this was hard to come by. People don't say cruel things in obituaries, nor do they write comments about the speaking skills of others, except maybe politicians. However the blunt and honest Graham Macphee gave a fleeting glimpse of Frank as an after-dinner speaker when in September 1931 he was the principal guest at the annual dinner of the Fell and Rock Climbing Club. The Club journal reported the event with the jaunty comment, 'F.S. Smythe, fresh from the kicks of Kangchenjunga and Kamet, interested us greatly.' But Macphee in his diary thought otherwise. His entry that day had the usual routine facts — the physical jerks and cold bath, the travel to his dental surgery for one patient only, the drive to the dinner at Windermere in 2 hours and 29 minutes. Then came a caustic comment: 'Smythe was the chief speaker, and very poor at that.'

There was more embarrassment for Frank that weekend. Next day he and Kathleen accompanied a large group to Gimmer Crag. He was short of rock-climbing practice, so a leader was found for him on Ash Tree Slabs, a pleasant and straightforward Severe, with Kathleen sportingly going third on the rope. Meanwhile Macphee accompanied the brilliant A.T. Hargreaves up Joas, a strenuous Very Severe. Frank was then invited to climb another VS but it all went wrong for him. 'We took Smythe up Diphthong,' recorded Macphee, 'which he could not do at all, and made a poor show, then five of us did Chimney Buttress, while FSS watched.' It had been two years since Frank did any rock climbing. The Himalayas and skiing were no substitute for uncompromising British crags. He was never an outstanding rock climber, but the first climb after a long gap can be harrowing. A sweat breaks out, you cling to the holds harder than you need, the exposure yawns underneath, your movements are uncoordinated, and you don't trust your feet or your balance. A critical audience adds to the misery. Kathleen probably enjoyed the climbing more than her husband.

The Club speech had been a chastening experience, but now he faced another 50 audiences in an intensive programme of slide lectures. It might be thought that he found the prospect appalling, but he loved giving slide lectures. And it would be fair to say he was very good at it.

A slide lecture has almost no similarity with an after-dinner speech. The lecturer must use his subject to interest his audience, not his personality. With a subject like mountaineering the only effective way is with visual aids — projected pictures, whether stills or movies, or a combination of both. The lecturer's personality does matter, but only indirectly. Crucially he is in darkness. The audience's eyes will be on the screen, and what the speaker is saying is complemented by the picture. This last point was the key to Frank's success, and that of any good slide lecturer. As a disembodied voice he could talk about an expedition, illustrated by his photographs, confident in his expertise, and knowing that what mattered was his subject and the way he dealt with it.

I once went to a slide lecture on mountaineering given by a climber who, presumably thinking that his audience needed to see him, arranged that a bright spotlight should be trained on him as he stood at a lectern to one side of the screen. Throughout his talk his gaze swept from side to side of the audience even though the spotlight probably prevented him from seeing anything. The result was disastrous. You didn't know whether to look at him or his slides. We had come to hear his story and see his slides — which were in fact disappointing — but not to see him as well. He had ignored, or perhaps not appreciated, the importance of this subtle point.

As a boy I attended a lecture given by Frank at my boarding school. These were held on Saturday nights when everybody was in festive mood and a poor lecturer could be given a rough ride. Frank had no difficulty at all. He talked about an expedition to the Canadian Rockies. There were stories about a grizzly bear attacking him and his companion on a raft, and another bear rummaging for food that he got rid of by peeing on it from the top of some steps ('I exercised the only persuasion I could think of'). He described landing on a lake in the middle of unexplored country in a floatplane, and being caught by a thunderstorm near the top of an unclimbed rock peak. He told us how to build an igloo. There was a terrifying attempt to climb Mount Alberta, one of the most difficult of the high peaks. He had a high, clear, tenor voice. His timing was perfect, with the next slide appearing at exactly the right moment, illustrating what he was saying rather than the other way round, the mistake of so many lecturers. They were magnificent Kodachromes, gorgeous colours that would be hard to improve on, even today. At one point to demonstrate the exhaustion of climbing at great altitudes in the Himalayas he paced slowly across the stage in the full glare of the projector, taking half a dozen loud gasping breaths after each step, a riveting sight. When he came to the end everybody wanted more. The lights came on and he stood there beaming in the lengthy applause. It was a performance I've never forgotten.

His Kamet lecture at the RGS had been arranged for the beginning of November 1931, but just a week before this prestigious event in the Society's calendar he had all his teeth extracted. Arthur Hinks had already complained that his speaker had allowed himself and his subject to be poached by branches of the Royal Scottish Geographical Society, and now he had the prospect of a dentally-disadvantaged Frank in London. Raymond Greene assisted with the extractions on a Sunday afternoon, Frank's only free day, and it seems extraordinary that within a few days he could give a lecture.

'I've had rather a bad time having had all my teeth out at once,' he told the appalled Hinks. 'The anaesthetic has made me a bit groggy. I shall however be able to speak all right next week as my dentist is fixing temporary ones.'

He lectured intensively for the rest of his life. Talks were vital to his career, but sometimes it was hard going. There were the chairmen who after long introductions warned him that he must finish promptly before the caretaker came to lock up. One organiser, on being asked for water provided a glass of neat whiskey, undetected by Frank until the first large swig. The heat from a high-powered projector could ruin his slides. He ran the gauntlet of late trains, freezing hotels in mid-winter, and a plane that nearly crashed on the approach to Jersey. He had to remember to take the keys and coins from his trouser pockets because of his habit of rattling them as he spoke. He fell off a narrow platform halfway through a lecture, nearly breaking his leg.

Meanwhile the Kamet film was proving a problem. In his haste to get a film company to accept it he made the mistake of showing the raw footage to the professionals uncut. It got the thumbs down. It needed a plot they told him, and there was no 'love interest'.

The Times published a despairing letter from him. 'It would be interesting to know whether these sentiments really express the requirements of the British public,' he wrote. 'Whether they do or not, it is certain that no British Himalayan expedition in the future will go to the expense of bringing back to this country a record of their work and that in future the film-going public will have to subsist solely on the 'make-believe' of Elstree and Hollywood.'[2]

The response was immediate, and *The Times* published letters from all quarters of middle England demanding to see the film. The industry was vilified. A film company executive even attempted to justify the rejection, explaining that another film about the Himalayas had been poorly received. Frank knew that this was Dyhrenfurth's Kangchenjunga film, and wrote another letter pointedly referring to 'the *German* film of the Kangchenjunga expedition,' and suggesting that 'a little more optimism might have been expressed for what was after all, a film of a British expedition.'[3] This jingoistic ice-axe rattling had an unexpected result. Frank received a Summons — but not your ordinary kind. And on the afternoon of Wednesday 3 March 1932 by Royal Request he presented himself to show the film to their Majesties King George V and Queen Mary at Buckingham Palace. The performance took place in the big ballroom, three or four other members of the Royal Family attended, it all went smoothly, and George took Frank into his private study afterwards for a drink and a chat.[4]

It was the turning point. The film industry knew when it was beaten. It could refuse a film about a mountain. Anything made by an amateur had no chance. A movie that had no plot, no heroine, no romance, no soundtrack even — forget it. But a Royal Command Performance ... There was muttering through clenched teeth — *Who the hell is this guy, Smythe?* And soon after that, in a smoke-filled office in Wardour Street, a contract was drawn up. The film was tidied up and given a sound track. On 1 August it opened at the Polytechnic cinema in London, ran for 11 weeks, then reappeared intermittently for several years at cinemas throughout the country. It was re-edited and broadcast by BBC television in 1965 and 1983 before being consigned to the National Film Archives. It made some money for Frank and his companions although most of the box office takings were swallowed up by a long queue of agents and other professionals.

By modern standards the film is embarrassingly amateurish, a home movie of dire quality which constantly threatens to descend into unintended farce. It's tempting, if uncharitable to poke fun at everything — from the studio scene where Frank in a smart suit nervously introduces the film in a squeaky voice, to the abrupt finish on the top of Kamet where Shipton is seen lying exhausted in the snow like a landed fish. The expedition gets to base camp via numerous shots of porters bowed under enormous loads plodding this way and that. A lot of cooking goes on over smoky fires. The porters grin cheerfully but the sahibs usually have their backs to the camera except when the great length of Raymond Greene is seen stark naked, mercifully for an instant only, plunging into a pool. Holdsworth happily smokes his pipe while being carried across a raging river by a porter half his size. Stone temples are mixed confusingly with sewing machines and a yogi does a headstand on the top of a pointed rock. Climbing takes place at disconnected moments whenever the camera can be heaved out of its box, otherwise the mountain is seemingly ascended by levitation, perhaps with the help of the smiling yogi. Frank commentates and a piano provides frantic music throughout, whether it is Rupert the baby deer being filmed or an avalanche.

But just as future generations will giggle at our creative efforts today, so we should perhaps thank Frank and his team for bringing us intriguing glimpses of their trip under difficult circumstances.

His book, *Kamet Conquered* was published in August 1932. As a story it lacked the drama and spice of Kangchenjunga but the reviewers were generally appreciative, apart from one writing anonymously in the RGS's

Geographical Journal, who saw Frank's remarks about the distressed and frostbitten Lewa as 'unfeeling and ungenerous.' This critic also disliked Garhwali villages being described as filthy hovels and valley air 'reeking of disease and death.' Smythe's style was 'laboured,' and as a traveller he was 'not at home in the East.'

Frank was shocked and angry. He wrote to the President, a four-page letter that swung between defence of his own conduct in India and bitter resentment of the anonymous reviewer who had 'overstepped the limits of legitimate criticism' and made a 'personal and personally damaging attack.'[5] The Society had allowed an unsigned attack to be made upon one of its Fellows ... The reader would infer that he was not a fit and proper person to be entrusted with the conduct of an expedition in the Himalayas ... The good impression his party had left behind could be confirmed ... No one had greater admiration for their gallant Sirdar Lewa than he ... The reviewer had gone out of his way to attribute to him a meanness and uncharitableness which were most damaging and distressing ...

The letter landed on the desk of the incoming President, Sir Percy Cox. 'Legacy from my predecessor,' he scrawled on it. 'Record, I suppose.' However before the letter disappeared it was passed to a Council member, Tom Longstaff for his comments.

Longstaff was a highly respected figure in British mountaineering. At the age of 57 his record was outstanding: 20 visits to the Alps and almost as many further afield. More than mere enthusiasm was needed for an explorer; 'qualify yourself' was his stern advice. He was wealthy with private means, but before his first trip to the Himalayas in 1905 he had gained a medical degree, become a first-rate naturalist, and had a working knowledge of the languages he would need. He travelled light, with just one or two companions and a few porters. In 1907 he climbed Trisul, 23,360 feet — the highest summit then reached, a record unsurpassed for 21 years. He went to Everest in 1922 as a doctor and naturalist. He won the Founder's Medal of the RGS, the highest honour for an explorer, awarded to very few.

In 1929 Longstaff had written an encouraging review of *Climbs and Ski Runs.* He had attended Frank's Kamet lecture at the RGS and had come to the lectern afterwards to congratulate him. Frank had apparently been acceptable to Longstaff, who normally disliked on principal anyone making money from mountaineering. According to his daughter, Sylvia he didn't think mountains should be written about, and wrote almost nothing himself other than diaries until he published a single volume of memoirs later in life.[6]

There's no evidence that he held adverse opinions about Frank's book on Kangchenjunga, which was reviewed well in the *Geographical Journal*. The publication of *Kamet Conquered* however, changed everything.

He had been asked to write the review for the *Journal*, but had refused. According to another daughter, Sally he hated the title. Frank's dispatches in *The Times* had called it a 'Conquest' and some thought that Gollancz had persuaded Frank against his better judgement to use the word in the book's title, but this was not so. Frank had roughed out a list of chapters for the book under the name *Kamet Conquered*, his instinct for a popular title evidently overcoming any finer feelings he may have had.

But in Longstaff's view much worse was to come in the contents, and he wrote a memo peppered with criticisms of the book and of its author.[7]

> [Smythe] habitually assumes an attitude of superiority over peoples he does not understand ... P.108 Cheek to blame yak drivers. What does he know about loading yaks? P.263 last para. Dreadful! Why should he salute? Why call a perfect stranger a 'Congress Wallah'? P.264-5 'We elbowed our way ...' A European at Badrinath is really there on sufferance and should efface himself. P.239 They will know at Badrinath and ultimately at Gamsali that the schoolmaster is credited with a 'disreputable' appearance, and the head man with a 'filthy-looking abode.' P.105 Why allude to the nice locally woven cloth as 'coarse sackcloth.' Does he expect them to wear gala dress while at work?
>
> In general the attitude is very similar to that of the less intelligent English tourist of 1840 — 1850 towards the alpine villager: that attitude so charmingly derided by Töpfer.
>
> But I believe you will hear no more of the matter. TGL.

Had Frank known that Longstaff would become involved he might have been tempted to swallow his pride and ignore the reviewer's barbs. Longstaff was a formidable figure, a member of the Mount Everest Committee, and not somebody to cross swords with. It was an example of the way Frank's haste to defend himself could add to the difficulties he encountered when sometimes he wrote insensitively about local people on his travels.

In January 1932 he toyed with a plan to attempt Nanga Parbat, the fearsome 8,125-metre peak in the Western Himalayas, but soon scrapped the idea when he found that a party of Germans had already obtained permission for an attempt. He may have been lucky not to get involved. The Germans mounted four large expeditions to the mountain in the 1930s and in the process suffered terrible loss of life from storms and avalanches. To this day it remains one of the most dangerous of the 'eight thousanders.'

At Easter he camped with Kathleen on Snowdon, then settled for a climbing holiday in the Oberland in July with H.B. Thompson. Thompson was a keen but inexperienced climber who happened to be free when Frank was looking for a companion. He was new to the Alps and must have wondered what he had let himself in for. After two fine days when they traversed the delightful Blümlisalphorn above Kandersteg, the weather was consistently bad for three weeks. Encountering *verglas*, slush, drenching rain, deep snow sometimes overlying ice, blizzards and an electrical storm they climbed seven more peaks. They stayed in three huts, and hired two porters for the third, the Baltscheider, to help carry up the next ten days' food, but two hours short of the hut the porters sat down and wept, so they dismissed them and shouldered 80-pound packs themselves for the last bit of the 7,000-foot bash. They had the hut to themselves except for the resident ghost which according to Frank 'tramped round the place at night, talking and leaving footprints.' From there it took 11 hours to reach the summit of the Bietschhorn, wading for three hours in bottomless snow, and on the descent they were delayed by another blizzard developing into a white-out so that it was 18 hours before they reached safety. After that they called it a day and went home.

Perhaps it was as much a relief as a delight for Frank when Sir Francis Young-husband telephoned him a few days later with the news that the Tibetan government had given permission for the expedition to Everest in 1933.

Sixteen

Camp Six

The Everest Committee needed to choose a leader for 1933. Walt Unsworth, in his history of Everest wrote, 'Had the Committee been bold, they could have chosen one of the new climbers who had gained Alpine and Himalayan experience since 1924. There was in fact an obvious candidate for the job — Francis Sydney Smythe.'

However, as Unsworth then suggested, Frank with his reputation for 'irritability, tactlessness and being easily offended,' his record of being one of the Committee's most constant critics and unwanted advisers, his application to run a private expedition to Everest, and his frowned-on career as a mountain writer and lecturer, had ruined his chances.[1] Frank himself, judging from an entry in his diary, didn't particularly want the job anyway:

> Why must expeditions be run by committees in this country? It is to be hoped that the committee will be sensible — but I fear not. They will appoint a leader and in theory give him the last word, but only in theory. God help the leader!

The Committee appointed Hugh Ruttledge.

Each of the four full-scale British attempts on Everest from 1933, up to and including the successful one 20 years later, were dogged by leadership problems. And as events showed in 1933, the selectors were to blame. Ruttledge was a decent man, liked by everybody on his team, but wasn't ruthless enough when it might have mattered. He was 48 and surprisingly had almost no climbing experience. Following a single holiday in the Alps when he was guided up three climbs, he had joined the Indian Civil Service and devoted himself in the Himalayas to what would now be called trekking. An accident had left him with a slight limp.

The Committee had opted for safety. The job of leading an Everest expedition was seen more as a diplomatic post needing an older man who could command from the rear. Ruttledge was seen by the Committee as ideal — 'malleable', to use Unsworth's word. He was astounded at being chosen. Jack Longland wrote of his own first meeting:

> He spent much of that afternoon explaining to a young stranger that he was no great shakes as a mountaineer, but that he hoped that his knowledge of travel in the Himalayas, and of their peoples and languages, might be some use to the expert mountaineers who would do the climbing, and whom he was very proud to command. He was a genuinely modest man.[2]

Ruttledge had known Frank for two years and assumed he would be in the team:

> You may be assured that I will do my damnedest to help you in your struggle to the top. I need hardly say that, so far as I am concerned you are a certainty in the party; no one has a better claim, and I have a strong feeling that you are going to plant your own flag on the summit. I want a long chat with you as soon as possible.[3]

Those who had climbed Kamet formed the core of the squad, except Holdsworth who was left out after he had unwisely criticised the Alpine Club's attitude towards skiers in a lecture at the AC itself when the President, Sir John Withers, had been present. The official reason for his rejection was the frostbite he had suffered to a toe on Kamet. The party eventually numbered 14, with an average age of 34. The youngest was Tom Brocklebank, aged 24, who like the 22-year old Sandy Irvine in 1924 seems to have been chosen as much for his rowing ability — he was a Cambridge treble blue — as for his climbing experience (limited). I mention this because the Committee turned down an applicant who was probably the best rock climber in Britain at that time — Colin Kirkus — ostensibly because at 22 he was too young. It is generally accepted now that candidates for Everest in the 1920s and 1930s who had the 'wrong' background stood little chance. It's also realised that a skilled rock climber will quickly become good at snow and ice too.

The team was twice as big as Frank believed necessary and he directed a stream of quibbles at Ruttledge. He ridiculed the Everest Committee's belief that getting goods free of charge was beneath their dignity. He criticised the sub-committee formed to handle publicity. He declared it was scandalous that Holdsworth had being rejected. He objected to the inclusion of Crawford, who was 'lazy and too old.'

Frank was walking on thin ice. Graham Brown was actively opposed to his inclusion and lost no opportunity to lobby Strutt, Longstaff and Ruttledge. Strutt assured him that Smythe had 'nearly *not* been chosen' and that Ruttledge had been 'told about him.' A memo GB wrote showed that Frank's place in the team was far from secure:

> [I spoke to] Tom Longstaff. He told me Ruttledge had already determined to tell the Everest Committee that if he received any more silly letters from Smythe, he would not take Smythe with him. It would be good (so TL says) if R did so, for people are asking if he is strong enough with white men to keep the Expedition together.[4]

The Committee was further discomfited when the literary agent they employed, Leonard Moore (also Frank's agent) negotiated an offer of £3,000 for the official expedition book if it was written by Ruttledge — as the Committee wanted — but £4,000 if Frank wrote it. They chose Ruttledge. All members had to sign a contract agreeing not to write books or articles or give unauthorised lectures or broadcasts about the expedition for three years afterwards. Their photographs would become the property of the Committee. There was a minor flap when an article of Frank's about Everest appeared in the *Daily Mail* after the party had sailed for India. Then it was discovered he had submitted it before signing the contract and the *Mail* had waited until it was deemed more newsworthy before publishing.

During the preparations Frank's domestic life was complicated by two upheavals and a near-disaster. In August 1932 he and Kathleen moved to the recently developed Hampstead Garden Suburb. On 17 November Kath gave birth to their first child, my elder brother John, and three days after that Frank was involved in a car crash. He made light of the incident in his diary:

> My knees were damaged, but thank heaven nothing broken bar my nose cracked. Spent two weeks in Manchester Royal Infirmary just when I ought to have been helping Ruttledge — but well looked after. I remember recovering consciousness — got concussion and shock — stretching out each limb and saying to myself, Good! I can go to Everest.

But it was a potentially deadly accident. After lecturing near Bolton he was being given a lift by his host, William Humphrey when an oncoming car skidded on ice and collided with them head on. Both men were trapped and soaked in petrol. A crowd gathered, several people smoking. Two policemen appeared, but merely wrote details in their notebooks. Eventually an ambulance arrived and one of the officers travelled with them to hospital, but it was only at Frank's urgent request that he applied a tourniquet to control the bleeding from a severed artery in Humphrey's leg. Frank's lip was severely cut and he suffered from a spine injury that was not discovered at the time because no x-rays were taken, but would lead to trouble two years later.

After he had recovered the Everest Committee ordered a further medical examination. This he passed successfully, although his knees remained painful.

By the beginning of March the expedition had assembled at Darjeeling, and soon a huge procession of climbers, Sherpas and porters, wireless operators, ponies, together with a large number of mules carrying about 20 tons of baggage, set off on the long journey to the mountain.

The straight-line distance north-west from Darjeeling to the summit of Everest is 104 miles. A fairly direct approach lay through Nepal, but all the expeditions between the wars were denied access to that country so a circular route of nearly 300 miles to the north through Tibet was necessary — as and when that government gave permission. So Everest's northern flank was the only side available, and until the late 1940s it was the only part of the mountain known to offer a possible route. The historic march undertaken by the seven expeditions to Everest between 1921 and 1938 has become a part of British mountaineering folklore. In those 17 years things changed little. Each man faced the journey across one of the bleakest regions on earth. I've read half a dozen accounts of it in books, diaries, and letters and even in a memoir for grandchildren. My mind is crammed with images:

The humid, tropical paths of the Teesta valley in Sikkim leading uphill to cooler air and the Tibetan plateau. The colour, light and enormous views, with the Himalayas a sublime panorama in the south. The extremes of night frost, scorching sun, and the wind which blew into the eyes, nose, ears and mouth a mixture of fine red dust and the 'dried excrement of a thousand years of travellers across the high plateau.' The sore throats, sunburn, upset stomachs and diarrhoea. The accidents. In 1933 the postman Lobsang Tsering broke a collar bone falling from his pony, but when Raymond Greene administered chloroform prior to reducing the fracture his heart stopped. Two minutes later after the frantic Raymond had injected coramine directly into the organ, it beat again, and within an hour the cheerful Lobsang was smoking a cigarette. Frank had trouble with his pony too, twisting a knee while leading the frisky animal across a stream. The same knee had hurt since his car crash, but miraculously, after a stab of agony he was free of pain.

At each community fresh pack animals had to be hired for the next section and Ruttledge, dressed in his 'State Occasion' opera hat and Tibetan brocade coat entered negotiations with the governor, the Dzongpen, with interpreter Karma Paul at his side. The Europeans would remember the stopovers. Phari, reputed to be the filthiest place in Asia was beset with sewage discharge, dung heaps, foul smells, people with skins and clothes 'black with the dirt of ages,' who crowded round with 'horribly adjacent curiosity,' and dogs that howled all night. At Kampa Dzong the climbers were invited to tea and chang and a guided tour of the ancient building, perilous in nailed boots on slippery stone steps. Jack Longland demonstrated pole-vaulting and Bill Birnie organised a boxing tournament at Tenkye Dzong. The stunningly beautiful Shekar Dzong offered from its highest point a view of Everest, almost due south now, less than 50 miles away, its features forbiddingly clear under the banner of cloud streaming from the summit. At Shekar porters' boots and clothing were pilfered — by the yak drivers, it was assumed. Four of them were arrested and handed over to the Dzongpen, who ordered them to be thrashed unless, and until, they confessed. None did, and each man, after a hundred lashes on the bare buttocks with a rawhide whip, was declared innocent and released. Greene in his capacity of doctor witnessed the punishment and was astounded at the endurance of the suspects, who never even flinched. He concluded that one hundred pounds' worth of equipment — an incalculable fortune in Tibet — was considered by the thieves to be worth a bit of suffering.

The march gave Ruttledge a chance to assess his team. He now saw Frank as 'quiet and unassuming.' Frank however waited until he wrote *Camp Six* before expressing his real feelings about big expeditions:

These hordes of animals and hundreds of packing cases separated us from the simplicity of travel. I remembered a vow that one day I would travel in the Himalayas with the lightest and simplest of equipment; that I would be committed to no plan; that I would wander where I chose. Somehow this vast transport made Everest into a rather dull duty. The companionship of the camp-fire was absent and in its place was a rowdy mess-tent, which always reminded me of a Sunday-school treat. We had carried civilisation into the wilds, and civilisation is better left at home.[5]

The Gates of Altitude. Norton gave this evocative name to the portal of the Rongbuk valley, the last bit of the journey to Everest. Rising from the miles of desolate moraine on the valley floor and from the snowy wastes of the glacier beyond, the vast bulk of the world's highest mountain blocks the sky. The sight has stunned every visitor to the present day. It isn't the tallest mountainside in the world, you're starting from quite high up, but no other mountain has the same majesty. Those in Ruttledge's group who had already climbed high in the Himalayas could only shudder at the agonies of cold, lack of oxygen and exhaustion that awaited them.

The party visited the Rongbuk Monastery and received the blessing of the head Lama. 'He beamed upon us a welcoming smile,' wrote Frank. 'Humour, wisdom, kindliness, sympathy and understanding all shone in his large and mobile face.' Gifts were exchanged and the Abbot asked after the health of the 'General Sahib' — Charles Bruce who had been in charge in 1922. Then the blessings began, the porters first. 'When our turn came,' wrote Frank, 'for some reason my appearance provoked a roar of laughter from the Abbot. All of us had to say Om Mani Padme Hum, but he was not at all satisfied with my pronunciation of the prayer and made me repeat it several times.'

Climbing Everest from the north is straightforward. The normal route today is still virtually that attempted by the early expeditions. You walk up the valley and then up a gently sloping glacier, for about 14 miles, going from 17,000 feet to 21,000 feet. You continue up a 2,000-foot snow-slope to a saddle on a ridge, and follow this ridge, which is broad, rocky and quite easy, for about 2,500 feet — say the height of an English fellside — to a point about 3,500 feet below the summit. From here it's steeper, but still only a scramble. The view from the top is amazing.

I said straightforward, as in uncomplicated. I didn't mean easy, as Frank seemed to think. 'If we keep as fit as we are,' he wrote to Hugh Slingsby, 'Everest is doomed, barring of course the weather.'

And so the build-up began. Ruttledge was determined not to hurry it, to allow time for vital acclimatisation. Altitude sickness in its extreme form — pulmonary or cerebral oedema — is the body's potentially lethal production of excess fluid in the lungs or brain. In the 1930s little was known about this reaction and it was often diagnosed as pneumonia. In 1933 the porter Ondi collapsed and very nearly died after an early carry to Camp 1 at 17,700 feet. He pulled through with the aid of oxygen treatment, a tough constitution and evacuation down to Kharta. Frank, who was with him on Kangchenjunga and employed him on Kamet, lay awake in a nearby tent listening to him fighting for his life.

By a twist of fate, in these early days the upper part of the mountain was clear of snow and the weather sunny and calm — perfect conditions for climbing Everest. They had reached Rongbuk on 16 April, nearly two weeks earlier than in 1924. But there was no way they could speed their progress.

Over the weeks several of the party fell ill and some of the complaints were far from trivial. Raymond Greene later went too high too quickly and strained his heart. George Wood-Johnson developed a gastric ulcer that forced him down to the rest camp at Kharta, never to rejoin the action. Frank had a digestive weakness with frequent painful stomach upsets. At Shekar Dzong he was 'unwell with severe colitic pains and vomiting,' and on the mountain at Camp 1, 'we had curry for supper and it gave me hell.' At Camp 2, 'I had a very bad night as something I had eaten died a lingering and agonising death within me.' Kathleen said that during this period there were so many things he couldn't eat or drink mealtimes were minefields.

Shipton developed his own food fantasy; 'Oh for a few dozen eggs,' he would whisper hoarsely, until at last, at Base Camp his dream was realised — eggs, Tibetan eggs, were on the menu. They appeared one morning at breakfast, poached, and the party started to tuck in. Soon however there was an 'exclamation' and an egg was 'returned to a plate looking decidedly the worse for wear.' Shipton arriving late strode to the place recently vacated by its disgusted occupant. He looked down and rubbed his hands together, gloating over the mess on the plate before him. 'Eggs!' he whispered. 'Eggs! My favourite way too — scrambled!'

Camp 3 at the start of the steeper climbing was set up two weeks after leaving Base camp. It was situated in a wide glacial bowl below the 2,000 feet of slopes leading to the North Col. The mere equivalent of a British hillside now separated them from this pivotal point on Everest. There was no other route; all other parties before and almost all since have been obliged to use the North Col as a staging post on this side of the mountain.

But with blizzard after blizzard it took another two weeks to make progress. Frank's diary entry for 6 May, 'Another bloody day' made its way into his published account and has often been quoted. For the record though, he began 7 May with 'Yet another bloody day.'

The delay caused tensions. A letter Frank wrote to his mother suggests that his reluctance to get involved in arguments was being put to the test:

I made a resolution at the beginning of this show not to lose my temper. So far I've kept it. A bit hard sometimes, but even at high altitudes it takes two to make a quarrel, and the sense of gratification in not answering back because one knows the other fellow is merely feeling altitude is immense ... There's nothing worse than loss of control. One feels oneself simply boiling with rage over something absolutely trivial that would pass unnoticed at sea-level ... [6]

A higher camp was pitched nearer to the bottom of the North Col slopes, to save the energy of the climbers working on the route on the days they could get to it. The slopes began at an easy angle but steepened to about 60 degrees. The relatively safe 1924 route on the right-hand side was now threatened by séracs, but the slopes on the other side were too steep for porters at the top, so a way up the middle had to be found. This could be very dangerous, as the 1922 expedition had found when seven porters were swept to their deaths in an avalanche. The route was made awkward by a large crevasse running across the middle and a 40-foot ice wall above it.

At last on 12 May, a rare calm day, Frank and Shipton, supported by Wager and Longland with two porters, made the breakthrough. The ice wall provided almost the only technical climbing on the mountain, and Frank took the lead and tackled it. It was a fine effort, although he was ill-equipped by modern standards, lacking even crampons. A rope ladder donated by the Yorkshire Ramblers' Club was later rigged over this section to make it possible for porters and Frank and Shipton continued almost as far as the col where they found a large sheltered snow ledge where the next camp could be sited.

The expedition was now poised for the assault. Experience had shown that two more camps above the North Col would be needed, then climbers making the final attack on the summit would be on their own. The pairs selected by Ruttledge as being the fittest and most likely to succeed were Smythe and Shipton, and Wyn Harris and Greene. To make history perhaps, but to return safely it was devoutly hoped.

On 19 May a weather report brought the shocking news that the monsoon was early and could reach Everest in as little as 10 days' time. But for the moment there was an improvement. Clouds still trailed across the upper part of Everest but the glaciers below were bathed in sunshine. The wind dropped. 'We saw Kangchenjunga glowing above a level sea of cloud,' wrote Frank. 'Was it possible, faintly possible, that the weather was mending?'

It was. A window of opportunity like the fine spell they had enjoyed on arrival, was about to open. Crucially the upper rocks were clear of snow — the recent gales had seen to that. And for a little while a blessed calm would fall upon the mountain.

Next day Wyn Harris and the two army officers, Birnie and Boustead set off with 11 porters to pitch Camp 5. This needed to be 2,700 feet up the North Ridge. From there a single tent, Camp 6, would be placed as high as possible to give successive pairs of climbers the best chance of reaching the top.

For several hours the party moved up, tiny dots on the vastness of the ridge. Then to the mystification of the watchers below they stopped, paused a while and started down again. Eventually it became clear that they had simply dumped their loads a full thousand feet short of their objective before heading back to the North Col. They had retreated because Birnie, supported by Boustead, had decided the porters were endangered by the cold wind — a concept scoffed at by the porters themselves. There was a huge row, Ruttledge was furious, Wyn Harris went ballistic, but two precious days had been wasted, a delay later seen by Longland as the ruin of their 'one thin chance of success.'

On 22 May the same party with Wyn Harris as leader reascended the ridge, establishing the camp at the intended height, 25,700 feet. Greene, Longland and Wager went up too — three climbers who, with Wyn Harris would potentially be involved in operations higher up including a first summit attempt. However Greene retreated to the North Col with a strained heart and Longland returned with a sick porter.

And that was the end of the fine window. Next day, in the teeth of a rising gale Frank and Eric Shipton struggled up to Camp 5 as arranged, to find however that the existing occupants had been deterred from setting out to install Camp 6. One pair of climbers would have to go down to relieve the congestion. Frank wrote that Wyn Harris and Wager generously volunteered; Wyn Harris wrote that he and Wager were 'sent down by the senior party.' Whatever the truth it must have been a relief for them to escape from Camp 5, where things had been hellish since the previous night. They were due to get much worse.

The evening was settled and Frank was tempted outside to photograph the sunset until the extreme cold drove him into his sleeping bag. Then the wind rose again, blowing fine snow into the little tents, and the next day stayed foul, with the gale preventing any movement of the party. Of the second night Frank wrote:

The wind responded to nightfall by rising to a fury such as I have never before experienced in a tent. Three yards away was the edge of Everest's north-east precipice and the wind was blowing straight over it. Suddenly one guy tore loose. The side of the tent nearest to Eric billowed in. He endeavoured to press it back by lying against it with the whole weight of his body, but the fabric was held by the wind pressure as tightly as a football. It another guy went we might be blown, tent and all, over the precipice.

Somehow or other I extricated myself from my sleeping-bag and dragged on my windproof trousers, then went through the exhausting acrobatics of getting my windproof jacket over my head and shoulders. Lastly I pulled on my granite-like boots. I crawled out of the tent on hands and knees. A smother of snow was raging across the rocks, and through this I saw the errant guy. It had pulled away from two large stones which cannot have weighed less than one hundredweight but had been shifted bodily. I reattached and tightened it. I managed to find additional stones to reinforce the guy. Finally, exhausted by the effort, I struggled into the tent and flopped down on my sleeping-bag. After an hour or so I managed to restore circulation to my fingers, but my feet remained like marble slabs all night.[7]

In the morning the wind had dropped and there was talk of pressing on, of attempting to reach the summit from Camp 5, but common sense prevailed. They had taken a terrible battering; all the porters were frostbitten, two severely enough to lose parts of fingers eventually. The party went down.

Himalayan weather was and is, terrifyingly unpredictable. Modern forecasting has improved but sudden storms have resulted in many tragedies over the years. Infuriatingly, the day they came down from Camp 5, beaten and exhausted, was another of the days to be heading uphill. For throughout the next three days, while everybody ate, slept and recovered, the weather was perfect, even better than during the last window.

On 28 May, 12 fresh porters headed by Longland and Birnie together with the first assault pair, Wyn Harris and Wager, went up to Camp 5. Next morning, as before, Frank and Shipton followed, in the role of back-up pair to try for the summit. It was 20 years to the day before the mountain was successfully climbed. But the confidence of the victorious Hillary and Tenzing as they headed for the top on the far side of Everest would contrast starkly with Frank's grim mood:

We were both of us a stone or so down in weight and as a result more vulnerable to wind and cold, whilst, in my case, my frostbitten toes were hurting when I put my weight on them … Our throats were in poor shape … Eric was almost speechless, and it was obvious that his strength was being slowly worn down by the constant discomfort.

Then a ray of cheer:

There is no man with whom I climb better than Eric. In pace and rhythm he is the beau-ideal of a mountaineer. He flows rather than climbs uphill and it is an education to climb with him. There was never any need to halt, and height was gained as calmly and inevitably as a clock hand mounts to the hour.[8]

At Camp 5 in worsening weather they waited anxiously for the return of Longland with the eight porters who had carried up the equipment and provisions for Camp 6. They arrived at last, exhausted but pleased, having left Wyn Harris and Wager with the single tent pitched at 27,400 feet, the highest camp ever. But they were hit by a sudden blizzard during the descent, and Longland had been desperately anxious that he might have been heading too far east and down the steepening rocks of the north east face. The men were so tired that he knew he could never have persuaded them to retrace their tracks uphill. In the whirling snow, coming suddenly upon the Camp 5 tents was not just superb route-finding, it was cheating almost certain death. His achievement has long been regarded as one of the finest in mountaineering history.

Had I thought of asking Frank which was his worst camp ever I feel sure the answer would have been Camp 5 on Everest in 1933. I have drawn on his description of the session when their tent nearly blew away in the night. Now in his second spell at the unloved place he and Shipton decided their Meade tent was so poor they would move in with Birnie, a tight squeeze for three. Frank got no sleep. All was silent except for someone's Cheyne-Stokes breathing — the gasping at intervals — common among climbers at altitude and sometimes at lower levels among the dying.

He and Shipton set off for Camp 6 on a fine windless morning. Shipton was far from well and looked for chances to stop and rest. Eventually they reached the tent, pitched at over 27,000 feet on a narrow sloping ledge with its outer edge unsupported. They brewed tea, the pathetic little solid-fuel cooker producing only a single lukewarm cupful each after an hour.

The 1933 expedition, like its predecessors was undecided about the best route up the final part of Everest. An ascending traverse across the north face brought the climber onto shelving slabs, likened to the tiles on a roof, and then to the Great Couloir, a gully with steep walls around its head. This would have to be crossed or climbed in order to reach the easier ground of the final pyramid. It appeared much simpler to avoid all this traversing by heading directly up to the north-east ridge and following that to the summit pyramid. This ridge, which forms the left-hand skyline of the mountain when viewed from Rongbuk, rises gently and at first glance it looks a better proposition than a route across the face below. However when the early climbers trained their telescopes on it they were dismayed to see three distinct steps. The first and the third appeared to be quite small, but the second was formidable, probably a hundred feet high. Could it be climbed or bypassed easily? If not, the traverse was the only way.

Wyn Harris and Wager knew that this question had not been resolved in spite of three major efforts to reach the summit. In 1922 George Finch and Geoffrey Bruce had tried to follow the ridge but were forced onto the face and then turned back by the failure of Bruce's oxygen apparatus.* Two years later Edward Norton and Howard Somervell favoured the traverse on the face and Norton reached a record height in the Great Couloir before turning back through shortage of time and exhaustion. A few days later Mallory and Irvine famously disappeared while apparently making an attempt on the ridge.

So the first pair in 1933 was a reconnaissance party, with Ruttledge's blessing to go for the top if all went well. Finding no easy way to the ridge bypassing the second step they followed the traversing line Norton and Somervell had taken. There they found treacherous loose snow on steep slabs, no belays in the event of a slip, and with Wager becoming exhausted and time running short they turned back. Their attempt is often remembered for the fact that Wyn Harris discovered an ice axe, later identified as Irvine's. He brought it back and after advising Frank and Eric Shipton that their best bet would be Norton's traverse, took it with him in place of his own when he and Wager set off down.

---

*On all the expeditions to Everest between the wars supplementary oxygen was used for a summit attempt only by Finch and Bruce, and Mallory and Irvine. In the 1930s the Everest Committee and respective leaders decided against it other than for medical use. There was a confusing mixture of technical reasons given, together with ethical considerations. Frank was undecided about the use of oxygen, feeling that Everest could and ideally should be climbed without its help. However in his contributed chapter in Ruttledge's *Everest 1933* he agreed with Wyn Harris's proposal that oxygen should be used specifically for the difficult 300 feet above the Great Couloir on Norton's traverse. Then in 1942 when his Everest days were over he wrote, 'It may be expedient to climb Mount Everest with oxygen apparatus, but speaking personally I would prefer to fail on that mountain without oxygen than I would to climb it with oxygen.'

Frank and Eric Shipton ate a meagre supper of beef extract followed by a concoction of condensed milk and café-au-lait. Most of all they craved liquid for their sore and congested throats but this the 'wretched little cooker resolutely refused to produce.' Then they tried to get comfortable for the night on their sloping rocky shelf. The weather augured well, as Frank noted:

> The evening was calm, the calmest we had known above the North Col. The smooth, outward-dipping slabs glowed in the fast setting sun and, at an immense distance beneath, clouds concealed the valleys and lesser peaks. There was nothing to obstruct the tremendous prospect ...
>
> It was cold. Space, the air we breathed, the yellow rocks were deadly cold. There was something ultimate, passionless and eternal in this cold. It came to us as a single constant note from the depths of space; we stood on the very boundary of life and death.
>
> The night spread out of the east in a great flood, quenching the red sunlight in a single minute ...

He spent a moment looking at the night sky:

> I remember dimly an appalling wealth of stars, not pale and remote as they appear when viewed through the moisture-laden air of lower levels, but brilliant points of electric blue fire standing out almost stereoscopically. It was a sight an astronomer would have given much to see, and here were we lying in our sleeping-bags concerned only with the importance of keeping warm and comfortable.[9]

But comfortable they were not. Frank spent the night 'rolling onto Eric, and Eric spent the night being rolled on by me.' 'From sheer self-preservation,' Shipton wrote, 'I had to kick him with my knee or jab him with my elbow. I did not sleep at all and I do not think Smythe fared much better. Several hours before dawn we gave up and started to prepare for the climb.'

They had planned to start at 5.30 a.m. but before this it began to snow. Soon there was a rising blizzard. It was hopeless to think of starting, and for hours they lay in their sleeping-bags, occasionally discussing their situation. If they did manage to make a bid for the summit next day, Frank wondered, what would the snow conditions be like in the Great Couloir? And what about the monsoon? Any time now it could unleash snowfall for days on end. What then? They had food for three days, four at a pinch, but there was fuel for only another two days. They would try to descend, but the slabs of the yellow band would be lethal in deep snow.

Shipton worried about how long it was possible to live at 27,400 feet. Their physical deterioration must now be rapid. Would the danger be apparent? Or would they perhaps just die in their sleep? It was a 'dreary day,' he wrote with great understatement.

But Chomolungma, Goddess Mother of the World, seemed only to be teasing. In the late afternoon the wind dropped, the clouds lifted and through the little window at the back of the tent they saw the summit, 'ridiculously close,' wrote Shipton. ' … 1,600 feet … without the powder snow on the rocks, and at sea-level, one could climb it in an hour!'

After another wretched night they prepared to start on what seemed an almost hopeless quest to reach the summit. The sky was clear, but intense cold with a brisk wind forced them to delay until 6 a.m. when it suddenly fell to a lasting calm. They set off an hour later. They were dressed for the occasion, as Frank wrote:

I wore a Shetland vest, a thick flannel shirt, a heavy camel-hair sweater, six light Shetland pullovers, two pairs of long Shetland pants, a pair of flannel trousers, and over all a silk-lined 'Grenfell' windproof suit. A Shetland balaclava and another helmet of 'Grenfell' cloth protected my head, and my feet were encased in four pairs of Shetland socks and stockings. [I wore] a pair of woollen fingerless gloves inside a pair of South African lambskin gloves, also fingerless.[10]

Shipton felt about as suitably equipped for delicate rock climbing 'as a fully rigged deep-sea diver for dancing a tango.' Packed lunch consisted of slabs of Kendal Mint Cake stuffed into pockets and Frank had his pocket-sized Etui camera with him plus a length of light climbing line. The need to travel light precluded their carrying any bivouac gear — being caught by nightfall high on Everest was — and still is — not far from a death sentence.

They headed diagonally upwards towards the head of the Great Couloir, finding that the sandstone slabs had been swept clean of snow by the wind, but drifts had collected on ledges and in crevices and gullies. Frank felt on good form. 'Exercise was loosening my cramped and stiffened limbs, and I [felt] warm blood flowing vigorously in my veins.'

Unhappily though, Shipton felt 'as weak as a kitten.' The extra day at Camp 6, far from resting him, had drained him of strength. After a couple of hours, when they were immediately below the first step he called a halt, unable to go on.

There was a short discussion and it was agreed that Frank should continue on his own while Shipton would rest and either follow slowly or return to camp. Separating on a mountain is never a good idea, and Frank later came in for some criticism, but Ruttledge and his party had discussed the problem and agreed that providing a man could return safely on his own and was happy to do so, it was acceptable for his partner to carry on alone.

Shipton would be the only man to go on all four of the Everest expeditions of the 1930s. He would become involved in the post-war reconnaissance of the mountain's Nepal flank and very nearly become the leader of the expedition that was successful in 1953. Like Frank, he was a 'small expedition' man at heart and often regretted committing himself to Everest and the accompanying 'hullabaloo' and 'the risk of bedsores' from incarceration in tents. But the mountain was irresistible, as it was for Frank. Yet each man would never again get as high on it as he did that day.

Frank went on. He followed ledges that took him directly under the second step* — 'It looked utterly impregnable,' he wrote. Convinced that Norton's route offered the only chance of success, he moved along the slabs towards the Great Couloir, hugging the sheer wall on his left. Progress was slow but steady and eventually he saw the final pyramid appear. 'There came to me for the first time that day,' he recorded, 'a thrill of excitement and hope. I was going well now, better than when I had parted from Eric, and for a moment there seemed a chance of success.'

At this point he couldn't see into the bed of the Great Couloir but could inspect the wall around it. This was part of the black band of steeper rock above the easier-angled strata of the yellow band slabs. The black band formed the second step and continued horizontally westwards as a barrier across the north face of the mountain. It would have to be climbed somewhere to reach the final pyramid, but there was clearly no hope immediately above the Great Couloir. This area, which would otherwise have provided access to the ridge above the second step, was impossibly steep, 'like a sea cliff,' and overhanging in places. The only alternative was to find a way up beyond the couloir. Here a subsidiary couloir apparently provided a breech in the cliff, although a buttress dividing it from the Great Couloir would have to be climbed or traversed first.

I gazed at the buttress. It was considerably steeper than the rocks I was traversing, and snow filled every crack and was piled deeply on every sloping ledge.

---

*The crest of the ridge including the second step was the route taken by the first climbers to scale the mountain from this side, three members of a Chinese expedition in 1960. It is now the standard way up from Tibet, aided by a ladder the Chinese installed on the second step.

Was it climbable in such a condition? In the Alps perhaps, but not at 28,000 feet by a man nearing the limit of his strength. And the subsidiary couloir? Even supposing the traverse of the buttress proved practicable, what kind of snow should I find in this narrow cleft? Most likely unstable powder affording no certain footing and impeding every movement …

One thing alone gave me hope: once the subsidiary couloir had been climbed and the rock band passed there seemed every reason to suppose that the principal difficulties were behind. I could see the face of the final pyramid and it did not look difficult. There was a scree slope at the base of it and higher a slope of light-coloured boulders. Energy alone would be required to surmount it. Of course, it may hold its surprises, for Everest will remain a stubborn opponent to the last; but I feel confident that once the rock band is below, the change from difficult and dangerous climbing to safe and easy climbing will inspire the climber to outlast fatigue and altitude over the remaining 600 feet to the summit.

Soon Frank stood near the edge of the Great Couloir. It was about 40 feet wide and in angle 'fully 50 degrees.' Higher up it ended abruptly under the cliff of the rock band. Lower down it dropped out of sight in a pitch of unknown height, below which it widened out in a small hanging glacier, then fell steeply again towards the Rongbuk Glacier, 8,000 feet below. It was a 'savage place.'

To reach the snowy bed of the couloir he had to follow a ledge which bent round a steep little corner.

This ledge was comfortably wide until it came to the corner, then it narrowed until it was only a few inches broad. As far as the corner it was easy going, but to turn the corner I had to edge along, my face to the mountain, in a crab-like fashion. The rocks above projected awkwardly, but it was not a place that would have caused a second's hesitation on an Alpine climb. One step only was needed to take me round the corner. This step I funked. The balance was too critical. With arms spread-eagled above me I sought for steadying hand-holds. They were not essential; balance alone should have sufficed, but I felt I could not manage without them. I could find none; every wrinkle in the rocks sloped outwards. For a few moments I stood thus like a man crucified, while my heart bumped quickly and my lungs laboured for oxygen, and there flashed through my mind the possibility of a backward topple into the couloir — an interminable slide into belated oblivion.

Backing off he went down to an easier ledge that brought him into the couloir at last. The snow in it was firm, and a dozen steps hacked with the ice axe took him across to the bottom of the buttress. Here he saw that he would have to climb straight up for about fifty feet before traversing into the subsidiary couloir:

> Snow had accumulated deeply on the shelving ledges and it was the worst kind of snow, soft like flour, loose like granulated sugar … As I probed it with my axe, I knew at once that the game was up. So far the climbing had been more dangerous than difficult; now it was both difficult and dangerous, a fatal combination on Everest. The only thing I could do was to go as far as possible, always keeping one eye on the weather and the other on the strength I should need to retreat safely.
>
> The weather at all events was fair. In the shelter of the buttress there was not a breath of wind and the sun shone powerfully … It seemed to sap my strength and my resolution. I was a prisoner, struggling vainly to escape from a vast hollow enclosed by dungeon-like walls … The final pyramid was hidden; if only I were on it, away from this dismal place … The climber who wins across the slabs to the final pyramid must conquer a sickness of spirit as well as a weariness of body.

He floundered up for an hour, until a nerve-racking incident finally persuaded him to turn back:

> So slow and exhausting was the work of clearing the snow that I began to rely on feel alone. I realised full well the danger of this, and whenever possible used my ice-axe pick as an extra support by jamming it into cracks. This last precaution undoubtedly saved me from catastrophe. There was one steeply shelving slab deeply covered with soft snow into which I sank to the knees, but my first exploring foot discovered a knob beneath it. This seemed quite firm and, reaching up with my axe, I wedged the pick of it half an inch or so into a thin crack. Then, cautiously, I raised my other foot on to the knob, at the same time transferring my entire weight to my front foot. My rear foot was joining my front foot when the knob, without any warning, suddenly broke away. For an instant, both feet slid outwards, and my weight came on the ice axe; next moment I had recovered my footing and discovered another hold. It happened so quickly that my sluggish brain had no time to register a thrill of fear; I had acted purely instinctively and the incident was over almost before I knew it had occurred.

When as a young lad I read Frank's description of his ultimate struggle with Everest I became totally absorbed by it. I became unaware of my surroundings. Reality became suspended. The printed words on the page vanished. As though in a dream I was there with him, willing him to succeed. I too panted in the thin air and felt the powdery snow and icy rock freezing my hands. I sensed the terrifying void underneath. But I urged him on. Just a last effort and we would win through to the final pyramid!

Of course it was not to be. But his compelling description of that day has often reappeared in anthologies of mountain writing, and his solo climb is seen as an imperishable moment in Everest's history. His highest point was calculated as 28,200 feet, or about 8,600 metres — a mere 250 metres from the top, but an impossible gap to overcome under the circumstances of that time.

So often climbers find that the greatest dangers on Everest lie in the descent and Frank was to experience the truth of this. His return as far as Camp 6 went without problems, although there were two strange moments. During one halt he turned to offer a piece of mint cake to the 'companion' he felt had been with him all day and was shocked to find no one there. Others have had a similar experience in the hills and it could be attributed to strain and the mind playing tricks. Then came something far weirder. While resting again he saw two balloon-shaped objects floating in the sky over the north-east shoulder, pulsating 'as though they possessed some horrible quality of life.' They were 'bulbous in shape, and one possessed what looked like squat underdeveloped wings, whilst the other had a beak-like protuberance like the spout of a tea kettle.' He conducted mental and visual tests in an effort to prove that this was not a hallucination before the objects vanished behind drifting mist. Frank's tea kettles have aroused curiosity and occasionally ridicule ever since.

Shipton elected to go down that afternoon leaving the exhausted Frank as the sole, more comfortable occupant at Camp 6. Amazingly, on this third night he did not wake until seven next morning, having slept the clock round, a unique experience on the mountain at that height:

> I was greatly refreshed; as long as I lay without moving I felt almost as though I were at sea-level; my heart was beating slowly, steadily and rhythmically, and my brain was more active than it had been since leaving Camp 4. Perhaps I might be able to settle once and for all the vexed question of the second step before descending to Camp 4.

But then he discovered that the tent was full of snow from a blizzard the previous night, it was intensely cold, and one glance at the threatening weather and lack of provisions and fuel disabused him of this mad idea. He gathered his few possessions together and headed down without a backward glance at the forlorn little tent.

The previous afternoon Shipton had battled against a sudden gale and thick cloud on his descent, and now Frank was caught too. A 'fuzziness' in the west was followed by a wind blast of such strength he was forced to crawl, using his ice axe to prevent himself being blown off the mountain. His goggles iced up, driving snow lashed his face, and he could only see a yard or two. Luckily he was close to the crest of the north ridge and he was able to reach a sheltered ledge on the other side. Here he was completely protected from the wind that roared over the rocks above — he could even sense the warmth of the sun through the flying cloud. Circulation returned to his frozen hands, but his feet remained lifeless, and he was lucky to escape later with minor frost-bites on his toes. When the wind eased and the cloud cleared he got all the way down to the North Col camp without further trouble.

The episode was more traumatic than he was prepared to admit publicly. This is clear from a letter he wrote some months later to his mother, to whom he sometimes confided his darker thoughts:

> There was the problem all the time if we should get down from 6. If the weather had completely gone to bits we should have lived a few days getting weaker until our food gave out … But I think we should have tried to get down. Better to die on a mountainside than in a tent. It's not at all an unpleasant death. I know because I was near it descending from 6. I shall never forget that strange numbing weariness in my limbs, that staggering of a few yards, then legs just doubling up and collapsing, and then another great mental effort and a few more steps and the wind roaring and beating me with snow and nothing to be seen but a few yards of slabs. I know I relied on forces outside myself and it was something far greater than me that decided that my worthless existence should not end then.[11]

Frank was obsessed with Everest. He went twice more in that decade but 1933 would remain the high point of his climbing career, not just in altitude but also more subtly in youthful brio. Never again would life seem quite so uncomplicated and limitless. In 1938, just before heading for Everest for what turned out to be the last time, uncertainty and depression over his marriage caused him to voice privately that he 'would leave his bones on the mountain.'

He gave away his ice axe as a gesture that he had finished with Everest. Yet during and just after the Second World War he hadn't quite given up the idea of going back there. In a chapter of *The Mountain Vision* published in 1941 he relived the final part of the climb:

> I remember pausing, and when my lungs had ceased their laboured pumping, of hearing the loosened snow slide swishing down the precipice. And when that was done, of straining myself against an almost intolerable silence, as though to resist like Atlas the whole weight and power of the universe. Then of gazing up, up and over those terrible walls of overlapping slabs to that untrodden summit, a thousand feet, no, a thousand weary miles, above me, the piled-up yellow rocks heaped crag on crag and cliff on cliff, the plastered snow chalkily white in the glaring sun, the summit plume streaming with an endless enormous energy against the blue-black sky. I remember, too, the northward vision down the brown desolation of the Rongbuk valley with its shaley slopes and huddled moraines, past the speck of the Rongbuk Monastery and away over the golden plains of Tibet, where the wandering clouds were couched on their own shadows, to the blue distance where the earth bent over into the fastnesses of Central Asia.[12]

Seventeen

Down to Earth

Camp Six, Frank's account of the 1933 Everest expedition finished where the climbing had begun, at Base Camp: 'Perhaps one day we would tread again the stony path beneath the deep blue of the Tibetan sky and see that yellow pyramid with its white plume writing the endless message of the west wind.' It was an elegant rounding up, but his diary showed that the journey home was a bit more rough and ready:

26 Jun.   Jack's birthday so that evening we celebrated … two dozen bottles of champagne … Eric under the table was carried to bed … more and more boisterous … To bed under my own steam … What a horrid feeling when the bed slowly tilts up and one find oneself spinning into a bottomless abyss …

28 Jun.   Managed to get hurt today … A friendly sparring match with Tommy [Lieut. Thompson] … He let out with a fist and got me under the heart so that unexpectedly I went down for the count. A nasty bruise and ribs very sore …

3 Jul.   A tragedy has befallen us … Two boxes of biscuits were to have been left at the Rongbuk Monastery … The wrong boxes were left … One contains bottles of rum, which were to form the principal ingredients in a punch for my birthday …

9 Jul.   Unfortunately Willy [McLean] has been very rude to Hugh and Raymond … He talked like a madman … fictitious statements that they had tried to drug him late at night … he had hit Raymond and knocked out two of his teeth …

There was plenty more. His sleeping bag smelt like 'a fox's earth' and his frost-bitten big toes turned septic. Raymond Greene's box of zoological specimens, months of collecting, was stolen one night and not recovered despite threats by Karma Paul that the village would be reported to Lhasa, cursed by smallpox, or even bombed and burned. The porters got drunk and had a punch-up with the locals. A woman missionary rebuked the team for accepting an un-Christian blessing by the Abbot of Rongbuk — an 'evil spell' might have been cast on them; Crawford remarked that if Buddhism was capable of that there must be something in it.

Frank once wrote about the delights of Courmayeur after climbing Mont Blanc: 'The climber may fight his way down through a blizzard in the afternoon and spend the evening at his ease under the trees of an out-of-doors café listening to an orchestra. In such abrupt and pleasant contrasts lies one of the charms of mountaineering.' However his arrival home at the end of August at the trim Brunner Close in Hampstead may have been a contrast too far. A reception party was waiting — Kathleen, her mother, his mother, and a nanny with John, his active and noisy nine-month-old son.

His remedy for expedition blues was to go away again immediately, and within days he had pushed everything to one side and set off for Skye with Kath in his new Alvis car.

After his disastrous brush with motorcycles he had persevered for three years with the Austin Seven. Then on getting married he'd bought an old Riley saloon. This was noisy, badly-sprung and slow. 'When you lifted up the bonnet,' said Kathleen, 'it was just empty space with the engine in a corner.' They got rid of it when Frank decided he could afford a new car of decent quality. Alvis was a respected company that made cars with performance and finish well above average. He chose a Firefly sports four-seater, which he changed later for a drop-head coupé version of the same model. It cost just under £500 — equal to about £30,000 at the end of the century. A year later he would trade it in for a top of the range Alvis costing over twice as much.

Spending like this was at odds with his mother's thriftiness. She had worried about money ever since his father had died, although her inheritance had enabled her to live in good hotels at home and abroad in Austria and Switzerland during Frank's engineering training. However he never forgot the struggle to escape from uninspiring jobs. In a spare bedroom he kept a joke ashtray with a chicken on the rim and the inscription, *You Have to Scratch Damned Hard for a Living.*

Frank and motoring made for an uneasy partnership and from time to time he wrote about the follies of the open road. Once, when he had been driving slowly to run-in a new car, he was shocked when a woman held up behind shook her fist. He mused what her response to being held up by a party on a climb would have been:

> Would she shake her fist and hurl rude remarks? Of course not. It is the lust for speed or the germ of speed, or whatever negative quality is peculiar to speed, which turns a pleasant person into an unpleasant person.
>
>   When travelling it is impossible to be peaceful, for rapid motion, whether on land or through the air, is inimical of true peace. It is pleasant to arrive in the mountains after a rapid journey by rail and road. For a day or more the traveller has seen the countryside flash past him as a welter of fleeting and illusive impressions. There is something unreal about rapid transit from one place to another, except in the ultimate change of scene. He who girdles the world in a fast-moving aeroplane sees less than he who sits himself down in a quiet country place.[1]

Skye should have provided the perfect rest cure after Everest. Wonderful September weather laid a haze over the Cuillin, the ridge presenting a two-dimensional jagged skyline through long days of sunshine. They found ideal places to park up and camp and Frank took pictures of Kathleen doing camp chores and skimming stones on a river. Later, clad in capacious new breeches she was a foreground figure when they climbed Blaven. On the summit he balanced the camera on a rock to include himself. A jumble of gabbro blocks, the Elgol coastline disappearing into the misty Sound of Sleat, Kathleen, her pleased face shining, and Frank, still emaciated from Everest, gazing into the distance. Unable maybe to forget that mountain in Asia.

By the end of the century Everest had become a huge media-fuelled event, a mountain important to the economy of Nepal and China. It had been climbed by 15 different routes, the summit a trophy to be collected by hordes of guided clients paying huge sums to tackle it from both the north and the south. Balloons and powered hang gliders flew over the mountain. It was descended by ski, snowboard and paraglider. Records were set for the fastest ascent, and by the oldest, the youngest, and by people handicapped by various disabilities. The summit was camped on, stripped naked on, and a bright red Frisbee was flipped down the east face for the world's longest glide, adding incidentally to the mountain's accumulation of rubbish. Climbers from obscure countries were keen to be their nation's first citizen on top. There was an endless flow of books and articles, TV documentaries and lectures, and the list of successful summiteers topped a thousand. There was a downside of course. There were deaths from falls and exhaustion and in storms and avalanches. Survivors were mutilated by frostbite and corpses too difficult to retrieve lay exposed to view. There was a court case brought by the relatives of a victim who was thought to have been wronged by his guide. Some climbers who collapsed were left to die, walked past by others single-mindedly going for the summit. The public's interest was titillated, but ordinary mountaineers were disgusted. Newspaper columnists had a field day. The contrast between this latter-day circus and the situation between the wars could hardly be greater.

After 1933 there were debates on how Everest should be tackled next time. Longland admired the aggressive style of Bauer's team on Kangchenjunga and pushed for using oxygen, pitons and two camps above Camp 5. He believed Alpine safety margins were unachievable and that support parties cluttering up high camps were counter-productive since it would not be possible to rescue incapacitated climbers high up. He suggested that bivouacs or descents in darkness to camps lit by electric beacons should be allowed for, and that the future would see small private parties, not big expeditions.

Longstaff proposed that climbers should acclimatise fully up to 23,000 feet then make a quick summit dash, a technique that most climbers use now. He believed that Frank's climbing at high altitude in the previous three years had been a factor in his good performance on Everest.

General Bruce picked out Frank's 13 hours' unbroken sleep during his last night at Camp 6 as an astonishing achievement. He finished with the comment, 'A touch of sadness! The Lama of Rongbuk, the Tsouy Rimpache, the pure Lord, died this summer!' However in 1924, unknown to Bruce the Head Lama had spoken to each porter separately in his own tongue, instructing him to 'obey the Sahibs, but not so that they reach the summit, because this would be a bad omen for your families, for the monks here at Rongbuk, and for the local people.' Did the wily Head Lama tutor the porters similarly in 1933? We may never know since Ang Tsering, who had been on both expeditions, died shortly after revealing the secret of 1924 at the age of 98.[2] However if any such instructions had been given to Ruttledge's hired men they had ignored them.

Frank had plunged into post expedition agonising even before the party had reached Darjeeling, and sent a detailed analysis of events to Sir Francis Younghusband.

Younghusband was on the Everest Committee and had known Frank since writing a foreword for *Kamet Conquered*. A close friendship had developed. He had been the Committee's first chairman prior to the reconnaissance to the mountain in 1921, and although he relinquished the post a year later, he remained an Everest oracle. His connections with the mountain went back to the very beginning of hopes and plans to climb it. In 1893 at the age of 30 he had proposed an attempt with Bruce, but their military careers and political difficulties got in the way, even though Lord Curzon, Viceroy of India, was enthusiastic about the plan.

Younghusband had earned a reputation for boldness and endurance as a Guards officer during the 'Great Game' — the political manoeuvrings between Russia, China and British India for control of Tibet. He has been described as the last great imperialist adventurer. He was a geographer, map-maker, journalist and spy in Manchuria, the Pamirs, in Chitral, and across the Gobi desert. With little mountaineering experience he crossed the Mustagh Pass, a formidable glaciated obstacle, at one point hacking steps in an ice slope for his yaks with a pickaxe. As British Commissioner he led a 'mission' — an invasion — into Tibet in 1903, to compel respect for the British. The results were bloody but Younghusband was later acclaimed a hero, at one point riding unarmed into a fortified Tibetan camp and imposing demands by the force of his will alone. His secretary and interpreter, Frederick O'Connor remembered his small stature but quiet confident manner, his large walrus moustache, the simplicity of his wants and his disregard of discomfort and altitude.

In England Younghusband began a busy retirement. Patrick French in an introduction to his biography listed some of these activities. 'He began to preach free love to shocked Edwardians, and set up a strange patriotic movement during the First World War with *Jerusalem* as its specially composed rallying song. He wrote over 30 published books, founded numerous outlandish societies, attempted to start a new world religion and organised the first four expeditions up Mount Everest. He took cold baths at low temperatures, had great faith in the power of cosmic rays, and claimed there were extra-terrestrials with translucent flesh on a planet called Altair.'[3]

Stringing together selections like this is one way of catching a reader's attention. But French produced a well-researched and stylish account, quite an achievement considering there had been four unsuccessful attempts to write Younghusband's life. Two would-be authors had given up, one had died, and another had suffered a breakdown after 30 years of research.

Of the people Frank knew well Younghusband was one of the most complicated. In the last 30 years of his life he was devoted to a search for spiritual fulfilment, a quest inspired by a revelation on a hillside near Lhasa. Some of his ideas were bizarre but his letters show that he kept a grasp on reality. Because of his illustrious career, reviewers, readers and audiences usually took him seriously. He received many awards and honours. He became a mystic. He had complete faith in humans as a superior species. 'An eagle has even finer eyesight than a man possesses,' he wrote, 'and at will it can soar along the Himalayas and look down upon the most glorious forests and exquisite flowers and heavenly mountains. But it will see none of the beauty. The eye of the body is perfect, but it has no eye of the soul.'[4]

His soldierly skills gave him confidence, but he was aware of times when he fell short of his own high standards. At an outpost in Tibet he was woken in the night by shots being fired into his tent during a mass attack. He was led 'in a horrid fright' to a place of greater safety while his Indian soldiers managed to drive off the enemy, but he deeply regretted his own moment of cowardice. In contrast, when a horse drawing his carriage in Calcutta bolted he immediately climbed up front, seized the reins from the panicking driver, and hauled the animal to a standstill. He was equally proud of his quick-thinking at breakfast one morning when his hostess's curtains caught fire; he leapt onto a table and ripping them down scrunched them against his chest to stifle the flames before the woodwork could ignite.

He was an astute man with an agreeable sense of humour. He was probably the only person who could tease Arthur Hinks at the Royal Geographical Society. When Hinks proposed calling the long hall of the RGS the 'Ambulatory', Younghusband replied, 'If that is the Ambulatory, then you shall be known as the Perambulator.' Referring to Mallory in his inaugural speech as RGS President in 1920 he said, 'If I am asked what is the use of climbing this highest mountain, I reply, No use at all: no more use than kicking a football about, or dancing, or playing the piano, or writing a poem, or painting a picture.'

It's easy to see why he and Frank were drawn to one another. Both were adventurous at heart. Common ground, Tibet and the Himalayas, had provided each man with his greatest inspiration and demanded from him the greatest efforts. Neither man was religious except in a broad spiritual sense. Frank sensed that a power greater than anything man could imagine pervaded the universe; Younghusband's great desire was to unite people of different faiths in 'a spirit of fellowship through religion.' Perhaps if they had been

inclined towards a particular faith both men would have chosen Buddhism.
Both were intensely patriotic, true Empire believers deeply interested in India.
Each wrote and lectured about his experiences, and Frank wanted to climb
Mount Everest while Sir Francis wanted to see it climbed. There was plenty
to talk and argue about especially when the conversation turned to England's military adventures and the justification of going to war. Frank felt
comfortable with Younghusband, as he had felt with other paternal figures,
Roberts, Young, Bruce and Ruttledge. And Sir Francis was flattered by the
respect given him by the youthful and highly successful mountaineer.

Occasionally Frank visited Younghusband at his home, Currant Hill, a
rambling mansion at Westerham in Surrey. Sir Francis and his wife, Helen
both came from distinguished families. Their marriage was a failure — 'sad and
sexless' to use French's words — but Younghusband remained caring towards
his disgruntled wife and was deeply fond of his rather staid unmarried daughter,
Eileen. His letters to the latter show his mischievous side, and are full of digs
at the self-important people he met on his travels. Joining Younghusband and
his circle at Westerham was stimulating for Frank. And although he wouldn't
have admitted it, it was a handy escape from his own domestic surroundings,
with the noise, mess, trivia and other distractions of family life.

In November 1933 the Everest lectures began. Proceeds went to the Everest
coffers, apart from the speaker's expenses and the agency fee. Things did not
always run smoothly. Frank arranged to speak at a Yorkshire Ramblers'
meeting in Leeds two days before he was due to give an official lecture in that
city, and a complaint was made. He was incensed. 'I certainly do not intend
having my private affairs interfered with in this way,' he wrote to the Committee's Secretary Sydney Spencer, reminding him of the YRC's gift of caving
ladders that had been vital on the North Col slopes. However, mindful of
George Finch's 1922 excommunication after he had pocketed the proceeds of
unauthorised lectures in Europe, Frank admitted to a couple of other private
engagements that were 'honorary, save that my out of pocket expenses are paid.'

Shortly after Christmas Kathleen joined him for skiing in Austria. But it wasn't
a success: 'With K to St Anton. Minor runs for only a few days. Arlberg Pass
– Ulmer Hut, etc. Then to Innsbruck. Weather and conditions bad.'

He was restless. It was the New Year, 1934. It could be a long time before
another Everest expedition took place. The visit to Austria had been unproductive, but it triggered an idea. He told Gollancz that he intended to make

a ski journey from one end of Switzerland to the other, mountaineering where possible. He would employ the great Josef Knubel as his 'guide, philosopher and friend.' His aim was 'not merely to relate mountain adventures, but to describe the people of the villages, to impart a historical background, to bring in folklore and legends and the deeds of the past by the pioneers of mountaineering.' Gollancz, undeterred by the plodding image this evoked, offered a contract for a book. He warned however, 'Don't let Moore open his mouth too wide in the matter of the advance!'[5]

Frank was influenced by a boyhood hero, Sir Martin Conway, who in 1894 with a team of guides and porters made the journey that inspired his classic book, *The Alps from End to End*. He was enthralled by the adventurous life led by the Victorian pioneer whom he had met four years earlier at a dinner before Kangchenjunga. Conway had climbed Aconcagua in the Andes, explored Spitzbergen, and reached record heights in the Karakoram with Bruce. He'd won the prestigious Founder's Medal of the RGS. He'd written Alpine guide books with Coolidge. At 45 he publicly retired with an ascent of the Breithorn with his daughter but had quietly gone on climbing ever since. At 77 he was still in robust health.

What appealed to Frank was Conway's approach, which mirrored his own. Conway was a wanderer. If possible he never slept two nights in the same place. He hated centres, crowds and tourism. He was interested in meteorology, he preferred snow and ice climbing, and he enjoyed equipment innovations — in 1892 in the Himalayas he was probably the first to use crampons outside Europe. He was a keen photographer. And significantly for Frank, Conway's writing had a lyrical touch.

He pinpointed little details in the daily trivia of travel. After his boots had been burnt by drying too close to a fire he went to a village, found a cobbler, and left one of his men to watch that the repair was done properly. 'From the inn I despatched a litre of wine to the pair to take the place of conversation,' he noted dryly.

He recorded being lectured to at a hut by a 'delightful' German gentleman — a homily that must have had Frank nodding in approval:

'You young fellows,' said the German, 'are always in too much of a hurry. Why don't you spend the night here like me? You can't see the view properly because of the clouds on the tops of the peaks. Wait here till you do see it and then move on. You have no time, you say, and have more mountains you want to climb. I tell you that is a nonsense. You appear to be a free man; I am a slave, I have only 10 more days' leave, but I mean to spend them well and not to race around, passing beautiful scenes without seeing them. Climb fewer mountains, but see those you do climb. Getting to the top of peaks is not everything or indeed anything. The enjoyment of beauty is the sole excuse for your travel. But I see you won't take my advice. Wisdom only comes with age.'[6]

Frank began his journey at the end of March. He decided not to employ Knubel or any other guide, 'because the inconsequences and indecisions of travel could be indulged in to the heart's desire.'

He sent details of his progress to Gollancz. He had run into Swiss army manoeuvres and 'damned nearly got killed by a machine gun.' He was now writing from 'this charming little place [Elm] which was wiped out about 40 years ago by a mountain fall.' He was optimistic but cautious. 'It's going well and I've written up about 20,000 words already, and the four dozen photos I've developed include some of the best I've ever taken. [But] it's one thing to sign a contract saying you will do Switzerland from end to end and another to carry it out in the teeth of the weather Gods.'

Heavy snowfall obliged him to avoid the Bernese Oberland, the planned centrepiece of the trip. His predicament was that the risks he had to avoid as a solo skier were the things that interested a reader most. Only once was he caught out, and it was nearly fatal. On the way to the Hüfi Hut near the Clariden pass a sudden Föhn wind turned the slope he was crossing into a soggy mess. It avalanched when he was within yards of the hut, so nearly sweeping him away that a ski he was carrying smashed painfully into his thigh as he scrambled to safety. All that afternoon from the sanctuary of the hut terrace he relished the sight of thousands of tons of snow crashing down all around. It made a good story.

An Alpine Journey was a bizarre mix of sights, sounds, smells and events. The German in the hut with such a weight of belongings that two guides were needed to carry everything. The *blodsinnige* — an idiot — who pestered Frank on a bus, and was later replaced by a 'peasant woman dressed in black and smelling of cheese and mothballs.' The extra charge in a hotel for 'Sport and Musique' that so annoyed him that Gollancz's libel lawyer had to adjudicate on his manuscript. Dignified stationmasters, hard wooden train seats. The cut of Swiss clothes and the sadness of their night life. The omelette that never was after Frank's hotel proprietor hard-boiled the eggs she supplied him for his hut supper. 'She meant well,' wrote Frank, after hurling the offending humpty dumptys into the forest on heating his frying pan to no purpose. 'Let that be her epitaph: *She meant well.*' Then there was the bouncing boulder that seemed set to smash his skis stashed at the bottom of a slope, but thudded into the snow exactly between them. And the German joker who asked two heavily-loaded English climbers, 'Wünchen Sie ein Esel?' (Do you want a donkey?) and got the reply, 'Ja! Kommen Sie mit!' And Frank's poke at 'downhill only' skiers, goading Arnold Lunn afresh. And at the end of the trip a monologue on boredom and loneliness: 'I was simply tired of myself, tired of thoughts that had no outlet through the medium of speech, and tired of my own ridiculous little problems — problems which only loom large to a lonely man. I was becoming morbid, egotistical and idle. A good hearty kick would have done me a world of good.'

It was the last book of Frank's Gollancz published. He sang best for Victor as a Himalayan hero, not as a ski-tourist, however eccentric. And if the next thing Frank planned was a companion volume on Austria, it wouldn't be he who published it.

Gollancz's daughter, Livia who took over the business in 1967 remembered her father's excitement when *Kangchenjunga* was published. She suggested there may also have been a problem over royalties. 'He was doing all the interesting stuff then. He published just about every interesting writer between 1928 and 1934. He published their first books, but then he refused to pay them more, so their agents took them away elsewhere for their later books. He would not pay advances, money up front, in excess of what he felt sure they would earn. He had strong views on that.'

Gollancz had advanced £1,000 for *Kangchenjunga*, £750 for *Kamet*, and, with waning confidence perhaps, £500 for *Alpine Journey*. And yet Frank's subsequent publisher, Hodder & Stoughton who published 11 of his books during the last 15 years of his life, were no more indulgent over the advances they paid. They matched the £750 four times, but usually it was £500 and sometimes less. And the structure of royalty percentages was pretty much the same with both publishers.

Money seemed not to have played a part in diverting Frank to Hodder. Had he become tired of keeping to Gollancz's tight deadlines? Hodder's contracts showed that they were also strict taskmasters. Had there been a personal rift? Surviving correspondence with Gollancz shows nothing of this sort although the two men had little in common other than eagerness for commercial success.

Very little of Hodder's records and correspondence had survived the World War Two blitz of their Warwick Square premises in 1940. However Paul Hodder-Williams, a former chairman of the company, living in quiet retirement at the age of 91, shed some light on Frank's relationship with the company when I contacted him:

> In those early years from 1934 to 1939, when I was just a small part of the production department I had nothing whatever to do with authors. Even my uncles Percy and Ralph Hodder-Williams were kept distant from authors by their literary agents, who thought that too much friendship between author and publisher reduced their bargaining power when it came to money and contracts.
>
> Nevertheless I do remember that my uncle Percy, who was an old-fashioned Christian gentleman and very sensitive to what he called 'righteous work' (which did not mean holy or religious, but 'genuine' and 'from the heart') was very proud to be Frank Smythe's publisher. His courage and skill on a mountain coupled with his 'spiritual' sensibilities was a combination that the general public responded to too and therefore such an author's books would sell well — which is what a publisher always hopes for. In that sense Frank Smythe was one of our favourite authors. I shared in our enthusiasm for all his books. And we were proud to be his publisher. Certainly I was.[7]

Righteous work. Somehow the expression fitted Frank's aspirations, although he might have thought the term a touch pretentious. He was accused of many sins as a writer. Overwriting himself, an over-zealous eye for the money he could make, excessively colourful descriptions or 'purple passages,' and climbing solely in order to write about it. Raymond Greene told me in a friendly, well-meaning way, 'Frank was always trying to be 'literary' and somehow never brought it off because he was trying too hard, God bless him!'

The spiritual if not the Christian ethos generated by Percy Hodder-Williams would have appealed to Frank. And while no correspondence survives to prove it, he must have been in direct touch with his new publisher, as he was with Victor Gollancz and later with Jack Newth at A & C Black. He would never have tolerated obstruction by Leonard Moore. 'Uncle Percy' had joined the firm in 1896. He was a generation older than Frank, and probably appealed to him as a steadfast figure compared with the impulsive contemporary Gollancz. Frank must have seen Hodder & Stoughton, 66 years in the business, as highly respected publishers. They were soon to publish Ruttledge's *Everest 1933*, a weighty tome including Frank's chapter on his final assault and 60 photographs plus maps and diagrams. That was another thing. Livia Gollancz had told me that her father 'resisted' illustrations — he preferred words to pictures. Frank, on the other hand, had become fascinated by mountain photography and it would play a big part in his career.

It was a defining moment in his life as a writer. So far he had built a reputation with his climbing and skiing stories, in the British hills, in the Alps, and on major expeditions to the highest peaks on earth. This would continue with Hodder, but with an added philosophical perspective, a greater effort still to capture the immensity of the mountain experience.

EIGHTEEN

Unsettled

There were two more trips to the Alps for Frank in 1934. Before the first of these however there was a minor interruption, the birth in late July of his second child, which happened to be me.

The family album has a handful of snaps. Frank is holding me doubtfully, the ash of his cigarette drooping over my face; he's happier playing tennis with John in another part of the garden. Then I'm sharing a pram with John, who doesn't look too pleased either; he told me recently he was subsequently stopped from braining me with a cricket bat. At my christening in October I'm wrapped in a long white shawl in the middle of a group standing in front of Frank's latest car, an Alvis Speed 20. It's a bit rich that this picture, the only one I could find of the jewel in his motoring crown, was spoilt by me and my supporters.

On 18 August Frank escaped to the Alps. His plans were vague — something on Mont Blanc perhaps. But the old inspiration was missing. He arrived a week late, joined up with Macphee and Parry, and they climbed Monte Rosa by the ordinary route. Even this was too much. He had no acclimatisation left over from Everest and was dreadfully sick in the Margherita Hut. Then the weather closed in, and they were back in Zermatt. Undeterred, they headed for the Italian Ridge on the Matterhorn. After a night in the overcrowded Carrel Hut they set off late, got caught by bad weather near the summit, and were obliged to shelter in the Solvay refuge cabin below the Shoulder on the Swiss route. Marooned here, with all the emergency rations eaten by casual visitors and heavy snowfall preventing escape, Frank described their plight:

> We reviewed our resources of food … We had been disgusted to find numerous bread crusts scattered about. These crusts were now valuable. Some were

months, even years old ... Then, on the floor in a dusty corner I discovered a piece of bacon, rectangular in shape, black in colour, of age unknown, and of size as large as the upper joint of a man's thumb. This would flavour soup. Then there was a piece of butter, only slightly rancid. This would thicken soup. Lastly, we came on a slab of blackened and withered meat green with age. This, we decided unanimously, would make a perfect emergency ration ...[1]

Luckily they were able to descend on the third day, leaving Frank's emergency ration for the next stranded party. And after a few minor climbs they headed back to England. It was an Alpine 'season' to forget, but it wasn't quite over. A grim experience awaited him, one that would remind him that while mountaineering has the potential to inspire and delight, it also has profoundly dark moments.

On 18 September he was telephoned late at night by Geoffrey Young. Two Oxford University undergraduates, John Hoyland and Paul Wand had disappeared in the Mont Blanc range; could he fly to Geneva in the morning and organise a search party? Within a few hours he had joined Hoyland's parents at Croydon airport and they arrived that night in Chamonix. Meanwhile Paul Wand's guardian, Dr Wiggins had reached the Alps and on being told that the missing pair had last been seen at the Gamba Hut on the Italian side of Mont Blanc, had gone to Courmayeur. Frank and Hoyland's father joined him there.

The story slowly revealed itself. A month earlier the two students had left their tent near the Montenvers above Chamonix and crossed the Col de Géant, staying the night at the Torino Hut before descending to Courmayeur. They had eventually reached the Gamba Hut the following night at 10 p.m. on 23 August. Witnesses said they were very heavily laden. Next morning, they made a late start, having written in the hut book that they intended to climb the Innominata, a difficult and demanding route between the Brouillard and Péterét Ridges. That evening a blizzard had set in and the hut keeper expected them to return. They did not, but the fact that they had been at the hut did not emerge for some time after they had been reported missing, and only then did investigations become focussed on Mont Blanc.

At Courmayeur Frank hired Adolphe Rey, a highly experienced guide who had taken part in the first ascent of the Innominata in 1919, and they set off with a few picked men to the Gamba. On arrival they met two guides engaged by Dr Wiggins who told them that much fresh snow had fallen and in their opinion it was 'hopeless to search.' Nevertheless Frank retained one of these guides together with Rey and one of his men, sent all the others down, and early next morning, 22 September set off with Rey and the other two for the Col du Frêney. It was a hunch that paid off, if only to discover a tragedy.

Not far above the col Rey spotted the tip of an ice axe pick projecting from the snow. It proved to be the place where one of the victims had slipped, dragging the other with him down a steep couloir leading to the Frêney Glacier, 2,000 feet below. Rey led the descent of this, and soon they were seeing and collecting pieces of clothing and equipment shed in the fall. At the bottom of the couloir Rey cut steps at great speed across an exposed avalanche groove where cascades of rocks were frequently falling. The bodies of the two young men were then found on the glacier with injuries which had killed them outright. A team was organised to carry them down to Courmayeur and after a service attended by many sympathetic local people they were buried in the cemetery.

John Hoyland, although only 19, had exceptional climbing talent. In Wales he had made the second ascent of Longland's on Clogwyn d'ur Arddu and other very hard routes. Young had invited him to join the elite at his Pen-y-Pass gathering the previous April. That summer — his first visit to the Alps — he had stormed up the demanding Mer de Glace Face of the Grépon before heading with Paul Wand for the Innominata. Jack Longland doubted if there had been 'any young English climber since George Mallory of whom it seemed safe to expect so much.' But Longland took the traditional view about experience. 'I encouraged John to go out to the Alps,' he told Young. 'His party when I first heard of it was to include people more experienced and cautious than himself ... But he seems to have got bored, or over-excited, and run off on his own, and shed the deadweights, as I suppose he thought they were. After that it's just a miserable story ... tired boys ... the too-heavy packs ... the pushing off in poor weather ... '[2] The deaths caused head-shaking among elders of the Alpine Club, and the situation was complicated by the fact that Hoyland came from a renowned mountaineering family; he was a great nephew of Howard Somervell who had distinguished himself on Everest in the 1920s.

Frank shared the mood of sadness and disapproval. He wrote to *The Times*.[3] He recounted the story of the accident in one of his books.[4] Privately though, he knew there had been uncomfortable similarities in his own climbing noviciate to Hoyland's, with some very close calls in the Alps. And many years later Kathleen told me that seeing the dreadful results on a body of a

2,000-foot fall down a rocky mountainside had deeply shaken him. Perhaps the last words should come from his own writing in which he came to a somewhat enigmatic conclusion:

> It is so easy to preach, so easy to lament the accidents that must happen now and then as the result of 'young fools' not taking guides. Youth must climb mountains and it must take risks, not ridiculous risks, but those risks inseparable from the acquiring of experience. Mountaineering would hardly be worthwhile otherwise. Mountains are kindly disposed towards youth; in that way they are like the sea. They condone ignorance if the spirit is right, but on intemperate recklessness they exact a swift penalty.[5]

'Three months bed rest.' This was the prescription handed out to Frank by his doctor in the final weeks of 1934. His digestive problems now plagued him more than ever and the stomach ulcer was blamed. There seemed no way he could follow such drastic advice, but when he began to get severe headaches and boils he became desperate. By chance a friend from the Alpine Club, whose identity Frank never revealed, told him that during a séance with a spiritualist he learnt that Frank had 'three spinal displacements' and was advised to go to an osteopath called MacKenzie who worked near Regent's Park. Ready to snatch at any straw Frank made an appointment. The diagnosis was correct — obviously the injury stemmed from his car accident two years earlier — and MacKenzie's first manipulation completely eliminated the headaches, with the stomach trouble clearing a few months later.

Frank had regarded spiritualism as quackery, but now he was curious. His climbing friend told him that the medium had claimed to be in touch with a seventeenth-century mystic and poet called Shah Abdul Latif. Frank decided to make an appointment with the spiritualist to 'talk to' Abdul Latif, and later he described the extraordinary events at that time:

> The evening before [the séance] I was seated by the fire with my small son on my knee when I noticed that his eyes were fixed intently on something there. Then he said, 'Nice man, daddy; nice man.' I had then the most extraordinary feeling that someone was in the room. The medium knew nothing of this, and you may imagine my astonishment when (next day) the medium having gone into a trance, the first words that issued from her lips were, 'Your small son has already seen me'.
>
> I then had a most interesting conversation, which told me so many things about myself that only I knew that I must confess that the theory that I had long

clung to, that spiritualism is thought-reading, broke down. During this conversation Abdul Latif said that it was quite unnecessary for me to talk to him through a medium, as I was naturally receptive and could communicate with him through my own mind. I determined to try this in the form of automatic writing, and a most astonishing series of communications came through. I wrote at the rate of 3,000 words an hour, and from beginning to end these communications, which were deeply learned and philosophical, and the work of an obvious scholar, were couched in the most beautiful English, which I could not do myself, yet with a curious Eastern phraseology, which again is quite beyond me. In one communication he wrote: 'At this moment a religious procession, accompanied by music, is passing through the streets of Baghdad'. Something made me open *The Times* next morning at the foreign news page, and my eye was drawn irresistibly to a column dealing with a religious festival and procession through the streets of Baghdad. I found, however, that so much force seemed to go out of me during this work that my ordinary work would obviously suffer, and maybe my health. I decided, therefore, and very reluctantly, to abandon this gift of mine, as I have a family to provide for, and such work, if taken seriously, and scientifically, as it should be, is a whole-time job. But I often wonder if I was right.[6]

This detailed description by Frank of his brush with spiritualism is part of a long letter he wrote some three years later to a sufferer of severe migraines who had been put in touch with him. He explained how the osteopath, MacKenzie diagnosed his old injury and manipulated his spine. He wrote candidly about how spiritualism had provided the vital link. But he finished with the request that what he had written would be regarded in the strictest confidence. He had no wish to 'parade his experiences.'

Unfortunately none of Frank's automatic writing has survived. He was never temped to revive his contact with Abdul Latif. It also transpired that the migraine sufferer unfortunately obtained no benefit from his treatment by MacKenzie.

Throughout 1934 it was assumed that permission for another Everest expedition would not be granted for many years. In May the Everest Committee had been reconstituted with a new Chairman, Sir Percy Cox, and devoted itself to analysing what had gone wrong in 1933. Statements were taken, including one from Frank on 5 November. But hugely frustrated by the situation he devised a secret plan, which I came across by chance at the back of a diary:

EXPEDITION 1935

First conceived on November 11th. My idea is to make another attempt on Everest. I had lunch with Leonard Moore at the Devonshire Club on 12th and confided in him — he will be necessary to run things this end. I rely on him absolutely. He calls it 'the Stunt' and thus it must remain — hateful word. I have been seriously wondering whether or not to take Eric into my confidence, but incline towards a solo effort. It's not really a solo effort at all. I don't think anyone realises what the Sherpa can do. I consider an attempt made with them is as safe as an attempt made with Swiss guides. I'm very opposed to big elaborate expeditions, though in the way Everest is run at present they are necessary. I don't think it will ever be climbed with two camps and a rush above N. Col. My idea is to cross pass at head of Lhonak with about 15 men [and] Karma Paul (shall take him and men into my confidence when we get to Lhonak) then via Tashirak to Arun. Avoiding Dzongpen at Kharta around Kharma Valley, cross pass to Kharta (1921 route) and cross Lhakpa La to Camp 3. Send some men back possibly with Karma [Paul] to Kharta for more coolie food. Go on with 10 men. Establish Camp 4 — hope we may find Arctic tents and food. It may be possible to dig down to them. Then on to Camp 5 with every available man. Send four back, retain six. On with six men. Establish Camp 6 under Yellow Band. Keep three men — sending three men down under charge of veteran. Then with three men put [Camp] 7 as high as possible — on face of final pyramid, roping up bad bit. Will leave men, go on and try for top same day if going well and plenty of time.[7]

This was followed by five pages of calculations for food, fuel, cooking gear, tents and equipment required.

It was an alarming indication of Frank's desire to climb the mountain at almost any cost. Had he put the plan into action and managed to avoid finishing up in a Tibetan jail (or worse) and had he against all the odds got to the top and down again in one piece, the accompanying notoriety and political explosion would surely have ruined him. But the plot was overtaken by events. Unexpectedly, in early March 1935 the Everest Committee was informed that another expedition had been authorised. Charles Bell, English diplomat supreme in Lhasa had worked a miracle. It was too late to mount a full-size attempt in 1935 but the Tibetans agreed to a reconnaissance that summer, followed by the main expedition in 1936. The good news however, marked the beginning of an administrative nightmare.

A year previously Hugh Ruttledge had resigned from the leadership of any future Everest expedition. Put simply, the young guns of 1933, meaning Longland, Wager and Brocklebank, had wanted a new leader, a climber who led from the front, and had chosen Ferdie Crawford. As it happened, the old brigade, consisting of Frank, Wyn Harris and Shipton preferred to keep Ruttledge, and the reasonable Ruttledge, in the face of this deep division had stood down. And now the Everest Committee, out of courtesy, offered him the leadership again. They assumed he would refuse, but he promptly accepted. The anti-Ruttledge group then became openly hostile, and he resigned again. The Committee, now desperate for a resolution but basically not wanting Crawford, offered the leadership in quick succession to no fewer than seven other men — Norton, Geoffrey Bruce (General Bruce's nephew), Major-General Wilson (a friend of Ruttledge), Kenneth Mason, Strutt, Longstaff and John Morris from the 1921 expedition. All refused or set unacceptable terms. Finally at a meeting on 28 March the six uninvolved members of the Committee were asked to choose between Crawford and Ruttledge. The split was even and the Chairman, Sir Percy Cox made his casting vote — for Hugh Ruttledge.

Meanwhile Shipton had been appointed to lead the reconnaissance and take with him a group of six climbers, most of them candidates for 1936. Organised very quickly, it was to be a low-budget session of exploring and surveying in the Everest region — and they sailed for Bombay on 2 May. The party included Bill Tilman who had accompanied Shipton to the Garhwal the previous year on the first Himalayan trip to be made by this redoubtable pair.

Frank was given the less glamorous task of assessing a few more Everest possibles in the Zermatt area that August, and in the weeks before that he intended to make another traverse of the Alps, and hope to gather material for a new book. First though, in early June he had to deal with another of those disruptions most of us endure at intervals — moving house.

The previous autumn he had bought a plot of land in the Surrey hills between Guildford and Dorking. He'd longed to escape from town life, and the weekend tramp with Hugh Slingsby before the RAF sent him to Egypt had shown him a fine area to settle. The house was built at over 500 feet on Abinger common with magnificent views to the South, and its accompanying one and a half acres sloped down towards a part of the surrounding forest called Tenningshook Wood. No other properties existed at that time on the bracken-clad common, but a track in front of the house linked with an overgrown lane that plunged down in a couple of miles to the valley and the main road to Dorking.

Privacy was complete, but there was quick access to civilisation.

As with all new houses there were glitches when Tenningshook was built. When you sat on the upstairs balconies the parapet wall was too high to see over. The architect managed to design the larder to face south. The decorators painted the fine front door with pink primer and then said, 'Oh sorry, didn't know you wanted it left oak.' John drank from a tin of cream paint left open in the garage — luckily grandmother Mollie, a trained nurse knew what to do. ('I think I've been brain-damaged with the lead ever since,' he said). Frank, in his passion for fresh air insisted that all windows should open — small, metal casement windows, more than 60 of them, the draughts in winter must have been memorable. He built a model Mount Everest in clay on the terrace, but the resident moles thwarted all efforts to make a lawn. 'We were having breakfast one morning,' John remembered, 'and father came in, triumphantly holding up a trap with this mole in it, all earthy and filthy, and saying, "GOT ONE!" And I thought, Oh no … *Poor* mole!'

There were jollier moments too. Father Christmas walked into the sitting room, stayed a little while, then went out chuckling 'Ho-Ho-Ho' from his big white beard. Shortly followed, said John, by Frank coming in and amid the excitement telling everybody that No, he hadn't seen Father Christmas, but he *thought* he saw something 'fly over the moon.' When Frank came back from an expedition he had a smelly, prickly, gingery beard. Jim Bell stayed on his way to the Alps bringing a magic sixpence that sprang in the air, and Kathleen made him a big bowl of porridge for breakfast, watching nervously as he ate. When the bowl was empty he pushed it forwards without a word to be refilled — what a tribute. Frank brought us a train set that we weren't allowed to touch, to begin with, anyway. 'Typical father/son train set stuff!' said John. 'Frank was thrilled to have his train set!'

At the end of June Frank flew to Zurich to begin a month-long traverse of the Austrian Alps.

He had two objectives, both nicely interdependent. He wanted to gather material for a book, and he needed to achieve good climbing fitness ready for the job Ruttledge had set him in August — assessing the Everest candidates.

Like his Swiss journey the previous year he started near Bludenz in the Tyrol, but now he would be heading in the opposite direction, eastwards. And this time he had company — Campbell Secord, aged 22, a lean and energetic Canadian with an impressive climbing record in the Rockies. Secord viewed Austria's comfortable huts and restaurant service with amused contempt and had a disconcerting preference for steep strenuous rock when easier ways beckoned. One consolation for Frank was his own quick improvement in form helping him keep up with his youthful partner. 'We took life easily,' he wrote disingenuously, 'but on occasion climbed 10,000 feet in a day.' There were lively moments. Secord was lucky to survive when he happened to be testing a long cable for harmonic movements at the moment a lightning bolt struck it. Italian soldiers sent a burst of machine-gun fire in their direction on the frontier ridge. They saw a large guided party on the Gross Venediger stop for breakfast on a snow bridge over an enormous crevasse. And Secord won a battle with a bossy woman over whether a hut bunkroom window should remain open.

When Frank arrived in Zermatt he was holding a poisoned chalice, and he knew it. Ruttledge had decided there would be 12 in the 1936 Everest team, four fewer than in 1933. This would include a transport officer, two doctors, and a wireless officer. Excluding the leader this left seven climbers' places, of which four had already been filled — by Frank, Eric Shipton, Wyn Harris and John Hunt. Hunt, ultimately the leader of the successful Everest expedition in 1953 had gained fine Himalayan experience while serving with the army in India and was a certainty for the 1936 team. Finally Shipton was likely to recommend at least two climbers from his reconnaissance group, leaving just one place to be filled from the *nine* climbers (including Secord) Frank assessed. Later this became two when Hunt was rejected after the Medical Board judged — incorrectly — he had a heart problem.

Frank chose a mix of climbs on rock and snow. He climbed with up to four at a time; those not involved climbed together elsewhere. Bad weather intervened during the two weeks. Not everyone was there all the time. By the end he had decided that just one man stood out — Peter Oliver, aged 26 and like Hunt a serving officer in the Indian Army, with Himalayan experience. Ten years later Frank had the sad task of writing Oliver's obituary when he was killed in Burma in the Second World War. Even taking into account the limited value of obituaries, an extract strongly suggests that Frank thought very highly of him and they were to climb together in the Himalayas in each of the next three years:

In 1935 he was one of a party of Everest possibles in the Alps. The most gruelling day was a traverse from the Margherita [Hut] to the Breithorn and Zermatt in soft snow under a broiling sun. Throughout this and other expeditions he proved himself thoroughly sound on all types of ground and exceptional in strength, stamina and speed. These qualities, allied to his personal qualities and Himalayan experience, especially in the handling of natives, made his inclusion in the 1936 Everest expedition a certainty.[8]

In Frank's view two other climbers, Jim Gavin and Colin Kirkus competed for what proved to be the last place, and his eventual choice of Gavin became a very controversial issue. Plenty of facts were available for him to take into account. Gavin was 24, Kirkus a year older. Concerning education and careers — aspects which carried weight in those days — both men had been to excellent schools, but Gavin as an army officer had the edge over Kirkus, who was a reluctant insurance office clerk (he lived for climbing). Regarding Alpine and high-altitude climbing, Kirkus had been on Marco Pallis's expedition in 1933 to the Gangotri Glacier region in the Central Himalayas, and had climbed several peaks of up to 22,000 feet, whereas Gavin, up to 1935, had just two Alpine seasons. Both men were well-liked, with equable temperaments and a wide circle of friends. But there was one enormous difference, one which today would command great attention from a leader assembling a climbing team for a high, difficult mountain. Jim Gavin had average rock-climbing ability, but Colin Kirkus, who had briefly been considered for Everest in 1933, was a superb rock climber, probably the best in Britain, (see Chapter 16). Frank would certainly have known this; Kirkus came from Liverpool and was a close friend of Graham Macphee, who had climbed with him regularly, often on very hard new routes.

At this point other factors influencing Frank's choice become speculative since unfortunately there are few other clues within the archives. However his decision in favour of Jim Gavin is referred to in a letter he wrote to Macphee on 23 November. In what appears to be an attempt to soften the blow he wrote:

> Tomorrow the final decisions will be made about the Everest party. I'm afraid Kirkus won't receive an invitation. I'm very sorry indeed for him. I like him personally immensely and only wish he was a first choice. But when I tell you that out of the nine people I climbed with this summer only one is likely to be invited you will see what a difficult business it is … I did not know there was any prejudice against Kirkus by people who hadn't climbed with him. Why? The only prejudice, if you can call it so, has been due to his accident and its possible effects on him. Have you observed any effects?

The accident Frank mentioned was a very serious fall Kirkus had suffered on

Ben Nevis at Easter in 1934 in which his companion, the highly talented Maurice Linnell, had been killed. Kirkus had bad head injuries and it was some months before he ventured back to the mountains. He eventually appeared to regain full confidence on rock — it had been the collapse of a snow step overlying ice while leading on a long run-out which had caused the disaster on the Ben — but many detected a change in him. John Watson, a long-standing friend remembered that Kirkus, although a quiet man, could be 'in lively and unbuttoned mood if the situation arose' but that in later years 'the more sombre side of his character pre-dominated.' The accident must have been a depressing reminder for Frank of the deaths of John Hoyland and Paul Wand on Mont Blanc a year previously, a disaster which had reinforced his belief that most young rock climbers, however brilliant had some way to go before becoming competent all-round mountaineers. In this respect Kirkus may have been unfairly disadvantaged. The Gangotri expedition — in which he and Charles Warren undertook arguably the hardest climbing at altitude at that time — had yet to receive the recognition it deserved, since Marco Pallis's book was not published until 1939. Their alpine-style first ascent of Bhagirathi III, 22,060 feet. later commanded great admiration.

By contrast with Kirkus's subdued personality, Jim Gavin according to Ashley Greenwood who had climbed with him in the mid-1930s, was 'a sparkling character with enormous charisma and humour.' Like Oliver, he was able to secure secondment from the army for six months. Significantly he too continued to climb with Frank in the years after Everest.

When Frank assessed the Everest candidates it was probably inevitable that however detached he attempted to be, there were elements in his own personality that played a part in the decisions he made. John Hunt, who knew him well in later years described him with customary directness as 'a sensitive soul, touchy, impulsive and petty at times … a bit of a 'prima donna' and jealous of his reputation … proud, and a trifle vain about his remarkable record.' There is no doubt that Frank got on best with people who were relaxed and tolerant of his sometimes difficult ways. It is easy to understand how he was drawn to Oliver and Gavin.

Whether Kirkus would have succeeded on the upper part of Mount Everest, weather and climbing conditions allowing, remains a hypothetical question. But it appears that the consensus view — which I share — is that compared with any of the others who went on the 1936 expedition he was by far the best climber, the one most likely to snatch that greatest prize, and by not choosing him Frank made a serious error of judgement.

NINETEEN

Midpoint and Stalled

When Frank got home from Zermatt at the end of August 1935 he discussed the Everest candidates with Ruttledge, made his recommendations, and the team was a little closer to being finalised. This was followed by an ugly incident which showed that the leadership struggle that Ruttledge had won so narrowly earlier that year hadn't quite gone away. A sense of grievance still existed.

Frank had proposed Jim Gavin for membership of the Alpine Club, but to his dismay, when the Club's committee met on 1 October the application was rejected. Gavin's climbing record was thought inadequate and it was decided that he should be asked to do another season's climbing. At that stage he had not officially been invited on the Everest expedition, but when his inclusion in the team was announced in November it was realised that the Club risked ridicule; if a man was good enough to climb the world's highest mountain, how come he wasn't good enough for the Alpine Club? At the urgent request of the President, Colonel Strutt Frank resubmitted Gavin's application at the end of December to await the committee's vote early in 1936. Approval was now assumed to be a formality.

But there was a last flurry of opposition. The anti-Ruttledge faction, largely absent from the December meeting and outraged by what they saw as the underhand shoe-horning of an under-qualified climber into the Club, plotted to blackball Gavin when votes were cast at the committee meeting on 3 March. Gavin however *was* elected — had the plotters backed off? No they had not! I discovered a fascinating footnote to the affair, a classic example of the skulduggery in the Club at that time, when I was investigating Tom Blakeney's papers in the British Library. Here I came across a letter Frank had written to Sydney Spencer, the AC Secretary on 19 February 1936 just before he set off for Everest. He thanked Spencer for his good wishes then lamented the threat to Gavin in the coming ballot. But he need not have worried. At the head of the letter Tom Blakeney had written a memo:

> An effort was made to blackball Gavin, and in fact blackballs were cast at the ballot. But it is notorious that Strutt removed a number and put them in the 'white' ball box!

In the autumn of 1935 the first of Frank's books published by Hodder & Stoughton came out. *The Spirit of the Hills* was constructed a bit like *Climbs and Ski Runs* in that it had unrelated stories of climbs, but these were chosen to accompany particular themes. There were chapters with titles such as 'Childhood', 'Youth', 'Low Hills', 'The Highest Hills', 'Dawn', 'Night', 'Storm', 'Friendship' and 'The Spiritual'. It was an appraisal of these things and their place in Frank's mountaineering life.

'Psychological bilge,' wrote Strutt, the *Alpine Journal* Editor in a postcard to Graham Brown when a copy landed on his desk. 'Will you review it for next *AJ*? Your initials need not appear.' GB, to his credit, refused on the grounds that he was biased and that it would be cowardly to remain anonymous. The job was accepted by Henry Tyndale, who later became Editor and stayed in that office for the rest of Frank's life.

Tyndale thought that Frank had attempted something 'as difficult, perhaps, as the last thousand feet of Mount Everest.' He contrasted Frank's approach to mountains with that of the 'young climber of today, a hard-bitten fighter, for whom there is only victory or defeat, never reconciliation with the enemy.' Frank was at his best, Tyndale decided, 'where he relates his own experiences … One is reluctant to turn to homilies on things rhythmic and cosmic … Digressions on education and wartime sermons accord ill with the grandeur of his vision of Nilkanta beneath a rising moon.' But Tyndale's esoteric comments apart, *The Spirit of the Hills* was a success, outselling every book he had written so far. Perhaps significantly, virtually all his books were published either during the 1930's recession or during World War Two and its hard-times aftermath.

So Percy Hodder-Williams' instinct that the general public would respond well to Frank's work had been sound. Paul H-W saw his uncle Percy as an 'old-fashioned Christian gentleman' but this label didn't fit Frank, for whom concepts such as heaven and hell were suspect. He felt that some kind of divinity existed, a 'Power beyond human understanding' he once described it. But he was inconsistent over whether the mind, the spirit, the soul, endured.

At the end of a moving description of the death and burial of Chettan on Kangchenjunga, he wrote, 'Death seemed to me a simple matter; something neither important nor unimportant, but absolute. And simple; too simple to understand.' He was accused of constructing a religion, but he was merely outlining his own approach to life's great unknowns. In its way, *The Spirit of the Hills* was about mysteries best contemplated among hills.

The 1936 expedition was an utter failure. Lavishly equipped and supplied with excellent clothing, tents and equipment, the latest radio gear, the tastiest and most varied food, it was an enterprise planned to take account of every detail including all the mistakes made in the past. But it made less headway than any of the other three full-blown attempts so far.

It was as though the weather gods had decided to have yet more fun. Across Tibet the sun blazed, the temperature soared, and as the team came near Everest, the great mountain basked, bare of snow, the atmosphere calm, and offering one excellent summit day after another. From Rongbuk the build-up went smoothly to the North Col. Then it snowed a lot, and they had to retreat. There was a clear spell. Again they tried, got to the North Col, and the same thing happened. All this occupied weeks, and now the monsoon arrived, earlier than at any time in living memory. A final desperate effort in what seemed to be a break in the bad weather got to just short of the North Col before a huge and lethal wind-slab avalanche started, then miraculously stopped, saving a party from disaster. Soon after that the expedition quit for good.

At least five members wrote an account. Ruttledge's official book, *Everest: The Unfinished Adventure* was boosted by 60 plates of photographs together with pencil sketches of each member by Oliver, and a set of appendices almost as lengthy as the text itself. Gavin, Wyn Harris and Oliver wrote memoirs, and Frank had his diary, although this petered out and he wrote letters to Kathleen instead. These survived, giving glimpses of a strange existence:

26 Apr.　At 9 a.m. we all went to the [Rongbuk] monastery … We were kept waiting three-quarters of an hour, the reason being that the old Lama had not the strength or energy to descend from his room. At length he managed it and amid booming drums and wailing horns we passed into the main courtyard of the Monastery. Then we were all blessed. As a final mark of appreciation and holiness the liquid from a teapot was used to

anoint the porters. Kharma Paul — a devout Tibetan — went so far as to pour a goodly proportion over his face and head. Fortunately we, not being Buddhists were spared this — fortunately, because the liquid in question was nothing less than the urine of the Abbot …

5 May   [Camp 1] I'm writing this between 6 and 7 a.m. and am muffled up in the excellent eiderdown jacket, which together with eiderdown shorts has been supplied to the climbing party. At 6.30 a.m. it began to snow … But there doesn't seem much malice about the weather — can't be more than 10 or 15 degrees below freezing this morning. So intensely dry is the air that we all suffer from congested throats. Otherwise I'm O.K. and can smoke a pipe all day long.

Just before I went to sleep last night you seemed very close. I seemed to see John and Tony very distinctly. It must be glorious at Tenningshook in May. I can picture that very well — the fruit trees out in bloom and Tenningshook wood in vivid green, with a carpet of bluebells drifting beneath the trees. What a contrast to this utter desolation. There is nothing so beautiful as an English countryside.

11 May   [Camp 3] Well here's our first big check. The North Col is hopeless now for some days …

Very disconcerting news on the wireless. John [Morris] is seriously ill at Camp 2. High temperature and unable to walk. Malaria again. Both the doctors and a stretcher party have gone off to take him down to Camp 1 or the Base Camp. He ought never to have come on the expedition as quite apart from his tendency to malaria he's had TB and has half one lung gone. But John has done splendid work with the transport and it's ungenerous to criticise — except that he ought never to have come.

22 May   [Camp 3]. When Eric and I with 41 porters went up to North Col (Camp 4, 23,000 feet) the weather was good. But the signal for our advent on the North Col was the heaviest snowstorm I've ever experienced in the Himalayas. Two feet came down. The camp was half buried. There was nothing to do but lie up for two whole days in our sleeping bags with the Primus stove between us cooking hot drinks to keep warm. After consultation with Hugh on the wireless I decided to descend. It was a big responsibility — 41 men's lives — and one I hope I never have to face again. The snow held except in one place, there was a nasty 'whump' as the snow split — a windslab [avalanche] that did not come away.

Then came a funny incident. I thought I had tied onto a rope and was connected with Ondi. Actually I had tied onto the end of the fixed ropes on the slope above. I cursed at Ondi for not letting the rope out … Finally, on realising the error — to Ondi's intense delight — I untied and tied onto the rope he threw out. Then came the long traverse over a broad shelf in abominable snow — bottomless stuff waist deep on occasions — but we all got down in safety. I've never breathed such a sigh of relief.

25 May   [Camp 3]. When we left camp 1 we were staggered to learn by wireless that the monsoon had reached Darjeeling and must be expected to reach Everest in two or three days' time. Was it — is it — possible that so happy a party could be treated so scurvily by Providence? To come all the way here, to throw up one's means of livelihood just to reach the North Col — and that dangerously — it would be too cruel.

A few days later they withdrew to Camp 1 where the weather cleared and spirits rose. A report said the monsoon was weakening in north-east India. Ruttledge decided to make another attempt. Again a group re-established itself at Camp 3, but heavy snowfall defeated two efforts to reach the North Col, both being threatened by a severe avalanche risk. They withdrew and eventually discovered that the Col was accessible from the western side. But any thoughts of climbing there were snuffed out by more snowstorms. Frank became resigned to failure and his letters were increasingly concerned with other issues.

2 Jun.   [Camp 2]. I'm glad (in a way) you can't see me now because I am not a pretty spectacle. My face is a dirty red and still peeling. My beard — now about three inches long — is full of 'foreign bodies' which I periodically remove with a comb — not I should explain, living matter. My lips are crusted, cracked and swollen. My eyes have a permanent bloodshot appearance about them, suggestive of an over-indulgence in alcohol. My nose — well, words cannot properly describe it. It is swollen far beyond its normal shape (Hugh says it reminds him of Gladstone) — it is blotchy red, cracked, raw and covered with congealed blood. Altogether my appearance is an unsavoury one, and were I to appear in the streets of London then I should almost certainly be hauled off to the nearest hospital for contagious or infectious diseases.

15 Jun.   [Camp 1]. Before I arrive I want you please to order another five yards of sandstone. And by the way have we paid for the last lot — please do so if we haven't. My idea is to construct a little Everest garden, with a small pool for moisture-loving plants. It will be the most glorious memory possible of this country and this expedition.

16 Jun.   [Base Camp]. We leave tomorrow. We must make peace with the old Lama as a lot depends on his report. If we can come next year we should be able to recover the stuff on the N. Col. Did I tell you my telescope is there, about 1,000 feet of film, Mother's volume of Shakespeare and various other things of mine — a bit annoying to lose them. It's about 25 days to Darjeeling. Our earliest ship is the *SS Corfu*, which sails on July 25th I think, so I should be back about August 12th. As above all I want to avoid the 'regrets' and condolences of the AC and RGS pundits at Victoria will you be an angel and meet me with the car at Dover or Folkestone? I see you all the sooner too, dear.

Now above all I want to take you away for a holiday. What about September after the August rush? Could the children be parked somewhere? I've a great idea. We'll get a folding canoe and combine this with motoring. It is grand fun according to Wyn and Hugh and it is a very safe contraption and you can even sail it. It's possible for instance, to combine the Thames and Severn but it would be great fun to go further afield and visit the Scottish Lochs. I can't imagine any jollier holiday than canoeing, camping and motoring and fishing. What do you think? But perhaps first of all we could take John and Tony to the sea? They would so love it. Couldn't you do this before I return? I want to find out from Moore what chance there is of the Land's End to John O'Groats book. A lot depends on that. I've told Christy I can't do any lecturing on this show — it really isn't worth it, but I might well lecture on Land's End to John O'Groats. And if the Tibetans give permission for next year it's going to be a squeeze. But I'm sure you'll understand dearest, how impossible it is to accept such a defeat as this year as final — it's simply not to be borne. Everest is becoming almost a life's task.

Frank enthused about the pressure cooker he was acquiring, 'unpacked and brand-new' to revolutionise Tenningshook cuisine — 'wonderfully successful on this show, they have converted the toughest and oldest Tibetan sheep into the tenderness of new-born English lamb. And my tent is ours —

the best tent I've ever had — and I hope to pinch a Whymper tent, so we shall be able to camp really luxuriously.' Warming to thoughts of his return to domesticity he continued:

> I've suddenly remembered the car. As it must have done 10,000 miles it needs an 'all in' overhaul. The clutch needed adjustment when I left. Decarbonising is NOT necessary as she was done at 8,000 miles. Would you see to this, old thing before I return as we shall use it a lot if we go off on a tour. We must go to one of the test matches — if there is still one to see. I hope you have got a good nurse by now, and what about the domestic problem? I wish we had a man like some of these Sherpas about the place. I've been seriously considering bringing home a man and his wife — they are worth a dozen of English domestics, but though they might be all right for a year, how could they be happy in the long run away from their own people and the bazaar etc.? They all say of course how they would like to come, but I'm afraid it wouldn't do.
>
> Well darlingest, I mustn't ramble on any more. Tell John Daddy is soon coming back from the big mountain. What changes I shall face. A few months make such a difference in children. I expect Tony with a big vocabulary. All my love darling. Your old Frank

After Frank's despair on the mountain, the storms, his trials and tribulations on the North Col slopes, and now his imminent homecoming and plan for trips in a folding canoe on Scottish lochs, Kathleen could console herself with one thought: a Sherpa family was *not* about to set up camp in her kitchen.

The 1936 Everest expedition was a failure, but during it Frank made an extraordinary discovery, one so sensitive that its details emerged only a year later, and then only privately. In an exchange of letters with Colonel Norton, leader of the 1924 expedition, the subject of the ice axe found by Wyn Harris and Laurence Wager above Camp 6 in 1933 was discussed. Frank wrote:

> I feel convinced that it marks the scene of an accident to Mallory and Irvine. There is something else, which I mention with reserve — it's not to be written about, as the press would make an unpleasant sensation. I was scanning the face from the Base camp through a high power telescope last year [1936], when I saw something queer in a gully below the scree shelf. Of course it was a long way away and very small even when seen through a high-powered telescope, but I've a six/six eyesight and do not believe it was a rock. I remember when searching for the Oxford men on Mont Blanc we looked down on to the boulder-strewn

glacier and saw something which wasn't a rock either — it proved to be two bodies. This object was at precisely the point where Mallory and Irvine would have fallen had they rolled on over the scree slopes below the yellow band. I think it is highly probable that we shall find further evidence next year.[1]

Mallory's body was of course found, although not for a further 63 years — in 1999 by an American expedition. It was subsequently confirmed by Graham Hoyland, a British member of the team, that from his description of the position of the mystery object, Frank had almost certainly seen the frozen corpse of George Mallory.

TWENTY

Return to Garhwal

At the end of June 1936, after the Everest party had finally quit Base Camp, Frank wrote to his mother, 'When the August rush is over I want to take Kath away for a holiday. She will need one away from all cares — somehow we must park the children — she mustn't always be tied to them. I've suggested to her that she comes out to the Central Himalayas next year — the loveliest part of the world.'[1] This was the first clue that he intended to return to the Garhwal in 1937, but the hope that Kathleen would come with him seems to have been wishful thinking. She had carefully preserved his letters from Everest in 1936 but there was no such invitation among them. In any case Frank knew that Kathleen would never agree to 'park the children' for more than a few days. When he got home in August he was hard at work immediately, allowing himself no holiday with Kath, children or no children.

There were sackfuls of letters to deal with. Ruttledge wanted him to write a memo about snow conditions and photography. The Everest film needed editing. Hinks was fussing over the commentary and ticket allocations for the film première at the RGS. And most important, there were suggestions for two more books to consider. He had been approached again by Jack Newth, now the managing director of A & C Black, whose offer to publish *Kangchenjunga* six years earlier had been trumped by Gollancz. Newth now wanted a book about mountaineering as part of an adventure series, but this proposal had foundered when Leonard Moore pointed out that the advance and the royalty percentage offered were too small. However Newth's postscript interested Frank:

> I have often thought what a magnificent quarto book could be made from a selection of your photographs, really well reproduced in good photogravure, with merely a brief introduction and short captions. Would you care to discuss it?[2]

Frank did discuss it. 'I have been thinking of the same thing myself for some time,' he replied, arranging a meeting. 'I have more than once been paid the somewhat doubtful comment that my books were purchased for their photographs!'

The Mountain Scene appeared the following August, the first of nine albums of Frank's photographs published by Black in the next 11 years. But there may have been times when he regretted the sheer labour in this kind of book. It could take days choosing up to 80 photographs and arranging them in groups covering different mountain ranges. The layout was delivered to the publisher for fine tuning, then forwarded to two companies that specialised in making high-quality enlargements from negatives and transferring the images to copper photogravure printing plates. He had to write a preface and an introduction and a page of text for each photograph. He and Newth communicated almost entirely by letter; there were some 40 exchanges between them during the production of the first album.

The other publishing deal was also unexpected. In December 1936 the Everest Committee cleared him to publish a book about the 1933 expedition and he signed a contract with Hodder. However they wanted it quickly and needed the manuscript in a month's time, at the beginning of February 1937. They assumed he had only to transcribe the contents of his diary, but he rewrote the story entirely, changed the title from 'My Everest Diary, 1933' to the punchier *Camp Six*, and still delivered it on time — an astonishing effort, especially as a big distraction had occurred in the New Year — permission had unexpectedly been given by the Tibetans for another expedition to Everest. And along with Shipton, Tilman and Warren he was invited by the committee to discuss plans for an attempt on the mountain in 1938.

It can only be guessed how he felt about all this regarding his family. Kathleen had always made it clear that she wouldn't leave the children and come with him to the Himalayas, and in any case she had become pregnant again. Now, as well as the trip to Garhwal there was Everest again the year after. He must have felt uncomfortable about being away for so long three years running. He knew he was thought selfish. On Everest he had felt the pull of home and family and the English countryside. And now Kathleen was expecting their third child just a couple of weeks after his departure for India in mid-May. But none of this caused him to change course. His need to climb and write and take photographs simply overwhelmed everything else.

He and Peter Oliver had toyed with a plan to climb in Tibet, but political difficulties caused them to switch to the Garhwal Himalaya, the region of

Frank's expedition to Kamet in 1931. He aimed to arrive in advance and make for the Bhyundar Valley, his 'Valley of Flowers', an evocative name later to be formally adopted by India. There he would spend a few weeks collecting seeds and bulbs for his own and friends' gardens, at the same time fitting in climbs on nearby peaks with a few experienced Sherpas. Then in late July he would meet Oliver for more ambitious ascents. Just north of the valley was the Banke Glacier and Plateau, virtually unvisited and surrounded by unclimbed peaks of between 21,000 feet and 24,000 feet, a fantastic prospect. Oliver, serving with the army in India was able to obtain long leave from his unit.

Frank's interest in Himalayan plants had begun six years earlier on his Kamet trip. Since then he'd become an enthusiastic gardener, and two Everest trips had been opportunities to learn more and do a bit of seed and plant collecting, although he was the first to admit it had been pretty amateurish, and was likely to stay that way. But three months before his departure a big slice of luck changed everything. During a Scottish lecture tour he visited Edinburgh's famous botanical gardens. There he met Sir William Wright Smith, Regius Keeper of the Garden and his Deputy, Dr John Macqueen Cowan. Both men became interested in his expedition, and he was asked to collect seeds for the gardens, little collecting having been done in Garhwal since the 1840s. Cowan gave him a crash course in packing and preserving specimens and undertook to dispatch to Bombay all the equipment he would need. He also promised to notify a string of prominent garden owners in Britain who would pay handsomely for seeds and tubers of certain Himalayan plants. Frank calculated later that the cost of his trip was almost entirely covered in this way.

It was a complicated journey to the Bhyundar valley that would take a full month. The voyage to Bombay was followed by two sweltering days and nights on the Frontier Mail train in temperatures up to 120 degrees fahrenheit, relieved finally by the cooler heights of Naini Tal and the hospitality of Sir Harry and Lady Haig at Government House. Then Ranikhet at last, and the familiar Forest Bungalow and its wonderful view of the Himalayan snows. And reassuring news from the life he'd left behind — a telegram to let him know Kathleen had given birth to their third child, my younger brother Richard, and all was well.

Four experienced men from Darjeeling now joined him, as arranged. He knew each of them from previous expeditions and he saw them as companions rather than porters. Acting as sirdar or leader was Wangdi Nurbu, also known as Ondi, who would eventually accompany him on all of his six Himalayan expeditions in the 1930s. Frank wrote:

He will be familiar to some readers as the man who fell into a crevasse on Kangchenjunga and remained in it for three hours before he was found. He was badly knocked about and was sent down to be cared for, but two days later insisted on returning to the highest camp. Then on Everest in 1933, he was taken ill with double pneumonia and was sent down to a lower valley apparently in a dying condition, only to reappear one month later carrying a heavy load and clamouring for work on the mountain ... He is a little fellow, all bone and wiriness, and has one of the hardest countenances I have seen; he looks a 'tough,' but in point of fact he is sober and law abiding. His eyes are usually slightly bloodshot in the whites, which gives them a ferocious, almost cruel look, but Wangdi is not cruel; he is merely hard, one of the hardest men I know ... Like many of his race he is an excellent handy-man but failing his kukri prefers to use his teeth, and I have seen him place the recalcitrant screw of a camera tripod between them and turn the tripod with the screw as an axis until the latter was loosened, then calmly spit out such pieces of his teeth as had been ground off in the process. Last, but by no means least, he is a fine climber.[3]

On 5 June the party set off with 11 local porters and half a ton of equipment and supplies, covering the first 40 miles in a ramshackle lorry, possibly the same one with bald tyres that had horrified Frank in 1931. Then came another 70 miles along paths through the forested foothills, past a string of small villages, the men carrying loads of up to 80 pounds each. Images from Frank's account of this stretch come to mind. His guilt at the sight of the porters sweating under their burdens in 100 degrees fahrenheit heat, and his estimation that for each man a 5,000-feet climb was 'equivalent to shovelling 75 tons of coal into a furnace.' The myriads of flies by day, replaced at sundown by vicious midges. The mother of all thunderstorms in which it was possible to 'read uninterruptedly' in the continuous blaze of lightning. The monster spiders in the forest, squatting in huge webs so strong that 'stout twigs to which they were affixed were bent at right angles.' The whirlwind that plucked his tent off the ground, ripping out its pegs and carrying it towards a river. 'I threw myself on it and was joined by Wangdi, Nurbu and Pasang, all evidently convinced it was a huge joke.' And the Kuari Pass, where he came across an old friend, a pine tree he had photographed in 1931, 'a solitary sentinel gnarled and weather-beaten by countless storms, an embodiment of that enduring force which epitomises the spirit of the hills.'

They had a day's rest at Joshimath, a village on the Alaknanda River a few miles short of the Bhyundar Valley. Frank stayed in a small bungalow where the bathroom housed the largest spiders he had ever seen, and he bathed 'with one eye on the dilapidated ceiling lest some huge brute should descend upon me.' But he had reached that moment of a journey into rugged country when the worries of civilised life are left behind:

> I reclined in an easy chair on the veranda, while a gentle breeze stirred an apricot tree above me, then fell gradually to a complete calm. A rosy glow invested the great rock faces opposite and dusk gathered in the deep Alaknanda Valley. The last mist vanished in a sky of profound green, and the first star shone out. There came to me for the first time since leaving Ranikhet, an indescribable exaltation of spirit, which most travellers experience at one time or another in the Himalayas. For days past I had walked over the foot-hills, rejoicing in the scenery; yet never for one moment had I escaped civilisation; it had been always at my heels, and I had walked with one eye on time and another on distance, my mind occupied with futile matters. Now I had in some way escaped from this slavery to schedule and was free to enjoy some of the grandest country of the world.

In the morning they joined the pilgrim path leading up-river towards Badrinath. Frank saw fakirs, or nomadic religious men with 'wild, haggard, sunken faces and unkempt beards, their bodies smeared with ashes.' There were 'fat bunnias [shopkeepers] squatting like bloated bull-frogs on charpoys borne by sweating coolies, their women-folk plodding dutifully in the rear, carrying the family bedding, cooking-pots and food.' The strangest sights were the little old men and women, 'so old it seemed impossible that life could persist within their fragile shrunken bodies, hunched uncomfortably in wicker baskets on the backs of coolies.' Most people were on foot; 'first father, striding unencumbered along, and wrapt in meditation, then mother, often as not a poor weak little creature perhaps 15 years of age, bowed down beneath an enormous burden, sometimes with a baby in addition on her shoulder. So they venture on their pilgrimage … some toiling along in rags, some almost crawling, preyed on by disease and distorted by dreadful deformities. And the stench! Fifty thousand pilgrims for whom sanitation and hygiene have no place in the dictionary. And not least the flies, millions upon millions of flies. Small wonder that cholera, dysentery and typhoid are rife along the route.'

Blunt descriptions of this sort can cause embarrassment or condemnation today, and even in the 1930s eyebrows would have been raised among some of Frank's contemporaries. In my chapter on his Kamet expedition I mentioned how the author Jonathan Neale found Frank's attitude towards his badly-frostbitten sirdar, Lewa, paternalistic, but that he was also a good source on Sherpa history because he noticed individuals, talked to them, and wrote about them. He was curious too, about ordinary people. 'Something sustains these pilgrims,' he wrote. 'Few seem to enjoy their pilgrimage, yet their faces are intent, their minds set on their goal. They are over-awed, too, by their stupendous environment. Europeans who have read and travelled cannot conceive what goes on in the minds of these simple folk, many of them from the agricultural parts of India. Wonderment and fear must be the prime ingredients. So the pilgrimage becomes an adventure. To the European it is a walk to Badrinath; to the Hindu Pilgrim it is far, far more.'

Five miles along the path Frank and his group turned north-east up a side valley. This at last was the Bhyundar Valley, about 15 miles long and rising into the heart of the high mountains. Half way up, its river bent sharply eastwards through a gorge giving the feeling that the higher part of the valley was cut off from the world below, a 'Shangri La' Frank called it. And it was here that he found a site for his Base Camp.

> I had several weeks to spend in the valley and desired perfection. My camping site must be so beautiful that I could never tire of it, a site where the march of light and shadow would charm me the day through, where there was shade from the noonday sun, and fuel unlimited for my camp fires. My eye was caught and arrested by a shelf on the far side of the valley, an alp with birch forests above and below ... an almost level lawn. Here if anywhere was the perfect place. Within a few minutes the men, with that peculiar facility of Tibetans for digging themselves in, had converted a nearby hollow into a kitchen, and collected firewood and water; so that within a quarter of an hour I was comfortably ensconced in my rickety folding chair drinking a cup of tea.

Frank saw botanising as the priority before Peter Oliver's arrival, but he fitted in a lot of climbing, reaching the summit of five peaks. He had to be careful in introducing men who although fit and strong and lived among mountains were raw novices to mountaineering of the type practised in the Alps, with its subtleties of rope handling. He quickly discovered their shortcomings. Pasang, a tall man and reliable at most things, 'more than once demonstrated his inefficiency on steep snow. The first thing he did when he slipped was to let go his ice-axe and leave it to Providence or his companions as to whether or not he was to slide on into eternity.' Tewang was a veteran who had been on Everest in 1924, carrying a load to Camp 5, but Frank now found him

too slow and usually left him to look after Base Camp. He earned his keep
as an excellent cook. Frank had to act when a blister on Tewang's foot became
septic, the poison spreading right up to his groin. He was unconcerned by
the gush of blood and pus from Frank's probing lance and made a full recovery.
Nurbu was the youngest, and although he had been to Everest as a porter,
he had almost no mountaineering experience. He had potential though:
'He was a natural climber, neat and careful, and quick to learn the finer points.'
Then there was Wangdi, who confirmed himself as a superb climber with
immense determination.

An early climb on a 17,000-foot peak above the camp was a shambles.
Frank developed his usual first-day altitude headache and couldn't even enjoy
the unique descent, a 4,000-foot snow glissade. 'Except for Wangdi, who
was soon out of sight, it was a melancholy procession. First of all myself, able
to glissade only a few yards at a time, then Nurbu, and lastly the unfortunate
Pasang, scrabbling about like a beetle on a sheet of glass.'

A week later they had a better day, reaching an easy summit of nearly
20,000 feet but then Frank tackled something considerably harder and got into
a very dangerous situation. After a spell of bad weather a clearance allowed
him with Wangdi, Nurbu and Pasang to reach a snowy pass on the north side
of the valley. His attention was drawn to a striking rock peak immediately
alongside. It was no place for all four of them, so leaving Nurbu and Pasang
to await their return, he and Wangdi started climbing.

They cut steps up a slope of frozen snow — they had no crampons —
climbed a belt of slabs leading to a level ridge, but were then faced by a rock
step 100 feet high. Making sure that Wangdi was well placed and belayed,
Frank climbed a crack, followed by an awkward step onto a slab. There was
a risky moment when Wangdi announced there was no more rope and Frank,
uncomfortably perched on small holds and with no belay, had to bring up
his second to release some rope.

They reached the summit of the peak, but the descent became a nightmare.
With too little rope to abseil the 100-foot step, Frank decided to make a
descending traverse joining their ascent line lower down. It was a mistake.
Wangdi going first ran out the full length of their pathetically short rope
and called to Frank to follow. 'I did so, devoutly hoping he was well-placed,'
wrote Frank. 'He was not, and when I reached him I found him perched on
a tiny ledge, supporting himself with one hand whilst taking in the rope
with the other. It was a miserable stance, with no vestige of a belay and I
implored him to climb very slowly and carefully.'

At the bottom of the rock Wangdi came to an ice slope, not the snow they hoped for, and began to cut steps. When the rope ran out again he was unable to drive in his axe for a belay. 'The slabs did not end as they appeared to end,' wrote Frank, 'but continued, covered by a sheet of ice about one inch thick, which in turn was covered by an inch or so of powdery snow. All Wangdi had been able to do was to cut nicks in this ice plating just large enough for the extreme toes of his boots. It was the most evil place I have ever climbed and was fraught with every potentiality for disaster.'

It was a horror story and even allowing for the limited techniques of those days many would think that Frank broke too many rules, risking his life and that of his Tibetan companion. But a few hours later he was relishing the tense moments. 'I was able to appreciate the joys of climbing in Garhwal,' he wrote. 'Now we were among the flowers; the perfect mountaineering contrast ... a great day's climbing.'

He found immense satisfaction in the remote valley away from all outside contact:

> For the first time in my life I was able to think. I do not mean to think objectively or analytically, but rather to surrender thought to my surroundings. This is a power of which we know little in the West but which is a basic of abstract thought in the East. It is allowing the mind to receive rather than to seek impressions, and it is gained by expurgating extraneous thought. It is then that the Eternal speaks; that the mutations of the universe are apparent: the very atmosphere is filled with life and song; the hills are resolved from mere masses of snow, ice and rock into something living. When this happens the human mind escapes from the bondage of its own feeble imaginings and becomes as one with its Creator.
>
> My pen has run away with me; it often did when recording my impressions in the Valley of Flowers ...

In an *Alpine Journal* article he described the climbs but side-stepped the botanising.[4] His book restored the balance with copious descriptions of plants seen, along with liberal use of their proper names. I have not been inclined to do likewise in this chapter, but I enjoyed vicariously some of the other things he encountered. I imagined the taste of tea brewed on wood fires that he described as 'liquid rhododendron smoke.' In spirit I wore his leaky boots which led to numb feet and much wringing-out of socks, sometimes

ACCIDENT ON MONT BLANC

In September 1934 Frank was involved in a search for two Oxford students, missing after attempting the difficult and demanding Innominata Route. He employed three guides, **pictured above (52)** with him at the Gamba hut after finding the bodies of the victims. From left: the very experienced Adolphe Rey who took part in the first ascent of the Innominata in 1919, FS, Camille Grivel, Edouard Bareux.

53 (below): The group of Courmayeur guides who attended the funeral service. The father of one of the students, John Hoyland was also present (back row, third from right).

AFTER EVEREST

54 (above left): In September 1933 Frank and Kathleen climbed Blaven on holiday in Skye.
55 (above right): Sir Francis Younghusband, an Everest guru since the earliest attempts and good friend of Frank in his final years.

FAMILY MAN

56 (below left): No John, it's mine! **57 (centre):** Jim Bell gives John an exciting tricycle ride.
58 (right): Not sure about this one … (Tony's arrival in July 1934).

59 (below): Tenningshook in 1935, custom-built for Frank in the Surrey hills.

60 (above): Frank's pride and joy, his latest Alvis, a 1.5-litre Firefly DH Coupé. Esmond and other family members lending human interest …

61 (below): Deckchairs at Tenningshook. Frank with John, Kathleen with Tony, and Florence.

ASSESSING APPLICANTS FOR EVEREST

62 (above): At Zermatt in August 1935, Frank climbed with groups of 'potentials' for Everest in 1936. Left to right in this picture taken by Colin Kirkus: Charles Nicholls, Jim Gavin, Peter Oliver, Frank Oakes Smith, FS.

63 (below): Everest candidates traversing the Lyskamm westwards from Monte Rosa.

THE VALLEY OF FLOWERS

64 (above): In 1937 Frank travelled to the Garhwal region of the Indian Himalaya to climb and botanise, initially on his own with a few experienced men from Darjeeling. **Pictured:** An outpost pine on the Kuari Pass en route to a base in the Bhyundar Valley, later to become known famously as the Valley of Flowers.

65 (below): With his team in the Valley. Left to right: Nurbu, Tewang, FS, Wangdi, Pasang.

66 (above left): Frank enjoying the evening hour in the Valley of Flowers.

67 (above right): A training climb. A new 20,000-foot summit with the skilled Wangdi.

68 (below): The fabulous Nilgiri Parbat. A previously unpublished photograph of the mountain that provided one of FS's greatest climbs. **69 (inset):** Wangdi (left) and Nurbu on top of the 21,264-foot peak that involved a 6,000-foot ascent in one day from their camp.

Peter Oliver — self-portrait **71 (inset)** — joined Frank for the last part of the Garhwal trip.
This included an ambitious attempt on the Mana Peak, 23,860 feet — in the background of the
main picture **(70)**. Oliver is resting on the Banke glacier during the long approach.

72: Frank on the summit of the Mana Peak. With Oliver becoming too tired to go on, he soloed the last 800 feet up a difficult buttress on the south ridge, completing what was arguably the finest climb of his mountaineering life.

73 (above left): Frank (left) with Nona Guthrie on the ship returning to the UK after Everest in August, 1938.

74 (above right): FS and his mother at Yew Tree Cottage with Nona.

75 (below left): Camping in Glen Lyon in June 1939 en route to Skye, where in a poor summer there were few photographic opportunities. **76 (below right):** 'A Glen in the Cuillin Hills' published by Jack Newth **(77, bottom left)** in Frank's album, *A Camera in the Hills*.

MOUNTAINEERING HOLIDAY

In August 1939 Frank had three weeks climbing with Jim Gavin in the French Alps just before the outbreak of war.

78 (above): Gavin enjoying a camp fire at a bivouac prior to their first climb, Les Bans.

79 (below): View south-east from Mont Blanc's summit shortly before their return to Engand.

MOUNTAIN WARFARE

In 1942 Frank was appointed to command a unit at Braemar training troops in movement and survival on mountains in winter. **80 (top):** Ski-equipped soldiers set out on a patrol. **81 (above):** FS (right) surveys the bleak Cairngorm landscape.

Later the Canadian Rockies were considered more suitable and Frank was assigned to command a base near Jasper. **82 (below left):** Lovat Scouts crossing the Columbia Icefield. **83 (below right):** Lt Col. Smythe in February 1945, shortly before the end of the war.

CANADIAN ROCKIES

In 1946 Frank returned to Jasper — he had been denied climbing there during wartime. Among the mountains he tackled, Mount Alberta, **84 (above)** at 11,873 feet the Rockies' sixth highest and one of the most difficult, gave him his toughest challenge. This previously unpublished aerial photograph shows the more difficult north and west faces. With Dave Wessel, **right (85)**, he followed the route of the peak's only previous ascent — on the far side, the east face — and was forced to retreat just short of the summit ridge.

Frank returned to Canada the following year, 1947. He hired a float-plane, **above left (86)**, and with six others including Nona flew to Howarth Lake, **top right (87)** in the remote Lloyd George range in northeast British Columbia. **88 (lower right):** The team (less FS) left to right: Rex Gibson, Henry Hall, John Ross, Dave Wessel, Nona, Noel Odell.

89 (below): Much of the climbing was on peaks around the Lloyd George Icefield, a magnificent sight visible from an aircraft over a hundred miles away.

90: The Canadian Rockies were where Frank Smythe did his last climbing in his short life. This fine portrait of him by Morris Taylor on the summit of Mount Hardesty near Jasper in 1947 is offered as a farewell to a writer and a climber soon to be parted for ever from his beloved mountains.

SCOTTISH HOLIDAY

In August 1948 my brothers, John and Richard and I joined Frank and Nona at Gatehouse of Fleet in Galloway.

91 (above left): We stayed in a beach chalet.

92 (above right): My picture of John, Frank and Nona during a drive across the moors.

93 (right): Frank photographed me and John on the summit of Cairnsmore of Fleet.

94 (below): John photographed me, Frank and Richard at Loch Trool.

THE LAST PHOTOGRAPH

By Frank: 95 (right):
A shot of Kangchenjunga
that was skewed, over-exposed
and poorly focussed, suggesting
that his final illness was already
affecting him.

Of Frank: 96 (below):
Breakfast with his hosts
in Darjeeling, Jack and Jill
Henderson (on left) on the
terrace of their tea garden
at Rungneet.

on freezing summits. I shuddered at Tewang's boots with their lethally-smooth leather soles that first horrified Frank then angered him when he discovered that the new, nailed boots Tewang had been given had been saved for re-sale in Darjeeling. I too felt the wind of a rock 'the size of a grand piano' that fell past them on a climb, and shared his surprise at the freak ejection of a stone from a waterfall that just missed his head. I was uneasy about the planned murder of the pheasants; a flock of these birds had been spotted flying out of a cave and Frank on being told they would return to roost, and savouring the thought of a delicious supper had sanctioned a night ambush. A raiding party closed the escape route with blankets and a man crept in to find … nothing (exit thwarted party, laughing heartily). And I was saddened by the death of Montmorency, the goat purchased on the march in. Frank craving meat, finally ordered the animal's dispatch. His edible parts lasted a fortnight kept in a snowdrift, while his skin made a carpet for the floor of the porters' tent. 'But here,' wrote Frank, 'Montmorency got something of his own back. Even the Tibetans have a power of smell, though it is seldom obvious, and one night I woke to hear a chorus of oaths, then the sound of something being hurled into outer darkness. It was the skin of Montmorency.'

Shortly before Oliver arrived Frank reached one more summit, and it was his best so far. He had long admired Nilgiri Parbat, the Blue Mountain, a superb snow peak of 21,240 feet straddling the watershed to the north. But the mountain looked too difficult to tackle from the Bhyundar Valley and he decided to make an encircling approach in the hope that a route existed up its northern side.

Accompanied by the whole group except Tewang, and with food for five days he had reached a glaciated pass when he came across large footprints in the snow. His men were terrified. It was the Mirka, the Yeti, the *Abominable Snowman*, the man-eating creature on whom to set eyes meant instant death! Intrigued, Frank followed the tracks for a short distance, the men agreeing to remain with him only because they believed that the Snowman walked with his toes facing backwards. Soon it was clear that the creature had made a complicated descent of the glacier and could be tracked no further. Frank later sent the photographs and measurements for an opinion by experts from the Zoological Society and the Natural History Museum, and he was to learn the results before he left the valley.

He discovered that Nilgiri Parbat might be climbed from the north, but much depended on camping as high as possible. The tents however were pitched rather low, committing them to a 6,500-foot climb in one day. Was it possible?

Frank wrestled with the problem, but next morning it was calm and clear and he was convinced that he must go for it. He set off with Wangdi and Nurbu at 6 a.m.

Essentially they needed to reach a small plateau below the final slopes of the mountain, and this first part was a climb of 4,000 feet. It was complicated, posing every kind of problem on snow and ice. But they were fired up now, Wangdi and Nurbu wanting the summit too, the terrors of yesterday forgotten. They reached the plateau at 10 a.m. Four hours for 4,000 feet. 'My mouth was very dry and I longed for a drink,' wrote Frank. 'I moistened it with snow and ate some chocolate, though I had no desire whatever to eat. Wangdi and Nurbu both refused food, but I told them that if they did not eat we should not be able to reach the top, to which Wangdi replied, "Of course we shall reach the top!"' The challenge now was to keep up the momentum. At 19,000 feet the air was thin, a gathering mist suffocated them under the broiling sun, and there was a new danger of avalanches. They needed to make a long ascending traverse of the north face, although this passed underneath séracs and across slopes which, if they avalanched would sweep a party over precipices below. But Frank judged the séracs were stable and the snow slope was 'in good order', so they set off.

After an exhausting hour the mist cleared and he was appalled to see the distance remaining. Surely they were beaten? He turned to the waiting Wangdi, but the order for retreat somehow changed itself into 'Go ahead and take a turn at leading.' It was a decisive moment. The little man with colossal energy stormed ahead, and the others felt renewed heart and strength. There was a nasty moment when they had to creep under an ice flake 'the size and weight of a fortress wall', but an icy corner Frank climbed was the last problem. Now it was mind over matter, soft snow, false summits, a freezing wind demanding every stitch of spare clothing, the 'nightmare ridge along which the mountaineer is doomed to climb without ever getting to the end.'

Frank's photographs from the Banke Plateau show Nilgiri Parbat as a steep peak, its upper mist-draped snows creamy and fabulous in the morning light. The summit appears quite broad, but the reality was 'a perfect point of pure snow lifting into the blue of heaven, and so small there was room for only one man at a time. The atmosphere that day was blue; everything was blue, the sky profoundly blue, the hills, the shadows and the distances. In the north, storm clouds were banked up along the edge of Tibet and beneath them I could see the Tibetan plateau, and that was blue and level like an ocean.'

And many hours later, after the long, dangerous and exhausting descent to camp, and the endless thirst-quenching, Frank lay sleepless thinking about what they had achieved. Later he put it into words:

We had climbed nearly 7,000 feet up a peak which remains unique in my recollection for its beauty and interest, indeed the finest snow and ice-peak I have ever climbed. Much that is worthwhile in life had been packed into the space of thirteen hours, but from all that I remember the summit stands pre-eminent, and I can picture it as though it were yesterday, simple, beautiful and serene in the sunlight, the perfect summit of the mountaineer's dreams.

Peter Oliver arrived on 22 July and the party concentrated on the problem of ferrying everything over the Bhyundar Pass, prior to the exploration of the Banke Glacier and surrounding mountains. The ultimate target was the Mana Peak, 23,860 feet. Frank had first set eyes on it when he came to the region six years earlier. Some three miles south-east of Kamet and linked to it by the watershed ridge east of the Alaknanda River, it was a shapely pyramid, and though dwarfed by its giant neighbour, it was a magnificent challenge in its own right. In his search for information, Frank had been in touch with Lieutenant R.A. Gardiner of the Survey of India who had recently explored the Banke glacier system.

An important discovery Gardiner made was a series of linked snowfields forming a plateau high above the Banke Glacier. If this plateau could be reached, Gardiner suggested, it could provide a straightforward route that might lead in about six miles to the foot of the Mana Peak's south-east ridge. He was pessimistic about the only alternative, a long trek up the winding Banke Glacier, although he admitted he had not explored this since it lay beyond the reach of his survey.

Unfortunately this information proved to be a red herring, although it's unlikely that Frank regretted the outcome. He and Oliver, with their combined team of five porters, expended much effort climbing a gorge to reach the Banke Plateau where they spent a week advancing north-westwards, setting up four camps and climbing two peaks on the way. Eventually they were brought to a halt when the plateau finished, and well short of the Mana Peak they were confronted by the depths of an enormous cwm enclosed by vast precipices. But the lofty Banke Plateau was extraordinary, and Frank's photographs give glimpses of a freezing, silent, almost surreal world of snow and sunlight, space and distance, unvisited since the beginning of time.

They withdrew to their base camp where they could rest and restock with provisions from the nearby settlement of Gamsali. Then the whole party, minus Tewang who had been sent down to Joshimath with troublesome bronchitis, began a second reconnaissance, up the Banke Glacier. Even if there proved to be no route up the Mana Peak they had planned to finish this part of their holiday by crossing the Zaskar Pass at the head of the glacier and descending to Badrinath in the Alaknanda Valley, an interesting finale.

Two intermediate camps were needed to reach the Zaskar Pass. The weather was magnificent, but the prospects for climbing the Mana Peak seemed hopeless. As they drew closer to the pass it was clear that an array of icefalls and buttresses blocked any approach to the mountain from its southern side.

However there was one last chance. If they could reach a peak standing above the pass — later designated Peak 21,500 — it might give access to a hidden plateau which in turn should allow them to reach the Mana Peak's north-west ridge. It was a question to which Frank and Oliver urgently wanted an answer, so urgently that even though they were tired from the carry to the pass, they set off that morning up the peak, leaving the men to establish the camp.

It wasn't an easy climb; they had to follow a ridge that presented every kind of feature — icy sections, rock problems, delicate moves over enormous drops, even awkward crevasses. But eventually they stood on the summit of Peak 21,500 feet, and walking a few steps more they viewed the descent to the plateau. It was easy! Just a gentle snow slope, quite short. And the plateau did provide a route to the north-west ridge of the Mana Peak. When they returned to the camp they were jubilant.

But lying awake that night Frank wrestled with a problem. Supplies were short, and they were due to go down to Badrinath in the morning. It would be a week before they could return and the good weather was unlikely to last that long; it was now the monsoon season. Suddenly he saw what they should do. If enough food and fuel could be scraped together, they should ask the men to install a tent as high as possible on Peak 21,500 tomorrow. He and Peter would then occupy it that night and make an attempt on the Mana Peak the following day.

Next morning the normally-cautious Peter Oliver agreed reluctantly with the plan, but there were grumbles among the men at the delay in the descent to the flesh pots. Nevertheless Wangdi saw that Frank was determined, so a great rearranging took place, and by late afternoon the two climbers were camped well up the ridge, on a ledge carved out of a snowdrift above a hair-raising drop. The men were instructed to return later the following day.

The good weather was holding and the two climbers got away when it was light enough to see. Making good progress they stood on the top of Peak 21,500 an hour and a half later. However when they crossed the plateau they were appalled to find that the slopes leading to the north-west ridge were steep and consisted of floury snow overlying hard ice. The thousand-foot slope would take a full day of step-cutting, even two, assuming they had the strength to do it. They appeared beaten almost before they had started.

One last possibility remained — the Mana Peak's south ridge. This was straightforward to reach from the plateau, but it was steep, rocky and with a formidable step about 800 feet below the summit. Neither man believed they had any hope of success but they decided to try it. They each had that mind-set that urges you to go for what is apparently impossible, knowing that the worst thing is to worry afterwards that it *might* have been possible. As Frank wrote, 'The game was up, but was it quite up?'

Oliver did the lion's share of step-cutting up slopes leading to the ridge. When they arrived they sat in the sunshine. It was 10 o'clock. Their throats were parched, and their only nourishment — chocolate — was almost impossible to swallow. Oliver took off his boots and rubbed his numbed feet. Eventually they started up the ridge. For nearly two hours it was mixed snow and rock, with cornices and towers to be avoided, the climbing never easy. At last they came to a point where the ridge swept steeply upwards towards the summit, a thousand feet higher. Here Peter Oliver said he was too tired to go on.

Frank was climbing strongly, the fire that had brought him so many successes now burning fiercely with the goal in sight. He wanted to go on, on his own, but had to ask himself whether he was justified in leaving Peter. The weather was magnificent, there was time in hand, and he knew his companion was too good a mountaineer to push himself to the point of being unable to retreat. They sat and discussed it. Oliver was unhappy about Frank's solo bid — not for his own safety, but for Frank's — however he did not openly oppose it. It was a dilemma many climbers have faced. Frank went on.

Before long he faced a 100-foot rock slab buried in insecure snow. The sun however had melted the snow from its highly exposed left-hand edge, and he crept up the length of this hair-raising ledge — a Himalayan version of the *Route aux Bicyclettes* on the Grépon. It led to the feature that had worried him most, the step in the ridge, which he now saw was 150 feet high and overhanging in places. But again, luck didn't desert him; to the right of the cliff he could kick steps up a little snow-filled gully, so steep that at each stop for a rest his chest was pressed against the slope, his axe driven in for safety. At 100 feet up he found he could step sideways onto a ledge a few inches wide and traverse under overhangs to a point where he could climb to the top using holds consisting of thin but solid rock flakes. The worst was over — or so he thought.

A difficult 25-foot, largely-holdless slab which he climbed with free use of his knees led to easier climbing but now, with no stimulating problems to focus on, he became aware of a deadly fatigue. While in this depressed state of mind a friendly Fortune smiled on him yet again.

> I approached the most remarkable obstacle I have encountered on a mountain. By some extraordinary geological chance a boulder the size of a cottage had wedged itself athwart the ridge. There was no climbing over the top of it, for it overhung, nor could I see a way of clambering over a vertical wall of rock to the [right] side. There was no hope of turning the obstacle to the left, for here the precipice fell with appalling steepness, but there was one way — and it is this that makes the obstacle unique in my recollection of Himalayan climbing — there was a way *underneath* it.

Stooping, Frank saw a gleam of light at the far end of a tunnel of glistening black ice wide enough for him to enter. He started to crawl through. The situation had a dreamlike quality, it was absurd, and at one point he laughed aloud. 'But my laugh deteriorated into a gasp; laughter is hard work at high altitudes.' Exiting the tunnel was difficult for it finished overlooking the western precipice. But yet again he was saved by a benevolent Fate. A tiny ledge existed for him to squeeze onto, there were handholds, and a hair-raising swing followed by some climbing moves left him exhausted, but safely back on the ridge.

When he started again he was drawing on his last reserves of energy. He came to yet another obstacle, a rock step in the ridge 50 feet high, which was too strenuous to climb in his exhausted state. However another gully came to his rescue. He traversed left into a steep chute and sank knee-deep in powdery snow, luckily with a firm base. With the loose snow pouring down the precipice, his ice axe driven in, he put every last ounce of effort into struggling up. The angle grew easier. He was back on the ridge above. He was fearful of cornices. A point of snow appeared. He clambered towards it and 'a few minutes later, at about 1.30 p.m., I sank down in the soft snow, the Mana Peak beneath me, after the hardest solitary climb of my life.'

I have gone into some detail in describing this final part, the climax of the Mana Peak, drawing of course on Frank's own memories, because it was a quite exceptional achievement. Taking into account the remoteness of the situation with no chance of help if things went wrong, the exhausting difficulties of the climbing at nearly 24,000 feet after an eight-hour approach including nearly 5,000 feet of ascent, the year and period in which it took place, and above all, the astonishing fact that the last, most demanding part was a solo effort — all these things suggest to me that the Mana Peak was his greatest ever climb, better than anything else he did in the Himalayas including Everest, certainly more impressive than any of his routes in the Alps, or on British rock, or later on in the Rockies. The Mana Peak wasn't climbed again for another 29 years, and then, after two failures, from the north. Frank's more difficult route to the summit was not repeated for 51 years.

After quitting the Zaskar range they re-grouped and attempted two more virgin peaks — Nilkanta, 21,640 feet, a shapely spire west of Badrinath, and Dunagiri, 23,184 feet, north of the Rishi Gorge, which had already been tackled without success by Peter Oliver and also by Eric Shipton. On both mountains they were turned back by continuous bad weather. Perhaps the worst moment came when they camped in a wet forest en route to Dunagiri. 'The height of misery was reached,' said Frank in a BBC radio talk later that year, 'when an open two-pound tin of black treacle deliberately turned itself upside down in my tent during the night, all among my sweaters.' The broadcast was replayed to me at the BBC Sound Archives, and at this moment in the scratchy recording I distinctly heard a stifled chuckle from Freddie Grisewood who had introduced the programme and stayed in the studio, possibly to Frank's discomfort.

On 21 September Oliver set off south to return to his unit, and Frank spent a last week in the Bhyundar Valley to finish his seed and bulb collecting. Oliver had obtained the loan of a rifle for him to stalk the 'Snowman' but Frank was disappointed if hardly surprised to receive a telegram from London informing him that the tracks had been made by a bear. Nevertheless he set off with the nervous Wangdi one morning in the hope of finding the creature. He mused over the legal implications of shooting it but later professed relief that the hunt had been unsuccessful. It was a strange little episode, in keeping with the culture of that period that killing wildlife was normal and acceptable for visiting Englishmen. Frank enjoyed shooting when an opportunity occurred, but he would have seen it as a separate issue from his lifelong search for a nirvana among mountains.

The Valley of Flowers would not remain as peaceful as he found it. In 1982 the Indian Government designated it a National Park and after that it received World Heritage Site status. It has grown into a great tourist attraction with paved paths, roads providing vehicle access to the valley entrance, and proliferating hotels in the Alaknanda Valley. A botanical survey identified 520 different species of plants including 112 with medicinal properties, and 23 species rare and endangered. There are regulations for visitors. No camping is permitted and access is limited to daylight hours, with no entry after 3 p.m. I typed 'Valley of Flowers' into Google and saw there were 43 million websites listed — samples from the first thousand showed that almost all were concerned with the one in Garhwal, most of those holiday and trekking agencies. 'The only thing that bothers me,' wrote one man who had posted a gallery of photos, 'why such a bland name to such a breathtakingly beautiful and majestic place?'

It was a fair question to which Harish Kapadia, a well-known Indian climber, writer and historian perhaps had an answer. In an article in the *Himalayan Journal* he described a journey he made to the Valley in 1996. He ended: 'This valley is the tribute of Frank Smythe to the flowers of the Himalayas. Because of this catchy name and easy access many Indians, non-mountaineers and common pilgrims, now know that there is more to the Himalayas than shrines and snow. This valley is a celebration of the Himalayan flowers.'[5]

When I met Harish in 2003 he told me he had met a local man, Nanda Singh Chauhan aged 82, who had carried Frank's botanical specimens from the Bhyundar Valley to Badrinath in 1937, and remembered his employer. Harish gave me Chauhan's address and I wrote. Sadly though, he had died and with him my chance of a last glimpse into the past.

TWENTY ONE

Nona

Frank and Kathleen's marriage failed largely because they had almost nothing in common. They were far apart in temperament and in their family backgrounds and upbringing. They shared few interests, and they were never really in touch with one another's feelings. There was a great lack of communication. Kathleen was probably uneasy in the face of Frank's drive and intensity, and became resigned to their drifting apart from one another, although she may have realised that they had never really been a couple. Frank ultimately became deeply frustrated and unhappy. A lot had gone wrong for him. In February 1940, about a year after he had separated himself from Kathleen, he wrote an extraordinary letter to Francis Younghusband, pouring out his despair about a mass of problems stemming from his earliest years:

> I had an appalling upbringing. My father died when I was two. My earliest memories are of being bullied by my step-brother, then a young man. My mother unhappily ought never to have had a child — she is a religionist in the wrathful and vindictive God sense. She possessed me body and soul and I was always struggling against this. I had no home, a succession of private hotels. I had no friends — I was always ill, bullied at school, a dunce and a weakling.
>
> I had a nurse who used to lock me in a dark cupboard and tell me the devil was coming for me. And then when I grew older I was made to believe that sex was utterly degrading and beastly, a mistake on the part of the Almighty. I was a day boy at school — my mother would not let me out of her sight. I wanted to study the arts and was forced to become an engineer, a trade at which I was useless. My saving grace was a deep and abiding love for nature and particularly for the hills. And then unhappily I married entirely the wrong woman. I wanted to love her, but could never get behind a sort of unfeeling indifference. I fear I have brought her a great unhappiness and too late have aroused feelings that never existed in our married life

— I am a passionate, romantic person and the results were well-nigh disastrous. Meanwhile there were three children. I am devoted to them and they were made to seem strangers to me. I was a stranger in my own house — despised as a literary crank and an impractical idealist, particularly by my wife's mother, who exercised an appalling influence on our lives. We lived a sluttish lower-class life on a decent income. It was impossible to entertain, so terrible was our household.

As a result I withdrew completely within myself. I became moody and self-centred, throwing myself into my work to the exclusion of my family duties — going away on expeditions where I temporarily rehabilitated my self-respect, but in general going steadily downhill. These were the circumstances when you saw me off to Everest [in 1938] and I was vaguely hoping that I should leave my bones on the mountain because life seemed entirely pointless and futile.[1]

Frank wrote this anguished summary of his life, but at the time the devil lay in the detail. The sadly impractical Kathleen had problems choosing and managing staff — only a single live-in nanny or nurse was needed at any one time, but seven came and went during a period of four years. Frank liked to host dinner parties but entertaining at Tenningshook was chaotic, although in spite of her domestic ineptness Frank's friends liked Kathleen. A typical upset was when she left the greenhouse door open on a frosty night and some precious plants perished, and of course three young children made for a very noisy and distracting household. Mollie, his mother-in-law caused great difficulty. He accepted that when he was away she would come and help with the children — Tenningshook after all was remote in the countryside and Kathleen had moved away from her friends and interests in London and Berkhamsted. But he disliked Mollie coming when he was at home, hating it if she was there when he returned from an expedition, and he dreaded the prospect that soon she might live with them permanently. Shortly before his return from the Valley of Flowers, he wrote to his mother:

I wonder what my in-law intends to do. Much as I am indebted to her I really cannot have her to live with us. She is for all her virtues a most difficult person to get on with. I know she disapproves of me and all my works and I must confess I find her one of the most uninteresting and narrow-minded persons I've ever encountered. I shall be quite firm on the point I cannot have her. Married people must have their own lives …

You can always be certain that as far as Kath and I are concerned you are an honoured and welcome guest at Tenningshook. It is an amazing impertinence that another guest should pose as the doyen of the household. I quite see I shall have to make myself very plain on my return, even at the risk of mortal offence.[2]

Life hadn't been easy for Mollie in recent years. The severe slump of the 1930s had wreaked havoc on the working lives of her two sons. Ken, after qualifying as an electrical engineer in 1924 had worked at a succession of jobs until finally unemployment had driven him to join a ship as an ordinary seaman. However with improving fortunes he found settled work, married a childhood friend, Gladys Waterfield in 1936 and settled in Buckingham. Sadly fate would deliver a terrible blow when Gladys died from a botched routine operation three years later. Ken's brother, Esmond after gaining a Classics degree at Oxford had taught at Pocklington School in Yorkshire for three years before joining a colleague to found a new private school in 1929. This venture proved to be a disaster. After a year the school failed with considerable financial loss to Mollie, and Esmond was unemployed until he was offered a post at a school in Northampton. Mollie then moved to Northampton, rented a house near the school, and Esmond joined her.

The Everest Committee had at last accepted the virtues of a small expedition, largely because the huge costs of the 1936 fiasco had left the coffers almost empty. For a while it looked as though there would be no expedition at all in 1938, then Tom Longstaff, a wealthy veteran of the 1922 attempt on the mountain and a man with a marked preference for lightweight ventures, stepped in and offered £3,000. He attached conditions. The leader must be Bill Tilman or Eric Shipton, and members of the party must contribute towards the cost. The Committee agreed to the deal, and Tilman was appointed leader.

Bill Tilman is now regarded with awe as one of the greatest explorer-mountaineers of the twentieth century. A small, craggy, taciturn man with a famously wry wit and notoriously spare in his needs for conversation, equipment and food, he amassed a lifetime of expeditions to rugged and remote parts of the world, sometimes with a single companion, sometimes on his own. In 1936 he had made a personal breakthrough in Himalayan climbing in reaching, with Noel Odell, the summit of Nanda Devi in the Garhwal, at 25,645 feet a new record for the highest peak ascended. He was a brilliant writer, combining a measured style with delectable observations on the follies he encountered, whether they were the results of his own blunders, or those of a companion, or simply the machinations of fate. In later life he bought a small ocean-going boat and sailed to mountains inaccessible by land.

In 1961 when I was working at a temporary job in London I heard that
Tilman was looking for crew members for a voyage to Greenland in his boat,
Mischief. I wrote to him, offering my (totally inexperienced) services. We met
at his Club, and the interview consisted of Tilman taking me on a tour of
the premises, removing the pipe from his mouth at intervals to remark
gruffly, 'Lounge', 'Library', 'Gymnasium', 'Swimming-Pool', and so on.
When he got to 'Dining-room' I hoped we might stop for lunch, but we didn't.
Finally, not having been asked a single question, I ventured one of my own.
What would I need to bring for the voyage to Greenland? The pipe was
removed. 'Rucksack-full of things,' rumbled the great man, and soon I made
my exit. Hearing no more I assumed I was now a crew-member, but eventually
I lost my nerve and wrote to Tilman resigning my post, perhaps before it had
been offered. I have never decided whether to be thankful or disappointed
that I did not go. Sixteen years later Tilman, aged 79 disappeared in the South
Atlantic aboard a younger friend's boat, no trace of which was ever found.

Tilman, calm and thoughtful, was very different from Frank, and it isn't
surprising that they were wary of one another. 'They kept each other at arm's
length,' Peter Lloyd, another member of the seven-man team told me. And
Tilman confirmed his distrust of Frank in a letter to Odell in March 1937
before his own position as leader had been confirmed. 'The thing is to keep
F.S. out of the lead,' he wrote, 'because that would be the devil.'[3]

An early monsoon had ruined the chances of the 1936 Everest expedition
and Tilman, determined that this should not happen to his party had sailed
from England earlier than ever — in the last week of January. Shipton went
with him to help with the preliminaries — hiring porters and organising
equipment and supplies — and the rest of the team except Frank would join
them two weeks later. Frank, giving himself a bit more time to finish his
labours at home planned to catch a ship later still and would trail the group
across Tibet by a week or two.

On each trip to India in recent years Frank had taken the train to Marseilles
and caught the ship there, slicing over a week off the three-week voyage from
Tilbury to Bombay. Now he did the same in 1938, arriving in Marseilles on 26
February and boarding the P & O vessel, SS Strathaird. There he met Nona.

He had first met Nona Miller, or to use her married name Guthrie, in 1932
when Younghusband had invited him to Currant Hill in the build-up for
Everest the following year. She was a young nurse from New Zealand who
came to England in 1927 and some four years later became employed by the

Younghusbands to assist the partially disabled Lady Helen. She was intrigued by the distinguished family she found herself amongst, and had soon made herself indispensable to them. She was an attentive listener for Lady Younghusband, who was happy to educate her in the ways and wiles of the British aristocracy. She became a close friend of Eileen, the Younghusbands' only child, a rather dowdy girl four years older. She teased and flirted with Sir Francis, whose marriage was a sexless humdrum affair and who responded to Nona's outgoing nature with great glee, happily breathing the draught of colonial fresh air that she blew through their staid household.

Her father, David Miller, owned a sheep station near Christchurch in the South Island, having emigrated in 1878 at the age of 13 with his family from Scotland. Nona was born in 1906, the third of seven children, and after her education and nursing training had followed the trend of many young women from New Zealand at that time in coming to the 'Old Country' to seek her fortune. However soon after she had joined the Younghusbands she blundered badly by becoming engaged to Bob Guthrie, a Scot some eight years older who was a partner in an insurance broking business in the City. Sir Francis disapproved of her choice, but Nona, attracted more by her fiancé's wealth and style than anything else, married him in short order at St Andrew's Presbyterian Church, Hampstead on 21 December 1932, Younghusband signing the register as a witness to what he believed was folly. Sure enough, the union was a calamity and didn't last long. It was out of character for Nona to make such a mistake, but it was unlikely that she saw it as more than a temporary setback to her aspirations, a painful experience to be learnt from.

Patrick French, in his biography, *Younghusband* wrote that after Nona had married Guthrie she still visited Currant Hill regularly and it became a 'home from home' for her. What drew Nona particularly, he stated, was the frequent presence of Frank Smythe, who was 'at his best' at Younghusband's gatherings. They took to 'spending a lot of time together and a love affair began.'

When I decided to write the story of Frank's life I knew of course the outcome of his getting together with Nona. He had died when I was 14, but my brothers and I had stayed in touch with Nona after that until her death nearly 50 years later. She was friendly towards us but revealed little of her early life with Frank, and now I wanted to know more about it, particularly about the timing of their real attachment to one another. There was a lot of evidence that he had urgently attempted to breathe life into his failing marriage to Kathleen for a number of years; it seemed unlikely that he would stray willingly into the arms of another woman until he had decided that all was lost between him and Kathleen. Patrick French seemed to suggest that a love affair had begun a long time before he boarded the boat at Marseilles. Where did the truth lie? I contacted French and asked him to help me. He wrote that he had no hard evidence of the relationship beginning much before 1938. In a biography he advised me, it was often best to 'trust your instinct', and if I thought their relationship began in 1938 then I was 'probably right.'[4]

Nona wrote draft notes intending to publish a biography about Frank's life, and luckily these escaped the bonfire she made of many of his papers shortly before her death. Referring to his arrival on board the *Strathaird* in 1938 she wrote, 'It was on the ship at Marseilles en route to India that I first met him, from an introduction given to me by Sir Francis Younghusband.'[5] This was clearly untrue, they had met years earlier at Currant Hill, but it raised the question of whether it was a planned rendezvous. Nona was on her way to New Zealand to visit her family, something she liked to do at least yearly and would obviously plan and book in advance. Frank caught the same vessel, which called at Bombay on the way from Tilbury to Auckland and this was the third year in succession he had gone to India by this route, boarding at Marseilles. Their meeting could have been a coincidence.

But it was unimportant. It made no difference to the outcome, and somewhat ironically it was an unguarded letter that the normally secretive Nona wrote some three months later, on 12 June from Wellington, New Zealand to her close confidante Eileen Younghusband, that heralded the news that something more than a casual affair had begun:

> Dear Beastly little Child,
> Well my dear, you will have heard from my beloved how he 'magnanimously' (is that how you spell it?) allowed me to stay until a later boat* and was I thrilled? Unfortunately I had left the South Island and my dear Ma and Pa when the cable came, and as I couldn't go through all those terrible Good-byes again I'm staying here with my sister, and going up to the Wairarapa to another sister next week.
> My welcome has really been so overwhelming!! (strange as it may seem, little cat!) — and this visit only convinces me more and more how I adore my beautiful NZ and its inmates of course!
> I think my beloved thinks this trip will cure me of wanting any more trips, but Darling it's the reverse, but don't say I said so!
> When I arrived the family were shocked to find I was so thin, so I told them

---

*The 'later boat' referred to the ship Frank directed Nona to catch from Auckland, the one that he would be boarding at Bombay after Everest.

I was in love and that has a disastrous effect on the figure!! And as for the shock F.S. Smythe got on further acquaintance I'm pleased to tell you it was an extremely pleasant one, so there! It won't bear repeating so I'll refrain, and don't tell dear Papa — he's already written and scolded me for keeping F.S.'s mind from the top of Everest!

I don't know what you're all doing to my beloved but his letters are about as cheerful as three weeks of wet weather!! I expect you'll tell me he's been enjoying himself 'no end' and that's only for my benefit!!

No more now 'cos you don't deserve it for not writing to me.

Much love, dear child, from Nona

PS Be tactful when you see the beloved and say how much I'm living for the moment I sight the white cliffs of Dover!!! Sounds romantic don't it? [6]

Nona was an exuberant and decisive young woman, physically attractive with dark hair and a good figure. She smiled and laughed a lot and her bubbling personality brought her numerous admirers. She had captivated Younghusband, but had been careful to keep him at a certain distance to avoid complications. He appeared to cooperate in this, although when they were apart he wrote to her lovingly.

It's difficult for me to judge what her feelings were towards Frank — perhaps a son has a problem in estimating his father's sex appeal. She undoubtedly admired his achievements as a writer and mountaineer. She basked in his fame, and saw him as a glamorous figure from those perspectives. But it's hard to imagine how the organised, astute and social Nona could fathom Frank's dreamy philosophy and spiritual leanings, or share his need for regular escape from the civilised world into the mountains, or understand his preference for his own company at times. Maybe once she saw he was smitten by her, and had decided he was a real catch her instinct was to make herself attractive to him rather than concern herself unduly with what was attractive *about him*. And following this, she was shrewd enough to see that her best route to his heart was to provide what Kathleen had failed to give him — companionship, conversation, understanding, an organised life, fun, good food, wine and sex. Friendship along with these things yes, but not necessarily a deep emotional attachment, to start with at any rate. In fact Nona's failed first marriage may well have laid the foundations for a lifelong resolve to keep her feelings under control and never again make herself vulnerable.

That she succeeded in attracting Frank is obvious from surviving fragments of letters he wrote on his return from Everest:

> You know it's just my idea of heaven to go through life talking with you, flirting and frivolling with you and loving you. We should get on so tremendously well. There's something about you — I'm damned if I know what it is — that draws out everything in me. Not once in my married life have I talked as I talk to you. It's been politenesses and platitudes. Your sympathy, your power of meeting me half way is something I've never before encountered. When I talk to you I feel a part of you somehow, and I want to be with you for always and always. I loved the Nona of the ship, but this Nona I'm getting to know is infinitely more wonderful.
>
> Well darling, I suppose you'll say I'm getting 'tense'. Don't inhibit my feelings. Just let me love you.[7]

> It's impossible to tell you all I feel. Let it suffice that you have made me very happy and every time I see you I find myself happier still. There is so much about you I'm always finding out — so many sides to you. You amaze me with your versatility. Darling how hard I'm going to try to make you happy — if I can make you as happy as you've made me it will be wonderful. I want you to forget these weary years just as I want you to make me forget. We are two people starting life again — at least that's how I feel.[8]

However such expressions of love and tenderness came later. On the Strathaird Frank's mind was in turmoil. If the shackles of his marriage seemed to be loosening he knew that he had to keep up a certain pretence that all was well at home, and a letter to his mother during the voyage suggested also that he felt responsible towards his children:

> I've never enjoyed a voyage more. I seem to have renewed my youth and thrown off all the cares of this past winter. I only wish Kath could have been here. I would give a lot to be able to take her for a voyage to say, New Zealand. There are several New Zealanders on board — all extraordinarily nice people. I feel more and more unsettled these days, that life in England is narrow, hedged around by all kinds of restrictions. I want to bring up our boys to be men. To ride, shoot, lead a hard open-air life, and how is one to get this in England. New Z sounds a marvellous place and it will be well away from the War when it comes. I would like to go there for a few months and explore the possibilities of making a living there. I suppose I've got the pioneering spirit and because of this I'm not as happy as I might be. But above all I want to keep the boys away from a narrow groove and war.[9]

TWENTY TWO

Broken Home

Little was published about the 1938 Everest expedition. Tilman wrote a slim book of 80 pages, although this didn't appear until 1948.[1] Walt Unsworth in his weighty history of Everest allowed it just 14 pages out of a total of some 700.[2] Shipton, who'd been to Everest three times before and made no secret of his disenchantment with the mountain, wrote five pages,[3] and Frank wrote nothing at all. The reason for this apathy from seasoned professionals was simple; the expedition failed as dismally as the last one, in 1936. Nor did it help that it took place during the plunge towards war in Europe.

Tilman seemed more inspired by the preliminaries. Asking the Tibetans for permission to climb their sacred Chomolungma was, he said, 'like asking the Dean and Chapter for permission to climb Westminster Abbey.' He wrote four pages defusing his critics over the expedition food ('As Shipton and I once lived perforce for a few days on tree mushrooms and bamboo shoots there is a general impression that this is our normal diet, eked out with liberal doses of fresh air, on which, thanks to a yogi-like training, we thrive and expect everyone else to do likewise. Nothing could be farther from the truth.'). He reviled the proposed use of oxygen, and with amused contempt, listed the rest of the scientific paraphernalia that Odell had brought. He admired Purba the mail runner who, arming himself with a long Tibetan knife, 'walked or rode great distances, travelled alone and carried nothing at all.' He told how Purba had 'very apologetically' asked for extra travelling expenses, explaining that on his last march he had been obliged to boil his shirt in order to make a cup of tea. An infusion of shirt might have tasted better than Tibetan tea, Tilman observed.

Frank caught up the main party before it reached Rongbuk. The bitter weather had blown all the snow off Everest, turning the mountain black, but wreaking havoc on the expedition's health. They struggled up the familiar

East Rongbuk Glacier, suffering from flu, coughs and sore throats, and escaped over the Lhakpa La to recover in the forested Kharta Valley, a haven 5,000 feet lower than Rongbuk. Then at the beginning of May it started snowing higher up. And didn't really stop. The monsoon had broken, earlier than ever.

There were brave efforts to climb the mountain. The North Col was attacked from both sides despite great risk of avalanches. They got there, and even pitched Camps 5 and 6 above, and Frank and Shipton set off in waist-deep snow from the top tent at 27,200 feet. But it was little more than a gesture. Shipton said that it would have taken a series of shifts for a week to dig a way to the top. There was a sad price paid by one of the exhausted porters who had carried a load to Camp 6. Pasang, one of Frank's men in Garhwal became paralysed by a stroke at the North Col. The other porters refused to help, regarding him as a victim claimed by the mountain God. Leaving him, they argued would save one of them from being chosen in his place. Tilman told them this wasn't an option, and the wretched Pasang was dragged and lowered down to Camp 3, put to bed in a sleeping bag and eventually carried to Base Camp. He managed to get back to Darjeeling, but never worked again.

They started back on 20 June. Frank had arranged to catch a ship from Bombay at the end of July and during the last 100 miles to Gangtok he and his Sherpa companion, travelling ahead of the main party had a nerve-wracking experience which he told his mother about, in the interests of persuading her that there were worse things than Mount Everest:

> In point of fact it's a far easier and safer mountain than many I climbed last year, but because it's Everest you let it worry you. Actually on the way back I had a more unpleasant experience than any on Everest, as we ran into a gang of bandits, robbers and murderers and were potted at. I got a rifle bullet unpleasantly near my head, but as we were riding and the bandits were not we got away. This was a most unusual thing to occur in that part of Tibet.[4]

At Kalimpong he stayed with the hospitable Odlings. He weighed nine stone after losing a quarter of his normal weight and suffered from a deep septic wound in a heel. He occupied himself writing letters, going over the same topics — Everest in its most hellish mood, the iniquities of Tilman and the penny-pinching Committee, Hitler and the approaching war and the beauty of escaping it in New Zealand or Canada. By way of light relief he rode the Kalimpong ropeway platform to the Teesta River, enjoying en route a close encounter with a 12-foot king cobra. He symbolically finished with Everest by bequeathing his ice axe to Jill Henderson at Rungneet tea garden in Darjeeling. Eventually it was taken into care by the Alpine Club where 60 years later I found it was exactly the right size for me.

Together with Shipton and Odell he joined Nona on the *SS Strathnaver* at Bombay. Three weeks later a mischievous Younghusband wrote to his daughter, Eileen who was having a holiday on the Scottish island of Canna:

> Our one and only has returned today from New Zealand, and I went down to St Pancras to meet her on her arrival from Tilbury. In a burst of confidence she told me she was not at all pleased to be back! However 'Frank' and 'Eric' had done their best to cheer her up — and I got some good gossip about Everest from her. I gather that the leadership ... had not been all that was to be desired. I asked her if she had been a 'good influence' over them, and she assured me that she had — and if 'Frank' stayed too long in the bar she would go and fetch him out. Also she had been a good influence over the Captain and the ship's officers generally, and had wangled a cabin to herself all the way (I was nearly writing a 'berth' to herself!)[5]

Frank had disembarked at Marseilles and taken a train to Paris where he had arranged to meet Kathleen for a couple of days. It was a difficult time and there would be no attempt at reconciliation. Meanwhile Sir Francis brought Eileen up to date with the latest gossip. He had invited Nona and her husband, Bob to dinner at Currant Hill. 'They are rather cross with each other. Bob doesn't like her goings on with Smythe! And Bob's sister thinks he would be better without Nona. So there's another jolly row ... '[6]

Frank put Tenningshook up for sale. There were no prospective buyers but in October he separated from his family, renting a flat for himself in London and a house on the outskirts of Dorking for Kathleen and us three boys. I was four but I have memories of Downway. The garden had laurel bushes to hide in, and the sickly smell of their crushed leaves still takes me back there. John wielded his bow and arrow. A railway ran across the bottom of the garden and trains made the ground quiver. I had my tonsils out in a hospital up the road and my throat was terribly sore. But I knew nothing about the heartache.

On 20 October Frank signed a contract with Hodder for *Edward Whymper*, a biography of the Victorian mountaineer whose classic *Scrambles Amongst the Alps* had fired his imagination in childhood. The manuscript had to be delivered to the publishers by 31 March — in just over five months' time — an unbelievably short time for such a project. He was used to working quickly and the six years of 1937 to 1942 were the most intensive of his writing life when 14 books, exactly half of his whole output were published.

He had moved to Hillsborough Court, a large block of flats in South Hampstead, and at that same time rented a flat for Nona in the nearby Priory Road. It had become impossible for her to go on living with Bob, who, although his marriage had been a charade for years, was furious with Nona now he knew she was unfaithful. Frank, whose closeness to Nona would soon become common knowledge, was aware of the threat to his reputation. Two or three generations on, society is mainly indifferent about people from broken marriages living together, but in the 1930s no such liberty was tolerated. The five-minute walk between his flat and Nona's represented a discreet but important separation. This was evident from an exchange of letters he had with Mollie some weeks after he had moved to London. She had written two letters criticising his behaviour — neither of which has survived unfortunately — but Frank's response from Hillsborough Court on 9 December 1938, although sparing with the truth about Nona, spells out the sadness, frustration and guilt he professed to be feeling after separating himself from Kathleen:

My dear Mater,
I appreciate your letter and the spirit in which it was written. After your previous remarks I never expected to hear from you again.
    On two points I feel I must correct you. Firstly I am living here on my own, secondly I did not leave Kathleen on account of an infatuation for someone else. It was not a case of yielding to temptation. Kathleen and I have been unhappy for a long time. You cannot have failed to have noticed there was a lot wrong long before this last Everest expedition. I failed to make Kathleen happy and she failed to make me happy. But the blame is mine. I know exactly what you and she think — that I was selfish and self-centred and neglectful of her and our family, and you are right. Why was I like this? I've asked my friends what they thought of me on expeditions — which are a pretty stern test of character — and they all tell me that I am unselfish, sympathetic and that the porters like me and would do anything for me. Why was I a different person in my married life? I knew I was a hopeless husband, yet it was impossible to remedy. I need not enlarge to you, her Mother, on Kathleen's wonderful qualities. She has done so much for me, nursed me, looked after me, helped me. I did little for her except provide a home and money. And to do this I had to work too hard when I was home. Yet there was always something lacking between

us and a barrier rose that grew higher and higher. It was my job to win her love, but somehow I never broke down this barrier of reserve, the lack of sentiment and romance and sympathy which characterised our life together. No doubt Kathleen felt it too. We were both afraid to confide in one another. We were cursed by a terrible puritanism. There seemed no common meeting ground intellectually and spiritually. And so we drifted. You think Kathleen was the only one to suffer, but I suffered too. Two years ago I wrote two letters. The first which was similar to this I tore up as [I] did not want to wound Kathleen. The second I sent — it was a plan for a better understanding. You will see how tragic it was. I could not even unburden my thoughts to my own wife. I was afraid to. And she was afraid to also. Yes, I gave Kathleen nothing and I look back now with horror at myself for what I was. But remember also how I used to slave away in the study beset constantly by financial anxieties. What would I not have given for Kathleen to come in and put her arms round me when I was so tired, but she never did. I think she scorned my creative artistic temperament. She had no use for it. Generously she tried to interest herself but it was no good. Even our friends were poles apart and I blame myself now for not trying to be a better host to her friends. Yes I am to blame all right. Under different conditions Kathleen would have been happy, but the first condition is a husband very different from me — someone sound, solid, unimaginative, stable, enduring. People like me tend to produce nothing but unhappiness — they need a woman of a very special temper and temperament as a mate — someone who will drive them out of themselves.

I would give all I possessed to see Kathleen happy, but I could never make her happy, or make myself happy. I'm not a believer in two people living together for the sake of children alone. An atmosphere of discord must react on children who are so sensitive to impressions. Believe me if Kathleen is suffering I am suffering too, but all bitterness I am trying to eliminate. It is necessary to get a new grasp on life and make a fresh start. Kathleen and the children will never want while I'm alive. In matters of upbringing and education I am going to do all I can. But it's terrible for me. I never realised how much the children meant to me.

Let me end by assuring you that if it were possible for Kathleen and me to start our life again I feel that neither of us would let anything stand in the way, but I cannot insult Kathleen by asking her to live with me as a friend for the sake of the children, nor would this have anything but ill effects on the children.

I pray that Kathleen will find happiness. Life has been very, very hard on her and I have been the cause of much unhappiness to her.
Frank[7]

Frank missed the deadline for his Whymper manuscript, getting it to Hodder in mid-June, 1939, spurred on by an Alpine holiday he'd planned for the end of July with Jim Gavin. He had paid Whymper's daughter, Ethel Blandy £50 for her father's diaries. Other sources were mainly historical records at the Alpine Club and members of the Whymper family. But before this Frank's writing had been almost entirely about his own climbing. Why did he write a biography?

He owed much to Whymper. His childhood present of *Scrambles Amongst the Alps* became his most treasured possession. 'I read and re-read it countless times,' he wrote. 'I lived and re-lived with Whymper and his companions the Golden Age of mountaineering adventure and, like many another before me, I was filled with a great desire to go and do likewise. I never met Whymper, yet I feel that I know him, for if personality may be handed on and perpetuated through the written word … he is very much alive today.'[8]

Perhaps, with Frank's dilapidated copy of *Scrambles* as evidence, those words answer the question. Whymper and Mallory, two of the most written-about English climbers shared one thing; they were witness or victim of a single dreadful event. Four of Whymper's companions fell to their deaths after the first ascent of the Matterhorn, an outcome that horrified the mountaineering world, and Mallory, the finest climber of his generation disappeared with his companion heading for the summit of Mount Everest. It was very likely, if not inevitable that Frank, fascinated by high achievers and spectacular moments in climbing history, would be drawn to write about one of these men.

He must also have seen parallels in Whymper's early life with his own — the loneliness, the hated trade imposed by his family, the ambition driven by the desire for a creative career and independence. And it was a strange coincidence that both men became interested in the Andes — although Frank never managed to get there after his job in Buenos Aires collapsed — and both visited the Canadian Rockies later in life.

In December 1938, half-way through his labours on the biography, Frank went to Zermatt on an intensive photographic foray for his next album. Four months earlier, while tidying up final details of *Peaks and Valleys* he'd put a new project to Newth:

> I have an idea for next summer … of travelling through the Alps with the aid of a car … and taking a really fine series of photographs with better apparatus than I have been able to use on expeditions. It seems to me that the Alps from end to end in pictures might attract a far wider sale than either of the two books so far done … [9]

Jack Newth was cautious. Ideas bounced back and forth. Frank became interested in an album of skiing shots and snow studies; Newth wanted more variety. Finally they agreed on an album of half winter and half summer photographs. There would be a handful of shots of British hills. Frank's original idea of travelling through the Alps by car was scrapped; Newth preferred pictures taken among mountains.

With the end of his marriage Frank now seemed energised. A weight had been lifted from his shoulders and fresh work beckoned — it was as though Nona had acted as a fault line to allow an earthquake to happen. The trip to Zermatt also marked a new beginning for him as a mountain photographer. Previously he'd used his camera for illustrating his books; now he wanted to make pictures in their own right. He was interested in the hardware too, although the cameras he had used for 10 years — the German Etui that came in two formats, 12 x 9 centimetres and 9 x 6½ centimetres — could scarcely be bettered. They were ultra-lightweight, pocket-thin folding bellows cameras of superb quality that had gone with him on every expedition and performed well in conditions varying from sweaty humidity in forests to great cold at altitude.

The new album, with its catchy title *A Camera in the Hills*, had 65 black and white photographs, all except six taken in the nine months between December 1938 and August 1939. Although he'd started to use colour in 1937 he didn't take it seriously for some 10 years, believing it too primitive to compete with black and white. He was lucky with the weather in Zermatt, shooting plenty of film from which 20 shots were chosen to form the winter section of the book. He roamed among hay huts in the evening sun and through snow-laden trees casting their shadows. He photographed frozen streams and velvety snow, and played with dramatic lighting on stormy days, and he shot the Matterhorn at sunrise with skiers on the bitterly cold Gorner Glacier. As before, each picture had its caption page alongside, but now he dealt with the circumstances surrounding the photograph, how it might have been improved perhaps, and the technical details of the exposure. He gave a BBC radio talk the following March entitled 'I photograph mountains.'

The book awaited a few pictures from the British hills, also its contribution from the Alps in the summer, and it would not be published until the end of 1939, but *A Camera in the Hills* was a winning formula. It ran to five editions including a final reprint in 1955, six years after its author's death.

At the end of June 1939 Frank and Nona drove up to Skye. The trip had echoes of his visit to the island six years previously with Kathleen. Now though, the Alvis cars had been sold and Nona endured the long haul in an Austin two-seater coupé. The weather didn't co-operate either, as a published picture showed; a tree, a stream and the cloud-wrapped Cuillin Ridge. One day he reached the ridge on Blaven and in a clearance took a photograph of exactly the same view in which Kathleen had posed for him on a day when the island basked in sunshine. Nona had chosen not to accompany him and Frank's postcard to his mother drew a firm line under Skye, 1939: 'Am shortly coming back. Rain every day for three weeks now. Much love, Frank.'

The three weeks he and Jim Gavin spent in the Alps in August were quite ordinary. It was the kind of trip that huge numbers of climbers have enjoyed before and since — a mountaineering holiday with no disasters and a minimum of alarming moments. They took an overnight train to Grenoble and from a village base warmed up on two medium-sized peaks in the Dauphiné. Then they travelled by train to Chamonix and from a hotel at the south-western edge of the Mont Blanc range reached two more summits before traversing the massif to Courmayeur. They finished their holiday with a fine climb on Mont Blanc itself. Frank took plenty of photos from which he chose 40 to make up the balance for *A Camera in the Hills*. And he wrote a book about the trip and called it simply, *Mountaineering Holiday*.

He now seemed to have developed a wry take on life. Experiences he'd found frustrating in his youth he accepted with good humour or at the worst, resignation and this was reflected in his writing. So the Channel crossing became fun with his stories about the gentleman with the large silk hat packed with drugs, and the one about the seasick Admiral terrified of being recognised. The first Alpine hut they tried was full so they bivouacked nearby, and his description of the fug in the hut next morning, comparing it with the inside of a submarine trapped on the sea bed, is memorable. The climax of the holiday came with an ascent of the Innominata, the very demanding climb high on the south side of Mont Blanc, a mountainside of many memories for Frank. To overcome the final difficulties they joined forces with a team of German climbers — decent friendly men who shared their food and openly regretted their country's unstoppable surge towards World War Two.

'We had a day or two of our holiday left,' he wrote, 'but why wait? It would be a sorry anti-climax to struggle up some peak in the teeth of bad weather. That evening in sullen ominous weather we set off for England. Our mountaineering holiday had ended. A few days later Europe was at war.'

TWENTY THREE

Yew Tree Cottage

With war imminent Kathleen gathered us children together and joined Mollie in Northampton where we lived in a small terraced house about a mile from the town centre. Northampton was best known for making boots and shoes and therefore assumed to be safe from aerial attack — a bomb that fell on a nearby lunatic asylum (as they were called then) was thought to be from a German plane emptying the last of its load after a raid on a more important target further north. However one hot summer afternoon I was walking past a big shoe factory just round the corner from where we lived, and saw through a basement window aeroplanes being made. I hoped Hitler wouldn't find out.

Frank also moved. While working in Hampstead he'd made frequent visits to Tenningshook, often with Nona, and he'd toyed with the idea of living there permanently with her. But the surrounding common had been developed and there were now too many people who'd known Kathleen for them to feel comfortable. There were bad memories. The garden was overgrown. Starting again somewhere else seemed best, although just after a war had begun wasn't the ideal time to move house.

Aged 39 Frank was still liable for recruitment, and soon after war had been declared on 3 September 1939 he'd written to the War Office offering to give morale-boosting talks to the troops on mountaineering. It was a rather weird letter which made much of the friendliness of the Germans he'd recently encountered on Mont Blanc: 'Although we are at war and are going to smash Hitlerism for ever, such a sharing of danger and such a comradeship is deserving of more than passing notice, particularly as the German [climbing] leader agreed that through such sports as mountaineering a greater under-standing could be derived than through more formal channels.' He also praised the Ghurkhas he'd employed on Kamet, and perhaps the men might like to hear about the Dalai Lama and the Tibetan system of government?[1]

In a department dealing with unsolicited letters from the British public, someone must have heard of Frank. Three months later he was called for interview and appointed a temporary Staff Captain. In January, 1940 he wrote to Jack Newth:

> It is gratifying to hear that yet another picture book is wanted. I would like to do nothing better, but I have been muscled into this blasted war and am now at the War Office where I shall sometime in the near future be one of the uniformed herd. I've a superheated office of my own and am attached to the CIGS [Chief of the Imperial General Staff]. What about lunch sometime? In fact come and lunch with me at the War Office itself and see the Brass Hats! Tel. War Office, extension 149.[2]

Frank's civilian career now appeared to be suspended, but apart from a few interruptions he was able to continue writing until he was posted abroad in September 1943 — well over halfway through the war. Meanwhile Jack Newth, exempted from service because of his company's educational publishing, was able to keep going with the photo albums. Despite paper rationing, he launched three more before the end of the war using unpublished photographs from the author's stock. Frank also found time in this period to write two more books for Hodders and one for the publisher, J.M. Dent. It might be thought from all this he had a 'good' war. Certainly it was easy at first, but a very tough time awaited him in the last 18 months.

His boss at the War Office, General Ironside, asked him to help design equipment for a force of ski-borne troops planned to occupy northern Norway and disrupt German use of valuable mineral ore. However the idea was abandoned, Frank was made redundant, paid £100 from special funds, and in March reverted to being a civilian.

Meanwhile he had domestic trouble. Nona's husband, Bob Guthrie started divorce proceedings citing him as co-respondent in adultery at Tenningshook. The suit was undefended, costs were awarded against him and with Kathleen in a state of denial and refusing to divorce him, Nona decided to make the best of the situation and changed her name to Smythe. Their neighbours at Tenningshook weren't deceived, but she and Frank hoped that with a move to a new district the uncomfortable truth about their relationship would stay secret. I was curious to find out more about the legal implications of this and called on my local registrar.

'Name-changing doesn't have to be by Deed Poll, which is gazetted and made public,' I was told. 'It can be done by Statutory Deed — sworn in front of a solicitor, a fee paid, and not made public. Several names can be put on the certificate, and normally are in the case of divorce or name-changing.'

On 12 March 1940 Frank's mother, Florence, died suddenly at the age of 75, and he went down to Bexhill to arrange her funeral. With her death he was freed from the last of the three women whose influence had dominated his life. For nearly a decade the sadly incapable Kathleen together with her strong-willed mother had frustrated him, but since childhood his own mother had often been even more difficult. Communication with her had only worked by letter. But when he had contemplated his mother's all too short married life, her long widowhood, her understandably fraught attachment to him, and her generosity in supporting him when he clawed his way up as a writer to escape the life he was doomed for ... At those times he had been appalled with himself.

I went down to Bexhill. Florence had died on a Tuesday, Frank had registered her death on the Thursday, and complying with the legal minimum three-day period required, had arranged her funeral for the following day. I had the receipt for his payment of five pounds eight shillings (£5.40) for a cemetery plot and an obliging attendant directed me to the final resting place of the grandmother I never knew. Her grave was unmarked, no stone or surround, just an oblong of grass among thousands of well-tended graves beside Great High Wood on the Sussex downs north of the town. It was a calm overcast December afternoon. Crows cawed and squabbled in the trees, there was a faint murmur of traffic and I could just see the gleam of the Channel. A lifetime suddenly seemed terribly short.

Frank got his opportunity to give talks to the troops later that month. He joined the ENSA team [Entertainments National Service Association] and was sent to France, where the British Army's Expeditionary Force, the BEF had assembled, ready to fight alongside the French to resist the German advance into western Europe when it came. He remained a civilian, but like the other entertainers, the musicians, comedians, actors, singers and so on, he was granted the honorary rank of Lieutenant. All wore standard army battledress to avoid being shot as spies (it was hoped) should they be captured by the enemy. Artistes were paid a standard £10 per week, whether they were superstars like Laurence Olivier or humbler entertainers glad to earn a crust. Performances varied, the scheme sometimes earning the epithet 'Every Night

Something Awful'. Frank limited himself to Mount Everest, but I never discovered how many marks out of 10 he got for that. He returned to England on 21 April, just 19 days before the German Panzer divisions smashed westwards, comprehensively ending the 'Phoney War.' The Allied forces were pushed back to the Channel coast, and the miraculous evacuation of the great majority of the soldiers from Dunkirk followed at the end of May.

Hitler then decided that Germany needed air superiority before an invasion of England could be made, and there began a near-overwhelming attack by the Luftwaffe on the Royal Air Force, culminating in the extraordinary success of the latter in the Battle of Britain later in the summer. This was followed by massive night bombing of London — the blitz — mainly in an attempt to demoralise the population, but this also failed to achieve its objective. And in May 1941 the threat of invasion was lifted when Hitler attacked Russia.

At last, at the end of June 1940 Frank and Nona quit Tenningshook. Jack Newth was among those he informed:

> I am purchasing a place in St Leonard's Forest. A Tudor style cottage and sixteen acres — which has the most beautiful garden and situation of its kind that I have ever seen … I thought that perhaps over a year or two I might make a collection of photographs depicting every season and aspect of the garden … The book might be called 'My Sussex Garden' or some such title, and I feel sure, judging from the excellent sales of *The Valley of Flowers* [it] would do well … What do you think? Do you publish any gardening books? I should like to buy *Living in the Country* and *Storing, Preserving and Pickling*.[3]

Jack Newth was cautiously encouraging but there's no record of what he thought about his favourite mountaineering author doing a bit of pickling and preserving in his spare time.

Yew Tree Cottage was on the outskirts of Colgate, a rambling village east of Horsham in Sussex. Some 15 miles of country roads separated it from Tenningshook, a clean break from the old life. The cottage stood near the end of a lane that curved south and west into extensive woodland. The previous owners, who had had the house built 10 years earlier, had cleared an area for a garden at the back. The house was constructed of warm red Sussex brick, half-timbered, with casement windows competing with masses of climbing roses and Virginia creeper.

Ursula Malloch Brown had lived at Colgate and the nearby village of Balcombe for most of her life and known Frank and Nona well. At 80 she was still spry, quick-witted and had clear memories of those long-gone days. As a young woman she had lived with her parents at the far end of the lane where Yew Tree Cottage stood, and after dark she would sometimes see the light in the garden shed where Frank did his writing. When she married at the end of the war her husband's best man could not attend so at short notice she asked Frank to stand in for him; she sent me a photograph of him outside the church, pale and gaunt in his uniform. She remembered the cottage being built. There had been a huge yew which was cut down to make way for it, and this she said was a great relief as she had always felt afraid when going past the tree. She then told me a strange and rather disconcerting story.

In the autumn of 1948 Frank and Nona had held a dinner party. They invited three couples — Ursula and her husband George, Prunella Stack and her fiancé Alistair Albers, and making up the party, Jean and Leo Zinovieff. Some of the guests were climbing friends of Frank's. It was the first time that Ursula had been in the dining room in Yew Tree Cottage. 'It immediately felt haunted,' she said. 'I thought it must be where the yew tree had been.' She then told me that after the dinner party within three years three of the four men who had attended — three quite young and healthy individuals — were dead. Frank had succumbed the following year from a severe illness. Albers, shortly after marrying Prunella Stack had fallen to his death while walking on Table Mountain. And soon after that Leo Zinovieff had been killed in a train crash.

I researched yew trees on the internet. It was 'The Death Tree and a source of poison'. It was associated with 'Celts, Druids, the Otherworld and Spiritual Guidance'. It was an 'ancient tree, its fossilised imprint dating more than 200 million years to the Triassic'. It seemed best to keep an open mind about yew trees.

At the end of December 1940 Frank drove up to North Wales to take photographs for a new album. His first stop was Capel Curig, the starting point for a walk over the Carnedds, and in delightful conditions of sun, mist and Brocken Spectres his camera was soon busy. He had only a few days and walked on his own, covering the Snowdon Horseshoe, old haunts round Gwynant and Aberglaslyn, then the Carnedds again with a school group and their teacher. Fifty-one photographs illustrated *Over Welsh Hills*, all taken on calm sunny days, the hills delectable in the early-winter snow.

The book was popular, perhaps because for the first time the pictures and their short captions were supported by an account in which Frank took the reader on a nostalgic ramble. He remembered a disastrous camping trip in heavy rain with a tent that weighed a hundredweight. He told the story about the sheep he surprised on Llewedd that leapt to its death. He joked about General Bruce's attempt to lose weight. And there was the horror of the insane climber who left two soaked and exhausted novices in his party to die of exposure on their way back from a climb. The pictures were enticing, but maybe for many of Frank's followers the writing more so.

Sir Francis Younghusband was a frequent guest in those early days at Yew Tree Cottage. Currant Hill had been sold and he and his wife had moved to premises near Victoria Station, a new base from which he promoted his visionary ideas. But with Lady Helen becoming senile, remote from reality and under professional care he now travelled more than ever, and Nona, with her cooking if not her cuddling, and Frank, with his splendid garden, offered a restful retreat. But one other person had become the focus of Younghusband's life. Sir Francis, in his dotage, had at last fallen deeply in love.

The most important of the societies he had founded was the World Congress of Faiths, which aimed to bring together the major religions, making wars an evil of the past. At a Congress gathering he had met Madeline Lees, the wife of a baronet from Lychett Minster in Dorset, and the two had established a rapport that had led to a grand passion. It was an unlikely union since Madeline was 32 years younger and had seven children. But Younghusband's charm, good humour and reputation made him welcome to all the family at Lychett, and when he and Madeline were apart they wrote to one another almost daily. Frank, knowing nothing about the affair was puzzled when their guest hovered near the phone. 'Who is this person ringing so much?' he asked Nona. 'Why can't Sir Francis have some peace?' But Nona understood what was happening. Younghusband however was frail and the end came a year later, in July 1942 in his 80th year. He fainted at a Congress meeting in Birmingham and Madeline took him to Lychett to recover. But her care was unavailing and one morning after a stroke he died.

Frank and Nona owed much to the 'Last Great Imperial Adventurer'. He was the man who had provided Nona with a pathway into English society. He was the hugely respected and influential figure who in earlier years had given Frank confidence and inspiration. To each of them he had been a good friend, even introducing them to one another.

Frank developed a routine at their new home. He usually wrote in the morning, in the shed in the summer months, as always in pencil in an exercise book on his knee. In the afternoons he gardened or went shooting rabbits, seen as vermin and a useful addition to the food ration. I was contacted by John Warren, a retired architect who at the age of nine had lived in Colgate and sometimes accompanied Frank on these outings, acting as 'bag boy'. 'He was what I would call lean and aquiline,' he told me. 'He wore breeches and an open-necked shirt, sometimes a sweater, and had that sort of easy lope through the woods. It was often difficult to get information out of him. I would say something like, 'What was it like on Everest?' If I hadn't spoken he'd be quite happy to tramp along silently, with me trailing a foot or two behind.'

Even rural Colgate didn't escape the great summer of 1940 aerial battle. 'We were watching a Heinkel when it was at about 10,000 feet,' Warren told me. 'It was damaged by a fighter. It circled, trailing smoke, and then blew up. The main bulk of it came down about half a mile from our house. The bombs went off — it was a terrible mess — the pilot had a huge hole in his head. One of them came down by parachute, but there were bits of the plane everywhere — little curls of smoke going up in the heather.' The school was bombed, with the house next door receiving a direct hit, killing its occupant, the district nurse. 'How naïve we were,' he said. 'We actually had a debate in the playground about whether we should be grateful to Hitler for giving us three weeks extra holiday, or annoyed with him for killing the nurse.'

Frank and Nona had a very upsetting problem in their first years at Colgate. At the time of Younghusband's death, Nona had told Madeline about her first marriage; how Robert Guthrie, not wanting a family, had coerced her into having abortions, and that these interventions seemed to have made her incapable of having the children she and Frank both wanted. Since starting to live with Frank she had conceived twice but each time had miscarried early in the pregnancy. Patrick French, researching for his Younghusband biography had learnt these intimate details when he met Katharine Rawlinson, the Lees' oldest daughter, half a century later. Katharine also told him about the postcards — the 'hate mail' sent by Frank's 'real wife'. 'They had such a dog's life,' she said, 'because they couldn't settle down and be accepted in any village they went to. She would immediately find out where they were and let the cat out of the bag. She must have been a dreadful woman.'

When a biographer is closely involved with the life of his subject — as I am — the job can become difficult. I have no doubt that Katharine was faithfully relaying to Patrick French what her mother had been told by Nona. And I am extremely grateful to Patrick for allowing me to hear and make use of the tape recording he made at his meeting. Earlier, when I read in his biography that my mother had sent postcards to Frank knowing full well that they would probably be read by strangers happy to spread salacious gossip, I couldn't believe it; it was so out of character. My mother died in 1991 and throughout her later life there was only one person she ever blamed for the failure of her marriage, and that was herself. She never blamed Frank, and Nona was never talked about. She refused for years to give him the divorce he wanted because she was convinced that he would come back to her, and when she did divorce him she used it as a bargaining chip in persuading him to pay for our education at a good school. I can only imagine that in the first year or two of her separation from Frank, when we children were very young and vulnerable, sheer despair caused her to write the postcards, not thinking or even caring that in the process of revealing Frank and Nona's secret she was also hurting the man she believed would return to us.

TWENTY FOUR

War Years

In January 1942 Frank suddenly found himself back in the war. A letter arrived from the Air Ministry (then the RAF's headquarters, proudly separate from the Army's War Office) asking for his help with an instruction book for aircrew. A writer was wanted for a pamphlet on survival in inhospitable terrain. Aeroplanes were of course more likely to crash-land in deserts or jungles than on mountains, but an expert was needed immediately so, as the official mind presumed, an author who'd been up Mount Everest would do. And remembering the old adage in the Military that whatever you're asked to do you do it or you'll be given an even worse job, Frank accepted.

You are lumbered with a problem, but this does not necessarily mean you are the person who has to deal with it. When I was halfway through flying training in the RAF I was posted with my course to a station where we were billeted in rooms in a hut. It was mid-winter and freezing. Each room had an iron stove and a supply of coal, and after trying unsuccessfully to light the stove I resorted to a can of petrol from my car. There was a minor explosion, I dropped the can and fled, and four of us quelled the fire with extinguishers. But the carpet was ruined, and I had signed for it. An older hand showed me what I had to do; with knives, steel wool and mud we made the whole carpet worn out, unserviceable. I took it to Stores, complained, and exchanged it for a new one. My brother in the Army had to reduce a camouflage net to two pieces and exchange them separately when he found he was one short on his inventory.

Frank's solution to his predicament was to write to the indefatigable Arthur Hinks at the RGS. The Secretary's answer was manna from Heaven. 'Our comparatively recent publication, *Hints to Travellers Vol. II*,' he told Frank, 'contains a very great deal that may be of use to Air Forces both in desert conditions and in others as the whole book is full of useful information on how to make oneself comfortable in all conditions dry or wet. Desert tents with special insulation are treated on page 26, desert camps on page 40, water supply in 55 and 85, clothing in 99, and so on. I have always thought that this book should be in use in all training centres, and when it came out it was brought officially to the notice of the military and Royal Air Force, but I don't think with much result at the time … I am posting you a volume.'[1]

Frank completed the pamphlet by mid-February then began visiting RAF stations throughout the UK. He was flown in all sorts of aircraft, from open-cockpit Tiger Moths to lumbering four-engine Stirlings. 'Today I had a most interesting trip,' he reported to Nona. 'I wanted not only to see the aeroplane on which the pupils learn to fly the Spitfire, but also to look at Snowdon from the air. So one of the instructors took me. There was dense haze up to 2,500 feet, but above that it was brilliantly clear. We flew round and round Snowdon, which looked magnificent snow-covered.' At another station he went into a decompression chamber and 'managed 15 minutes at 25,000 feet and five at 27,000.' He flew over Yew Tree Cottage and 'nearly knocked the chimney pots off.' He flew in a 'very hush-hush new plane' to 30,000 feet.[2] He spent Easter climbing in the Lake District with old friends, having previously checked the snow conditions on Scafell from the cockpit of a Hudson.[3]

But this life of Riley inevitably came to an end. In August he was summoned to a meeting at the War Office with Brigadier Robert Laycock, Commander of the Special Service Brigade, and asked to set up a new centre for training commandos in mountain and snow warfare. Given a free hand in selecting an area, he chose the Cairngorms, with the village of Braemar as the base, and the requisitioned Fife Arms Hotel as his headquarters. As commander of the unit he was promoted to squadron leader. He had no doubt about the potential of the Cairngorms for training soldiers in tough conditions. The weather on the high plateau could be Arctic especially in winter, compared with the more benign climate of the mountains on the west coast. Although the ground rose to little more than 4,000 feet, Frank reckoned that if a soldier could learn to survive there he could function anywhere.

He invited John Hunt to be chief instructor. Hunt was a regular army major whom he had known since 1935, and was a very proficient Alpine and Himalayan climber — experience which would culminate in his leadership of the successful Everest expedition 10 years later. Other officers appointed were Bill Mackenzie from the Scottish Mountaineering Club, David Cox from the Alpine Club, the Polar explorer David Haig-Thomas and Robert Chew an old friend of Geoffrey Young. These men would train more junior instructors ready for the arrival of the main body of commandos in January 1943.

They were depending on the Cairngorms to provide good snow, but unfortunately this didn't happen. As Frank commented, 'We had hoped for much skiing. The stores were packed with Greenland sledges and much else … But the winter of 1942-3 was unusually snow-free. Instead, it blew. It blew as it does in Tibet. There were five full gales a week and one hurricane. What happened on the seventh day no one cared — it was our rest day.'[4] He described one outing in exceptionally cruel conditions:

> We had set off from Derry Lodge, each man carrying some 70 pounds of food and equipment with the intention of camping for a week by Loch Etchachan. In Glen Derry it was merely blowing the usual gale, but when we turned the corner into Corrie Etchachan we encountered a hurricane. As we mounted the slopes towards the loch the fury of the storm grew and veritable tornadoes of sleet and hail swept down the glen. I was ahead prospecting for a suitable camping site, and behind me was the leading section, which was commanded by a certain cockney sergeant, one of the humorous grumblers that for generations have been the backbone of the British Army … Of a sudden a gust whirled me off my feet and flung me violently down on a rock several yards away. As I lay recovering my wind, which had been completely knocked out of me, I saw the section in single file toiling up towards me. Then came another gust which lifted every man off his feet. As they slowly struggled upright there was a momentary lull and in it I heard the voice of the sergeant: ''E can 'ave 'is Everest, every f***ing inch of it!'[5]

John Hunt in his autobiography *Life is Meeting*, was generous in his assessment of his commandant at Braemar: 'Frank and I got on well together and I think we made an effective partnership. He was a gentle, most unwarlike character, whose main contribution to the work at the centre was to impart his deep, poetic love of the mountains to the tough, high-spirited wearers of the Green Beret. His achievements and his obvious sincerity won him respect, the more so because of his very slight physique. I was able to supply an element of military pragmatism to the exercises, which had tended to be rather aimless mountain walks which Frank so much enjoyed.'[6] However years later, when questioned privately Hunt said, 'He was a most inappropriate choice as commandant; he had no military experience and the direction of the courses lacked purpose and organisation. Inevitably, we had strong differences in my determination to train the units for war. But after a few initial rows we settled down and he did not interfere with my training programme. His knowledge of military training and tactical exercises was zero!'[7] Hunt though remembered his first meeting with Frank, who had approved him for the 1936 Everest expedition only for an RAF medical board to discover he had a heart 'murmur' and reject him. 'I have an abiding memory of Frank's concern and sympathy,' said Hunt. 'He had wanted me to be a member of the team. I learnt later on that he had had a similar verdict in the 1920s on his own heart condition. He was a very caring person. This was the beginning of our friendship.'

Braemar had not been a success, and with an Allied invasion of northern Europe now on the horizon emphasis was placed on the commandos being prepared for cliff-assault. In August 1943 Frank and his staff were dispatched to Snowdonia, to Capel Curig and Llanrwst. From these bases teams of climbing novices sampled the delights of Welsh rock. 'I've been climbing in gym shoes on Tryfan today,' he told Nona. 'My men almost half my age climb like cats but I can show them a thing or two on a hillside, and yesterday took them up Snowdon at a speed of 3,000 feet an hour at my fast but rhythmical speed, and that made them think!'[8]

Frank was discovering that in the war you were like a leaf floating in a turbulent river; you didn't stay in the same place for long. After only a few weeks in North Wales he was called to the War Office again, where Brigadier C.N. Barclay asked him to become Chief Instructor of Training in High-Mountain Warfare in the Canadian Rockies. Braemar had been unproductive, but it had been decided to train one regiment to operate in alpine conditions, should the war in Europe need a force to take on the enemy in high mountains. The Lovat Scouts were chosen for this task, a famous Scottish regiment originally raised by a distinguished Highland laird, Lord Lovat to fight in the Boer War, and now one of the toughest and most highly-regarded in the army.

On 6 September Frank accompanied a military mission with Brigadier Barclay to the USA and Canada. In Washington members of the American Alpine Club helped him choose the latest clothing and warm boots with cleated rubber soles — a big advance on nailed boots. Then he headed for Ottawa and linked up with Major Rex Gibson, an experienced climber who had been appointed his Canadian liaison officer. He and Gibson flew to Calgary, proceeding by road from there to Banff, and then to Jasper in the heart of the Rockies.

From the aircraft his first sight of the mountains was captivating: 'The weather was perfect and when daylight came I saw the infinite leagues of prairie stretched below, brown and parched at this time of year. Then came my greatest thrill. Spanning the whole western horizon in a mighty curve bending along the perimeter of the Earth were the Rockies, a blue broken line of peaks far above the brown patchwork of plain.'[9]

He found that Jasper was ideal. It had access to the Athabasca Glacier and Columbia Icefield and the surrounding high snowy peaks. There were mountain huts, chalets and trails. As well as providing an excellent training ground for the Scouts, Frank noted other potential advantages: 'It was interesting to see peak after peak still unclimbed, and you can be sure I marked them down! ... This is going to give me magnificent material for a lecture — I'm taking photos both in natural colour and black and white.'[10]

On 24 September he flew back to Ottawa to report his findings and sit through a week of conferences before continuing by train to New York and Washington for yet more meetings, lunches and other commitments: 'I had to make a speech. I did so with the sweat pouring off me; doubtless they thought me nervous. I cannot tolerate the tropical heat in which Americans live. I would sell my soul for an open window, give anything for an honest to God British draught.'[11] Then it was back to Ottawa for more discussions before he and Gibson returned to Jasper on 7 October, charged with making a reconnaissance of the proposed training areas.

These long flights were to become a part of life for Frank, and he found them exhausting. A regular service by Trans-Canada Airlines had only started operating in the last few years, and it took 15 hours to cross the continent using Lockeed Electras, flying at about 200 miles per hour. Life was stressful in other ways. On top of the workload in a primitive office with little secretarial help he disliked the food and the routine for meals: 'I find it trying having to digest a huge supper at 5 p.m. with nothing more that day, and drinking tea stewed to the colour of ink.' And in another letter: 'Have been quite unwell and had recourse to medical treatment as was fairly knocked out by pains and sickness.'[12]

The reconnaissance took Frank and Gibson and a third member of their party, a Canadian corporal, to the closed Columbia Icefield Chalet hotel, where they used rooms on the first floor, connected to the ground by steps. Here they often spotted a grizzly bear rummaging for scraps — a worrying sight, although the animal ignored them. One night however Frank, in descending the steps to relieve himself discovered he was almost on top of the bear.

'I exercised the only persuasion I could think of,' he said. 'He gave one bound and rushed away as hard as he could go, exactly like a cat when from a window you hurl a basin of water upon it. We did not see him again.' Unfortunately the bear returned later, and now deemed to be interfering with military property, was shot.[13]

From the Chalet the three men climbed peaks including Mount Athabasca, 11,453 feet. The approach lay up the five-mile-long glacier of the same name, where conditions were very dangerous with numerous crevasses, some hidden under a crust of frozen snow. On the descent Gibson in the lead was carefully following their upward tracks when suddenly he broke through into a crevasse. The inexperienced corporal behind him had allowed slack to develop in the rope and this now viciously tightened under the weight of the falling Gibson, dragging the corporal and then Frank behind him, towards the crevasse. By a desperate combined effort they halted their slide, helped by the rope friction in the snow at the edge of the hole through which Gibson had dis-appeared. With the corporal — a big man — securely holding the rope, Frank cautiously approached the crevasse, and seeing Gibson dangling some 15 feet down a bottle-shaped chasm of unknown depth, reassured him that they would soon have him out. This was easier said than done. Frank placed his ice axe under the rope to ensure a smooth pull, then with a huge effort he and the corporal dragged Gibson to the surface. It was a lesson in strict rope handling on a glacier — very nearly learnt through fatal experience.

On 15 October Brigadier Barclay visited Jasper, and in the course of talks with Frank pledged his support, assuring him that he would recommend his transfer to the Army and promotion to Lieutenant-Colonel. Soon after this Frank made yet another trip to Ottawa, New York and Washington to report his latest findings. 'In a few days I'm returning to the Far West,' he wrote, 'and by Jove I'll be glad to settle down at Jasper. I've now done over 20,000 miles of travelling, and three-quarters of my nights have been spent on trains and aeroplanes — a most fatiguing business.'[14]

But there would be no let up. He had to requisition accommodation for the main body of the Scouts due to arrive in early January. Rations had to be ordered and storage arranged. Transport was needed — lorries, tracked vehicles, snow ploughs and even pack horses. First-aid training was important, communication equipment a headache. Two aircraft on loan from the RCAF would play a part in casualty evacuation, spotting, recce, aerial survey and photography. Plans had to be made for air-dropping supplies. And above all, there was the final selection of Instructors. Gibson put forward 85 potential Canadian Army instructors but few had glacier experience and Frank believed that none of them was a competent mountaineer. He planned an immediate three-week course in instructing the instructors. Conditions were sometimes extreme, as he wrote to Nona on 5 December:

> I'm just back from a two-day trip. Imagine thirteen husky people packed into a little cabin. I slept in a sleeping bag on the floor. In the night a high wind sent snow whiffling through a crack. Temp. 15 below zero [F]. Then the wind so rocked our abode that an avalanche of crockery descended upon me from a shelf. I woke with a wild yell thinking that the end of all things had come.
>
> Next day we were on a peak of 11,300 feet [Snow Dome] in the foulest wind I've experienced since Everest 1933. The cold, about minus 20 degrees and the snow blown on a 50 miles per hour gale burned like whip lashes. An icicle formed on my nose — a gust removed it together with a piece of skin. I'm very sore — my whole face and neck. Even my eye lashes stuck together. The bread was frozen too — fruit juice in a water bottle was solid ice. One of the party was frost-bitten — his feet were like marble blocks. In peacetime I wouldn't dream of taking on a job in weather conditions like today.[15]

Soon after this things went badly wrong for Frank. The stress of working long hours, often until after midnight, the poor food, the savage winter weather, the trips with the rookie instructors — these things had brought him to breaking point. While working in his office he was seized by a violent stomach pain. The medical officer sent him to Jasper hospital where he was told that his trouble resulted from a dodgy appendix. He was allowed to return to duty, but warned that if he had any more trouble he would need an operation. A few days later he had another attack. This time he was transferred to the University Hospital at Edmonton where the consultant told him that his appendicitis had been brought on by a diseased gall bladder and that this organ at least should be removed. But again Frank argued it was vital he kept working, and again he was reluctantly released, with strict instructions not to go 'into the blue' until he'd had the operation. Things then happened all at once. He had left the hospital to join up with his adjutant for the return to camp when he suffered a seizure. He was quickly returned to hospital. The following morning he was operated on. When he regained consciousness he had lost both his appendix and his gall bladder. It was Christmas Eve, 1943.

This collapse of his health effectively marked the end of Frank's command in Canada. He had been knocked out of action even before the Lovat Scouts arrived. His recovery in hospital was long and slow, with a dangerous relapse in early January when, on attempting to stand up he fainted and had to be revived with oxygen. Pneumonia and pleurisy were diagnosed — it had been a 'near thing' he was told. He was given radium therapy and sulphur drugs. He was nearly a month in hospital and the staff found him an unusual and sometimes difficult patient. He practised water-colour painting. He wrote huge numbers of letters. The American Alpine Club President, Dr Monroe Thorington sent him a package of climbing books. He had so many visitors that Anderson, the consultant told him bluntly that he must not convert his hospital room into a military office. When he was invited by the British Ambassador to attend a prestigious dinner in Washington, Anderson's patience snapped. 'He was quite adamant and won't let me go,' Frank said sorrowfully, but with private feelings of relief. The doctor was anxious that his patient should go somewhere sunny and warm for his convalescence, and eventually it was arranged that he should stay in New Jersey, at the home of a family called Cutting, who would be away but would leave staff to look after their guest. Six weeks of sick leave were authorised.

The job of commanding mountain warfare training in Canada seemed to be jinxed. When Frank had been offered the post five months earlier, he was a shoe-in for Colonel Rusty Westmoreland, an experienced mountaineer who'd had to drop out when he too needed a gall bladder operation. During Frank's absence control of the training was taken over by Major Sandy Wedderburn, second in command of the Lovat Scouts. Sadly, on Christmas Eve, 1944, exactly a year after Frank's operation, Wedderburn met with an appalling freak accident during the Italian Campaign. He slipped in descending the marble staircase of a hotel in Aquila and fell over low banisters to his death.

Frank arrived back at Jasper on 19 February 1944, two weeks before the end of his leave. Everything was running smoothly, there was little he was allowed to do, and frustration soon crept in. 'I'm like a bear with a sore head,' he wrote. 'In fact I heartily wish that I were back in England leading a peaceful carefree life.' For weeks he was involved in fringe activities. He became friendly with Belmore Browne, a visiting American instructor well known for his art and mountain exploration, who gave him tips on painting and showed him how to build an igloo, following which they slept in it, comfortably. He flew with the USAF to Fairbanks in Alaska. Locally a pilot obligingly flew him round Mts Robson and Alberta, and he picked out a route up the unclimbed rock spire of Mount Brussels. At last, with the training complete and the instructors disbanded, Frank travelled to Washington to make his final report. He embarked for England on 2 May 1944.

The last months of his war service began uneventfully. He was assigned to the Pool of Lecturers and could relax at home, waiting for work to come along, rather like a teacher on supply. But this didn't last long. In August he made the long and complicated flight to the Advanced Headquarters of the Allied Armies in Italy, at Caserta near Naples — where he was attached as an adviser to the Commander in Chief, General Sir Harold Alexander. After the Allied invasions at Salerno and Tarranto in September 1943 the advance northwards through Italy had been gruelling with a heavy toll of casualties on both sides. The Germans were currently defending a strong position in the Apennine Mountains about three-quarters of the way up the country.

Frank revealed very little about this part of his life and only a few bare statistics are to be found in war archives. However he wrote to Nona and a number of these letters survived. He was conscious of the need for secrecy about many details, but the letters give a flavour of the strange disjointed existence he endured, soon plagued by further ill health as the war in Europe ground on towards its end:

3 Aug. [1944]   I arrived here yesterday — I'm now on General Alexander's staff in advanced HQ [at Caserta] and have a job which is going to occupy me to the full. After arriving I went down to a nearby lake for a bathe. The water was perfect. I had got out and was sunning myself when a man came along in shorts and shirt — no badges. I entered into casual conversation and he was obviously a simple, charming fellow I took to on sight. But his face was familiar and a few minutes later I realised it was the CIC himself. He invited me to dinner. It's a most interesting and responsible job which is good to have after so much dithering about getting here. There's nothing worse than boredom. I'm on my own and I plough my own furrow as it were. I'm not feeling very fit — my innards are giving me trouble again. Saw the MO who gave me some opium mixture to quieten them down. He said I shouldn't have been sent overseas after a gall bladder operation. The weather is brilliant and I have the luxury of electric light in my tent.

12 Aug.   I'm now in Rome. I've just paid a visit to the Italian Alpine Club.
            It was most amusing — they were more than cordial and I had for
            courtesy's sake to drink a formal toast in strong Italian brandy at
            three-thirty on this particularly hot afternoon.

25 Aug.   I'm now attached to HQ 4th Indian Division … I've been at the
            front for a few days and am constantly on the move. My memories
            will be dust and rush, shattered villages, endless road blocks, constant
            packing and unpacking at a moment's notice, the thunder of guns and
            all the racket of modern war. I'm working with the GOC of this very
            famous division, General Holworthy. I've a jeep of my own and
            a driver called Isaac, who also acts as my batman. It's a great life this
            roving commission!

7 Sept.   I've not been at all well and the Camp MO insisted on my going to
            see the medical specialist at Base Hospital for an overhaul. Actually
            I think it is due in part from shock, as Isaac and I had a very near
            squeak the other day from a shell which burst on the road in front
            of us not more than five yards away. We were both stunned and my
            body has felt since as though it had been kicked. Although the jeep
            was bent we were untouched by splinters.

11 Sept.   I'm in the 93rd General Hospital which is right down in the south of
            Italy [In Naples] where I was sent by hospital ship. It's simply that my
            innards don't seem able to cope with this racketing life, and I can't
            keep anything down. They now tell me they don't think there is
            anything organically wrong, but it's a question of the right diet and a
            well-regulated life. All through the war I've tried to deceive myself into
            liking the life, but fundamentally I've loathed it more than I can say.
            But pray heaven it will soon be ended! I'm not gregarious. I loathe the
            lack of privacy.

20 Sept.   I have arrived at the Red Cross convalescent home at La Selva, which
            is delightful — up in the hills about six miles from the sea [near Bari]
            and I have a room on my own in a beautiful little villa. I'm being very
            lazy here, putting my feet up and reading and scribbling, and it's doing
            me the power of good. Unless my jeep, which was being repaired,
            turns up it's going to be a deuce of a job getting back north.

Frank did have difficulty getting back to HQ at Caserta. He was offered a
spare seat in a light aircraft, but the pilot had to turn back in bad weather.
The other passengers left by road, but he eventually got there in the aircraft,

enduring three hours of thunderstorms, severely bumpy air and a failed compass that 'resulted in our finding ourselves over the wrong ocean.' Safely back at his desk, he wrote a note to General John Harding, Alexander's Chief of Staff, asking to be returned to the UK since there was a better chance of a job for him there. General Alexander agreed, and meanwhile Frank went sight-seeing in Florence and Rome. But his weakened constitution couldn't survive even these activities:

23 Oct.   I've got a wretched chill and feel foul with a very tight feeling in my chest, so shall try to visit the MO tomorrow, but the last thing I want is to get into his clutches at this stage. I retired to bed and a Colonel Turner turned up in the afternoon and told me I must go to hospital immediately, as I was developing pneumonia. So he packed my bag — he wouldn't allow me out of bed — and an ambulance carted me off.

He eventually recovered and reached England in November. He was in Italy for three months, but had been in hospital or convalescent home for nearly half of that time. His involvement in the war was now over. He was granted the rank of Honorary Lieutenant-Colonel and released to become a civilian again on 27 March 1945.

Twenty Five

Switzerland Again

The war was over but the quiet life seemed to evade Frank. Graham Brown's book *Brenva* had just been published after five years in the hands of the publisher, Dent whose director Ernest Bozman was an Alpine Club member and had been worried by the 'discrediting' of Frank, as he saw it. GB had reluctantly made alterations, but Frank, who demanded that the proofs be seen by his solicitor, was still disgusted by his climbing partner's interpretation of the long-ago events on Mont Blanc.

Then there was Mount Everest. A year earlier an American pilot flying at 30,000 feet in Western China had seen a peak he thought was even higher, and Frank had agreed with American friends to launch an Anglo-US expedition to investigate this after the war. If they found no new world's highest summit their plan B was merely to transfer their efforts to Everest itself. The project fell apart however when the Everest part of the expedition was announced by the Americans. British establishment figures, Geoffrey Young at the forefront, huffed and puffed at the idea of a team like this intruding on such a thoroughly British mountain, and Frank, after receiving a tart and disapproving letter reluctantly bowed out, and so did the Americans. The new 'Everest', Amne Machin, was eventually found to be just 20,610 feet high, the first ascent being made 15 years later by the Beijing Geological Institute.

There was also an uncomfortable domestic situation for Frank. Seven years had gone by since he and Nona had got together and it had been four years since Robert Guthrie had divorced Nona. He and Nona were desperate to marry but Kathleen had refused to divorce him. Finally though, she agreed to meet him in Northampton to talk about it.

My brothers and I remember the meeting. Richard, aged seven and I, some three years older, were sent to meet him off the train and escort him home.

'I didn't recognise him,' said Richard. 'Not like you — you saw him at Castle Station and said there's Dad. I can remember walking up to the town centre — he was in uniform, and lots of soldiers were saluting him, and I thought this was quite an occasion.' At All Saints the three of us caught the bus up the Wellingborough Road, past Abington Park to the Trumpet Inn. From there it was a short walk to where we had lived for the last four years.

Kathleen had found it impossible to go on living with her mother, and in 1941 had moved a short distance to Weston Favell, a pleasant parish on the outskirts of Northampton. Here she rented a small semi-detached house in Ridgeway, a road backing onto allotments and a wood above the Nene valley. We spent the rest of our childhood there and Kathleen lived there for the rest of her life. To make ends meet after her £5 monthly allowance from Frank she taught music at a nearby primary school and after school hours and in holiday time gave piano lessons at home. She travelled back and forth on a sturdy black bicycle with a large basket on the handlebars to carry the shopping. We three children thought nothing of looking after ourselves when we were on our own or with friends; it was decades before society began to fuss and curb young people's independence. My early years were happy and exciting and I remember them with pleasure.

'It was always such a contrast, wasn't it,' John remembered about Frank's visit. 'There he was in colonel's uniform, looking absolutely the dog's dinner. And we went round the side of the house and that's where Mum came out of the kitchen to say hallo to him, and as kids do you know, I looked at the two of them, knowing that this was the first time they'd met for years, and it was a terrible contrast between the four of us, and him, and he was the one looking uncomfortable. You know, that's a moment that lives in my mind, and in a sense you could say it summed things up.'

Of course knowing nothing about the situation we hoped they would get together and we would have a father again. But Kathleen had now given up hope of reconciliation. With just the welfare of her sons important to her she struck the bargain with Frank, 'selling' the divorce for our schooling. They met once more to finalise this and on 11 February 1946 — ironically her birthday — the decree was granted in the divorce court. They had been married 15 years, but had been separated for half of that time. The divorce became absolute on 20 May and Frank and Nona using an accommodation address and obtaining a special Licence to avoid publicity, married three days later at Westminster Register Office. Nona could at last abandon the deceit over her name, and to make herself feel even more comfortable — and maybe an unknowing Frank too — she took four years off her age for the marriage certificate, giving it as 36, which happened to make her two years younger than Kathleen.

Jack Newth and Frank jointly planned the next two albums, *Swiss Winter* and *Snow on the Hills* which needed the author to go to Switzerland in February and March, 1946. Newth also single-handedly organised Frank's Swiss visa, extra foreign currency, priority Swissair reservations, business contacts in Zurich, and while he was about it, an extra petrol ration for his 'essential' travel in Britain. When Frank began to plan for Canada on the heels of the Swiss trip, Newth even fixed free travel for him on the Canadian National Railway.

He also dealt sensitively with his author's occasional bouts of pessimism. When Frank complained that the books of his rival, Walter Poucher were displayed prominently in London shops but there were none of his own anywhere, Newth refused to be drawn, reminding him of the efforts he'd made to keep the books in print throughout six years of war. Frank thought about it and apologised. 'I should like to tell you how grateful I am' he wrote, 'and more than this I value the personal association.'

This was his rather awkward way of referring to their friendship. They had known one another for 15 years and were now on Christian name terms, a rare thing in those days for men in a business relationship. It would be fair to say that Jack Newth, a man who otherwise kept his work strictly separate from his private life became one of Frank's closest friends. I met him a couple of times at my school, Wycliffe College, where he was on the Board of Governors. He had attended as a boy and had recommended Frank should send us there. And he took an interest in our careers after Frank died. Half a century later I got a backwards glimpse of the Jack Newth at work as a managing director when I talked to Charles Black, a retired chairman of his family's publishing dynasty:

> In those days there were no specialist titles. You either were a publisher or you weren't, and someone like Jack did everything. He was a very private person. He called my father Black and my father called him Newth. He was small of stature. He was senior, approachable, formal, quite strict in the way that things were carried out, and one of those people that compartmentalised his life so we in the office never heard a word about what he'd done at the weekend, or where he'd been on holiday, or his family. People like that today would be considered

too inward-looking, too introverted, but in those days it was the way everyone behaved — it was quite normal. They never had any formal meetings. They would discuss things literally by my father saying, 'Oh Newth, I wonder if you've got a moment.' They never had a meeting; they did all their business on the stairs.[1]

Jack and his wife, Bunty lived at Chesham and had six children, three sons and three daughters. He spent his entire working life with Blacks. 'Work, family and Wycliffe were the three legs of the tripod in his life,' his second son, John told me. Jack had died in 1973, but Bunty was in excellent health at the age of 87. When I phoned her she told me that his other interests were few. He'd walked in Austria. He gardened. She laughed at the memory of his stab at being a special constable during the war. She chuckled at the thought of Nona. 'She was terribly bossy to poor Frank. I remember they invited Jack and me to a theatre and dinner in London during the war. And all through dinner she was telling Frank not to put his arms on the table and to hold his fork properly, and all this sort of thing, which I found *highly* embarrassing, but Frank seemed to take it in his stride! I think Jack thought she was rather a joke. We all did. She gave herself such airs. But I think fundamentally she was a very kind person.'[2]

During his solo ski traverse through the Swiss Alps in 1934 Frank had encountered springtime avalanche risks and there had been some very dangerous moments. This time he began in the depths of winter with safer snow conditions and he arranged to have companions for most of the time. It was going to be a set of excursions in different areas starting with three days in Zurich dealing with publishing matters. So it was a business-cum-holiday trip that had none of the raw challenge twelve years earlier.

The difference between the two trips was reflected by Frank's age and mind-set. In 1934 he'd been an ambitious climber in his early 30s at the peak of his powers. Now he was approaching 50, recovering from wartime stress, looking for a secure future while capitalising on his fame, and there to enjoy the skiing. John Hunt summed up Frank's outlook when he was a guest at the Hunts' home on the Welsh border: 'After the war our friendship was resumed. My memory of him then was of a tranquil and domesticated Frank, deeply in love with Nona, and content with his life in a country cottage.'

So it's hardly surprising that Frank's book *Again Switzerland* is the story of a trip that was but a pale shadow of his pre-war mountain adventures.

He laboured to make it an interesting read, but for the first six weeks of a visit due to last less than two months he had rather uninspiring material to work with. For six days he skied cautiously on his own at Adelboden, understandably delighted to be back in the mountains again. His visit to the Lötschental was supposed to be the prelude to traversing the Oberland glaciers with a guide, but a storm forced them to retreat to the valley. There was more bad weather at Verbier, where he joined forces with a friend, Jimmy Belaieff, although they eventually reached Zermatt by road and climbed a modest prize, the Breithorn on the only fine day. They skied back to Verbier via the Haute Route without incident apart from Belaieff suffering from slight snow blindness.

It was a break in this plodding pattern that Frank should spend his last few days making a solo ski crossing of the Bernese Oberland. 'The glaciers' he wrote, 'were as safe as glaciers were ever likely to be owing to the heavy snowfalls, thaws and frosts of late winter which had effectively bridged the crevasses with firm snow.' His logic was unlikely to convince Nona, but in the plan there was a gleam in the eye, a nod towards the unstoppable madness of youth. He claimed he was running out of foreign currency and couldn't afford a guide but there was more to it than that. There was the promise of a stimulating trip in which he would need his wits to keep safe — the fix he would relish after some fairly tedious weeks.

The Oberland crossing took only four days but made for the longest chapter in the book. From Münster in the Rhone Valley he faced a hut bash up soft snow under a broiling sun with a heavy rucksack. But climbing has the potential to delight even the victim of its treadmills. The Galmihorn Hut, which he had to himself that night was superbly situated at the top of the timberline, and after supper he enjoyed a marvellous sunset. 'I remember the night spreading out of the east behind the glowing snows of the Galenstock, and the faint tolling of church bells from one of the villages, and finally, when all the lights were out, a solitary star and a world of snow left softly glowing like a vast pearl.'[3]

The weather was set fair at last. This was the Switzerland he knew. Almost too late a real trip had begun. The plan now was to cross the Galmilücke, a col which gave access to the central convergence of the Oberland glaciers, the largest area of permanent snow and ice in Europe. Once there he would divert to the Finsteraarhorn, using its hut before an early start next day to climb it, the highest mountain of the Bernese Alps. The peak was familiar — he'd climbed it in 1923 with Colonel Neame — but a solo attempt, even for an experienced alpinist, was suitably ambitious.

After leaving the hut he was stopped by a guide with two clients and asked about snow conditions lower down. Then came the inevitable question: Was he quite alone? Frank replied that he was, and wishing the guide good-day immediately moved on. 'I knew what was coming,' he wrote. 'Few guides can resist an opportunity for a homily on the follies of solitary mountaineering, and here was a heaven sent opportunity in the presence of his employers. I had no intention of presenting him with the opportunity. A little later I glanced back. The guide was gesticulating with his arms. I could easily imagine what he was saying. "There goes an *alleinganger*, a fool, a wooden-head. Look at him now. You will never see him again, nobody will. He will fall into a crevasse; he will perish in the first storm; he will be buried in an avalanche; he will …"[4]

After a long hard plod Frank arrived at the Finsteraarhorn Hut. Early next morning, with the weather still perfect, he set off on foot for his peak. It posed a 4,000-foot climb up slopes of firm snow into which he comfortably kicked steps, and it finished with the rocky north-west ridge. Finally he reached the summit.

For an hour he rested and marvelled at the view, an enormous one on one of the clearest days he could remember. It was a moment to treasure. In the next two days he would cross the rest of the Oberland glaciers to the Lötschental and from there reach civilisation, trains and home.

> It was easy to dream up there in the sun and the silence. In that panorama rested the friendships, the experiences and the adventures of 25 years. In those small shapes over which the eye passed tranquilly, on those shining summits where memory paused to refresh itself, youth was renewed. Our friends the mountains, our friendships on the mountains, can man ask for stauncher than these? Is there any sport, any pursuit in which a zest of living is blended more perfectly with a noble environment than in mountain climbing?[5]

The Alps had been both cradle and forge of Frank's high-mountain career. Successes on the greater peaks of the Himalayas had followed, and he would shortly return to the Canadian Rockies to explore and climb new summits there, but the Alps had always occupied a special place in his imagination and in his heart. And as I wrote these words I realised with a pang that the Finsteraarhorn was the last Alpine peak he ever climbed.

TWENTY SIX

Canadian Rockies

Frank had wanted to climb in the Canadian Rockies for over 20 years. His plan to go there in 1925 after becoming disenchanted with his job in Buenos Aires was impossible without his mother's support. Earlier still, when his engineering training in Switzerland stalled he toyed with the idea of doing survey work in Canada but that came to nothing. The war had propelled him into the command post in British Columbia, but the pressures of the job and the collapse of his health put the mountains out of reach. Now at last he was heading there on his own terms. On 8 July 1946 he and Nona arrived at Jasper after a 16-day journey from England by sea and rail.

The familiar town was a base for the succession of short trips and climbs he made in the next three months. For the first excursion he had agreed to be accompanied by Bruno Engler, a Swiss-born mountain guide and professional photographer who had been engaged by the Canadian National Film Board to make a publicity film, and after a few days he, Nona and Engler set off with a local packer and team of horses. For nearly three weeks they were exploring the little-known country to the north of Jasper, initially following the horses before being left with their equipment and supplies to camp beyond the Elysium Pass. From here they fished, botanised, climbed, and Engler shot film. They had to cope with mosquitoes, blackfly, horseflies, thunderstorms, rain, hail, a surplus of pork and beans, and the unrelenting Canadian bush. They climbed Monarch Mountain, where Engler narrowly escaped serious injury when a mass of boulders collapsed onto him, damaging his camera, and Frank on a fishing trip surprised a grizzly bear which, undeterred by his shrieks and brandished fishing rod, ran straight at him, swerving away at the last moment.

It was a testing start to the trip. Comments in Frank's diary suggest that at times he found Engler difficult to see eye to eye with, his own reserved nature at odds with the other man's pushy style. He needed to make adjustments when dealing with a typical North American, if there is such a person, and he got on best with calm, easy-going, cheerful people, tolerant of his sometimes petulant ways, climbers who were competent but not competitive, men who were happy to second him but would share the lead when necessary. Several friends fitted this profile — Jim Bell, Graham Macphee, Peter Oliver, Raymond Greene and Jim Gavin among them. Soon he would meet another mountaineer he liked immediately, a younger man he would climb with on almost all the rest of the peaks he tackled that summer.

At the beginning of August he and Nona, with Engler, had headed southeast to Banff, and from there went to the Canadian Alpine Club cabin at Lake O'Hara with Noel Gardiner, a local climber and his wife. For two days the men climbed and filmed on Mount Victoria, a shapely but straightforward snow peak with a dramatic summit crest. While they rested from their efforts back at Lake O'Hara a mixed party of Canadians and Americans arrived. 'Among them,' wrote Frank, 'was a young American, David Wessel. In the course of conversation he told me this was his first season in the Rockies, but he had spent years wandering about the mountains of Montana, his home. He had always gone alone, as there was no one in his town who was interested in mountains. Could I take him on a climb? Yes, I could. He was so obviously keen. I invited him to accompany me on the ascent of [Mount] Hungabee, which had been planned for the morrow.'[1]

Frank, Engler, Gardiner and Dave Wessel set off soon after dawn. The day was clear and sunny, the two-mile approach over the Opabin Pass straightforward, and the 2,000-foot west flank of the mountain easy scrambling, if exposed. 'Like E. side of Matterhorn,' as Frank noted. However before long Bruno Engler declared that they must retreat — a thunderstorm was imminent. Frank disagreed — justifiably it turned out, there was no storm — and the party split, Engler and Gardiner returning and Frank and his protégé continuing. 'David Wessel, I noticed, was going extremely well,' wrote Frank. 'He was a fast goer when walking uphill, but of course needed experience in the more difficult aspects of mountaineering, such as moving quickly and rhythmically over difficult ground and handling the rope accurately and skilfully at all times. He was not the one to fall off, and all those instinctive actions and reactions that are gained out of experience in mountaineering would soon be his.' They were soon on the narrow summit ridge of Hungabee. 'It was a sensational edge,' wrote Frank, 'overlooking one of the greatest single precipices in the Rockies, falling some 4,000 feet straight into the Horseshoe

Glacier and Paradise Valley. I doubt whether the Horseshoe Glacier would bring you luck if you were to step off the top of Mount Hungabee, but the Paradise Valley might make amends.'

Frank's next trip, an attempt on Mount Assiniboine was a disappointment. It began as a social foursome with him and Nona travelling by taxi from Banff with the Gardiners, switching to an army truck for the last few miles along a rough track to a lodge. The weather broke down totally, with several days of rain, sleet and a foot of snow. Frank and Noel Gardiner went fishing in Lake Magog catching one fish and a soaking, and on the sixth day tempted by a slight clearance Frank made a futile solo attempt on the imposing and now ice-plated 11,870-foot mountain. After this dispiriting experience he routinely asked Dave Wessel to join him. They attempted without success the difficult rock tower, Mount Brussels, but later, accompanied by Frank's wartime colleague, Rex Gibson, they made the first ascent of Mount Bridgland. Gibson joined them again for an attempt on the magnificent Mount Robson, highest of the Canadian Rockies, but hopeless weather forced them down early on.

In any Alpine season or trip to a greater range there's a chance that a climber will encounter a route or a mountain that will never be forgotten, perhaps because of its character or unusual difficulty or danger. Mount Alberta was that kind of climb for Frank and Dave Wessel in September 1946. Rising above the Athabasca river 50 miles south-east of Jasper, it was a huge wedge-shaped peak with two faces, the east and west, rising to meet at the sharp summit ridge like the sides of a broad-bladed chisel. At 11,873 feet it was the sixth highest in the Canadian Rockies and was considered to be the most difficult of the major peaks. Even today it is climbed only rarely. Frank published just one photograph of it, (in *Climbs in the Canadian Rockies*), selected from a couple he took from the air in 1944, and very forbidding it looks, with the typical horizontal strata and narrow snowy ledges rising steeply towards an imposing headwall. However this picture is of the more difficult west face, which remained unclimbed until 2007. In 1946 the first and only ascent of the mountain had been made via the east face, by a large team of Japanese climbers and Swiss guides in 1925, and Frank hoped to make the second ascent by this route. It's strange therefore that there is no photograph of the climb accompanying his description in *Climbs in the Canadian Rockies*, apart from an unsatisfactory one of Wessel standing by their bivouac tent looking towards the mountain, where the east face is largely concealed from view. Another thing I found odd was the way he described the climb, making it sound more like a technical report than the story of one of the most demanding and frightening climbs he ever made.

It began with 10 miles of very tough backpacking from the Banff road on the Sunwapta river, involving 4,500 feet of ascent through dense bush, up stream beds and boulder-strewn moraine, up rotten snow and ice-glazed rocks, over a col and across a glacier with concealed crevasses. They pitched their tent close to Alberta after a long inspection of the east face to identify the likely route followed by the Japanese. Next morning they set off.

Frank's description leads the reader page after page up the face. Up a 1,000-foot scree shute. Up walls, ribs, a chimney and stone-swept gullies. Up sloping ledges piled with wet snow or bare with loose stones. Up long run-outs of rope on a steep slabby wall with small holds and few adequate belays. Up a pitch of a hundred feet where neither man could find a belay, followed by another the same, with Frank candidly doubting that he could have held his companion in the event of a slip. And all the while a cliff of terrific steepness yawned below their feet, dropping 2,000 feet to the glacier.

Several things combined to persuade Frank to turn back just 200 feet short of the summit ridge and victory. The obvious difficulty of reversing an overhang just above him, the problem of protection with so few natural rock belays — they carried no pitons or other gear — the risk of a storm, and above all the exposure, which he sensed was now worrying his young companion. Maybe this concern for Dave Wessel still played on Frank's mind when he came to write about Mount Alberta, causing him to present the climb in a detached way. Had he been justified in pushing up as high as he did? There was a way for me to find out. I discovered that the 24-year-old Dave Wessel was still with us, aged 80, and still in Bozeman, Montana. So I got in touch.

Wessel enthused about the climbs he did with Frank. He liked Nona's cheerfulness and competence. He described the way they travelled — three on the front seat of his old Dodge car, Frank in the middle, 'like jam in a sandwich, with his legs mixed up with the gear shift.' He found Frank 'a fine person.' They hit it off personally. 'He trusted my climbing, and I trusted his, that's for sure.'

I asked him about Alberta. 'Of course that was beyond us,' he said. 'We didn't have the equipment that it takes. It's just not a safe mountain — if you know the Canadian Rockies you know how bad they can be, with hazardous rock. And we got up to the absolute limit of *his* climbing skill. And that was as far as I wanted to go, too! We couldn't have gone any further without the technical aids that other people employed. I was concerned because I was trying to belay him as he climbed the last piece of blank rock wall. We were close to the summit ridge and then he got spread-eagled on the holds, and he realised he couldn't go up any more, and he could just barely come down. I was standing on a tiny triangular scree shelf below him, with no chance to get an anchor belay or anything. A body belay — of course that would not hold, so I was quite uncomfortable. I didn't really worry about his falling off. I just knew that he *could* fall off but I trusted his skill. He was my mentor of course. An experienced climber and I in my second year and the first time in some really big tough mountains.'

With the climb reversed into a slow and unremittingly-careful push for safety, Frank's account relaxed:

> So I gave the order to retreat ... For however precious the prize it is always better to come back another time, and you cannot do this by leaving your mangled remains at the foot of the mountain ... These are not words of wisdom but of plain and unvarnished common sense ...

They dared not hurry and the descent took as long as the climb. Later that afternoon Frank flopped down on his sleeping-bag, promising himself an immediate sleep. But Dave Wessel had other ideas. 'Look at that stuff coming out of British Columbia!' he exclaimed. 'We ought to get out of here and cross that pass. It's the first big snowfall of the winter coming.' They packed and set off up the weary snow and scree slopes. On the col at last Frank surveyed the scene:

> We took our last backward look ... The storm clouds had for some time engulfed the summit ridge; now they were creeping down the precipices, enfolding them in grey curtains of hail and snow. Never have I seen any mountain look more menacing than Mount Alberta that evening ... We turned and set off as hard as we could go on our descent; we had less than half an hour of daylight left in which to reach timber-line.

Twenty Seven

A Last Expedition

As it forged slowly away from the shore of Stuart Lake at Fort St James the little German wartime communications Junkers never looked as though it could fly. The boxy floats had a suspiciously home-made appearance, suggesting that at one time the plane had possessed wheels. The fuselage, wings and tailplane seemed to be clad in corrugated iron. The single engine lacked a cowling and displayed itself as a mass of machinery that would be better hidden from view. It was alarming also to realise that the aircraft, with a full payload of pilot, mechanic, four passengers and a large quantity of baggage was scheduled to fly some 300 miles into a remote wilderness in the Canadian Rockies, there to land on a small lake surrounded by high mountains, in an area almost completely unexplored.

But the pilot Pat Carey, a small taciturn man with a lifetime of experience flying such missions was unconcerned. This was pretty much routine for him. After a careful warm-up of the engine he thrust open the throttle and with a shattering roar the Junkers started to plough down the lake. Faster and faster it went, bumping up and down in clouds of spray, but still not rising. Carey began deliberately to rock it back and forth, edging the floats out of the clinging water. Suddenly there were no more bumps. They were airborne. Turning and climbing, he set a northerly course. And Frank, together with three of the six other members of his expedition could relax for the moment.

It was midday on 2 July 1947. Planning had begun the previous year when Frank had learnt from Rex Gibson about the opportunities for exploration in the Rockies, in particular the north-east of British Columbia, where in an area of some 25,000 square miles between the Liard and Peace rivers there were whole ranges of mountains which no climbing party had ever visited. The great difficulty in travelling through the bush had always limited access to a few hardy Indians, trappers and prospectors, but the advent of the float plane now offered opportunities to climbing parties too, so long as there were handy lakes or suitable sections of rivers to land and take off from. Further investigation showed that a group of peaks named the Lloyd George Range was a tempting target. The range had been approached with great difficulty by an American explorer, Paul Haworth, in 1916 and 1918, and Haworth, who admired the British Prime Minister of that time and named the mountain group after him, also discovered a lake adjacent to the peaks. This stretch of water, Haworth Lake, was about five miles long and was the clincher for Frank. Provided a plane — and a willing pilot— could be hired, access was assured.

Of the four others joining Frank, Nona and Rex Gibson, there were two Frank knew well — Dave Wessel from the previous year and Noel Odell, the Cambridge geologist who had been with him on Everest in 1938. The other two were Gibson's friends, both American, Henry Hall and John Ross. Hall was an old hand but Ross, like Wessel the previous year, was in his first season of climbing. However he had already showed considerable ability. While the expedition was assembling in Jasper he had accompanied Frank, Gibson and Wessel on a warm-up climb, an attempt on Mount Colin, a difficult unclimbed rock peak in which the four men had split into two pairs to tackle simultaneously the north and south ridges. Both parties had failed, but after the Lloyd George expedition Ross would join Frank and Odell on the successful first ascent of Colin. An interesting point about this climb led by Frank was his use of a piton as a belay on what proved to be the crux pitch. It was the first time he had used one in his 30 years of mountaineering, and even though it had been for protection and not for direct aid he had felt guilty about it and expressed remorse for what he believed to be cheating.

As well as tackling the peaks of the Lloyd George Range Frank had listed other objectives: making a geological survey, making as accurate a map as possible, and collecting local flora. But first they had to get there, and they had to face the fact that flying across mountains and forests in a single-engine aircraft posed a great potential hazard. However when Frank discussed this subject with Pat Carey he had to be satisfied with the pilot's laconic comment: 'She's strongly made, I guess,' he said, 'and she'll plough through the tree tops like a toboggan.'

At last the Lloyd George Range came into view, its distinctive ice cap clearly visible from many miles away. Approaching closer they became aware of a deep valley below the south-western side, with two glaciers plunging into it from the icecap like frozen cataracts. Then as the plane lost height there was a view into the valley and their first sight of Howarth Lake.

'And there it was,' Frank wrote, 'a brilliant turquoise blue in a setting of olive green forest and golden limestone precipices with their diadem of gleaming ice and snow.' Carey executed a perfect landing on the water, taxied to the shore near the site of their intended base camp, shut off the engine as the plane grounded in shallow water, and the mechanic jumped out and secured it with a tow-rope. After a year of planning and preparing Frank had reached the starting point of his venture.

As the first group, Frank, Nona, Odell and Hall, made their way ashore the mosquitoes rose and attacked in their thousands, and the insect repellent was quickly located. Frank referred to this problem more than once, declaring that nothing was more voracious than the Canadian mosquito. His comment reminded me of a trip I made down the Yukon River in a powered dinghy during which we stopped for lunch one day on a sandbar in mid-stream. It was devoid of vegetation and several hundred yards from the nearest shore but within one minute there were half a dozen mosquitoes, five minutes later several hundred, and within ten minutes the usual huge swarm.

After unloading, the pilot took off for Fort Nelson to pick up Gibson, Wessel and Ross, and returned with them next morning. The priority was to set up a comfortable camp. They cleared an area of spruce and balsam fir, pitched the tents, including a large mess tent, and organised a kitchen for Nona, who would be spending much of her time preparing meals for six permanently hungry men.

Their immediate impression of the country was its dampness and the luxuriance of its vegetation. Animal life seemed sparse; a young cow moose was seen on several days and there was a porcupine which was chased up a tree and shot after having the temerity to raid the stores in the mess tent. The lake seemed devoid of fish and bird life was scant. Early on no bears were seen and Frank wrote about the occasions Nona would be left on her own: 'Should any intrusive bear appear she provided herself with a large tin and a stick with which to drum it off.' To compound their sense of isolation, their radio transmitter had been found to be useless, blanked off by the enclosing mountains. Yet in spite of these deficiencies Frank enthused about their unique situation:

> It would be difficult to imagine a more beautiful site for a base-camp. We could gaze towards the cirque of precipices supporting the icefield above, from which poured a great tongue of glacier so steep that it formed a continuous ice-fall of 3,000 feet in vertical height … Of all the lakes I have seen none has more colour than Haworth Lake and none in a finer setting of mountain and forest. Six miles long and over a mile broad, it stretches between the mountains …

The lake reflected every mood of the weather … In the dawn hour it slept motionless beneath a shawl of frosty mists … In the still evening hour it was the most beautiful, when the sun's gold on the snows of Cloudmaker was mirrored with faultless accuracy in its still waters.[1]

Unfortunately however, the sun was a rare commodity in the Rockies in 1947. It was an exceptionally poor summer, the wettest and coldest for 40 years, and they had to grab the chances when they came. It became possible to climb high on only eight days of the 26 they spent in the range.

The first job was to find a route to the ice-cap from where the two main peaks, Mount Lloyd George and Mount Glendower could be reached. This was complicated and involved the whole group splitting into two independent parties to explore the options on two separate occasions before a reasonably safe route was discovered. This lay up one edge of the Llanberis Glacier, a name suggested by Odell who saw a likeness with the glaciated valley alongside Snowdon.

Meanwhile on 5 July Pat Carey returned with the rest of their supplies that weight restriction had prevented him from bringing on his first trip, and Frank, with Hall and Odell used the opportunity to go for a reconnaissance flight. However they had no map and very little information about the huge numbers of peaks spread around them. They flew northwards to a region where the Canadian Survey had given the names Churchill, Roosevelt and Stalin to three mountains, but couldn't identify these and eventually with bad weather looming they returned for a useful look at the Lloyd George Range before Carey dropped them off at Howarth Lake and made his escape in deteriorating weather.

In recent decades the Canadians have produced superb maps to showcase every square mile — or even yard — of the Rockies, and sitting comfortably at my computer I have navigated around the region that Frank was unable to make sense of. As well as the peaks commemorating the three Allied war leaders I spotted numerous mountains with names connected with the conflict — Normandy, Caen, Falaise, Arnhem and Dieppe. Blenheim and Alexandria. The Battle of Britain Range. Yalta, Potsdam, Casablanca, to name a few. Those who go climbing in that part of the Rockies can hardly help being reminded of the events and sacrifices of World War Two.

The weather now closed down for over a week preventing all but local excursions. At last on 14 July Gibson, Hall and Ross succeeded in reaching the ice-cap and continued to the summit of Mount Glendower, 9,750 feet, the expedition's name for the range's second highest mountain. Two days later all six men combined to climb the principal peak, Mount Lloyd George, 50 feet higher.

This latter mountain provided one of those uneventful but deeply satisfying days that a lifetime's climbing grants often enough, a day for the ageing mountaineer in his dotage to remember and dream on. They started at dawn after a good breakfast. The streams on the gravel flats gave no trouble after the freezing night higher up. The icefall of the Llanberis Glacier was silent as they hurried past the dangerous places. Soon it was crampon time on the bare ice and Frank's backward glance as he bent to strap them on took in yet another of the lake's surprises, 'An extraordinary molten colour … a combination of blue and gold'. Then the icefield at last in blinding sunlight, its surface a thin crust to break through knee deep, but not a problem for six men taking turns. Two hours to the far edge where the last thousand feet of Lloyd George rose in snow slopes. A stop there on a scree patch, a rest for the eyes from the glare, a welcome trickle of melt water for parched throats. Then the work, the steady plod taking the easiest angles of the slopes, until the arrival at the summit at last, never before trodden. The laughter, the handshakes, the photographs, the view …

Strangely, Frank climbed Mount Lloyd George by the same route 10 days later. Smarting from his failure to climb Glendower due to his poor choice of route while Gibson's party had succeeded with theirs, he and his companions Odell and Wessel had spotted an opportunity to trump Gibson's efforts by traversing both peaks in a day. This they did, although judging from his account it was a joyless business, a long and exhausting day harassed by poor weather.

Perhaps Frank's most hazardous excursion that year came shortly before this traverse. On 22 July he and Dave Wessel set off at 6 a.m. to climb Cloudmaker, a twin-headed mountain on the other side of the lake, so-named because of its tendency to attract any bad weather around. The straight-line distance to its summit ridge from base camp was about five miles, but another couple of miles would be added in travelling round the northern end of the lake. To avoid the tedium of hacking through the bush they decided to use *The Nona*. This was a shaky raft built by the team for fun, launched by its namesake and consisted of four logs nailed together with cross pieces. An hour's walk brought them to where the raft was moored, then with Dave punting and Frank paddling they began their uncertain journey, keeping as close to the shore as possible. They had to bear in mind the water was too deep to pole in places and very cold in the event of a capsize. They carried three days food but no tent or sleeping bags, reckoning to bivouac at timberline where there should be plenty of dry wood underneath trees.

They had travelled for three quarters of an hour when suddenly Dave shouted, 'Look, a bear!' It was a moment Frank wouldn't forget:

> I looked, and there on the bank only five yards away, squatting on its haunches was a bear. It was a brown bear, much lighter than a grizzly and a good deal bigger. For a moment it continued to look at us, then it dashed into the lake, and commenced to swim straight for the raft.
>
> There was no hope of escape. It could swim far faster than we could pole or paddle the raft. In another few seconds it would have its paws on the raft, its weight would upset it, and we would be thrown into the ice-cold water. What chance would we have then?
>
> Somehow or other I managed to turn round in order to face the bear; it was a difficult manoeuvre, and it all but capsized the raft. I kept my balance by some miracle, and was now paddle in hand facing the oncoming animal.
>
> There was only one thing to do. I yelled at him. I yelled and beat with my paddle on the water in front of him. I yelled shrilly again. Only his head was visible and his eyes, large brown luminous eyes, were fixed on me. They showed no emotion, only an implacable purpose. The thought flashed through my mind that I must not strike him — keep that for an emergency, for it would only anger him. Now he was coming within range of my paddle and in another moment would be up to the raft. I raised my paddle and brought it down an inch or two in front of him, giving at the same moment a yell into which I concentrated everything within me. It was enough. He turned and made off to the shore, landed, and in a series of great bounds crashed into the forest. There was silence. Then Dave spoke: 'Holy mackerel! I sure would have liked to photograph him.'[2]

After this terrifying experience neither man enjoyed walking through the bush after they had tied up the raft and headed for their mountain, but worse was to come. By early afternoon they had made good progress to a point high on Cloudmaker, where they stopped to eat. Soon after this they reached the lower of the two summits of the peak, but became aware of a massive build-up of thunderstorms to the south-east of the range. This pall of cloud was 'slashed with white streaks of hail, inkily dark', and 'shimmered with lightning'. The main summit was now not far off, and desperate to reach it before the storm struck they cast off their jackets and rucksacks and rushed on. They were too late. They were at the top of a snow slope, nearing rocks that angled up to the summit when they realised it was madness to go on.

'Suddenly came one of those tearing cracks almost overhead, a sound like

Titan rending a length of calico,' wrote Frank. Rain and hail lashed down and they found places amongst the rocks which gave all too little shelter. Then a tremendous flash enveloped everything in a 'violet-coloured and brilliant light'. More strikes hit the ridge above them, followed by a 'blinding blaze of light and simultaneously an ear-splitting explosion … I was stunned by the impact and blinded by the brilliance of the discharge … the current went shuddering down my body, and my feet felt as though they were being driven into the ground and impaled on upright needles.' The lightning struck again and again, delivering its agonising effects to them both, until at last it moved on, leaving them to a steady bombardment of sleet and rain.

Shuddering uncontrollably from the effects of the lightning and cold, they staggered down to their kit, piled on all their spare clothing, then after speeding down some 1,500 feet and feeling warm again, they looked at one another. Both had the same thought, no discussion was needed. They *had* to climb this wretched mountain! They turned round, plodded and scrambled all the way back up to the summit in drizzling rain, and triumphantly built a cairn.

There was only an hour of daylight left and they raced the darkness down to the forest. There they spent the last of the light collecting fallen timber for an all-night fire. They brewed tea and cocoa in their single billy-can and ate a simple meal.

> We sat by our fire with its leaping flames revealing the ranks of trees around. The rain had stopped and the stars were spread between the tree tops. We were well-fed, warm and comfortable, and our damp clothing was steaming pleasantly as it dried in the heat of the fire. Now we could relax, both physically and mentally. It had been an adventurous day. Within a space of 18 hours we had faced an angry bear and then an angry heaven, we had been defeated and then achieved victory. We were well content. It was Dave who summed it up. He said, in that slow Western way of his, 'Well, Frank, I guess we can call it a day.'[3]

The expedition had a few days left in the Lloyd George Range, and Frank would then be active throughout August, September and October, climbing in the Jasper area and visiting friends after that with Nona in eastern Canada and America. But the Cloudmaker climb, with its weird risks and its hardship balanced by the fulfilment of the summit and the peacefulness of the camp fire — this was the type of adventure that had nourished his very spirit and soul throughout his life. With no more mountain days ahead quite like it, maybe with hindsight it could be seen as his swansong.

Twenty Eight

Full Circle

By 1948 the collapse of Frank's marriage to Kathleen and the trauma of the war years were well behind him. With Nona at his side he'd managed to put this dreadful period of his life to rest. He was looking to the future. In wartime Canada and Italy he'd become interested in art, briefly trying his luck with pastels and watercolour and later starting a collection of Victorian mountain aquatints. In his writer's capacity he suggested to Jack Newth a trio of large illustrated books entitled 'The English Scene', 'The Welsh Scene' and 'The Scottish Scene'. 'I find as age creeps on,' he wrote, 'I am as much interested in the ordinary landscape and town and village studies, etc. as in the hills, and I am very anxious to enlarge my scope ... It will not always be possible to photograph mountains ... I should like therefore to establish myself as a known photographer in landscape and even architectural studies.'[1] Newth however managed — not for the first time — to dissuade his highly successful mountain photographer from competing just yet with the common herd at sea-level. And in April, 1948 Frank duly signed a contract for an album entitled 'Swiss Summer', designed to follow the soon-to-be-published *Swiss Winter*. On the domestic front he was drawing up plans for building a new wing at the cottage to include a library, and as for leisure time — 'We could get no gardener,' he told Roberts, 'and you can imagine what the garden was like after six months' neglect. The vegetable garden alone is a good half acre and I've trenched the whole damned thing. I rather enjoy the exercise although we've 16 acres and work is never finished.'[2]

He was also conscious of the needs of his three sons, although his interest in us may have stemmed more from a sense of paternal duty than from any parental instinct since he had separated himself from us a decade earlier. John had injured his knee on a swing a couple of years earlier, damaging the cartilage, and this had caused persistent pain. Merely bandaging it, the routine advice at that time, was useless so after a bit of self-diagnosis in the school library — he and I were now boarders at Wycliffe — he wrote to Frank asking him to pay for an operation, this being just before the introduction of the National Health Service. Frank agreed to cover the cost. He also came to the school and gave a lecture on the Canadian Rockies, although this backfired for John, who shortly afterwards was taken aside by the headmaster and told, 'I had a letter from your father. He thinks you *slouch* rather a lot, you know. He suggested I sew up your pockets.'

Frank's involvement with his sons reached a new level however when he and Nona invited the three of us to have a holiday with them that summer. I suspect that Nona had a say in this. ('For heaven's sake Frank, *do* stop fussing about the boys. We're going up to Scotland in July. Why don't we have them to stay with us somewhere at the seaside on the way for a few days? Then you'll have *quite* done your duty.')

The seaside turned out to be a river mouth in Galloway. We got a train from Northampton and burdened by suitcases and bicycles changed at Dumfries onto a branch line for the final miles to the south and west. Here we were drawn briskly across the moors by a steam engine not unlike George Stevenson's Rocket. As townies we gazed in wonder at the rocks and pink heather and yellow gorse and glimpses of blue hills. A ticket inspector asked us kindly, 'will ye noo gahing t' Gatehoos o' Flee?' and while we were still puzzling about this the train stopped for us at a tiny station. Here an ancient taxi was waiting to convey us through the little town of Gatehouse of Fleet and beyond, along the shore of the Fleet estuary, to a small wooden chalet that was to be our home for the next three weeks.

Nona took charge. We'd hardly arrived before a rota of duties was established. Water had to be pumped from a well by hand. There was washing-up, table-laying, tidying and sweeping, and a stove to be tended. We were carried along by her sheer enthusiasm and jolliness. By contrast Frank kept a low profile, to such an extent that we each now remember very little of his presence there, although Richard says he heard him arguing with Nona in their room. I think he would willingly have swopped staying in the chalet with us for say, a tent on his own on Mount Everest, whatever the weather. There is no doubt that without Nona the holiday wouldn't have lasted three hours, let alone three weeks, although to John's delight the spats between them were sometimes resumed when they were on their own in the car. He remembered saying 'This marriage won't last long ... Good!' Then added, laughing, 'Shows how little I understood!'

But Frank's morale was restored when we got out and about. John and I walked with him up Cairnsmore of Fleet, a whale-like mountain ridge some miles from the road. We sped ahead of our plodding mentor but quickly tired, two hares in a losing battle with the tortoise. When we stopped at a stream he was shocked that I should worry about quenching my thirst. 'Of course it's safe to drink!' he told me impatiently. 'There's no purer water in the world.' At the summit John and I scrambled up the large cairn and Frank changed his shirt, laying out the sweaty one to dry while we ate our sandwiches. He talked about the Alps and how he would take us there when we were older, an impossible thing to imagine at the time.

Richard, who'd been taken to a doctor by Nona to have a boil lanced joined us for the next walk, up the highest hill of the region, Merrick. We drove to Loch Trool where Frank preferred to go fishing, leaving John as leader of our threesome. It was a very hot day, another long and boring trudge, and it wasn't surprising that after that nobody wanted to go up any more hills. Instead there were car outings and picnics, which suited Frank since he could make sure we stopped at the best places for photographs, one or two of which were later published in his album, *Mountains in Colour*. We became aware of what he was up to one day when we were called urgently to help search for a dropped filter, which to his great distress remained lost. I took photographs too with my first camera, which had been a birthday present on our arrival. It was an Ensign Full-View, a box camera of astonishing simplicity. You arranged your picture in the big glass viewfinder on top and pressed the shutter. And that was *it* — very primitive in the days before true automation. It had its disadvantages. With no control over exposure, only two settings for focus, and a lens like the bottom of a bottle the results would have been disappointing to a more critical eye than mine. It came with one roll of film providing twelve shots, almost all of which I used up on blurry countryside views.

One day Frank's film jammed in his camera and there was a demonstration of how his fame had spread. He walked into the local photographer's shop in Gatehouse of Fleet, identified himself, and the proprietor, with a sweeping bow (well nearly) immediately offered him the use of the darkroom. 'Never forget,' Nona warned us more than once in her well-bred tones, 'that your father is an *international mountaineer*.' He and Nona were also invited to take tea with the widow of a laird whose estate occupied a large slice of Galloway. We three scruffs were dispatched to the far reaches of the garden where we busied ourselves by damming a stream, only desisting when we were eaten alive by midges, my introduction to a lifetime's battle with this iconic north-of-the-border problem.

Frank concentrated on taking landscape photographs, over which he took immense care, but he never seemed to use his camera for family snaps. However many years later I discovered a shot he'd taken of John, Richard and me playing cricket on the beach. It's a great picture, three small figures of different sizes silhouetted against the last of the light — how he loved sunsets, I remembered. I imagined him stepping onto the bungalow's veranda to enjoy the evening air and unable to resist capturing the scene. What went through his mind? How much did he really care about us? We'll never know. But the picture John took of him at Loch Trool with Richard and me flanking him says much. In close contact with us he was uneasy, frozen, unable to be a father. But when he watched us playing and shouting, unaware of his presence that evening, maybe he experienced a pang, an awareness of a part of his life that he had avoided and therefore lost — that strange, frustrating but often amazing business of being a father.

John was an excellent cricketer, particularly that summer at school when he'd scored 79 not out in a House match. Frank had learnt about his prowess from school reports and arranged for him to play for a local club against an RAF team at Stranraer. We all went with him to lend our moral support, needed perhaps since he was only 15 and playing against men. He had vivid memories of the match: 'It was a concrete strip, with coconut matting on, which I'd never come across before and was a bugger because the ball bounced up past your head. And I was facing this pretty medium-paced bowling, and there was a real old salt keeping wicket behind me, and I played at one ball that was outside the off stump, and missed it. And the chap caught it, and the bail came off, and he called, 'Bowled! Well bowled!' And he'd done this old thing, you see, where he'd knocked the stump with his foot while he'd caught the ball, and pretended to the umpire that it had hit the wicket, but fortunately the umpire saw this … ' John acquitted himself superbly, scoring 24, but on returning to where we were watching on the boundary was greatly disappointed that Frank had nothing whatever to say, other than mentioning that he once saw Jessop hit a ball right over the stand at Lords. When I asked John why he thought Frank had been indifferent to his heroic performance he said, 'I can only suppose that he had very strict views about getting big-headed, about knowing your limitations. Upbringing was a matter of strictness, and we were running pretty wild … ' We also suspected that his complete lack of experience of dealing with young people accounted a bit for his ineptness.

Towards the end of the holiday he made a last effort to join in. He hired a bicycle, a big heavy police-style machine, and one morning we set off for a ride. I was some way ahead on the track from the chalet when I heard a tremendous crash and a shout. A couple of minutes after setting off Frank had fallen from his bike and was in great pain, lying on the ground with one leg mixed up with the frame. Somehow we extricated him and John and I supporting him on each side got him back to the bungalow, where the horrified Nona took charge, becoming concerned that the Press might learn of the disaster ('Everest Hero in Plunge from Bicycle'). When I collected the machine I found beside it a small twig with an oily groove cut into it. Freakishly it had somehow jumped into Frank's front wheel and caught between a spoke and the fork, locking the wheel and throwing him off. It seemed to say everything about the holiday, especially as that day happened to be Friday the 13th of August.

Frank had a badly swollen ankle, but refused medical attention and hobbled about gamely for the rest of the holiday. John and I met him again three months later when he paid a brief visit to Wycliffe in the autumn term. It was suggested that I should accompany him to the station for his train. We walked silently for a while, then he said suddenly, 'You know, I was an absolute fool not to go to hospital when I had that accident.' As I stupidly demurred that surely *he* could not be thought foolish he went on as though I hadn't spoken, 'My ankle was broken.'

Nothing more was said, and a little later his train disappeared from view. I never saw him again.

In December Frank was asked to write a foreword to *A History of Mountaineering in the Alps* by Claire Engel, a French climber he knew well. During a meeting with her he talked about his plans for the coming year, 1949. 'He was trying to choose between the various mountaineering programmes open to him,' Engel wrote in a later publication. 'The Himalaya, an expedition to Alaska, or to the Andes, or to the Alps and one of the great routes he had not tried up Mont Blanc, the Via della Pera. He chose the Himalaya and Fate chose death.'

It was a dramatic statement. I have occasionally thought about these four options facing Frank, knowing that in all likelihood he would have come home safely from any of the three he turned down and maybe lived to a ripe old age. The Alaskan expedition was an invitation from an American group to attempt Mount Logan, and an English friend had suggested the southern Andes. As for the Alps, he was probably still climbing well enough to tackle the Pear Buttress.

But it was no surprise that he wanted to go back to the Himalayas for what would be his seventh expedition to that peerless range. In a lifetime of climbing he had found that every mountain area, including the humble British hills offered its own satisfaction and rewards, but the Himalayas had that extra edge of magic. It wasn't just a matter of size and height and the physical demands imposed. There were mountains and valleys that had provided inspiration and the space and time to think, free of the clutter and triviality of Western life. Particularly in 1937, when his marriage was failing, he'd been able to find solace and peace of mind in the Valley of Flowers. On that expedition he had climbed, botanised and spent many an evening with his four employed men round a camp fire, a trip that lingered in his mind as the most memorable and satisfying of his life. So it was that region, the Garhwal that he had decided to make his destination in 1949. And he had already settled on an ideal target, a mountain he had seen from the summit of Kamet in 1931. A little to the north on the same ridge, beyond Meade's Col and the Abi Gamin rose a shapely summit, later named Mukut Parbat and found to be 23,760 feet, a mere 100 feet lower than the Mana Peak, the other side of Kamet and Frank's finest achievement of 1937. The ascent of the unclimbed Mukut Parbat would complete a superb triptych. And climbing it would fittingly celebrate the life of Peter Oliver, his companion during the final weeks in the region in 1937 and who sadly, had been killed in World War Two.

Frank had never been superstitious, despite having an incredible ability to detect danger in advance — he called it a sixth sense — notably using this awareness to save the lives of a group of men in a Bradford foundry.* So it was odd that he should irrationally change the date of his departure, as he confessed in a letter to Jack Newth at the end of January 1949. 'I fly to India on March 10th. They tried to make me go on the 13th, but not again. It was Friday 13th last year that I broke my ankle.' And there was something else which he probably hadn't noticed or thought anything of. He had typed this letter — the last he ever sent to Newth — on notepaper with a printed heading that was new in the letters I'd gone through in the publisher's archive. At the top of the sheet, as well as the Yew Tree Cottage address the design incorporated a short dividing line, a vertical bar with half a dozen decorative bobbles down its length. While idly studying this I suddenly realised that it precisely resembled a suspended knotted rope, and closer inspection revealed a small gap, *a break in the middle of the rope.* I'm not superstitious either, but it was a thought-provoking moment.

By 1949 Heathrow airport was fully operational after five years of development, and was absorbing all the international air traffic which had previously used Croydon. In late 1947 Britain had reached agreement with the newly independent Government of India to operate regular flights between London and Bombay and it was this service Frank had booked to travel to India. BOAC[3] used Lockeed Constellations, a great improvement on previous aircraft flying the route such as the Avro York or Handley Page Halton. The pressurised 'Connie' cruised at 300 miles per hour at up to 24,000 feet and carried 80 passengers. Even so, with a refuelling stop at Cairo the flight of 4,500 miles took the best part of 12 hours.

He spent two nights in Bombay resting and visiting the Army and Navy Stores, where he obtained some of the clothing and equipment needed for the couple of climbing Sherpas he planned to recruit in Darjeeling. Other requirements could be got more conveniently in Calcutta, but first he planned to spend some time in Delhi, and on 14 March caught the night Frontier Mail train to the Indian capital.

In the days of British administration, travellers and climbers moved fairly freely about the Indian Himalayas, but Frank now had to apply for a travel permit from the relevant department of the new Government. He eventually discovered this would be delayed and he would probably receive it in Darjeeling. However he enjoyed the hospitality of friends and his early days in Delhi were comfortable if busy. He was invited to give a lecture on Everest. He went sight-seeing with his hosts. He attended dinners, and unfortunately in the process of being wined and dined he fell victim to a severe stomach upset. Recovering from this he continued on 24 March by train to Calcutta, staying at a familiar haunt from pre-war days, the United Services Club. And while he was there he met a young climber, Trevor Braham, who was a fellow-member of the Himalayan Club and held the post of regional secretary.

Some 50 years later I asked Braham what he remembered of that meeting. He had been born in 1922 and lived in Calcutta, his father having established a business there. He'd become interested in climbing while at school in Darjeeling, when the Everest expeditions of the 1930s passed through. Later he moved to Switzerland after many years of journeys and climbs in the Himalayas. But he had clear memories of the single evening encounter with Frank. 'We talked about his plans. He was awaiting permission and he was rather concerned that he might not get it.' He found Frank not good company. 'I suppose I was a little disappointed,' he said. 'I didn't find him very forthcoming. He tended to be a bit aloof. He was sort of flitting from one subject to another in his conversation.'

Trevor Braham wasn't alone in finding Frank socially awkward. Claire Engel wrote, 'He had plenty of self-assurance on the heights, whereas at sea-level he was either shy or over-assertive.' Certainly the previous summer my brothers and I had found that at times he had been preoccupied to the point of ignoring us. Had his mood that evening in Calcutta been distant because of the difficulties he was having with Indian bureaucracy, or was there some other problem?

The following evening, 28 March, he caught the train for Darjeeling. Trevor Braham was familiar with the journey and described it vividly in his book *Himalayan Odyssey*. His images come to mind: The tumult of an Indian railway station at departure time. The dimly lit carriages unholstered in dark green leatherette and with windows fitted with Venetian, wire mesh and glass shutters, none of which worked. The steam engine, whistling through the hot night, its coal dust and smoke entering and smothering the carriage. From Jalpaiguri before dawn the startling view of Himalayan peaks, over a hundred miles away. Then Siliguri at 7 a.m., and with the great barrier of the forested foothills rising above the plain, the last stage of the journey at hand. Breakfast in the railway dining-hall followed by the selection of a taxi driver and his decrepit vehicle for the final 50 miles. Or if desired, the same journey by narrow-gauge railway equipped with miniature steam engine and carriages, and six or eight hours-worth of loops, hairpins and sidings.

Frank had been invited to stay at Darjeeling with his old friends, the Hendersons. Jack was the manager of Rungneet tea estate, one of the largest in the area, and his wife Jill tirelessly looked after the interests of the Sherpas employed by visiting expeditions. Frank had made a note of the names of two very experienced men he wanted to take with him — Dawa Thondup, who was a close friend of Tenzing Norgay, the man who four years later would stand alongside Ed Hillary on the summit of Everest, and Ang Tsering, who began work in 1924 when he was employed by the expedition on which Mallory and Irvine were lost. Frank still needed his permit for Garhwal however, and by way of a back-up plan should this not be granted he wrote to the Maharaja of Sikkim asking for His Highness's personal approval for a visit to photograph mountains and flowers in Sikkim, a State which enjoyed a degree of autonomy from India. The weeks passed, it became May, and nothing had been settled.

Of the photographs Frank took on this trip to India in 1949 only a handful survived. They're all Kodachrome colour transparencies, apparently from a single reel of 35mm. In Delhi there's a group shot, perhaps of his hosts, and five carefully composed pictures of formal gardens. The rest, apart from three landscapes apparently taken from a train, are of Darjeeling. Some of these are of a Sherpa wedding and include a picture of Karma Paul, the legendary Everest interpreter he knew well and who accompanied every expedition to the mountain between the wars. Then there are a couple of views of the town's market place and some of Kangchenjunga. There's also one of Frank at breakfast with the Hendersons on the terrace outside their bungalow. And this one was especially poignant to me when I came across it, since it must have been the last photograph ever taken of him. For around this time he became fatally ill with cerebral malaria.

In 1955 Tenzing published his autobiography, *Man of Everest*. He told how 'a sad thing happened' that Spring of 1949 in Darjeeling. Frank had arrived to a 'fine welcome' and he had helped him with his preparations. It became clear however that there was something wrong. When Frank was asked to sign the visitors' book at Sain's photographic studio he had difficulty remembering his name, and then had two attempts at the date, eventually writing December, when it was really May. Later, while walking and chatting with Tenzing his voice suddenly changed and with deadly seriousness he called for his ice-axe, believing he was on a climb. At the Henderson's, where his behaviour had seemed strange, he soon began to cause alarm when they found him detached from the present and instructing phantom Sherpas about his tent and boots. Soon after this he collapsed and was taken to hospital.

Even today cerebral malaria, which is a deadly complication of the *Plasmodium falciparum* genus, requires swift diagnosis and skilled treatment for a sufferer to have a reasonable chance of survival. A victim's condition may rapidly deteriorate from a fever, headache, shivering and confused conversation to delirium, coma and death in a matter of hours. The incubation period is usually between two and three weeks but can be longer, and anti-malarial drugs are not a guaranteed protection against this, the most virulent strain of the disease. It has a uniquely nasty feature in that the parasites transmitted by the mosquito not only inhabit red blood cells causing harm to organs but migrate to the brain, obstructing the blood vessels there and potentially causing terrible brain damage, even in a survivor.

To add to Frank's predicament the British surgeon who had headed the Victoria Hospital in Darjeeling had left, along with the rest of the British management after 1947. 'It was run by local people,' Trevor Braham told me, 'and I would think that they did not have skilled staff to deal with a case such as this. I would say it was not a suitable place for him to spend any time at, in his state.'

The Hendersons sent an urgent message to Nona. In the meantime Frank was visited by Tenzing, who wrote: 'He did not recognise me, but simply lay in his bed with staring eyes, talking about climbs on great mountains.'

Another visitor was a Ghurkha major, Charles Blaschek, who happened to be in Darjeeling. 'I met him, but only for a few minutes,' he told me. 'He was telling me of the problems of climbing Everest and suddenly started gasping for breath. It seemed that he was experiencing lack of oxygen as if at high altitude, and in fact hyper-ventilated and fainted.'

Nona was a resourceful woman. Within hours of getting the horrifying news she had chartered an aircraft and set off for India. An earlier letter from Frank had suggested that the country was still in chaos, with English residents leaving in large numbers. When I had asked Trevor Braham about this and told him that the deeply worried Nona had armed herself with Frank's service revolver, he was surprised. 'Feelings ran very high in the years up to Independence,' he said, 'but then the ill feelings died down considerably. There were a lot of English people living in India at that time. It was an awkward period for them, but not dangerous. I think she was over-cautious if she carried a firearm with her.'

Nona's harrowing journey to India and back with the desperately ill Frank took about six days during the middle of May. She was helped by an Indian, Dr Chatterjee, staff from the High Commissioner's Office and the crew of the aircraft. In England at last he was taken to the West Middlesex Hospital. A week later, on 27 May Nona wrote a despairing letter to her close friend, Eileen Younghusband:

> I feel a weak and helpless woman. I saw Willie on Thursday who had spoken to the specialist — the outlook was pretty grim as it was a virulent tropical germ attacking the nervous system. They are trying everything of course and I'm going to see them next week.
>
> Today is a bad day for me and I'm unable to pull myself together and concentrate on the enormous amount of work that has piled up.
>
> I cannot think why this should have happened to a good man like Frank. I simply must cling to the fact that while there is life there is hope. I really have great faith in his being restored to his natural self but I've been brooding all night and a deep depression has descended upon me.[4]

The efforts to save him were in vain. He appeared to improve, and even spoke about a plan to go to South America, but on 27 June, late in the evening after Nona had visited him that afternoon, a nurse urgently called a consultant, Mr Nethercote to Frank's bedside. A little later their patient, now unconscious, stopped breathing. It was nine days before his 49th birthday.

Epilogue

Within hours of Frank's death a post mortem had been carried out and the coroner ruled that no inquest was necessary. Nona arranged a private funeral at Golders Green crematorium to which only Eileen Younghusband, Jack Newth and Arnold Lunn were invited. Later she scattered her husband's ashes on Box Hill, as he had once suggested. She had an avalanche of correspondence to deal with, and eventually escaped on a tour of New Zealand, the USA and Canada to visit relatives and friends. Before this she invited John down to Yew Tree Cottage. She told him that Frank had written a letter to us to explain, in the event of his death why it had all gone wrong between him and Kathleen. However she then added, to John's disbelief, 'But it wouldn't have done any good, Sweetie, so I destroyed it.' She eventually married Viscount Malden who later became the Earl of Essex, thus achieving from her ordinary beginnings a notable triple of money, fame and a title. However she kept in touch with us three. She and Reggie lived at Wingrave in Buckinghamshire. I and my family lived closest, near Bicester, and she would drive over, disgorge a few items of Frank's and stay for a jolly lunch, her good humour never deserting her ('More wine, Nona?' 'Thank you, Sweetie, why not! After all, we're such an *awfully* long time dead!'). Sadly though, her desire to keep personal control of Frank's collection of photographs eventually led to its destruction. Becoming bored and irritated by unending requests for copies of his pictures, yet rejecting the idea of anyone else taking charge, she destroyed the negatives, some 50,000 of them, deciding perversely that the pictures already published in his books would have to represent his heritage to mountain photography. Gerald Evered, a nearby friend and Attorney of the Earl told me that a gardener had brought everything including Frank's papers by multiple wheelbarrow loads to the corner where Nona had her bonfire, but had been forbidden to stay and help.

Luckily she had earlier brought me Frank's colour transparencies, and after her death in 1997 at the age of 91, her niece Jenny Armstrong, while disposing of her possessions discovered a quantity of negatives, letters, diaries and other papers which had escaped the fire, and kindly passed them to me, but I have found it impossible to forgive Nona for her rampage.

Frank's last two books were published shortly after his death; *Mountains in Colour* in 1949 and *Climbs in the Canadian Rockies* the following year. In the Rockies two new peaks, one in the Jasper National Park and the other in the Lloyd George Range were climbed and named Mount Smythe in his honour. In Zermatt a memorial consisting of his hat and crampons was unveiled in the Alpine Museum. Of the dozen obituaries I gathered together I liked one written by the no-nonsense Ernest Roberts of the Yorkshire Ramblers' Club, Frank's first mountain mentor and lifelong friend. He finished:

> Laughter and joy fill my memories of Frank Smythe, he was an excellent correspondent — even from high camps on Everest — and all through he never lost touch with the Club. When we dined him in 1938, he reminded us that he had been half his life in the YRC He was a marvellous photographer and published many wonderfully illustrated books. Though many people think very highly of his *Spirit of the Hills* I have always liked his *Valley of Flowers* best, myself.

Let the last words come from India, where as I have suggested, Frank discovered both inspiration and peace. On my own first visit to the Himalayas, to Kulu, in 1972, I was struggling to find my way on a hot June night at Delhi main railway station. A friendly porter helped me with my equipment. He picked up my ice-axe, a dangerously inappropriate weapon to have loose in a crowd of people, although there was no place I could stow it safely. 'Aha,' he said with a smile, 'Frank Smythe!' I laughed, and soon we had found my carriage and the porter had disappeared in search of more work. It then dawned on me that since he could not have known who I was, he had spontaneously linked my ice-axe, that trademark mountaineer's implement, to my father, famous in India since the 1930s following his success on Kamet, and his expedition after that to the Valley of Flowers. Whether or not the porter was a mountaineering enthusiast I do not know — it seemed unlikely — but it was somehow a unique tribute to Frank, as memorable as any I have come across over the years.

Acknowledgments

I would like to record my profound thanks to the following individuals and organisations whose collective help has made my book possible. Inevitably some of these kind people are no longer living, but their names are included within the list:

Louis Allard; the Alpine Club, in particular George Band, Margaret Ecclestone, John Emlyn Jones, Bob Lawford, Margaret Pope and Yvonne Sibbald; Jean Altshuler; Nick Walker and Dave Culshaw of the Alvis Owners' Club; Library Director Francine Loft at the American Alpine Club; Sally Amos; Celia Armitage; Jenny and David Armstrong; Tony Astill; Philip Attenborough; Chris Mobbs at the BBC Sound Archives; David Pearce and Barbara Ecclesfield at Berkhamsted School; the Bexhill Museum; Barrie and Lucy Biven; Charles Black at A & C Black; Charles Blascheck; Jean Blest; Peter Blest; Maggie Body; Chris Bonington; Trevor Braham; Sylvia Branford; Jane Brian; Jan Faull at the British Film Institute; David Blake at the British Library; Ethel Broughton; Vicky Byatt; Robin Campbell; John Cleare; Liz and Andrew Cowan; Paul and Tony Cronk; Anthony Cullingworth; Elsie Dale; Ted Young and other helpful members of the Darjeeling (Planters') Club; Steve and Janet Dean, endlessly supportive; Archivists at the Ministry of Defence; Norman Dyhrenfurth; Graham Hardy at the Edinburgh Royal Botanical Gardens; Anne Locker at the Institution of Electrical Engineers; Susan Engler-Potts; Denise Evans; Gerald Evered; Viscount Falmouth; Hermione Fletcher for her frequent help and unrestricted use of the diaries of her father, Graham Macphee; Bill Samuel of Foyles; Patrick French; Ann Gander and the family of Adrian Bell; Billy Gayleard; Richard King and the Orion Publishing Group and in particular the rights holder/s of Tom Graham Brown's book *Brenva* whom I have unfortunately been unable to trace;

Livia Gollancz; Nawang Gombu; Veronica Cassie at Dr Graham's Homes; Raymond Greene; Ashley Greenwood; John Gregson; Harry Griffin; The Guildhall Library staff; Peter Harding; Rita Gibbs at Harrow School; Judy Hill; Meher Mehta, Priyadarshi Gupta and other helpful members of the Himalayan Club in Calcutta; staff at Hodder Headline Ltd.; Paul Hodder-Williams; Robin Hodgkin; Jennifer and Walter Hogg; Jean Holden; Nigel Hollingworth; Mr G. Horne; Charles Houston; Martin Howes; Graham Hoyland; Roy Humble; John Hunt; Elizabeth Hussey; Robin Huws Jones and his daughter Gwen; Guy Johnson; Harish Kapadia; Jackie Faye at the Kendal Library; the Kent Messenger; staff at the National Archives, Kew; Rosemary Kirkus; Chris Roberts of Kodak Ltd.; Maureen Kons; Peter Lloyd; Nick Longland; Jim Lowther; Peter Lunn; Brian Neaves, Church-warden at All Saints, Maidstone; Janice Cordwell at Maidstone Library; Ursula Malloch Brown; John Millar; Tony Moulam; Susan Newman; John Newth; Nona, Countess of Essex; Marlene Parks; Joanna Pateman; Tshering and Sonam, generous daughters of Karma Paul; Jane Pullee at the Pen-y-Gwryd hotel; Colin Harding, Director of the National Museum of Photography; Olive Pilfold; Prunella and Brian Power; Tom Price; James Rackard; Jean Rasmussen; Michael Bott at the Reading University Library; Bunty Redman (Newth); John Reeves; George Rodway; Chris Godfrey of Rother District Council; Bridget Palmer at the Royal Academy of Music; staff at Royal Air Force Records; The Royal Geographical Society, particularly Alasdair Macleod, Jamie Owen, Sarah Strong and Joanna Wright; The Royal Scottish Geo-graphical Society and Director David Munro; The Rungneet Tea Estate at Darjeeling and our guide, Ravi; Audrey Salkeld; Peter Bond at the Savage Club; Stuart Allan at the National War Museum of Scotland; The National Library of Scotland, particularly for help in accessing the archive of Professor Thomas Graham Brown; Chic Scott; Doug Scott; Sydney and Margaret Scroggie; Matthew Shaw; Roger Shaw; William Shaw; Pat Sherlock; Michael Simpson, Vicar of Ticehurst and Flimwell; Maggie Colpous at the Ski Club of Great Britain; Mike Spencer at the Eagle Ski Club; Graham Smythe; Maureen Smythe; Percy Smythe; John Snoad; Karen Winchester at the National Institute for Social Work; Jonathan Somervell; Gordon Stainforth; Peter Steele; Jackie Stratis; Susan Taylor; Mick Tighe; Beverley Matthews at Tonbridge School; Trevor Bale and Sue Wells at Travis Perkins Ltd.; Jon Barton and his team at Vertebrate Graphics, my publishers; Charles Warren; John Warren; Brad Washburn; Tom Weir; Dave Wessel; Dail Whiting; Ken Wilson; Neil Wooler; The OW archivist at Wycliffe College;

MY FATHER, FRANK

Steve Wyn-Harris; The Yorkshire Ramblers' Club, in particular Albert Chapman, John Godley, David Smith, George Spenceley, Bill Todd, and Chris Hilton who kindly loaned and allowed me to make use of letters FS wrote to Ernest Roberts.

Finally there are my brothers, John and Richard who shared their memories unstintingly, my inspired niece, Ruth, and all the other family members, 100 per cent interested and supportive, including of course my wife, Sonia, always encouraging and always ready to offer wise and calming words at the more fraught moments.

Notes

ABBREVIATIONS
AC The Alpine Club.
AJ The *Alpine Journal*.
BL The British Library.
EER Ernest Roberts.
EY Eileen Younghusband.
FS Frank Smythe.
FY Sir Francis Younghusband.
GB Tom Graham Brown.
GWY Geoffrey Winthrop Young.
N Nona (When followed by a number this indicates the document containing the information concerned, now in the author's collection).
NISW The National Institute for Social Work.
NLS The National Library of Scotland.
RGS The Royal Geographical Society.

ONE — THE CREVASSE
1. An account of an incident described by FS in *The Spirit of the Hills*, Chap. 5, p. 75-80, also in *The Mountain Vision*. Chap. 15, p. 208-15.

TWO — CHILDHOOD
1. N/421, FS to mother, 27/3/38.
2. In answer to questions from Jennifer Hogg, March, 2004.
3. *The Spirit of the Hills*, Chap. I, p. 2.

THREE — SCHOOLDAYS
1. *The Spirit of the Hills*, Chap. I. p. 15. (Includes other comments made about Berkhamsted and childhood).

FOUR — YORKSHIRE RAMBLER
1. *The Mountain Vision*, Chap. XV, p. 231.

FIVE — ALPINE APPRENTICE
1. *Over Tyrolese Hills*. This and other comments were made in the Preface.
2. FS to EER, 10/4/22.
3. FS to EER, 1/11/22.

SIX — REJECTED FOR EVEREST
1. *AJ*, 1940 (Obit.), p. 105.
2. AC, Bruce to Spencer, 13/4/1923.
3. FS to EER, undated (prob. 14/5/23).

4. Ibid.
5. N/47.
6. *The Spirit of the Hills*, Chap. XIX, p. 262.
7. *Climbs in the Canadian Rockies*, Chap. XVII, p. 218.
8. *The Mountain Vision*, Chap. IX, p. 109.
9. RGS, Somervell to Spencer, September, 1923.

SEVEN — TWO FAILED CAREERS

1. FS published an account of the Schreckhorn epic in no fewer than four of his books: *Climbs and Ski Runs* (Chap. VII), *The Mountain Vision* (Chap. XXII), *The Adventures of a Mountaineer* (Chap. VI) and *British Mountaineers* (Chap. VI). Descriptions also appeared in *Blackwood's Magazine* and in two editions of the *Alpine Journal*.
2. Sir Henry Birkin.
3. *The Spirit of the Hills*, Chap. III.
4. N/57-70, FS to mother, quotations and events from 17 letters FS wrote between 15/8/26 – 15/2/27.

EIGHT — THE SENTINELLE

1. *AJ*, May, 1967.
2. *AJ*, 1928. p. 62.
3. *Climbs and Ski Runs*, Chap. XIV, p. 224.
4. FS to GWY, 5/12/27.
5. *AJ*, May 1966, p. 51.
6. *Climbs and Ski Runs*, Chap. XIV, p. 219.
7. *AJ*, May 1966, p. 55.
8. *AJ*, May 1967.
9. *The Yorkshire Ramblers' Club Journal*, 1928, p. 284. *AJ*, 1927, p. 308.
10. *Climbs and Ski Runs*, Chap. XIV. *The Adventures of a Mountaineer*, Chap. VIII. *Brenva*, Chap. 3.

NINE — ROUTE MAJOR

1. *AJ*, May 1966, p. 56.
2. GWY to Author, 31/3/56.
3. *Climbs and Ski Runs*, Chap. IX.
4. NLS. GB to Waller, 21/11/32. GB offered to propose Waller for the AC. During an exchange of letters Waller cheerfully, if reluctantly agreed to answer written questions from GB about the Grépon climb, which he did in a letter to GB on 23 December 1932.
5. *Climbs and Ski Runs*, Chap. XV, p. 266.
6. John Hunt to John Millar, 17/7/98, in reply to Millar's written questions.
7. *Brenva*, Chap. 5, p. 60.

TEN — RECRIMINATION

1. FS to GB, 26/8/28.
2. GB to FS, 9/9/28.

3. FS to GB, 19/10/29.
4. FS to GB, 19/1/30.
5. GB to FS, 22/1/30. In his original handwritten draft of this letter GB laboured over the sentence, 'I have taken no part ... ', with heavy deletion and alteration, suggesting that he wavered a little over his response to Frank's evident keenness to settle the dispute. After this, however there were no signs of forgiveness by him.
6. NLS. GB, memo, April 1932, p. 45 (of 57).
7. NLS. GB, memo, 14/12/32.
8. GB to FS, 24/12/32, and 3/2/33.
9. FS to GWY, 7/2/33.
10. FS to GB, 28/12/32.
11. FS to GB, 21/6/34.

Eleven — A writer's Progress

No notes

Twelve — Kangchenjunga

1. Known now as simply, 'The Club'.
2. *The Kangchenjunga Adventure*, p. 176.
3. *The Spirit of the Hills*, p. 242.
4   *AJ*, 1930, p. 206.
5. N/134, FS to mother, 11/4/30.
6. *Himalayan Climber*, p. 90.
7. *The Kangchenjunga Adventure*, p. 250.
8. Ibid, p. 252.
9. N/144, FS to mother, 11/5/30.

Thirteen — Rising Star, Married Man

1. FS to Macphee, 19/9/30.
2. N/155, letter 12/12/30.
3. Gollancz to FS, 9/12/30.
4. *AJ*, 2001, p. 305.
5. FS to Gollancz, 1/12/30. The wording of the advertisement, which appeared in *The Times* on 25/11/30 reads: 'Published to-day: The greatest adventure story of our age: THE KANGCHENJUNGA ADVENTURE by F.S. Smythe, *The Times* correspondent on the Expedition. Heroism. The Avalanche. Defeat: and then — Smythe climbed the Jonsong Peak, highest summit ever reached by man! 48 marvellous photographs. 464 pages. 16/-. GOLLANCZ.'
6. Gollancz to FS, 3/12/30.
7. FS to Gollancz, 4/12/30.
8. FS to GWY, 31/7/30.
9. FS to Kathleen, 14/6/36.
10. AC, Shipton to Pamela Freston, 9/7/38.

Fourteen — Kamet

1. 6/5/31.
2. 29-30/4/31.
3. *Kamet Conquered*, Chap. V, p. 63.
4. Ibid, Chap. IX, p. 109.
5. Ibid, Chap. XIV, p. 194.
6. Crampons were not taken on the expedition since Frank believed that the danger of frostbite from their restricting straps outweighed their usefulness. In any case the technique and type of crampon for 'front pointing' to avoid step-cutting on steeper slopes had not been developed.
7. *Kamet Conquered*, Chap. XIV, p. 199.
8. Ibid, p. 202.
9. Ibid, p. 204.
10. *The Times*, 6/8/31 and *The Illustrated London News*, 15/8/31.
11. *Kamet Conquered*, Chap. XIV, p. 208.
12. Ibid, p. 210.
13. Ibid, Chap. XVII, p. 235.
14. *Tigers of the Snow*, Part 2, p. 111.
15. *Kamet Conquered*, Chap. XIX, p. 261.
16. Ibid, Chap. XXVI, p. 359.

Fifteen — Hammering on Everest's Door

1. RGS. From J.C. Walton, India Office, Whitehall, to the Royal Geographical Society and Mount Everest Committee, 9/8/32.
2. *The Times*, 4/2/32.
3. Ibid, 9/2/32.
4. Ibid, 4/3/32. (Court Circular).
5. RGS, FS to Sir William Goodenough. 7/1/33.
6. *This My Voyage*, 1950.
7. RGS, Longstaff's handwritten memo accompanying FS letter of 7/1/33.

Sixteen — Camp Six

1. *Everest*, Chap. 7, p. 160. A review of FS's life and character.
2. *AJ*, 1962, p. 393 (obit.).
3. N/192, Ruttledge to FS, 12/9/32.
4. NLS. GB memo, 15/12/32.
5. *Camp Six*, Chap. III, p. 25.
6. N/251, FS to mother, 3/5/33.
7. *Camp Six*, Chap. XIII, p. 192.
8. Ibid, Chap. XIV, p. 209.
9. Ibid, pp. 236-237.
10. This and all subsequent quotations from FS's description of the climb that day, 21 June 1933 and descent next day to the North Col were drawn from *Camp Six*, Chap. XV. Shipton's words come from his book *Upon that Mountain*.

11. N/309, FS to mother, undated.
12. *The Mountain Vision*, Chap. XIV, p. 206.

SEVENTEEN — DOWN TO EARTH
1. *The Spirit of the Hills*, Chap. XVI, p. 220, and *Mountaineering Holiday*, Chap. I, p. 29.
2. *The Guardian* (G2), 23/4/01, p. 8.
3. *Younghusband*, page xx (Intro).
4. Jane Brian collection, FY to Lady Lees, 7/2/41.
5. Exchange of letters FS/Gollancz, 30-31/1/34.
6. *The Alps from End to End* (Nelson Edn.), Chap. XIV, p. 301.
7. Hodder-Williams to Author, 6/3/01.

EIGHTEEN — UNSETTLED
1. *The Spirit of the Hills*, Chap. VI, p. 147.
2. AC, Longland to GWY, 2/10/34.
3. *The Times*, 28/9/34.
4. *The Mountain Vision*, Chap. VIII, pp. 79-84.
5. *An Alpine Journey*, Chap. XIII, p. 126.
6. FS to migraine sufferer, 11/12/37.
7. Written at the back of FS's third and final notebook used for his 1933 Everest expedition diary.
8. *AJ*, 1946, p. 212.

NINETEEN — MIDPOINT AND STALLED
1. FS to Norton, 4/9/37.

TWENTY — RETURN TO GARHWAL
1. N/371, FS to mother, 27/6/36.
2. Newth to FS, 19/10/36.
3. FS's book, *The Valley of Flowers* was virtually the only source of information about his expedition in 1937. Oliver left no record, FS's diary and his letters to Kathleen were unfortunately lost, and the handful of letters to his mother that survived were mainly unhelpful. I have therefore, following this initial reference to Wangdi on p. 20 in Chapter I, suspended the use of notes except in instances where my information came from a source other than *The Valley of Flowers*.
4. *AJ*, 1938, pp 60-81 (Substance of a lecture to the AC on 7/2/38).
5. *The Himalayan Journal*, 1998.

TWENTY ONE — NONA
1. FS to FY, 10/2/40.
2. N/407-408, FS to mother, 27/9/37.
3. AC, Tilman to Odell, 6/3/37.
4. Patrick French to Author, 2/2/06.
5. N/414.

6. NISW. N to EY, 12/6/38.
7/8. FS to N. Parts of two letters, the dates, address heading, and signature removed with scissors, but written on notepaper used at Tenningshook and probably written soon after FS's return from Everest in 1938, when he had separated himself from his family. The mutilated letters were given to me by Jenny Armstrong together with other effects belonging to or connected with FS after Nona's transfer into care in the 1980s.
9. N/416, FS to mother, 10/3/38.

Twenty Two — Broken Home
1. *Everest* 1938.
2. *Everest*, p. 210-224.
3. *Upon that Mountain*, Chap. 11 (part).
4. N/429, FS to mother, 8/7/38.
5. BL. FY to EY, 19/8/38.
6. BL. FY to EY, 23/8/38.
7. FS to Mary Johnson, 9/12/38.
8. *Edward Whymper*, Preface.
9. FS to Newth, 18/8/38.

Twenty Three — Yew Tree Cottage
1. FS to War Office, 21/9/39.
2. FS to Newth, 7/1/40.
3. FS to Newth, 14/6/40, 14/12/40.

Twenty Four — War Years
1. RGS, Secretary to FS, 27/1/42.
2. N/458-460, FS to N, 13/2/42 plus undated extracts.
3. FS to EER, 23/4/42.
4. *The Open Air in Scotland*, 1945, FS article 'Mountain Training in the Cairngorms'.
5. Ibid.
6. *Life is Meeting*, Chap. 4, pp. 63-64.
7. In answer to written questions by John Millar on 17/7/98.
8. N/466, FS to N, May, 1943.
9. N/474, FS to N, 25/9/43.
10. N/475, Ibid.
11. N/477, FS to N, 1/10/43.
12. N/479 and N/480, FS to N, 11/10/43 and 14/10/43.
13. *Climbs in the Canadian Rockies*, Chap. II, p. 21.
14. N/482, FS to N, 28/10/43.
15. N/486 and N/487, FS to N, 5/12/43.

Twenty Five — Switzerland Again
1. Conversation on 27/6/03.

2. Conversation on 1/8/03.
3. *Again Switzerland*, Chap. XI, p. 212.
4. Ibid, p. 215.
5. Ibid, p. 232.

Twenty Six — Canadian Rockies
1. *Climbs in the Canadian Rockies*, Chap. IV, p. 50.

Twenty Seven — A Last Expedition
1. *Climbs in the Canadian Rockies*, Chap. XV, p. 198.
2. Ibid. Chap XIX, p. 229.
3. Ibid, p. 238.

Twenty Eight — Full Circle
1. FS to Newth, 26/3/48.
2. FS to EER, 8/1/48.
3. British Overseas Airways Corporation, forerunner (with British European Airways) of British Airways.
4. NISW. N to EY, 27/5/49.

List of Illustrations

All photographs Frank Smythe collection unless credited otherwise.
* Indicates (57) previously unpublished photographs from Smythe collection.

38.* Kamet and the Mana Peak viewed from Nilkanta.

39. Nima Dorje with the cine camera.

40.* Holdsworth and Shipton facing the last 2,500 feet of Kamet.

41. Lewa, the sirdar. (*Frank Smythe photo; Royal Geographical Society collection*)

42. Kamet, view south-east from the summit.

43.* Everest 1933. Expedition members with Dr Graham at Kalimpong.

44.* Frank riding his pony at the start of the journey to Everest.

45. On the Tibetan plateau. (*FS photo; RGS collection*)

46. Raymond Greene. (*FS photo; RGS collection*)

47. Camp 3a and the North Col. (*FS photo; RGS collection*)

48. Climbing the North Col slopes. (*FS photo; RGS collection*)

49. Camp 5. (*FS photo; RGS collection*)

50. Camp 6. (FS photo; RGS collection)

51. View from 25,000 feet on Everest. (*FS photo; RGS collection*)

Section Two

52.* FS with three guides after the search for two Oxford students on Mont Blanc.

53. The group of Courmayeur guides at the funeral service for the two students.

54.* Frank with Kathleen on the summit of Blaven, Skye.

55. Sir Francis Younghusband. (*RGS collection*)

56.* Frank Smythe, family man.

57.* Jim Bell gives John a tricycle ride.

58.* 'Not sure about this one ... ' (Tony's arrival in July, 1934).

59.* Tenningshook in 1935.

60.* Frank's latest Alvis — a 1½ litre Firefly DH coupé.

61.* Family group at Tenningshook.

62. Everest hopefuls at Zermatt in 1935. (*photo C.F. Kirkus*)

63.* Everest candidates traversing the Lyskamm.

64. Outpost pine on the Kuari Pass en route to the Valley of Flowers, 1937.

65.* FS with his team in the Valley.

66. Enjoying the evening hour by the camp fire.

67.* A training climb. A new 20,000-foot summit with Wangdi.

68.* Nilgiri Parbat.

69. Wangdi and Nurbu on the summit of the 21,264 foot peak.

70.* Peter Oliver on the Banke Glacier en route to the Mana Peak.

71. Peter Oliver self-portrait. (*Oliver collection*)

72. FS on the summit of the Mana Peak, 23,860 feet.

73. Frank with Nona Guthrie in August 1938. (*Jenny Armstrong collection*)

74.* Frank with his mother and Nona at Yew Tree Cottage.

75.* Camping in Glen Lyon en route to Skye.

76. A Glen in the Cuillin Hills.

77. Jack Newth, Frank's publisher at A & C Black. (*Newth collection*)

78. Mountaineering holiday. Jim Gavin by the camp fire at a bivouac.

79. View south-east from the summit of Mont Blanc.

Bibliography

Allan, Stuart, *Commando Country* (National Museums Scotland, 2007).

Anderson, J.R.L., *High Mountains and Cold Seas: a biography of H.W. Tilman* (Gollancz, 1982).

Attenborough, John, *A living memory: Hodder & Stoughton, publishers* (Hodder & Stoughton, 1975).

Band, George, *Everest: 50 years on top of the world* (Harper Collins, 2003).

Bell, J.H.B., *A Progress in Mountaineering* (Oliver & Boyd, 1950).

Benson, Joe, *Souvenirs from High Places* (Mitchell Beazley, 1998).

Birtchnell, Percy, *Bygone Berkhamsted* (White Circle Press, 1975).

Braham, Trevor, *Himalayan Odyssey: When the Alps Cast their Spell* (Allen & Unwin, 1974; The In Pinn, 2004).

Brendon, Piers, *The Dark Valley: a Panorama of the 1930s* (Jonathan Cape, 2000).

Brown, T. Graham, *Brenva* (Dent, 1944).

Bruce, C.G., *The Assault on Mount Everest 1922* (Edward Arnold, 1923).

Calvert, Harry, *Smythe's Mountains* (Gollancz, 1985).

Clark, Peter (with Lyn Murfin), *The History of Maidstone* (Alan Sutton, 1995).

Conway, Martin, *The Alps from End to End* (A. Constable and Co., 1895).

Cranfield, Ingrid (Editor), *Inspiring Achievement: The Life and Work of John Hunt* (Institute for Outdoor Learning 2002).

Dean, Steve, *Hands of a Climber* (Ernest Press, 1993).

Desowitz, Robert S., *Tropical Diseases* (Harper Collins, 1997).

Dickinson, Matt, *The Death Zone* (Hutchinson, 1997).

Douglas, Ed, *Tenzing: Hero of Everest* (National Geographic, 2003).

Dyhrenfurth, Hettie, *Memsahib im Himalaya* (Verlag Deutsche Leipzig 1931).

Dyhrenfurth, G.O., *To the Third Pole* (Werner Laurie, 1955).

Edwards, Ruth Dudley, *Victor Gollancz* (Gollancz, 1987).

Edwards, J.M. (with J.E.Q. Barford), *Clogwyn d'ur Arddu* (guidebook) (Climbers' Club, 1942).

Engel, Claire, *A History of Mountaineering in the Alps* (Allen & Unwin, 1950), *They Came to the Hills* (Allen & Unwin, 1952).

French, Patrick, *Younghusband* (Harper Collins, 1994).

Gander, Ann, *Adrian Bell: Voice of the Countryside* (Holm Oak, 2001).

Gee, Christine (with Garry Weare & Margaret Gee), *Everest: Reflections from the Top* (Rider, 2003).

Gillman, Peter, *Everest: 80 years of triumph & tragedy* (Little, Brown, 2000).

Gray, Fred, *Bexhill Voices* (University of Sussex, 1994).

Greene, Raymond, *Moments of Being* (Heinemann, 1974).

Hankinson, Alan, *Geoffrey Winthrop Young* (Hodder & Stoughton, 1995).

Hastie, Scott, *Berkhamsted: An Illustrated History* (Alpine Press, 1999).

Hemmleb, Jochen (with Larry Johnson & Eric Simonson), *Ghosts of Everest* (Macmillan, 1999).

Humble, Roy M., *The Voice of the Hills: The Story of Ben Humble MBE* (Pentland Press, 1995).

Hunt, John, *Life is Meeting* (Hodder & Stoughton, 1978).

Jones, Kathleen, *Eileen Younghusband* (Bedford Square Press, 1984).

Kapadia, Harish, *Across Peaks and Passes in Garhwal Himalaya* (Indus Publishing Company, 1999).

Kingdon Ward, Frank, *Assam Adventure* (Cape, 1941), *Himalayan Enchantment* (anthology) (Serindia, 1990).

Longstaff, Tom, *This My Voyage* (John Murray, 1950).

Lonsdale Library (Volume 18), *Mountaineering (contributions from T. Longstaff & S. Spencer)* (Seeley Service & Co., c. 1935).

Lowe, George, *Because it is there* (Cassell, 1959).

Lunn, Arnold, *Mountain Jubilee* (Eyre & Spottiswoode, 1943), *A Century of Mountaineering* (Allen & Unwin, 1957).

Lyall, Alan, *The First Descent of the Matterhorn* (Gomer Press, 1997).

Mason, Kenneth, *Abode of Snow* (Rupert Hart-Davis, 1955).

Meade, C.F., *Approach to the Hills* (John Murray, 1940), *High Mountains* (Harvill Press, 1954).

Messner, Reinhold, *The Second Death of George Mallory* (St. Martin's Press, 2000).

Minto, James R., *Dr Graham of Kalimpong* (Dr Graham's Homes, 1974).

Morin, Nea, *A Woman's Reach*, (Eyre & Spottiswoode, 1968).

Murray, W.H., *Mountaineering in Scotland* (J.M. Dent & Sons, 1947), *The Evidence of Things Not Seen* (Bâton Wicks, 2002).

Neame, Sir Philip, *Playing with Strife: The Autobiography of a Soldier* (George C. Harrap & Co. Ltd., 1947).

Neale, Jonathan, *Tigers of the Snow* (Little, Brown, 2002).

Newth, J.D., *Adam and Charles Black: 1807-1957* (A & C Black, 1957).

Noel, Sandra, *Everest Pioneer* (Sutton Publishing 2003).

Norton, E.F., *The Fight for Everest: 1924* (Edward Arnold, 1925).

Parsons & Rose, Mike C. & Mary B., *Invisible on Everest* (Northern Liberties Press 2003).

Paynter, Thomas, *The Ski and the Mountain* (Hurst & Blackett, 1954).

Roberts, Dennis, *I'll Climb Mount Everest Alone* (Robert Hale, 1957).

Roch, Andre, *Climbs of my Youth* (Lindsay Drummond, 1949).

Russell, Scott, *Memoir to The Making of a Mountaineer* (G.I. Finch) (Arrowsmith, 1988).

Ruttledge, Hugh, *Everest 1933* (Hodder & Stoughton, 1934), *Everest, The Unfinished Adventure* (Hodder & Stoughton, 1937).

Scott, Doug, *Himalayan Climber* (Diadem Books, London, 1992).

Scroggie, Sydney, *The Cairngorms Scene and Unseen* (Scottish Mountaineering Trust, 1989).

Shipton, Eric, *Upon that Mountain* (Hodder & Stoughton, 1943), *That Untravelled World* (Hodder & Stoughton, 1969).

Smythe, Frank S., *Climbs and Ski Runs* (Blackwood, 1929), *The Kangchenjunga Adventure* (Gollancz, 1930), *Kamet Conquered* (Gollancz, 1932), *An Alpine Journey* (Gollancz, 1934), *The Spirit of the Hills* (Hodder & Stoughton, 1935), *Over Tyrolese Hills* (Hodder & Stoughton, 1936), *Camp Six* (Hodder & Stoughton, 1937), *The Mountain Scene* (A & C Black, 1937), *The Valley of Flowers* (Hodder & Stoughton,

1938), *Peaks and Valleys* (A & C Black, 1938), *A Camera in the Hills* (A & C Black, 1939), *Mountaineering Holiday* (Hodder & Stoughton, 1940) *Edward Whymper* (Hodder & Stoughton, 1940), *My Alpine Album* (A & C Black, 1940), *Adventures of a Mountaineer* (Dent, 1940), *The Mountain Vision* (Hodder & Stoughton, 1941), *Over Welsh Hills* (A & C Black, 1941), *Alpine Ways* (A & C Black, 1942), *Secret Mission* (Hodder & Stoughton, 1942), *British Mountaineers* (Collins, 1942), *Snow on the Hills* (A & C Black, 1946), *The Mountain Top* (St Hugh's Press, 1947), *Again Switzerland* (Hodder & Stoughton, 1947), *Rocky Mountains* (A & C Black, 1948), *Swiss Winter* (A & C Black, 1948), *Mountains in Colour* (Max Parrish, 1949), *Climbs in the Canadian Rockies* (Hodder & Stoughton, 1950), *Polar Journey* (Ernst Klett, 1951), *The Six Alpine/ Himalayan Climbing Books* (Omnibus) (Bâton Wicks & The Mountaineers, 2000).

Somervell, T. Howard, *After Everest* (Hodder & Stoughton, 1936).

Spencer Chapman, F., *Helvellyn to Himalaya* (Chatto & Windus, 1940).

Steele, Peter, *Eric Shipton: Everest and Beyond* (Constable, 1998).

Taylor, William C., *Highland Soldiers* (Coyote Books, 1994).

Tenzing, Norgay (and J.R. Ullman), *Man of Everest* (George Harrap, 1955).

Thetford, Owen, *Aircraft of the Royal Air Force since 1918* (Putnam & Co., London).

Tilman, H.W., *Everest 1938* (Cambridge University Press, 1948).

Tredrey, F.D., *Pilot's Summer* (Duckworth, 1939), *The House of Blackwood 1804 – 1954).*

Unsworth, Walt, *Everest* (Oxford Illustrated Press, 1989), *Everest* (The Mountaineers, 1999), *Savage Snows* (Hodder & Stoughton, 1986), *Because it is there* (Gollancz, 1968).

Venables, Stephen, *Everest: Summit of Achievement* (Royal Geog. Society, 2003).

Ward, Michael, *Everest: A Thousand Years of Exploration*, (Ernest Press, 2003).

Whiting, Dail, *Wateringbury Revisited* (enlarged from George Newman) (Privately published, 2001).

Whymper, Edward, *Scrambles Amongst the Alps* (Thomas Nelson, 1871).

Williams, Paul, *Clogwyn d'ur Arddu* (guidebook) (Climbers' Club, 1988).

Wrangham, E.A., *Selected Climbs in the Range of Mont Blanc* (Allen & Unwin, 1957).

Young, Eleanor & G.W., *In Praise of Mountains* (anthology) (Frederick Muller, 1948).

Young, G.W., *Mountains with a Difference* (Eyre & Spottiswoode, 1951), *On High Hills* (Methuen & Co., 1927), Mountain Craft (Scribner, 1920).

Younghusband, Francis, *Everest; the Challenge* (Thomas Nelson, 1936).

Index